Elementary

Aspects of

the Political

Theory in Forms
A series edited by Nancy Rose Hunt and Achille Mbembe

Elementary Aspects of the Political

Histories from the Global South

Prathama Banerjee

Duke University Press   Durham and London   2020

© 2020 Duke University Press
All rights reserved
Designed by Aimee C. Harrison
Typeset in Portrait Text and Univers LT Std by Copperline
Book Services

Library of Congress Cataloging-in-Publication Data
Names: Banerjee, Prathama, author.
Title: Elementary aspects of the political : histories from
the Global South / Prathama Banerjee.
Other titles: Theory in forms.
Description: Durham : Duke University Press, 2020. | Series:
Theory in forms | Includes bibliographical references and index.
Identifiers: LCCN 2020016390 (print)
LCCN 2020016391 (ebook)
ISBN 9781478009870 (hardcover)
ISBN 9781478010906 (paperback)
ISBN 9781478012443 (ebook)
Subjects: LCSH: Political science—India. | Political
science—Philosophy.
Classification: LCC JA84.I4 B364 2020 (print) |
LCC JA84.I4 (ebook) | DDC 320.01—dc23
LC record available at https://lccn.loc.gov/2020016390
LC ebook record available at https://lccn.loc.gov/2020016391

COVER ART: Rana Begum, *No. 394 L Fold*, paint on mild steel,
2013. Courtesy of the artist.

*To my little Chiku (2002–2014)
and his unforgettable courage and cool*

CONTENTS

ix   *Acknowledgments*
1   *Introduction*

Part I. The Self

23   1   Renunciation and Antisocial Being
44   2   Philosophy, Theater, and Realpolitik

Part II. Action

67   3   Karma, Freedom, and Everyday Life
87   4   Labor, Hunger, and Struggle

Part III. Idea

119   5   Equality and Spirituality
142   6   Equality and Economic Reason

Part IV. People

165   7   People as Party
189   8   People as Fiction

214   *Epilogue*
221   *Notes*
247   *Bibliography*
265   *Index*

ACKNOWLEDGMENTS

This book has been a decade in the making. I have accumulated innumerable debts along the way. The Centre for the Study of Developing Societies (CSDS), Delhi, where I work, is the most hospitable academic institution imaginable. My first thanks go to my colleagues and friends at CSDS, who heard me out with patience and responded with enthusiasm as I presented this book in bits and pieces. Many thanks also to the warm and friendly support staff of CSDS. A generous institutional grant by the International Development Research Centre, Canada, supported much of the field and archival work for this book. I also thank the staff of the National Library, Kolkata; the West Bengal State Archives; the National Archives, Delhi; and the Nehru Memorial Museum and Library, Delhi. Thanks also to Avinash Jha, scholar-librarian, CSDS.

Many friends from the academy, in India and overseas, are participants in this book, though they bear absolutely no responsibility for its shortcomings. I want to especially mention Aditya Nigam, Ajay Skaria, Aishwary Kumar, Anupama Rao, Arindam Chakravarty, Awadhendra Sharan, Baidik Bhattacharya, Boddhisattva Kar, Chandan Gowda, Debjani Ganguly, Dipesh Chakrabarty, Durba Mitra, Felicia Bishop Denaud, G. Arunima, Jinee Lokneeta, Kalpana Ram, the late and fondly remembered Kavita Datla, Mahesh Rangarajan, Malavika Kasturi, Mallarika Sinha Roy, Malini Sur, Murad Idris, Neha Chatterjee, Partha Chatterjee, Pradip Datta, Raffaele Laudani, Rajeev Bhargava, Rakesh Pandey, Ravi Sundaram, Ravi Vasudevan, Ravikant, Rochona Mazumdar, Ruchi Chaturvedi, Shailaja Paik, Shibaji Bandopadhyay, Soumita Mazumdar, Stephen Legg, Sukanya Sarbadhikari, Suren Pillay, Udaya Kumar, Upal Chakrabarti, Vinayak Chaturvedi, Wang Hui, and Yasmeen Arif. Colleagues and students at Ambedkar University, Australian National University, Azim Premji University, Bologna University, Columbia University, Delhi University, Jawaharlal Nehru University, Presidency University, University of Cape Town, University of Western Cape, University of Virginia, National University of

Singapore, and Tsinghua University, Beijing, have heard and commented on various sections of this book.

A very special thanks goes to the two anonymous readers of my manuscript, who pored over this work with great attention and offered incredibly insightful comments and criticisms. I am deeply grateful to Elizabeth Ault of Duke University Press for placing her trust in this intellectual project.

Finally, my family. My father, Diptendra Banerjee, himself a professor of history, passed away twenty years ago. I still miss him. He would have been the first reader of this work, would have criticized it ruthlessly and still been proud of his historian daughter! My mother, Jayasri Banerjee, has always watched over me like a guardian angel, though she still scolds me for not studying enough! My older son, Nishant, just turned eighteen, has voted for the first time in his life, and has left for college. It has been the most exciting aspect of my life, seeing him grow into a poised young man—strong, supportive, kind, wise, and the pride of any mother. My partner of more than twenty-five years, Shailendra Jha, is more passionate about politics than I am. We have been comrades in arms—in left politics in our younger days and now in the battle of life, which has thrown up unexpected challenges. He is my anchor and friend.

My younger son, Arita née Chiku, left us in 2014 at the age of twelve, having battled a rare form of brain cancer for two years. He remains for all of us the ideal of courage, wit, and élan in the face of death. He looked after us as we looked after him, made us laugh and party at his bedside, and shone with blinding brightness and mischief until the last moment. This book and everything else in my life are in his name.

INTRODUCTION

> Politics is a paradoxical form of action.
> —Jacques Rancière, "Ten Theses on Politics"

This is a study of the years when what we know as modern politics took shape in India and the world. However, this is not a book of political history—rather, it is one of "histories of the political." It asks the question that raises its head before we even set out to the write political history—namely, What is the political?, or rather, What is it that in modern times comes to be commonly recognized as the political?

Growing up in India in the second half of the twentieth century, my friends and I saw politics as the default condition of being. It seemed as if no aspect of life (art, philosophy, love, spirituality) and no space of habitation (classroom, household, workplace, theater) was free of the overt play of politics. Politics was destiny, we believed, even though elders often warned us against the evils of overpoliticization! We lived in a ready state of agitation and mobilization. It is this condition—of being always already political—that I wish to investigate in this book, by asking the question that we never asked in our younger days: What or how is the political?

Commentators attribute this condition of intense politicization to the colonial experience. Dipesh Chakrabarty argues that since modernity in the colony was inextricably tied to the experience of political conquest, modernity emerged here as first and foremost "political modernity."[1] Sovereignty, rights, representation, democracy, and so on emerged as the first questions in India, overshadowing other quintessentially modern questions, such as those of secularism, rationalism, individualism, and industrialism. As Sudipta Kaviraj notes, this made modernity in India very different in its sequentiality and configuration from the western European model.[2]

Because anticolonial struggle needed to mobilize the force of the people at large, democracy was, right from the start, the constitutive question of modernity in India. Anticolonial movements, heterogeneous in both ideology and constituency (after all, not all anticolonial mobilizations can be subsumed under nationalism), shared one thing across the board. They called on everyone—men and women, rich and poor, peasants and workers, upper and lower castes, tribes and untouchables, students and professionals, theologians and traders, Hindus, Muslims, and Sikhs—to come through as unconditionally political. Even those who were neither educated nor propertied nor civil enough to be recognized as "responsible" actors were invited to act, in the first instance, as political beings. This was very different from the historical trajectory of western Europe, where education, modernization, and governmentalization of society preceded by centuries the recognition of universal political franchise. In the colony, being political was prior to all else; it was the precondition to achieving not just freedom, equality, and justice, but also community, sociability, intimacy, and indeed the ordinary fruits and pleasures of human life.

The subaltern studies school of history writing belabored this point in the 1980s. Against Marxist social history, which saw nonclass popular rebellions as premodern and prepolitical, it argued that even the most marginalized peoples in India, such as landless peasants and forest and hill tribes, must be recognized as deeply political beings, if anything.[3] But even as subaltern studies fronted the moment of the political—against nationalist culturalism, Marxist economism, and upper-caste, middle-class statism—it never really interrogated the concept of the political. It never asked what it was about the subaltern that was recognizably political.

It was as if, irrespective of all philosophical or ideological disagreements, everyone recognized politics when they saw it. For what was modernity if not the triumph of politics over tradition, habit, custom, religion, culture? I feel that it is precisely this modern common sense—this faith in the self-evidence of the political that makes us see politics everywhere and invoke politics at every turn—that obstructs our understanding of politics today. For today it is politics that stands most unsettled across the world, often assuming unexpected if not counterintuitive forms. Our given ideological, sociological, and philosophico-normative parameters no longer guarantee political efficacy or insight. Clearly, we need to reinvent our political compass. And to do so, I argue in this book, we need to place diverse histories and counterhistories of the political right in the face of mainstream political theory and ask the question anew: What is the political?

I should clarify what I mean when I invoke histories and counterhistories of the political. I write from and about a location that is variously called Bengal, India, south Asia, "the subcontinent," erstwhile "third world," the global South, and so on—all of which are disciplinary regions with a certain geopolitical overtone. It is also often indexed as Indic, Islamic, or both—terms with problematic civilizational charge. Clearly, it is a struggle with language and lexicon when one seeks to step around binaries like national/international, provincial/universal, and local/global, while claiming a transhistorical salience for one's own work. While I write from and about my particular location, my aim is not to demonstrate colonial or historical or cultural difference, nor is it to stake a claim to theory as such. It is simply to mobilize "other" histories, which are only contingently "Indian," in order to open up new theoretical and conceptual possibilities for all to think about and debate. It also seems to me that this facility of thinking across histories and traditions, without being "comparativist," calls for a certain lightness of being that cannot be achieved so long as one appears to be carrying the great burden of history, be it colonial or national, or so long as one assumes only the stance of "critique" at the cost of creative play.

Hence I go with the currently popular term *global South*, as signposted in the title of the book, to express solidarity with the intellectual mobilization happening around that term in academies of distant regions, including the decolonial institutional sites of Africa and Latin America. As I see it, this book belongs to that deterritorial intellectual domain where, despite geopolitical obstructions, scholars find each other struggling to move on from the moment of (postcolonial/decolonial) critique and undertake the positive and experimental task of reassembling diverse philosophies and experiences of struggle from across the world. So when I ask, What is the political?, I ask it from a crossroads that is no one's country but only a modest meeting place, where we share our philosophies and histories with each other. The advantage with the global South is that it is indeed a nonplace. Hence, it might be interesting to rest here, at least for a while, with unexpected neighbors and wonderful strangers. What we might achieve is certainly not a universal political theory but perhaps unprecedented chords and productive "dischords," by way of making music separately together.

The Philosophy Question

So when I ask, What is the political?, I am not by any means seeking a universal philosophical definition. In fact, I seek to move away from the western European tradition of thinking politics via political philosophy. For in India, and most likely in other postcolonies, we remain caught up in a curious double bind. We believe that we are an intensely political people, and yet we lament the lack of political philosophy. We seem to "do" politics under the perpetual shadow of this lack and compensate by either borrowing concepts from western European political philosophy or showing up the latter's Eurocentrism and consequent inapplicability to other-than-European contexts. But we do not ask questions of philosophy itself, nor do we interrogate philosophy's claim to a privileged access to politics.

In universities and colleges in India, we teach politics through a narrative of great thinkers who make up the western European philosophical canon (Plato, Aristotle, Thomas Hobbes, John Locke, Karl Marx) or through a similarly structured narrative of great Indian thinkers (Mahatma Gandhi, Jawaharlal Nehru, Rabindranath Tagore, B. R. Ambedkar), who, often in spite of themselves, are made to perform the philosopher's role for the sake of the political. Of course, these figures do not always fit the properly philosophical persona, resulting in their fundamental misrecognition as "not-quite" political. They appear as always already contaminated by an undigestible surplus of the "nonpolitical"—spiritual, cultural, sexual—that seems to obstruct in the global South the rise of the purely political idea.

When we do not think politics through a narrative of great philosophers, we tend to think it through a narrative of universal ideologies—liberalism, nationalism, Marxism, Fascism, and so on. Ideology here works as a proxy for philosophy, the implicit assumption being that ideology is the form in which philosophical thought acquires a practical life outside isolated and elite spaces of contemplation. For the longest time, a certain variety of Marxism held sway over political understanding in India. The categories of "economy" and "class" reigned supreme, irrespective of the actual dynamics of everyday politics. Caste continued to be misrecognized for decades, by academics as well as "progressive" political actors, as a distorted variety of class identity that would automatically right itself as modernization and development turned all Indians into rational economic beings.[4] In the same vein, historians and economists searched for feudalism in India, tortuously trying to fit "Indian facts" into a global "transition narrative," in the hope that feudalism in India's past would ensure capitalism in India's present and hopefully socialism in India's future![5]

Currently, Marxism has been replaced by liberalism as the universal frame within which to think politics across the globe. Chris Bayly reads much of Indian political thinking between the 1820s and 1940s as flowing into a worldwide "age of liberalism," despite liberalism's complicity in the imperial project and despite the fact of colonial difference.[6] Even more tellingly, Andrew Sartori shows not only western-educated elites but also poor Indian peasants to be liberals, even if they might not have known it themselves. He sees Bengal peasants fighting for land rights against rent-seeking landlords as bearers of a vernacular version of the original Lockean idea of the property-constituting power of labor, without considering the fact that the peasants' common sense might very well have been the original version of this idea.[7] This is not the place to debate the validity of reading world history as a history of liberalism. Let me just register the real question at stake here: it is that of western European philosophy's presence at the heart of colonial (and postcolonial) politics, via a charting of philosophy's global career as ideology.

And if not ideology, we have normative ideals—citizenship, rights, secularity, civility, rationality, and indeed modernity itself—standing in for philosophy's claim over the political. Partha Chatterjee shows how European philosophy enforced normative principles across the world, through colonial pedagogy, on the one hand, and colonial governmentality, on the other, structuring the world in terms of a norm/deviation and norm/exception principle (such that those denied rights were first posited as deviations from the norm and then administered as exceptions to it, reinforcing the norms themselves in the process). That such ideals could assume the status of universals—even when blatantly flouted by their proponents and even when historical counterinstances flew in their face—was possible only because these norms, in Chatterjee's words, inhabited the "mythical space-time" of philosophical thought.[8] From this mythic space-time—empirically seventeenth- and eighteenth-century western Europe but conceptually posited as the founding moment of political philosophy as such—norms continued to legislate on politics, unperturbed by the latter's empirical diversities.

The issue for me, however, is not that so-called modern political concepts—historically produced as they were in a certain western European location and then pitched as universal—are unhelpful to the study of non-European contexts. That issue has been tackled by the many acts of "provincializing Europe" undertaken by postcolonial theorists in Africa, Asia, and Latin America. The issue at stake for me here is the relationship between philosophy and history and its implications for the understanding of politics as such.

Western European political philosophy as we know it today simultaneously mobilizes and erases traces of its own historicity—first by grounding itself in local historical events, such as the French Revolution or the Industrial Revolution, and second, by turning these empirical historical events into universal philosophical archetypes, the font of philosophical concepts such as liberty and equality, capitalism and communism. The result is a hierarchy not only between philosophy and history but also between history and history—between a history that claims to be philosophically and normatively salient, and other histories, such as histories from the global South, that cannot make such a claim. The latter remain confined to the register of the empirical. They offer counterfactuals to European history, and indeed "provincialize" it, but they do not dislodge philosophy itself from its hegemonic location.

It is this hierarchy between histories that I wish to interrupt—not by saying that histories from the global South can also function as a source of philosophical archetypes (which they indeed can if so written) but by denaturalizing the coupling of politics and philosophy. I wish to displace philosophy itself from being the natural ground of the political. This is not to say that I do not find philosophy relevant to thinking the political. Nor do I argue for some kind of political "realism" by scorning the power of ideas. In fact, I shall talk of ideas frequently in this book, in their diverse embodied and operationalized forms. I wish merely to say that philosophy must be seen as one, and only one, among the many protagonists that vie for supremacy around the question of the political. Hence, in this book, the question of philosophy will appear, as but one among many other questions. In chapter 2, for example, I show how it is in the tension between philosophy and theater that an image of the purely "political man" emerges in early twentieth-century Bengal and India. In chapters 5 and 6, I show how an idea becomes political by operating not as norm or ideology (not as philosophical proxies) but as a shared language that makes politics of various ideological hues mutually legible and translatable.

Politics and the Political

Therefore, when I ask the question—What is the political?—it is not a reference to the "politics" versus "the political" distinction made popular by contemporary French philosophy. Carl Schmitt familiarized us with the use of the political as a self-standing noun, when he defined decision/exception as the essence of sovereignty and friend/enemy as the essence of political community. He posited the political in opposition to what merely appeared as politics, namely, the routine and tame activities of law, representation, and government.[9] However, it was Claude Lefort who made the distinction between *la politique* (politics) and *le politique* (the political) popular in the academy in the 1970s. Lefort defined the political as the prior moment of giving form to society (be it democracy, bureaucracy, or totalitarianism) and politics as the ex post facto play of antagonistic forces within that society. To Lefort, what we ordinarily perceive as politics—elections, party activities, unions, revolts, movements—was a second-order set of activities predicated on the real political, which was the prior moment of the "institution" of a certain order of things.[10]

Needless to say, Schmitt and Lefort were very different philosophers. But they shared two assumptions that would come to be generalized in contemporary political thinking via this politics/political distinction. The first is the understanding that the political beyond politics can be accessed only through the work of philosophy. The second is an assumption of the unconditional priority of the political itself. When Jean-Luc Nancy and Philippe Lacoue-Labarthe set up the Centre de recherches philosophiques sur le politique in 1982, it was for the stated purpose of "the *philosophical* questioning of the political" and "the questioning of the philosophical *about* the political"—expressing at its most articulate the politics-philosophy coupling foundational to European political thinking.[11] Of concern to Nancy and others was the apparent emptying of politics from the political as such—as politics stood reduced in liberal democracy to the workings of law, on the one hand, and mass media, on the other.[12] To return the political to politics was thus to search for the ontologically political, a task for which philosophy had to be mobilized, no less, because the epistemologically oriented sciences of sociology, economics, history, political science, and so on and the ontically oriented empiricism of political activity itself were grossly insufficient.[13] Of course, these thinkers defined the political very differently from each other. If Lefort defined the political as the institution of society, Nancy defined it as disposition toward community, Alain Badiou as radical event, and Jacques Rancière as redistribution of the sensible (i.e., change in the order of what or who is seen, heard, and felt).[14] Despite these crucial differences, however, all of them defined the political in opposition to politics, policy, police—terms designating domains and activities that ordinary people recognize as political but the philosopher finds emptied of the political. And all argued for the priority of the political as the originary act of (re)ordering the world, wherein we lived life and played politics.

In this book not only do I wish to question philosophy's privileged claim to accessing the political, but I also want to investigate its assumption of the priority of the political, which I believe is an eminently modern historical phenomenon. So when I use the term "the political," I do not oppose it to "politics." I do not believe that ordinary politics—involving elections, parties, mass media, movements—is devoid of the political in the least. To say so is to express a philosopher's conceit and an inchoate fear of the routine, the everyday, the massified—a fear that has haunted western European philosophical thinking, right from the time of the French Revolution to the late nineteenth- and early twentieth-century debates around universal adult franchise, to mid-twentieth-century anxieties around the culture industry, to what Rancière aptly calls the late twentieth-century neoliberal "hatred of democracy," to our most recent perplexity about populist, demagogic politics.[15] But while I do not subordinate politics to the political, I do ask the following question of ordinary, everyday politics—namely, What is "political" about politics in the first place? In other words, I retain the adjectival connotation for the term "the political." I believe that subjects, ideas, acts, images, and affects that might not appear to do with politics at any one time can and do *become* political at another, redefining in the process the very concept of the political itself.

Let me then refine my preliminary question. Instead of asking, What is the political?, I now ask, What is it that becomes political and in modern times assumes a kind of constitutive priority? This is obviously more a historical question than a philosophical one because it does not presume that there is any one thing—a force, an essence, an orientation, a subjectivity, a site—that is a priori or ontologically political. The political is not just a self-standing noun but an orientation, a qualifier, that is sometimes assumed or worn by subjects, forces, acts, and images, irrespective of their origin. What is political becomes so and does not remain so forever.

Two further points then become crucial. First, to chart the movement of becoming political historically is also to step aside of the modern-day common sense—that "everything is political." This imagination of the political as pervasive and ubiquitous historically emerged (and was radicalized by feminist writers) in opposition to earlier imaginations of the political as confined to the state, the public sphere, and the realm of high politics. However, I feel that we have reached an impasse in this thinking of the political as everyday and everywhere because such a seamless generalization of politics renders the very category of the political toothless, shorn of both descriptive and analytical purchase. We are left with no history, no genealogy of the political—only with an unremarkable sense of our imbrication in everyday operations of power.

The motto "everything is political" rests, I believe, on a conceptual slippage between power and politics. Michel Foucault has taught us that power is everywhere—in schools, hospitals, prisons, and bedrooms. He has also taught us that power not only represses but also makes possible new subjectivities and positive practices. But talking regimes of power—coloniality, discipline, governmentality, biopolitics—and talking politics are different enterprises, and Foucault himself never conflated the two. Politics does presume power, but power does not necessarily presume politics. Perhaps the only definition, a minimalist one, that we can have of politics is that politics is one kind of orientation toward power, though not necessarily the only kind.

Second, to move away from the position that "everything is political" is also to move away from a universalist notion of the political. It seems to us today that the political can be conceived of only as a universal imperative. Some concede that in nonmodern times, politics might have been differently conceived and differently played out across peoples and places. But not so in modernity. With colonialism, the whole world came to share the same political grammar (a combination of liberal and Marxist concepts, such as rights, equality, autonomy, democracy, revolution), the same political forms (the nation-state, the representative assembly, the political party), and the same institutions and technologies of rule (discipline, governmentality, biopolitics). It is telling that even Partha Chatterjee, who critiques the hegemony of western European normative theory so sharply and differs with Benedict Anderson's claim that all modern-day imaginations of political community partake of a universal homogeneous time, accepts that in the imagination of political form (as opposed to the "inner," sovereign domains of culture, society, religion, domesticity) the whole world has thought in the same way since the nineteenth century.[16]

There is certainly some truth in this claim that, with colonialism, politics takes on a globalizing, if not universalizing, aspect, which I see as the obverse of the constitutive priority of the political in modernity. But if we take seriously the actual practice of politics, including its diverse enunciations across the world, very different stories come to the fore. My interest lies in exploring some of these differences. However, my project is not to demonstrate difference as such. Nor is it to relativize "political cultures" such that culture becomes the site of admissible difference, keeping the political undisturbed as a stable universal. By telling a different story of becoming political I seek to reopen theoretically what we, in our times, call politics.

Can the Nonpolitical Be Thought?

To study the movement of becoming political requires that we admit that there is something specific though not essential to politics. Rancière says that politics is a rare moment, when a given order of things is transformed by the enactment of equality by unequals. Otherwise, it is just the "police," that is, an established regime of the perceptible and the sensible wherein unequals occupy, without surplus or spillage, the proper places assigned to them.[17] While I agree with Rancière's formulation of the rarity of politics, I am uneasy with his universal, once-and-for-all definition of the political as the enactment of equality. Such a definition conflates the rarity of the political with an assumed purity of political essence. It refuses to recognize other kinds of claim making that do not speak in the name of equality.[18] As I shall argue in chapters 5 and 6, it is important not just to invoke equality and recognize it when we see it—which, in Rancière's telling, is in the "now" of politics rather than in some utopian future of a perfected society—but also to study how equality becomes a conceivable political idea in the first place, from being, for example, simply an everyday practical stance or a deeply spiritual idea. So while I agree with Rancière that politics is not a general condition of being, that things politicize or make a transition into politics, I also argue that the production of the political is not the production of an always already known orientation. In fact, I argue that the production of the political can be understood not by trying to predefine the ontologically political but by attending to the contingent and different ways in which the political gets differentiated from the putative nonpolitical. That is, becoming political is, at any one time, the unfolding of a certain political/nonpolitical relationship.

The nonpolitical, however, must not be confused with the prepolitical or the not yet political. The prepolitical (read premodern) has been a colonial epithet for so-called peoples without history—the colonized, the indigene, the poor, the effeminate—who have been struggling for at least a couple of centuries to prove that they, too, have history and politics. Much has been written about the tragic nature of this burden—of having to prove one's political acumen until the end of time.[19] But more important for my purpose is to recognize that the terms *prepolitical* and *not yet political* posit the political as the telos, the ultimate destiny, of all being—feeding into what I have called the constitutive priority and universality of the political in modern times. This blinds us to the crucial fact that in modernity the political actually gets instituted in opposition not only to the so-called prepolitical and prehistorical but also to changing imaginations of the nonpolitical. The nonpolitical has been variously imagined in modernity—as the spiritual, the intimate, the sexual, the social, the artistic, the scientific, and even the economic. Indeed, these various political/nonpolitical divisions have had institutional lives as modern disciplines. The history of each such discipline can be written as a history of how its relationship to the political played out over time—vouching for the fact that what is at stake here is indeed a political/nonpolitical dialectic. The eighteenth- and nineteenth-century imagination of politics, as having to do with the state and state-oriented activities, proposed that political logic was autonomous of religious (Max Weber), social (Thomas Hobbes), economic (Adam Smith), aesthetic (Immanuel Kant), and other such supposedly nonpolitical logics. Subsequently, twentieth-century critics demonstrated that each of these so-called nonpolitical logics was no less shot through with the political than politics itself. Feminists politicized the intimate, Marxists politicized the economic and the aesthetic, historians politicized the social, postcolonials politicized culture, and so on. In fact, all the influential debates of our times can be read in these terms. Thus, the never-ending secularism debate in political theory is about the division between politics and religion.[20] The event/everyday debate in anthropology and sociology is about the division between political action and life, glossed, respectively, as culture and social habitus by the two disciplines.[21] The state/market debate in economics is about whether production and exchange are best regulated politically or allowed to operate by the autonomous logic of the market.[22] And so on.

In other words, in modern times, we seem to be caught in a spiral. The political gets defined as being not-economic, not-religious, not-social, not-aesthetic, and so on, and then the economic, the religious, the social, and the aesthetic get shown up, inevitably, as also political. We may call this the persistent political/nonpolitical dynamic through which modern thought works, reproducing the political itself as the overdetermining concept of our times. To put it differently, it is only when framed by a universal and prior political that the social, the cultural, the psychological, the spiritual, and the aesthetic appear as particular to us. Interestingly, the economic works somewhat differently, even as it mobilizes its own status as a nonpolitical imperative. One of the lines of thought I pursue in this book is that the political assumes priority and universality in modern times not entirely by itself but by borrowing from the putative universality of the economic, which paradoxically gets posited as the ultimate instance of the nonpolitical, being about basic needs and bare life and hence, in the final instance, both before and beyond politics. (I consider this in chapter 6, where I discuss the animation and augmentation of the political idea of equality by the logic of economic reason.)

Running through all the chapters of the book, therefore, is an effort at understanding the modern political in terms of an ongoing process of differentiation—which consists of a simultaneous setting up and unraveling of antinomies between politics and society, politics and economics, politics and religion, politics and art, and so on. In other words, I argue that a history of the political is always already also a history of the social, the religious, the economic, and the aesthetic not only as categories of thought but also as organizing principles of life.

And yet, at the very heart of this political/nonpolitical dynamic, we also get glimpses of the extrapolitical! If the nonpolitical is that which gets posited as the other of the political, only to be in turn politicized, the extrapolitical appears as the excess that actively resists politicization, even refuses it. So religion gets posited as the non- of the political, in modernity's self-presentation as a secular age, only to return as political question par excellence in the twenty-first century. But spiritual intensities—such as those involving questions of the self's finitude and solitude—even as they animate politics in times of mobilization and martyrdom, remain always already a little bit extra. This extrapolitical appears as the limit of the political, specifying politics and making it conceivable in the first place. Many political actors in this book, including famous ones such as Gandhi, Ambedkar, Muhammad Iqbal, and Tagore, cut sad and solitary figures exactly at moments when they insist on the salience of the extrapolitical—that is, on spiritual, intimate, poetic intensities, which accompany the political but refuse to be exhausted or explained by it. At the edge of the political, as it were, these adored yet misunderstood figures come through, unsurprisingly, as the most sharply critical voices with respect to modern politics.

Why Elementary Aspects?

It is not easy, in our times, to suspend belief in the self-evidence of the political. In trying to do so, my strategy is to disassemble the modern political into what appears as its constitutive elements. As must be obvious, I borrow this analytical pitch from Émile Durkheim's classic *The Elementary Forms of Religious Life* (1912) and its subsequent reinvention in Ranajit Guha's masterpiece, *Elementary Aspects of Peasant Insurgency in Colonial India* (1983). Elements here stand for those constituents that work as building blocks of a concept—be it religion or rebellion or, in my case, the political as such.[23] Concepts, because they are often denoted by single words, are sometimes confused with selfsame entities such as keywords and jargon. We must remember, however, that concepts are not just words or even special words. They are philosophical operations in the way that functions and equations are scientific operations. Concepts become concepts, as Gilles Deleuze and Félix Guattari remind us,[24] by articulating in themselves multiple propensities and potentialities, which is why concepts work more as expressive events than as signifying terms. That is, a concept is internally heterogeneous and, for that reason, highly amenable to disassembling into its constitutive elements.

I disassemble the political into its elementary aspects, so that one is able to think the political in terms of not merely, to use Guha's phrase, "specific encounters" (colonized/colonizer, Brahmin/Shudra, capital/labor, or landlord/peasant) but also "common forms and general ideas" that are shared across such distinct historical encounters and combine differently at different moments in order to produce particular historical complexes of the political.[25] And yet I must also go against the grain of the foundational presupposition, shared by Durkheim and Guha, that elements are necessarily the most primitive, originary, or simple entities that are known to us; that elements become visible only when one analyzes early formations such as aboriginal religion (Durkheim) or pre-twentieth-century peasant insurgency, prior, that is, to the ideological overlay of nationalism and socialism (Guha). On the contrary, I argue that elements of the political, as we think of them today, are highly elaborate, complex, and coded formations and by no stretch of imagination natural, basic, or simple units "without [civilizational] embellishments" à la Durkheim.

I disassemble the modern political into four elementary aspects—subject, act, idea, and people—following the conceptual division posited by modern political philosophy. Needless to say, this imagination of the political as predicated on subject, act, idea, and people has passed into common sense today. When asked what is the political, we sometimes invoke a newly emergent subject— worker, poet, guerrilla, revolutionary, jihadi, black, Dalit, woman. At other times, we define the political as action—strike, fast, civil disobedience, war— which suspends or at least overdetermines ordinary activities of life. At yet other times, we define the political as "commitment" to an idea or ideology, such as freedom or equality, that helps us transcend particular locations and come together in solidarity. At other times still, we see the political as the rise of a new community under the sign of the people—nation, proletariat, race, *qaum*, multitude, and so on. Sometimes these elements appear in conjunction—with self, act, idea, and community seamlessly coming together to produce a particular formation of the political (as is the fantasy of nationalism). At other times, one element appears to replace another. Thus, when a self-identical political subject appears impossible, an idea appears to gather under its umbrella incommensurable peoples (as has been the fantasy of communism).

Having thus disassembled the elementary aspects of the modern political, I then set out to unpack the assumed elementary status of the elements themselves. So when I say *elements*, I use the term (originally defined in chemistry as the basic constituents of mixtures and compounds that cannot be further broken down by subtractive or operational means) somewhat differently than intended by Durkheim or Guha. In fact, I use *elements* somewhat ironically. Elements of the political for me are not an objective set of stable and simple entities. Instead, I see elements as codified entities that actively *resist* further decomposition—for, once decomposed or disassembled, they no longer appear as political or even productive of the political. Elementary aspects of the political, in this sense, are aspects that simulate the ontology of "first principles"—by performing their role as entities that are both historical (because modern) and extrahistorical (because universal). A study of elementary aspects of the modern political for me, then, is also an interrogation of the presumed simplicity, stability, singularity, and universality of the elements themselves.

But my argument is not only a historical one. I am not just saying that the concepts of subject, act, idea, and people unravel when tested against historical or empirical reality. For example, I am not just making the point that the people—whether the nation or the proletariat—are always socially, culturally, and ethnically divided, which indeed they are. I am also making the additional point that the "people" does not cohere even as a pure concept. Nor do the concepts of subject, act, and idea with respect to the political. In fact, I believe that at the heart of each elementary aspect of the political lies a secret implausibility, which must remain coded for the element to appear as a stable element in the first place. Thus, I show that the political subject is split by the contrary pulls of self and selflessness, interest and sacrifice, renunciation and rule. Political action is thwarted by life, as action comes to be pitted against the everyday, the routine, and the quotidian. The idea founders on the irresoluble idealism/materialism dichotomy. The people appear always already strung between the distinct ontologies of population and crowd, mass and society—as that dangerous "part" that seeks to be "whole." Moreover, one element sometimes appears to contradict another. Thus, the subject may undercut the conceptual valence of the people, when the latter is reduced to being an object of manipulation and mastery, as we see today in the context of hypermediatized and hypermanaged politics, in India as in the United States. Action may undercut the valence of idea and ideology. Again, subject and action may appear contrary. Thus, when an act such as the strike is defined as inherently political, irrespective of who the agent of that act might be, the subject question itself becomes redundant. And so on.

If elementary aspects of the political do not cohere conceptually or even sit together comfortably, how do they perform their elementary status in the first place? By being codified as such, I argue, through the mobilization of the persistent political/nonpolitical dialectic that marks modernity. Subject, act, idea, and people become elementary aspects of the political, each by positing a division between itself and something else, which appears for that moment as its definitive nonpolitical. But to effect this very differentiation yet another non- or extrapolitical imperative is mobilized, in which the political seeks its grounding. Thus, for example, the constitution of equality as a political idea in the twentieth century involved a simultaneous mobilization of the spiritual and the economic. When defined as nonpolitical imperatives, the spiritual and the economic appeared as rival grounds of the political. But when defined as extrapolitical, as that which remained before and beyond politics, they worked together to index life as such, and in the name of creaturely life marked out the limits and the failures of the political. A quick description of the chapters might clarify this further.

Subject, Act, Idea, People

I write about each elementary aspect of the political in chapter pairs, the separation into the two chapters highlighting the internal tension, indeed the split, within the element itself.

Chapters 1 and 2 explore the rise, from the late nineteenth century on, of the image of the quintessential "political man" via the critical recasting of two distinct precolonial Indic traditions—renunciation (*sannyas*) and realpolitik (*artha/niti*). Embodied in two iconic figures—Vivekananda, the young renouncer who talked of a resurgent global Hinduism but also of socialism and Shudra revolution, and Chanakya/Kautilya, historical author of the ancient treatise of statecraft, the *Arthashastra*, and kingmaker and political strategist of legend—these two propensities, of renunciation and realpolitik, pulled in opposite directions and yet shared a common search, namely, for a purely political mode of being. Such a mode of being, I argue, was imagined as two distinct types of asocial, even antisocial, orientations—that of the renouncer who makes an irreversible exit from household life for the sake of public service and that of the realpolitiker who holds all social norms hostage to the cause of unconditional political efficacy. The social facts of caste and gender, unsurprisingly, played out in interesting and complex ways with respect to these figures, as they struggled to emerge as exemplars of the antisocial orientation.

Here the process of becoming political shows up as a process of differentiation from the social, which gets defined as the ultimate nonpolitical of the times. And yet this antisocial orientation comes to be grounded in two extrapolitical forces—the spiritual for the renouncer (such that Vivekananda would insist that what he did was not politics at all) and the philosophical for the realpolitiker (such that Chanakya would be recast in modern times as the original political philosopher of India). Spirituality in chapter 1 and philosophy in chapter 2 thus appear as the unmistakable extrapolitical supplements to the purely political mode of being of the political subject—returning us to the two defining issues of our times, namely, the relationship of politics to religion and the relationship of politics to philosophy.

Chapters 3 and 4 explore the modern sensibility of politics as action and nothing if not action (we call politics *activism* and political actors *activists*). Chapter 3 studies new uses of the familiar concept of *karma* as it came to be invoked from the late nineteenth century on, in response to the perplexed question of how to differentiate political action from the sea of unceasing activities that was the business of life itself. Note that this question was the opposite of what anthropology asks today—namely, Can everyday practices of life be seen as intrinsically political?, or, more recently, How do quotidian life activities engage and mediate spectacular political action and exceptional events?[26] Traditionally, *karma*—action, duty, imperative—denoted the very essence of the human condition, which was nothing other than an inescapable series of actions leading to more actions ad infinitum, such that not just this life but all future lives were always already determined in a chain of causality and consequence. Political action, it now came to be argued, was action that could break out of this cruel circularity—of cause leading to consequence and consequence becoming further cause. Hence, the imagination of political action as *nishkama karma*—a particular kind of nonteleological and unattached *karma* that achieved unconditional freedom by relinquishing stakes in consequences. The problem, however, was that in so defining political action, action no longer appeared political in its capacity as action per se but in terms of the renunciatory disposition of the agent of action. Action, in other words, failed to appear as political qua action and dissolved into the subject question.

Here was a paradox in the very constitution of the political. On the one hand, to define politics as action implied that any subject could be political, so long as s/he acted in recognizably political ways. On the other hand, to define politics as subjectivity implied that the subject was always already political, irrespective of her/his action (or indeed inaction). In response to this paradox, I show in chapter 4 how political action came to be reimagined in analogy to labor, since the 1920s. Labor simultaneously denoted a subject, a noun, and a modular form of activity, a verb. To be able to function in this double capacity, however, labor had to be first abstracted from the diversity of concrete work practices engaged in by people of different classes, castes, and genders. As Ambedkar never tired of saying, there was nothing called labor, only laborers—only a contingent hierarchy of intellectual, manual, and menial work, an intricate gradation of pure and polluted, masterful, and degraded bodies.

To model political action after labor thus required the abstraction of labor as an unmarked universal concept, irrespective of its imbrication in actual laboring bodies. Gandhi performed this abstraction by pitching labor—and politics—as a moral disposition, communists and socialists as productive/creative purpose, Tagore as poetic/artisanal disposition. The shared sensibility was that anybody who labored was, presently or potentially, a political actor. But if labor was politics and politics labor, it was paradoxically so only insofar as labor could be indexed as ultimately an extrapolitical force. Labor henceforth came to be glossed as "struggle," that is, a mode of bodily comportment. This was more easily done in images than in discourse. Images of labor now came to be copiously produced in India, often placed side by side with images of hunger, proneness, and passivity, and eventually subtly transcoded, in the name of the political, into a warlike comportment that was however never quite war. The very body from which labor had to be initially extricated and abstracted thus returned as that extrapolitical aspect that made the imagination of politics as action possible in the first place.

Chapters 5 and 6 are about the emergence of the political idea. Here I study how equality becomes thinkable in Bengal and India as the central political idea of our times. Chapter 5 explores early attempts at conceptualizing equality. It argues that equality initially gets posited as a spiritual idea—drawing sustenance from incommensurable philosophical and theological traditions such as nondualist Vedanta, popular Islam, and a recast Buddhism. Central to this moment was the struggle to imagine equality-in-difference, difference being the point of departure for the very thinking of equality in the colony. This challenges our common sense, drawn from the story of liberalism in western Europe, that historically equality gets thought first as formal equality and is only later inflected, in the writings of early feminists and race theorists, by the concept of difference.

In the early years of colonialism, freedom itself appeared predicated on a preliminary setting up of equality between unequals, colonized and colonizer, across the fact (which no one denied) of cultural and civilizational difference. If such an imagination of equality across the colonial interface was the bedrock of nationalism in India, nationalism itself, from the very beginning, was beset by the question of (in)equality between different constituents of the nation. Thus, what we had here was the play not only of difference as such but also of competing criteria of difference. One of the main arguments of chapter 5 is therefore that equality looked different when thought via the fact of gender difference than when thought via facts of caste, religious, or class difference. Hence, instead of working with a normative ideal of equality or with pregiven binaries, such as formal versus substantive, political versus economic, or liberal versus socialist equality, perhaps we should ask, What happens when we have competing inequalities,[27] inflected by competing experiences of difference, which resist being gathered under a singular conceptual rubric such as Difference with a capital *D*?

Ajay Skaria, in his insightful reading of Gandhi's philosophy of equality, argues that equality-in-difference, being that which is without any basis in equivalence or commensuration, can perhaps be thought only in terms of a spiritual aspect. I try to show that spirituality indeed was central not only to early imaginations of equality as an idea but even, in certain cases, to later ones. B. R. Ambedkar, otherwise known as a great rationalist, felt compelled to return to spirituality after thinking with Karl Marx and John Dewey for quite some years. In most of chapter 6, however, I dwell on early socialist and communist thinking in Bengal—and study how economic reason came to be mobilized as a way of circumventing the question of difference, of setting up equivalences where none seemed plausible—as a way of measuring the immeasurable. And yet, I show that while the economic did inspire mass mobilization in the name of equality, what it made thinkable as an idea was not really equality as such but inequality. Equality, an impossible idea in its own terms, thus came to be pitched in the primary sense of a double negative—as that which was not inequality. In order to think equality as a positive idea, the economic itself had to be resignified—through the work of sociology, on the one hand, and literature, on the other. Chapters 5 and 6 thus are a study of the difficult "politicization" of an idea—in its circuitous travels through distinct spiritual, economic, literary, and social registers. The implicit query animating this study is about the very "normative" status of a universal political ideal and the necessary play of the political, the nonpolitical, and the extrapolitical in its constitution.

Chapters 7 and 8 study the "people." Modern politics can be described as the repeated making and unmaking of the people, in whose name popular will and popular sovereignty are invoked. As we know, the people are never ever a preexisting entity. Different communities—race, nation, class, caste, religious community—claim the name of the people at different times, only to be dislodged from that privileged position by other emergent communities. In the last two chapters, therefore, I ask not so much, Who is/are the people?, but How do a people assume form and presence? That is, instead of working with normative concepts such as popular will or popular sovereignty, I attend to specific historical modes of "staging the people," the term *stage* implying here both assembly and artifice in the constitution of political community. Therefore, I am not so much concerned with the different categories of the people posited by political philosophy—class, mass, people, folk, nation, crowd, multitude, and so on. Instead, I dwell on the particular forms that in modern times claim to make the people both thinkable and palpable as an entity.

Chapter 7 is concerned with the rise of the modern political party, which seeks to give people a coherent body. I argue—through a study of the intimate yet fraught relationship between a nationalist party, the Indian National Congress (which claimed to encompass the people as a whole), and a vanguardist party, the Communist Party of India (which claimed to represent the working classes)—that the history of the people as political community is centrally animated in our times by a persistent part/whole dynamic, embodied in the party form. Even though classically a party is meant to represent "a part" of the people, in its modern democratic form it seeks to always already simulate a totality—be it nation, state, people, or the proletariat as a universal class. So while nationalists and communists appeared to stage the people differently—as, respectively, mass party and vanguard party, as the whole and "the part that has no part" (to quote Rancière again), they remained inextricably tied to each other—each feeding on the other's constituencies, representational techniques, mobilizational forms, and rhetorical and pedagogical address. That is to say, both partook in a generalized part/whole dynamic constitutive to the form of the people as community. Equally, both shared the position that the party was the people in its purely political form. Hence the Congress's need to distinguish itself from social and religious organizations, which represented the people in their social and cultural aspects, and the Communist Party's need to distinguish itself from trade unions and peasant leagues, which represented the people in their economic aspect—returning us to the persistent political/nonpolitical dialectic without which the people appeared unthinkable.

In chapter 8, I approach the same question of the people and its form, from a very different angle. In opposition to the structure and solidity ascribed to the people by the party, I now posit the *fictionality* of the people, as it comes to be shaped in Bengal in the first half of the twentieth century. I use the term *fictionality* advisedly. I argue, through a reading of novels, short stories, poems, songs, and drama and a study of the newly emergent figures of the "literary ethnographer" and the "people's poet," that it is precisely the literary—and more specifically the dramatic (not in a generic sense but drama as an effect that cuts across genres)—which in modern times materializes the people as a credible fiction, with a charged yet evanescent presence.

Animating this final chapter is a crucial debate of the times—about the relationship between politics and aesthetics. Many aspects of the debate are familiar to us as having to do with globally salient disputes on aestheticism, naturalism, realism, socialist realism, Nazi art, and so on. But these do not preoccupy me so much as does the question of how culture and aesthetics operate as different, indeed rival, grounds of political community in modern times. Culture indexes what the people are by default—by habit, tradition, history. Culture thus is a claim of a preexisting people that politics must address and mobilize. Culture is about identity. Aesthetics, on the other, hand indexes what the people can become in the future. It is an imagination of the people's potential. It is thus literally about fiction. Hence, the question at stake is not about representation (can a people that is "yet to come" be represented?) but about which modes of staging make the people appear more viable and credible at a certain point in time. In other words, I argue that it is not so much the nature of a people but the mode of its staging that determines the political—a fact that must, however, be hidden, or at least disguised, if the people (the demos) are to function as the founding moment, the stable ground of modern politics.

Part I

The Self

I

Renunciation and Antisocial Being

> Even as the lion, not trembling at noises,
> Even as the wind, not caught in a net,
> Even as the lotus-leaf, unstained by water.
> Do thou wander alone,
> Like the rhinoceros!
> —Vivekananda, quoting from *Dhammapada*

I begin with the question, Who is, or who becomes, a political man in our times? I use the word *man* advisedly, for modern politics emerged across the world as a masculinist formation, even though, as we shall see, women—human and godly—were absolutely critical to its constitution.[1] But I also say *man* in order not to use, a priori, the Enlightenment term *subject*. I believe that the self in political deployment is always already unstable—shorn of self-possession, coherence, even identity, qualities attributed to the subject by modern political philosophy. For at stake at the moment of the institution of the political is the perplexed question, If the political man must speak for others, can he ever really be himself?

The Difficulty of Social Being

Modern politics emerged in India under the shadow of a new binary—state versus society or the social versus the political.[2] Modernity arrived in the colony via colonial conquest.[3] To placate this experience of political humiliation, colonial intellectuals began claiming that the nation's true history lay not in the vagaries of politics but in the deep continuities of *samaj* or native society.[4] The national self was a deeply social self, unperturbed by surface ripples like foreign invasion and regime change. The poet-philosopher Rabindranath Tagore (1861–1941), for example, argued that conflict and so politics were traits peculiar to the West—unlike the East, which was fundamentally socially oriented.[5] The transformation of *samaj* into "society" thus happened in India not through the governmentalization of populations by an absolutist state in the way of early modern Europe but through the operations of an antistatist imagination brought on by colonial experience, an imagination that would often slip into an antipolitics rhetoric, enlisted ironically by even the most political man of our times, Mahatma Gandhi.[6]

But then, denying the political was also the ruse of the colonizer. After all, colonial legitimacy depended on disguising the fact of conquest and staging colonial rule as the rule of law and reason, attributes of an evolved society rather than simply of military prowess or strategic cunning.[7] This indeed was the seduction of modernity, the promise that the colonized, too, could become sovereign once they evolved socially—that is, once they became "reasonable" in their approach toward social victims like women and outcastes.[8] This promise produced a great wave of social criticism in India—which, in its enterprise to reform unjust social practices such as bride burning, enforced widowhood, and caste discrimination, thwarted the nationalist valorization of society. In fact, social reformers did not shy away from enlisting the help of the colonial state, even at the cost of being labeled antinational, on the ground that it was precisely the foreignness, the social disconnect, of the colonial state that allowed it to move firmly against entrenched social orthodoxies. But the very same externality that made the state a potent instrument of intervention in society was also the state's limit in the face of the power of caste and sexual constitutions in India.

The relationship between state and society—the social and the political—was thus a highly charged issue in modern India, as was the very question, What is society? Nationalists, who prioritized political freedom over social justice, and social reformers, who prioritized social justice over political freedom, were locked in a bitter face-off.[9] This was best captured by philosopher, constitutionalist, and Dalit leader B. R. Ambedkar (1891–1956). Ambedkar said that the social question was the first question of modern India and that favoring political freedom over social reform was nothing other than casteism in the guise of nationalism.[10] At other times, however, Ambedkar resented Gandhi's insistence on caste being a social issue, which he felt prevented caste from becoming a full-fledged political cause.¹¹ While this might appear self-contradictory, what Ambedkar actually exposed was the difficulty of working with a given social/political binary in India. For India was no society in the first place, he added with great perspicacity, even though it might be a nation. India was a hierarchical network of caste communities sans sociability. Here caste communities exercised sovereign power (like polities unto themselves) over social subjects, regulating contact, communication, sexuality, and even accidental touch and exercising punitive violence if needed. Hinduism was neither religion nor culture—it was law and, hence, nothing short of a political regime.¹²

In other words, the state/society or the social/political binary appeared in India in the form of a conceptual impasse. The colonized could not simply own up the political, because it was the technology of the colonizer, nor could it ensconce itself in the social, because it was always already conflicted and fraught.

Renunciation and Return

Renunciation became politically salient in the context of this vexed double bind. This was around the 1890s through the 1910s—an in-between and underwritten moment in Indian history, coming after the time of social reform and of peasant and tribal rebellions but before the rise of organized mass nationalism. Debates raged around what would be an appropriate stance for the colonized in her two-faced being, one turned toward the colonizing West, the other turned toward the indigenous social. Not always was the political explicitly invoked in these debates. The talk was often of religion, culture, nation, civilization, and such like, prompting today's historians to read these debates primarily in terms of reformism/revivalism, liberalism/nationalism, communalism/secularism, and so on. I suggest, however, that to reduce these debates to issues of only nation and community is to miss out on a rather significant, instituting moment in the history of the political, namely, the moment when the question—Who is a political man?—was thrown open to theoretical contestation. The ways in which the political was simultaneously owned up and disavowed were crucial to this moment.

Critical to our story is the rise to prominence of Swami Vivekananda (1863–1902). Vivekananda, originally Narendranath Datta, was born to a middle-caste Kayastha family in Calcutta and lived initially the unremarkable life of a moderately well-off (at least until his father's death), middle-class, college-educated young man, who frequented the reformist Sadharan Brahmo Samaj and read John Stuart Mill, August Comte, Herbert Spencer, William Wordsworth, and Thomas à Kempis. In 1881 he came into contact with the rural Brahmin mystic

Ramakrishna. After intense struggle with the idiosyncratic persona of Ramakrishna and his version of ecstatic devotion to Kali, the goddess of destructive primal force, Narendranath was transformed. He became a *sannyasi*, an ascetic, and with fellow brothers set up a *math* or monastic order dedicated to spiritual cultivation, the reading of Indian and European texts, physical labor, and care of the poor and the sick. Vivekananda also embarked on a seven-year journey across the country as *parivrajaka* or spiritual traveler. He spent some of this time alone, in contemplation, travel, and occasional hardship. At other times, he studied with traditional scholars and lived with poor, low-caste, mendicant peoples as well as with native princes and urban elites. Eventually, he set out for America, alone and on a daring journey without much in the way of support or contacts, where he grabbed the world's attention as speaker in the 1893 World's Parliament of Religions. His return to India was met with tremendous enthusiasm but also with criticism from theosophists, missionaries, and the Hindu orthodoxy. Vivekananda died young, but by that time he had set up the Ramakrishna Math (a still-extant monastic institution that recently claimed a religious identity separate from mainstream Hinduism); traveled extensively across India, England, and the United States; and spoken and written substantially, becoming in the process one of the most powerful political icons of modern India.[13]

I am not interested in Vivekananda and his ideas per se. In fact, given the fact that he spoke in public address more than he actually wrote, I feel that an "intellectual" history of Vivekananda as "thinker" is not quite appropriate. In fact, when reading his collected works, one is often struck by his contradictory statements, addressed to diverse publics. I see this as a sure sign that Vivekananda was of the nature of an unresolved moment, his corpus resistant to "content analysis" because it leads to sterile debates over whether he was pro-caste or anticaste, pro-women or antiwomen, pro-Muslim or anti-Muslim, political or spiritual, global or national. What interests me is precisely that Vivekananda was self-contradictory, troubled, and vulnerable to competing political appropriations by groups as diverse as revolutionary nationalists, Hindu militants, socialists, communists, and caste radicals. For the same reason, he is also amenable to new readings. I therefore read Vivekananda—his words, acts, and persona—as a difficult expressive performance of what it means to be a modern political man, but not quite.

Vivekananda embodied a struggle, and perhaps a partial reconciliation, of three traditions—western intellectual, precolonial intellectual, and rural-popular. With all three, Vivekananda engaged with difficulty and intensity as befitted the colonial condition. He also embodied the mutual imbrication of the spiritual and the political, the reclusive and the public—each impulse pulling against the other and by that very detraction animating each other. Vivekananda also skillfully enacted a double address—one directed toward the West and the other toward his own people—producing the effect of an equipoised and impartial self, distinct from the hyperpolitical, passionate, overcommitted nationalist subject. In what follows I read Vivekananda in this framing, while also addressing some later recensions of him by Irishwoman-turned-disciple-turned-Indian-nationalist Nivedita (1867–1911), *swadeshi*-revolutionary-turned-spiritual-master Aurobindo Ghosh (1872–1950)—both central to Vivekananda's afterlife—as well as early socialists and communists. I also invoke motifs of renunciation as found in the common sense and literature of the time in order to explore how, in modernity, renunciation came to index political being, as opposed to being, as it earlier was, a timeless existential question.

Vivekananda came into prominence by becoming an ascetic at a very young age—not in the earlier mode of turning away from the world but in a new mode of reinhabiting the world, but only after first seceding from it. He was laboring against the colonial accusation that renunciation was an otherworldly impulse and lay behind the political ennui of Indians. Vivekananda in fact argued to the contrary—that renunciation was a particularly active way of owning up the world but without stakes, that is, without turning the world into an object of desire, interest, or attachment. When M. G. Ranade (1842–1901), a prominent social reformer and economic nationalist from western India, said that the renouncer could not conceivably be a political man because he had no experience of ordinary social life, Vivekananda retorted that monks were militants because they acted without any sense of "recompense" or "putrid duty," that is, without any economic motivation or social stake.[14] The renouncer's dwelling in the world was thus qualitatively different from the social mode of inhabiting the world.

Vivekananda was one of the earliest public figures in India to invoke the Buddha as political ideal.[15] Buddha refused his personal liberation, *moksha*, many times over, so that lesser creatures in the world could first be saved, Vivekananda said, citing the traditional Mahayana ideal of the *bodhisattva* as one who can achieve nirvana but delays it to stay with suffering beings. According to Vivekananda, Buddha, the "perfect agnostic," acted without the comfort of a personal god or personal soul.[16] Also, history proved that the Buddhist ideal of renunciation and effective imperial power (of the Mauryan king Ashoka who supported Buddhist *dhamma*) emerged simultaneously in India.[17] (Many of these opinions resonate, as we shall see in chapter 5, with Ambedkar's later reconstruction of Buddhism as a religion of equality.) Thus, even though Vivekananda refused to be labeled a political man, he clearly saw renunciation and political being as closely related. Nivedita quotes Vivekananda as saying that "monk and king were obverse and reverse of a single medal";[18] and, again, "what the world wants today is twenty men and women stand in the street yonder and say that they possess nothing but God."[19] Notice the unexpected similarity between the ascetic who possesses nothing and the proletarian who too possesses nothing and therefore is constitutively political!

Renunciation, Colonial and Precolonial

It is easy to slip into reading Vivekananda's ascetic ideal as a precolonial spiritual concept cannibalized for the purpose of modern nationalist politics. Most recent academic writings place Vivekananda in just such a teleology.[20] But let me propose an alternative argument here—namely, once we take Vivekananda out of this teleology, it becomes quite apparent that his kind of renunciation was not easy to harness to nationalism.

There is much evidence in early Indian history of an uneasy relationship between the renouncer and Brahminical and kingly power. The Rg Veda and the Atharva Veda refer to the favorite pastime of the king of gods, Indra, as that of hunting and subjugating ascetics. The *Arthashastra*, the early Indian treatise on statecraft ascribed to Kautilya/Chanakya, gives the injunction that no ascetic should be allowed to settle in the *janapada* or country, lest he fan dissident sectarianism, even rebellion.[21] It was *samaj* or the caste-based social constitution that was to judge whether an individual had the right to renounce society. (Shudras, for example, were not allowed to renounce their life of compulsory labor.) Patanjali's *Mahabhasya* says that the conflict between Sraman (ascetic) and Brahmin is eternal. And a *Shabak Jataka* story describes the Buddha, in his birth as a Chandala or an untouchable scavenger, extolling the virtue of renunciation—a potent analogy between the outcaste (who is prohibited from settling inside the *janapada* for fear of polluting touch) and the renouncer (who must shun *jana samaj* or common society).[22]

William Pinch sees monks, belonging to various heterodox sects, as common and critical figures who transformed the power dynamics of the northern and eastern Indian countryside in the seventeenth and eighteenth centuries. Often as armed warriors reckoned with by kings, monks mobilized middle- and low-caste peasants (as divinely ordained warriors or Kshatriyas rather than cosmically created slaves or Shudras) into dissenting political blocs or *sampradays*. Early colonial power had to "pacify" such groups militarily. The "political *sannyasi*" therefore appears as a threatening figure in the colonial archives.

While in secular historiography, the *sannyasi* appears as a nonmodern, Hindu "communal" figure who jeopardizes the nation's modernity and unity, the *sannyasi* continues to inform—in changed yet persistent manners—modern imaginations of the political in India.[23] Even in the twenty-first century, *sannyasis* remain active in politics, including socialistic ones such as Swami Agnivesh, Hindu militants such as the recent United Provinces chief minister Yogi Adityanath, and women *sadhvis* such as Uma Bharati and Ritambhara, front-ranking members of the Hindu majoritarian Bharatiya Janata Party. Interestingly, in his victory speech after winning the 2019 national elections with a record majority, Prime Minister Narendra Modi called himself a *fakir*, a renouncer, whose empty bag was now filled with the love of the people.

Pinch argues persuasively that Gandhi himself became legible to the masses precisely through this familiar combination of humble peasant and simple monk. Gandhi's minimalist clothes, his spare meals, his *ashram* or sanctuary, his celibacy, his uncompromising nonviolence, and his daily routine of meditation, prayer, and service—all evoked ideals of spiritual asceticism and rural simplicity and allowed, I would add, a renewed politicization of poverty, patience, and suffering in modern times. Interestingly, hundreds of *sannyasis* attended the 1920 Indian National Congress session at Nagpur, and Gandhi invited them to spread the message of noncooperation across the countryside, much to the unease of other congressmen.[24] Hindu *sannyasis* and Muslim *fakirs* mobilized Bengal peasants in the Khilafat movement in the same years.[25] It is important, however, not to focus solely on Gandhi as we often do under the sway of his putative exceptionalism.[26] In fact there were other modes of renunciation in late nineteenth-century and early twentieth-century India that competed with Gandhi's. Swami Sahajanand Saraswati (1889–1950) in Bihar, for example, broke publicly with Gandhi in the mid-1920s and worked toward his vision of a Vaishnava obligation to serve the oppressed peasant through ideals of caste equality and socialism.[27] There was also the earlier ascetic figure of Sri Narayanaguru (1856–1928) in Kerala, who mobilized low-caste Izhavas in the late nineteenth century through a dissident interpretation of Vedanta, a school of early Indian philosophical thought also invoked by Vivekananda.[28]

Bengali fiction, too, deployed the figure of the *sannyasi* to great political effect. The most famous early example is the novel *Anandamath* (1882) by Bankimchandra Chattopadhyay, the "father" of modern Bengali prose.[29] Set against the backdrop of the great 1770 famine of Bengal, the novel features a heroic band of *sannyasis* battling the Bengal nawab, puppet of the English East India Company. The novel was a major hit and contained the poem "Vande Mataram" (I worship thee, mother), India's future national song, and created the image of country as mother goddess, inspiring militant Hindu nationalism and Muslim criticism of nationalist idolatry.[30] Bankimchandra took inspiration from the actual historical rebellion of *sannyasis* and *fakirs* that occurred in northern parts of Bengal in the early 1770s.[31] But he also set up renunciation as a modern political problematic—exploring the possibility of ordinary householders becoming ascetic beings for a few years before they returned to society, after the moment of the political, as it were.

In 1909 and 1910, Prabhat Kumar Mukhopadhyay (1873–1932) wrote *Nabin Sannyasi* (Young ascetic), a novel that was serialized in the popular Bengali magazine *Prabasi*. The poet Hemchandra Bandopadhyay wrote *Bharat Sangeet* (Song of India, 1870), describing a young renouncer, with a noble forehead, standing atop a mountain, calling on the millions to rise up in freedom.[32] Saratchandra Chattopadhyay (1876–1938), the most widely read Bengali novelist of all time, wrote *Pather Dabi* (Call of the road) in 1926, which had as its hero a wandering revolutionary, lonely and celibate, with an ascetic and plastic disposition, able to take on any disguise and blend into any crowd across Bengal and Burma. The novel was a major hit. It was proscribed and its theatrical performance banned by the British, until it came to be staged with much fanfare in the Rangmahal theater in Calcutta, right after independence. Not surprisingly, Saratchandra himself spent some time in his youth as a wandering ascetic—as did, incidentally, the maverick scholar of Buddhism and Marxism Rahul Sankrityayan—and was labeled the "vagabond messiah" by his biographer.[33] The militant communist theater activist Utpal Dutt also staged the play *Sannyasir Tarabari* (The ascetic's sword) about the *sannyasi* rebellion.[34] And communist organizer and musician Hemanga Biswas remembered how growing up in and around a local ascetic's ashram in eastern Bengal gave him skills for future communist politics.[35]

Vivekananda's was thus not a maverick position but neither was it merely a reiteration of the precolonial tradition of militant monks. The existence of such a tradition surely made Vivekananda more easily intelligible. But the nineteenth century added other dimensions to renunciation. Popular discourses on the *kaliyuga* (the age of decline, as per the imagination of the Puranas) criticized the excesses and pleasures of modernity, attributing to the renouncer a renewed legitimacy.[36] After all, Gandhi's own spare lifestyle derived from his 1909 *Hind Swaraj* critique of western civilization as consumerist and wasteful. But more important to the political recasting of renunciation was, I believe, the unhappy question of the social.

The Antisocial Ascetic

In modern India, the renouncer became a privileged position of critique vis-à-vis the social in its twin connotation, as the sovereign domain of national life and as the supreme object of criticism and reform. As mentioned earlier, the reform/revival debate had reached a kind of dead end by the end of the century, when Vivekananda appeared on the scene and condemned the nationalism/reformism debate as useless and shameful.[37] Denouncing the reigning ideals of utilitarianism, he said that ethics of public good could derive only from a spiritual ideal, not a social ideal: "Any system that wants to bind men down to the limits of their own societies is not able to find an explanation for the ethical laws of mankind. The utilitarian wants to give up the struggle after the Infinite . . . and in the same breath asks us to take up ethics and do good to society. . . . If the end is not there, why should we be ethical?"[38] In Vivekananda's formulation, society was a contingent human construction. There was nothing sacred or eternal about it. In fact, society was merely a passing phase in human history until humans learned a more evolved form of togetherness than the merely social.

Nivedita, too, vouched that Vivekananda saw social customs as arbitrary and transient. Only by acknowledging this could one critique society, though with empathy. In Nivedita's reading, Vivekananda viewed society with poetic indulgence, sensing the beauty and suffering of the social being while showing up its inessentiality and ephemerality.[39] Vivekananda disavowed both the disciplinary strictness of the reformer and the blind complicity of the conservative. Distinguishing his own campaign from existing models, he said that the social reformer behaved like a philosopher to a drowning boy—lecturing him while forgetting to step into the waters! He also questioned the lack of "political sanction" behind social reform: "First create the power, the sanction from which the law will spring. The kings are gone, where is the new sanction, the new power of the people. Bring it up."[40] Vivekananda is known to have said that the modern state—the faceless, impersonal structures of bureaucratic government—was particularly unkind to the poor because, unlike in the times of kings, the poor no longer had access to an embodied ruler whose discretion and mercy could be called on, and who, one might add, could be assassinated because, as Claude Lefort reminds us, the place of power had fallen empty in modern times.[41]

Vivekananda was making two simultaneous moves here. He was arguing—by invoking love and empathy—for a particular orientation that could be assumed only by one who had no stakes in society and, therefore, no relationship of necessity with it. At the same time, he was arguing that the legitimacy of political being lay not in a *social* contract—because society was a limiting condition—but in the political man's intelligibility and accessibility to common people. Presumably, the renouncer answered to both these demands—in his being indifferent and external to the social (like the modern state) and in his being embodied, peripatetic, and proximate to the poor (unlike the modern state). That is, Vivekananda was trying to imagine a political being that was other than that of both the state (which reformists invoked) and society (which conservatives invoked). To my mind, it is here that one can fleetingly glimpse the instituting moment of the modern political—in this nonstatist moment of political being's differentiation from social being. Here the social gets posited as the nonpolitical moment against which politics gets defined, and the spiritual comes across as the extrapolitical force enabling the difficult but necessary exit from the social.

Let us read this in the context of European history. We know that the rise of the absolutist state in seventeenth-century Europe made possible the invention of society as an ordered and governable field and the modern state as an abstract, rationalized entity outside the domain of civil society. The invention of society was also a precondition to the rise of the social sciences, sociology, demography, statistics, and so forth and made possible "social reform" as a standard mode of public action. It also led to the possibility of imagining a purely social organism, an imaginary that was quite the favorite of Indian nationalists raised on Herbert Spencer. In other words, the state/society binary made possible the political/social binary in modern Europe. In the colonial context, however, it was clear that the state/society binary produced a political impasse. Here the state appeared as a foreign imposition—inadmissible both as the location of the nation's political self and as the conceptual counterpoise to national society. And national society appeared as always already fraught with inequalities tending to spin out of control. The renouncer, on the other hand, offered an alternative, nonstate way of distancing from *samaj*. The renouncer critiqued society by a priori giving up stakes in it and yet refused to align with the colonial state as did social reformers and liberal nationalists. Renunciation was a refusal of the recently imposed social/political binary. To put it rhetorically, the renouncer, fueled as he was by spiritual energy and intensity, was a quintessential antisocial being.

The Crushed Ego

It is not enough, however, to simply acknowledge the ascetic as a figure with renewed political significance in modernity. One must also try and feel the texture of this new political being. As is well known, Vivekananda drew on early Indian philosophical traditions in order to enunciate a certain version of Advaita (nondualist) Vedanta, into which he, with characteristic opportunism, infused Sankhya and Yoga elements.[42] He then presented this transformed "ancient" philosophy as practical Vedanta—a principle of public action based on nonduality between West and East, elite and poor, Brahmin and Shudra, human and amoeba![43] (I return to Vedanta in greater detail in chapter 5.) Vivekananda argued that without a spiritual realization of nonduality between the self and the other, all projects of emancipation inevitably turned into projects of power—as they did in the hands of reformers, legislators, philanthropists, and nationalists. Nondualism, he added, was possible only in conditions of democracy. Yet, the democratic West, having lost sight of spirituality, turned its poor into passive objects of ameliorative action.[44] The East, for its part, lacking democracy, reduced nondualism to an abstract cognitive principle without practical implications. In an 1898 letter to Mohammed Sarfaraz Husain of Nainital, Vivekananda said that Vedanta needed inputs from "practical Islam," a tradition that valued activism and equality. India needed a "Vedantic mind and Islamic body," he said, in a turn of phrase that later became a famous Vivekananda quote.[45]

One should note that nonduality—neither oneness nor otherness—was a relationship distinct from relationships of both equivalence and identification. In that sense it was like neither liberalism nor nationalism, neither about formal equality nor about unity/community. It was, by that logic, also not about social representation. The political man, Vivekananda seems to be implying, was not a "representative" of the people—for he was neither entirely like the people nor entirely unlike them (no one was entirely like or unlike another). He was merely in a nondualist relationship to them. But nondualism, to be made operative, had to be first materialized in political being—through the cultivation of impartiality, equanimity, and equidistance from all social identities and interests. Only such a perfectly ascetic, even agnostic self, shorn of personhood, could become truly open and hospitable to the needs and demands of others.

In other words, nondualism did not promise to generate a subjectivity in the strict sense of the term.[46] At stake here was the *atman*, a term with no cognate in modern European languages. "The idea does not exist in Europe," Vivekananda said. German philosophers translated *atman* as the self, which was merely a rough approximation.[47] The *atman* could be sensed only through the negation of negation—it was neither mind, nor soul, nor intelligence, nor ego, nor memory, nor individuality. In this world, Vivekananda argued, everything was in flux. Therefore, there was no individuality: "There cannot be any changeful individuality, it is a contradiction in terms."[48] One's embodied self was inconstant, contingent. Hence, identity was impossible. Renunciation was based on this primary realization, which made it possible for one to transcend particular interests and partake in the universal. It was as if renunciation mobilized a nonself, a being without memory, ego, identity, interest, or attachment, and for precisely that reason unconditionally committed to the world. Such a nonself was not the godlike subject of the Enlightenment, who intervened, armed with indisputable scientific knowledge, in the object world. Nor was it the withdrawn, contemplative philosopher of Greek antiquity who cultivated, as Peter Sloterdjik provocatively puts it, a mode of being "as dead as possible" in life, so as to achieve absolute immersion in thought.[49] The renouncer was a powerful yet modest being, socially and culturally indeterminate, at one with the world by virtue of its fundamentally antisocial and impersonal character.

But this nonself did not come about merely through spiritual realization. One had to methodically labor to achieve it. Here Vivekananda brought into play the concept of *yoga*, taken from early Indian Sankhya philosophy. He translated *yoga* as a method of joining or yoking the self to the world. The two critical techniques of *yoga* were *abhyasa*, or reiterative practice, and *vairagya*, or cultivated indifference/nonattachment.[50] Among all the *yogas*, Vivekananda laid special emphasis on *karmayoga*, the discipline of activism. Action by the renouncer, he said, was free action—a formulation, as we shall see in chapter 3, shared by many others of his time. Free action was propelled by neither a sense of duty (for duty was a socially predicated imperative) nor conscience (for conscience remained constrained by the fear of unintended consequences). Free action was based on a humbling sense of the compromised nature of all action: "We cannot breathe or live without injuring others, and every bit of food we eat is taken away from another's mouth. Our very lives are crowding out other lives."[51] Such a realization made action free of pride and ego, for the renouncer acted with a sense of neither efficiency nor importance but a generic indebtedness to the world. The world allowed one to act even though it did not need it—"Be grateful to the man you help."[52] Action by the true renouncer, thus, did not consolidate the self so much as render it redundant.

It is, however, quite inadequate to read Vivekananda only in philosophical terms. Most academic writing, by concentrating exclusively on Vivekananda's philosophy, reads him as a neo-Vedantist, a modern "thinker" who made an ism out of disparate Hindu principles and practices. In this reading, Vivekananda becomes one of many moments in a unidirectional history of modernization, instrumentalization, and nationalization of Hinduism. But Vivekananda, we cannot forget, was also a product of other encounters, such as with popular spiritual and expressive traditions, which cannot be fully accounted for within the analytical framework of modernity, religion, secularism, and nationalism. The most studied encounter is that between the young Narendranath, before he turned ascetic, and the rural mystic Ramakrishna, who became his initiator into the world of spirituality. By all accounts, this was a difficult relationship. Narendranath was as skeptical of the idiosyncratic and unpredictable ways of Ramakrishna as he was of the latter's devotion to the grotesque figure of Kali, the mother goddess. There was also an intense homoerotic love that Ramakrishna showed for Narendranath, forgiving caste and gender mixing in the latter's case, which caused unease in the younger man. And yet, Narendranath's initial incomprehension soon turned into a deep empathy for the intense, almost insane way of life that Ramakrishna shared with other *fakirs* and *sannyasis* of the time. Nivedita recalls Vivekananda reciting a poem regarding these popular figures:

> Sometimes naked, sometimes mad
> Now a scholar, again a fool
> Here a rebel, there a saint
> Thus they appear on earth, the paramhamsas.[53]

Ramakrishna was only one among many such ascetic figures that Vivekananda encountered. Another great influence was Pavahari Baba of Gazipur, whom Vivekananda visited often. Legend goes that he considered becoming Pavahari Baba's disciple, until Ramakrishna appeared in his dreams to reclaim Vivekananda for himself! To Vivekananda, Pavahari Baba had what Ramakrishna did not—namely, a taste for public action.[54] Nivedita recalls how Vivekananda, on meeting a wandering *fakir*, instantly declared that he was a *paramhamsa* as evinced by "every line and curve of his body."[55] Then there was Raghunath Dass, a sepoy who escaped the British army to become a *sannyasi*, despite the very real threat of being shot for desertion. There was also Trailanga Swami of Banaras, who kept mute and responded to people's queries in writing. He went around semi-naked and slept with his feet up on the idol of Lord Shiva—in an act of antisocial irreverence that only a true ascetic could display.[56]

However we may read these encounters, it is clear that Vivekananda recognized in these ascetic figures an illocutionary force that was extradiscursive and extraphilosophical in intent and effect. His guru Ramakrishna's mode of *sadhana* or spiritual practice, after all, was not that of study—he was a nonliterate, poor Brahmin—but of an intimate, bodily enactment of different schools of *askēsis*. Ramakrishna took instruction in various forms of religious practice, both Hindu and non-Hindu, from wandering ascetics who passed by his village. He was instructed in Vaishnava devotion, Shakta *tantra* or esoterics, and Vedantic metaphysics. Under instruction from a Sufi master, Ramakrishna chose to live as a Muslim and apparently even ate beef. Legend has it that Ramakrishna touched human excreta as a way of liberating himself from disgust, the obverse of desire, just as he scrounged for food, alongside a dog, from a garbage dump. In his devotion to Rama, Ramkrishna became Hanuman, the divine monkey, eating roots and fruits, leaping and jumping around. In order to overcome erotic desire, Ramkrishna became a woman, cultivating femininity and acquiring, to his own admission, love and desire for beautiful young men.[57] Though Vivekananda's own instruction was more textual and his persona more vividly masculine, his travels partially reproduced this mode of embodied learning of different ways. His instruction in *darshana* philosophy was undertaken in residence with traditional scholars in traditional settings—Sikh gurus in Punjab, Jain masters in Gujarat, Pandit Narayan Das in Khetri, Suraj Ram Tripathi in Junagadh, and the Vedanta scholar Pramada Das Mitra in Banaras.[58] He also lived with a family of untouchable sweepers in central India and spent time with Muslim peasants in Kashmir. He personally navigated the complicated caste customs of Malabar in the far south.[59]

Nivedita recalls Vivekananda saying that the physical enactment of other ways was akin to learning other languages. After all, only thus could an Irishwoman like Margaret Noble become Nivedita, devotee of the alien and terrifying goddess Kali and an Indian nationalist.[60] Perhaps it was this polyglossia, this learning to speak across traditions and languages, that gave Vivekananda his multiple personalities—alternately an abstract philosopher addressing the West, a mad devotee of the goddess Kali, a political leader exhorting the masses, a humble disciple to a guru, an aimless traveler, and a reclusive ascetic.[61] That is to say, in Nivedita's eyes, Vivekananda was a plastic figure who operated without seeming to fall into the trap of any enduring individuality. It is telling that Kazi Abdul Odud, a prominent Muslim intellectual from East Bengal, distinguished the Hindu identitarianism of Bankimchandra Chattopadhyay, credited with idolatrous worship of the motherland, from the nonidentitarian spirituality of Ramakrishna and Vivekananda. Odud was writing in 1935, when Hindu-Muslim hostility was at its peak in Bengal and India.[62]

No less crucial than his travels and encounters was Vivekananda's devotion to Kali, the goddess of primal force, imaged as a four-armed naked woman, with lolling tongue and flowing hair, one foot on the chest of her consort, cut heads and sabers in her hand dripping blood, genitalia covered by severed limbs strung together. Her worship, the worship of *shakti* or primal power, was a precolonial tradition well entrenched in Bengal and was often associated with heterodox esoterics. She was called the mother and worshipped by the devotee assuming the guise of her infantile but demanding son. In the twentieth century, Kali worship remained popular, though many middle-class reformers saw it as an uncivil practice, involving "vulgar" iconicity, animal sacrifice, and the consumption of meat and alcohol. More acceptable to them was Vaishnava bhakti or Krishna devotion, with the devotee desiring god after the image of a lover at *lila* or play. The devotee in this case assumed *radhabhav*, or a feminized, adulterous affect, craving the attention of Krishna. Kali worship and Krishna worship thus mobilized two kinds of gendered love—one of the son for the capricious mother, and the other of the woman for the unattainable lover. If Vivekananda's choice of Kali worship was a rejection of the feminized self of longing in favor of a masculinized self that dared to embrace infinite cosmic power, it bears remembering that this was also an infantile self.

The following is a poem that Vivekananda wrote about Kali, well known but rarely interpreted:

> It is darkness, vibrant, sonant
> In the roaring, whirling wind
> Are the souls of a million lunatics
> Just loosed from the prison house
> Wrenching trees by the roots
> Sweeping all from the path . . .
>
> Of Death, begrimed and black
> Scattering plagues and sorrows
> Dancing mad with joy
> Come Mother come!
> For Terror is thy name
> Death is thy breath.[63]

Vivekananda told Nivedita that these words were straining inside him, and once he put them down on paper, he fainted from exhaustion. However we read this poem, one cannot but notice the psychosomatic intensity of the experience of madness and terror. Facing Kali was an ego-crushing experience, one of utter subjection and abandonment, of "becoming a slave" to Kali.[64] Vivekananda also spoke of embracing death and worshipping terror. In a lecture to young monks at the Belur Math, he defined renunciation pithily as "the love of death."[65]

Renunciation cannot be understood without this affective intensity that inflected the abstract Vedantic ideals of nonattachment. The charge displayed by the renouncer as a modern figure was thus derived from the difficult coming together of two incommensurable orientations—indifference and desirelessness, on the one hand, and a terrible and all-consuming love, on the other, not for a beautiful distant lover but for a hideous and driven mother-woman. Hence, in this imagination death appears central. Death here is both the social death of the renouncer and the literal death, the obliteration, that always already lurks at the edges of challenging love.

Renunciation and Nationalism

Renunciation in Vivekananda was thus a complex configuration. In what way did this produce the figure of the political man in turn-of-the-century India? The conventional reading is as follows. Vivekananda modernized and rationalized Hinduism and turned the figure of the ascetic into a rallying point for the nation. The politicization of the ascetic inspired the renunciation of personal interests in public service. It also inspired the actual sacrifice of life for the motherland. True, militant Hindu nationalism was one of the legacies of Vivekananda. However, my argument is the opposite—namely, that Vivekananda appeared as a quintessential political man precisely at the point where he resisted nationalism.

Nivedita, who tried more than anyone else to translate Vivekananda into nationalist terms, recalls Vivekananda's relentless struggle against nationalist sentiment and patriotic anger. Attachment to country and history was the same as attachment to home and family, he believed. The *sannyasi* was an ascetic and only that, and must remain equidistant from all races, societies, and cultures.[66] He must be an impersonal "witness" rather than "for or against India" and must avoid all politics of ressentiment.[67] Nivedita admitted ruefully that if Vivekananda was a nationalist he was so in spite of himself—for "of the theory of this [nationalism], he was unconscious."[68]

Sarala Devi Chaudhurani (1872–1945), *swadeshi* writer and patron of Bengal revolutionaries, complained that Vivekananda failed his followers by refusing to become their leader and ideologue.[69] Vivekananda even shocked his contemporaries by saying that Indians should not be given freedom because they did not deserve it. He wrote, "Slaves want power to make slaves."[70] Vivekananda preferred universal equality over nationalism. Hence, he performed a double address to the West and to his fellow Indians—advocating for equality between colonizer and colonized and among castes and classes in the same breath. This was an enacted universalism unlike the aggressive epistemological universalism of modern reason. It explains Vivekananda's desire to be called an ascetic and only that, as well as his advice to followers that they must not follow the path of either nationalism or social reform—that is, neither culturalism nor liberalism—but stay with the "old grounds of universal salvation and equality."[71]

Vivekananda thematized the question of equality via the figure of the Shudra. The Brahmin (the priestly caste), the Kshatriya (the warrior caste), and the Vaishya (the producing and commercial castes, recently exemplified by the British) had ruled successive phases of history. Currently there were emergent signs of the final phase of history, when Shudras would gain supremacy across the world not by emulating Brahmins or Kshatriyas but in their own full-blown "Shudrahood." Directly translating modern political ideologies into his version of nondualism, Vivekananda stated: "Socialism, Anarchism, Nihilism and other like sects [are] the vanguard of the social evolution that [is] to follow."[72] Muslim and British rule had ended hereditary caste privilege in India, he said. The Shudra now had the option of converting out of Hinduism; therefore, Hindus had no choice but to admit to equality.[73] Vivekananda saw himself as leading a band of ascetics, possessing nothing but knowledge and educating the poor, because caste privilege, he said, was based above all on a denial of knowledge to the underclass. Today, learning was every man's struggle, "alone or in combination."[74]

Lower-caste movements had become powerful in Bengal by the early twentieth century. Vivekananda also traveled extensively in Madras and Malabar and experienced firsthand caste dissensus in the south. A middle-caste individual, he himself had been accused of daring to represent Hinduism to the world despite not being a Brahmin. The *Indian Messenger*, the journal of the reformist Sadharan Brahmo Samaj, wrote on July 31, 1897: "How can Vivekananda, who is a Shudra, assume the role of a sannyasi, a religious teacher of the people?"[75] Caste radicals often invoked Vivekananda as a source of inspiration. For example, the moral critique of Brahminical hierarchy made by the untouchable Chamars of Lucknow, as R. S. Khare shows, drew on the ideals of asceticism and nondualism posited by those like Vivekananda, rendering Buddha into one of the supreme ascetic exemplars of past spiritual and philosophical traditions.[76] In fact, so did latter-day communists, including Vivekananda's own brother Bhupendranath Datta (1880–1961).[77] Datta started his political life as a nationalist revolutionary; traveled to Germany, the United States, and Russia; and eventually turned to communism. But unlike many orthodox Marxists of his time he retained sensitivity toward India's caste sociology and devotional traditions.[78] In an essay on becoming Marxist in 1960s Bengal, Dipesh Chakrabarty writes that he and his peers moved directly, though not seamlessly, from being fans of Vivekananda to being followers of Marx. As a young neocommunist, Chakrabarty remembers having to disavow his own middle-class upper-caste ancestry. This was far more than just "declassing." It was a rite of passage involving renouncing (and denouncing) one's social station.[79] Needless to say, communists and caste radicals, like Vivekananda's ideal renouncer, never invested as strongly in nationalism as did those who valorized national society. Communists and caste radicals sought to be, with various degrees of success, antisocial in the best sense of the term.[80]

Renunciation and Its Limits

And yet there is no denying that an irresoluble tension beset the renouncer as political man. This was the tension between two expressive idioms, of self-mastery and self-effacement, that co-constituted the ascetic's public face. At the Alambazaar Math in 1897, addressing young monks, Vivekananda proclaimed, quoting from the Bhagavad Gita: "There is no sin in thee, there is no misery in thee; thou art the reservoir of omnipotent power. Arise, awake, and manifest the Divinity within."[81] Vivekananda was exhorting listeners to be extraordinary, purified, ascetic selves, with power akin to god's own. As Shamita Basu says, Vivekananda replaced the self-ironic tone of late nineteenth-century colonial intellectuals with a performative idiom of power—"manliness"—proper to the renouncer.[82] And even as she notes the uncertainties involved in the project, Parama Roy says, quite rightly, that Vivekananda fashioned a masterful male self (unlike his guru Ramkrishna's assumed femininity), eliciting desire, notably from white women, only so that the celibate, virile, hard-hearted beautiful monk could rebuff it.[83]

It was this masterful aspect of the ascetic self that nationalist revolutionaries mobilized in the name of self-sacrifice. Aurobindo Ghosh (1872–1950) entered political life under the inspiration of Vivekananda and with support from Nivedita. His political career contributed a great deal toward Vivekananda's later nationalization. Aurobindo wrote a blueprint text in 1905 called *Bhavani Mandir*, in which he planned a Kali temple as the organizational hub of ascetic self-fashioning and revolutionary political action by the Indian youth.[84] Here renunciation became the font of a sacrificial supersubjectivity—masterful, violent, Hindu, and nothing if not Hindu. Apparently, this was the lesson Aurobindo drew from Vivekananda. Contrast this with a well-known incident in Vivekananda's own life. When told, during his travels in Kashmir, of a temple that had been destroyed by a Muslim king, instead of expressing resentment at "foreign" conquest, Vivekananda heard the goddess Kali say: "Do you protect Me? Or do I protect you?" "So there is no more patriotism," Vivekananda is known to have said. "I am only a little child."[85] If, for Aurobindo, Kali's primal force fueled a passionate and hyperactive political subject, in Vivekananda's own exemplary rhetorical posture, Kali rendered the self shadowy and feeble. Thus, if renunciation in Aurobindo was a heightening of the effect of the self through the spectacle of its exemplary sacrifice, in Vivekananda it was an arduous effort to articulate a nonself, one that could assume the clarity needed to mirror and manifest the world at large. After all, if the political man was to express—but not represent in the modern liberal sense—the people and the poor, then his own self, his personhood, must be minimized, rendered reflexive like a mirror. (We shall encounter the mirror metaphor again in chapter 5, in the context of the other Vedantist and theorizer of equality, Sri Narayanaguru.) Incidentally, when Vivekananda started his own organization of ascetic activists, he concluded the initiation ceremony not with worship of Kali, like Aurobindo, but with the offering of flowers at the feet of the Buddha.[86]

This tension in renunciation between mastery and modesty, self-righteousness and self-effacement, was by no means peculiar to Vivekananda. In fact, it was constitutive of the very idea of the political subject as it emerged in modern times. In modernity, we define the political in two ways—as a new subject or as an exemplary act. The dilemma that besets the modern political, then, is as follows. Is the subject—the working class, the people, the ascetic, the Dalit, the black—always already political, irrespective of her action and/or inaction? Or is the act—strike, war, fast, civil disobedience, renunciation, class struggle—a priori political regardless of the agent of the act? That is, must the political, to be efficacious, accentuate or understate the subject? Or, to put it differently, must the political act bear the signature of its agent, or must the signature be erased for the act to become a sui generis political act? The renouncer, it seems to me, strives to have it both ways—that is, foreground an excellent and extraordinary subject (the idiom of mastery) and, at the same time, mitigate the agential claim of just such a subject (the idiom of modesty). As one who conquers ego, desire, and social station, the renouncer demonstrates unqualified self-mastery, which may stealthily blur into a mastery of the world. But as one who lets actions speak for themselves, the renouncer is also a nonself who renders the subject question superfluous. I believe that this tension between subject and act, mastery and modesty, constitutes the modern problematic of the political, which is why I call Vivekananda an instituting moment. I return to this problem in chapter 3, when I deconstruct the modern definition of the political as action and nothing if not action.

Not surprisingly, then, renunciation as a mode of political being reached its limits over the question of who renounces. At one place, Vivekananda asked whether a beggar, who had nothing to give up, could be called on to renounce.[87] Was renunciation accessible to one always already shorn of property and words? Or would the poor forever remain in an ironic relationship to the renouncer—jeopardizing the latter's claim to political acumen? Was renunciation really a parody of poverty—as communists implied when they insisted that Gandhi's asceticism was no more than self-indulgent role-playing? But then Vivekananda also argued that renunciation must be put to work "in the cottage of the poor man": "If you teach Vedanta to the fisherman, he will say, I am as good a man as you. I am a fisherman, you are a philosopher, but I have the same God in me as you have in you. And that is what we want, no privilege for anyone, equal chances for all; let everyone be taught that the Divine is within and everyone will work out his own salvation."[88] Vivekananda would even go on to say, like a latter-day Marxist: "It depends on you who have no money, because you are poor you will work. Because you have nothing, you will be sincere, you will be ready to renounce all."[89] As if the poor were renouncers by default! In other words, the question of Who is the political man? stumbled over the question of whether politics inhered in a particular subject (the poor, the Shudra, the ascetic) or in the very act of renunciation, irrespective of who renounced.

Let me end by invoking the other exemplary ascetic figure of Indian politics, Gandhi, who embodied in his own person this subject/act impasse. As mentioned, Gandhi was very much a product of the turn-of-the-century idiom of renunciation; he fashioned a unique political self, seamlessly moving through a series of disavowals—nonviolence, nonattachment, nonpossession, noncooperation—all ways of giving up claims of agency, activism, and efficacy. (Interestingly, Vivekananda also stated in so many words that "nonresistance" was the "highest position of power.")[90] The other side of Gandhi's efforts at achieving this exemplary and disinterested nonself—through prayer, fasting, and celibacy—was his unceasing attention to the exact nature and texture of the political act itself. He proposed intricate theorizations of *seva* (service), *satyagraha* (truth-quest), fasting, and sexual protocols, and he held them up against other kinds of actions, such as war, passive disobedience, the strike, and so on, which he felt were inadequate because they were not sufficiently charged with spiritual integrity.

Despite his emphasis on the autonomy and integrity of the act as such, Gandhi would feel compelled to return to the question of the subject. Thus when faced with so-called prostitutes as political subjects, Gandhi felt profoundly challenged, even unnerved. Was renunciation by a prostitute—who gives away all her gold ornaments, tools of her trade as it were, to the Tilak Swaraj Fund—equivalent to renunciation by other more morally acceptable social subjects? Or despite the profundity of her act, does she remain irreversibly improper and undeserving? In 1921, 350 prostitutes in the East Bengal district of Barisal volunteered to become members of the Congress Party in response to Gandhi's call to "broaden membership." But when they wanted to seek office in Congress committees, Gandhi categorically refused.[91] In the context of widespread mass mobilization, proper political subjectivity became an impossible question as the subject/act impasse took on newer faces. Gandhi's repeated withdrawals from mass agitation, of which the 1922 Chauri Chaura incident was the most famous,[92] was on the grounds that the ordinary man or woman on the street always already fell short of being the true *satyagrahi*, the truly ethical political subject. The communists countered this charge by arguing that if the act itself was political, then the question of the moral worth of the subject was irrelevant. This subject/act impasse, I argue, would never get resolved, only sidestepped, as the twentieth century rolled on. And the question—Who is a political man?—would always remain besieged by the counterquestion, What is a political act?

2

Philosophy, Theater, and Realpolitik

> What do I fear? Myself? There's none else by:
> Richard loves Richard; that is, I am I.
> —Shakespeare, *Richard III*

The realpolitiker is as different from the renouncer as can be. Yet he, too, is an antisocial being who holds social norms and relationships hostage to the cause of political efficacy. He, too, is a solitary figure like the ascetic, but that is because he is unloved and untrusted. And he is dangerous, being without spiritual or moral grounding. He is a purely political being, if such a being can indeed be imagined.

In early twentieth-century India, the figure of the realpolitiker emerged after the image of the ancient political Brahmin Chanakya (also known as Kautilya and Vishnugupta)—putative author of the *Arthashastra*, the earliest Indian treatise on statecraft. Chanakya was also popularly believed to be the freethinking Brahmin minister of King Chandragupta Maurya (340–293 BCE) and the real brain behind the rise of the Maurya Empire, the earliest imperial formation in Indian history. Historians disagree on the exact date and location of Chanakya and on whether the Chanakya of legend was indeed the author Kautilya of the *Arthashastra*.[1] But despite uncertainties around the real historical figure, Chanakya/Kautilya has remained a popular figure through the centuries, mentioned with wary respect in precolonial political treatises, classical Sanskrit plays, and collections of popular tales. Even today, he is frequently invoked in theater, cinema, journalism, and even comic books. In this chapter I recount the story of Chanakya's reinvention as the supreme figure of the political man in modern times.

Artha and Politics

In early India, politics was subsumed under the broad concept of *artha*. *Artha* had a range of meanings—purposive action, object of desire or purpose, intended meaning of a word or sentence, statecraft, wealth, and success. *Artha* was also one of the three (later four) *purusharthas* or ends of human life (namely, *dharma* or social or moral activity, *artha* or worldly success, *kama* or erotic pleasure, and *moksha* or liberation from the cycle of lives). Patrick Olivelle translates *artha* as "success." I prefer to define it as "efficacy" because *arthashastra*, the science of achieving *artha*, was really about how to exercise power and deal with counterpowers. This is as close as we can get to a definition of politics as we know it today.[2]

Kautilya's *Arthashastra* dealt with matters of governance, civil and criminal law, land, forest, manufacturing, mining, property, taxation, city planning, fort architecture, chariot making, information and intelligence gathering, warfare, alliances, and enmities, making no distinction as such between *polis* and *oikonomia* regarding the efficient management of a polity. Following this early text, *arthashastras* and *nitishastras* proliferated in India in later centuries, including in diverse adaptations by Buddhist and Muslim authors, and the figure of Chanakya/Kautilya was recalled as an exemplar of political acumen. While the science of *artha* was originally addressed to rulers of men, in the form of *nitishastras* it came to be popularized through well-known animal stories of the *Panchatantra*—the five techniques for worldly efficacy. The *Panchatantra* proliferated not only in folklore in diverse Indian languages but also in multiple adaptations in Pahlavi/Persian, Arabic, Greek, Hebrew, Chinese, and Latin.[3] In this dispersed anecdotal form, the science of *artha* was meant no longer just for kings but for all those who sought power—wealth, social standing, and success—in life. *Artha*, in other words, was the generalized art of "being politic." (More on this distinction between "being politic" and the modern notion of "doing politics" is presented in chapter 3, where I discuss the modern concept of politics as action.)

In precolonial imaginations of *artha*, there was no operative division between state power and economic power, one being unthinkable without the other, though today the term *artha* has been erased of its political connotations and reduced to economics. *Artha* simply implied an efficacious and worldly orientation toward power as such. If *artha* worked in opposition to anything, it was *dharma*. *Dharma*, again a word with many meanings, is often misconstrued as religion, and the *dharma/artha* dichotomy is wrongly translated as the dichotomy between the religious and the secular. In the generic division between *arthashastras* and *dharmashastras*, however, *dharma* stood not for religion but for law. Law here refers to *varnashrama*, or the order of castes and "stages of life" (*brahmacharya* or celibate studentship, *garhastha* or the household, *vanaprastha* or retirement, and *sannyasa* or renunciation, with all stages but the household prohibited to the laboring and menial castes). Evidently, *varnashramadharma* was about a social hierarchy of unequals (by birth and occupation) and was a juridical imagination consisting of differentiated rights, privileges, and duties; strict regulation of intimate relationships (sex, marriage, and commensality); and a hierarchical gradation of penalties and penances for transgression of caste prohibitions. *Varnashramadharma* was encoded in the genre of *dharmashastras*, most famously the *Manusmriti*, the text that B. R. Ambedkar publicly burned on December 25, 1927, on the occasion of the Mahad Satyagraha.

Historians have shown that *dharmashastras* and *artha-/nitishastras* were competing genres in precolonial India, the former celebrating the supremacy of the social constitution, the latter celebrating political intelligence that could cut through the social constitution and achieve success in spite of juridical obstacles. Philological studies of multiple *Arthashastra* manuscripts show that caste was not mentioned in the original text. Passages asserting Brahminical exceptionalism and the injunction that the king must at all costs ensure caste conformity in his realm were later interpolations.[4] Studies of medieval south India also confirm that political efficacy often challenged Brahminical *dharma*—as evidenced by myriad low-caste kingships that compelled Brahminical acquiescence to "illegitimate" political power.[5] We see a parallel in Mughal times in the dichotomy between *siyasat* and *shariat*—*siyasat* denoting political acumen and thematized in the *akhlaq* literature, rivaling the *shariat*, the textual format of Islamic jurisprudence.[6] In both *dharmashastra* and *sharia*, law was pitched as the transcendental order of the world, preexisting the institution of kingship, *rajatva*, or *sultanat*. In other words, in precolonial India, political power was imagined not as the power to make law (and declare exception)—the classical Judeo-Christian definition of sovereignty[7]—but as the ability to cut through a law that seemingly always already existed. Indeed, political efficacy sometimes consisted in mobilizing "other" laws such as regional customs and *lokavyavahar* (popular practice) against *dharma* and *sharia*—such as during Turkish and Mughal rule, when governing a multilingual and multireligious subject population required an explicit suspension of the *sharia*, despite objections by theologians. Needless to say, this precolonial *artha/dharma* or politics/law binary was very different from modern-day binaries of state/society and political/social.

Philosophy versus History

When Chanakya/Kautilya came to be discussed in modern India, the terms of the debate had shifted under the influence of colonial epistemologies, though a critique of the social continued to animate the conversation. The discussion was now about whether Chanakya was a political philosopher or simply a historical figure who exemplified the canny art of politics. Faced with the European imagination of the political as philosophical, the colonized felt it necessary to reclaim Chanakya as their very own political philosopher, even better if he was of great antiquity, like Plato and Aristotle. And yet, there was also the influential colonial opinion that Indian philosophy was idealist and lacking in political salience. The need to show up Chanakya as being steeped in the actual practicalities of politics was thus no less compelling.

The early twentieth-century interest in Chanakya can be traced to the "discovery" of two manuscripts of the *Arthashastra* by a Tanjore pandit, their handing over to the Mysore Government Oriental Library, and the 1905 publication of a paper by R. Shamashastry in *Indian Antiquary*. Shamashastry published an edited version of the manuscript in the same journal in 1909 and its full translation as a book in 1915. Not that Chanakya was unknown before then. References to Chanakya were ubiquitous—in precolonial *niti* texts, stories, and drama—in Kamandaka's *Nitisara*; Banabhatta's *Kadambari*; Vishakhadatta's *Mudrarakshasa*; the Buddhist Somadeva's *Nitivakyamrta* as well as *Panchatantra*, *Kathasaritsagara*, and *Nandisutra*; and even as late as the fourteenth-century text of Mallinatha. In Bengal, *niti* was already being translated in the nineteenth century. Manmatha Nath Dutt translated Kamandaka in 1896.[8] Even though an extant manuscript of the *Arthashastra* was unknown, Indologists discussed the "political science" of Chanakya through studies of other texts that cited him.[9] *Chanakyasutras*, or Chanakya's aphorisms, were sold as low-priced chapbooks in local markets, and some were even incorporated in readers for colonial schools. And yet, there was something exciting about the rediscovery of a full manuscript of the *Arthashastra*, beyond the general nationalist celebration and colonial skepticism around the possibility of a classical political figure for India.[10]

An intense debate about Chanakya took place in the mid-1920s in the pages of the *Indian Historical Quarterly*. Benoy Kumar Sarkar (1887–1949)—polyglot, sociologist, economist, and philosopher, who founded *Arthik Unnati*, the first

Bengali journal of economics, and in 1914 edited and translated the medieval political treatise *Sukraniti* (which also invoked Kautilya as the font of political skill)—argued that Chanakya and the *Arthashastra* were philosopher and philosophy, respectively. The political could be thought only as a universal imperative, he argued, and therefore was of the nature of a philosophical principle.[11] If one paid attention to the unmistakable similarities between Chanakya's and Machiavelli's treatises, it became obvious that political reason was a universal philosophical operation irrespective of the particular time and place of its enunciation. Neither Germans nor Indians understood this. Only Italians did. This was because they read Giambattista Vico, transcended empiricism and historicism, and grasped the dynamics of philosophical history![12]

Chanakya, we know, was famous for his alleged "end justifies the means" political rationality, referred to, among others, by Max Weber in his "Politics as Vocation" lecture.[13] Sarkar implied that even if Chanakya was about politics without moral or spiritual grounding, his philosophical integrity compensated for this lack of foundation. The historian Kalidas Nag, however, disagreed. He argued, in his book *Les theories diplomatique, de l' Inde ancienne et l'Arthacastra* (1923) that Kautilyan political (a)morality had been historically abandoned by India.[14] The *Arthashastra* was actively rejected, within a century of Chanakya and Chandragupta Maurya, by the latter's successor, King Ashoka, when he turned from *artha* to Buddhist *dhamma* as the basis of just rule. Thereafter, the tradition of pure political reason came to be subsumed under ethical and normative discourses.[15] (As we know, Gandhi also counterpoised realpolitik to his vision of righteous public life based on *dharma* and the morality of means.)[16] Nag further argued—quoting the seventh-century poet-playwright Banabhatta's derogatory statement that Chanakya *niti* was *maranatmaka*, or "of the spirit of death"—that evidence from early Indian *kavya*, or literature, confirmed India's civilizational turn from the political toward the moral. It was a fatal confusion identifying the fate of Chanakya as character to the career of the *Arthashastra* as text and tradition, Nag added. While Chanakya continued to be nominally invoked through centuries as a theoretical reference point and a literary protagonist, the *arthashastra* as an intellectual tradition stood co-opted by moral and legal discourses of the *dharmashastras*. There was thus a critical disjunction between Chanakya and the *Arthashastra*, between the dramatic life of the man and the epistemological life of the text—preventing the coupling of philosopher and treatise that was a basic protocol of European metaphysics and that Sarkar invoked in order to pitch Chanakya as a Machiavelli analogue.

In other words, Kalidas Nag and many other contemporary historians like Narendra Nath Law and R. P. Kangle felt that an overarching normative framework was necessary in order to regulate cynical and opportunist politics. R. P. Kangle, known for his own edition of the *Arthashastra* and for his association with both Ambedkar and the communist S. A. Dange, did agree with Sarkar on the relative autonomy of political reason in India's past. He, unlike Nag, believed that only aspects of law, and not politics as such, were later appropriated by the *dharmashastras* from within the *arthashastra* corpus. But he too felt compelled to argue that Chanakya was not entirely an amoral person, because he instructed kings in high moral principles and practices of self-discipline.[17]

Benoy Sarkar, on the other hand, invoked Chanakya and Machiavelli as philosophical pioneers who for the first time instituted a distinction between political reasoning and normative reasoning. According to Sarkar, Kautilya emancipated politics from rules of everyday social life based on moral or *dharmic* injunctions.[18] After all, politics began only when preexisting moral frameworks fell into crisis. Sarkar's stake in creating an analogy between Machiavelli and Chanakya was evidently to consecrate Chanakya as the inaugural moment of political philosophy in India, just as Machiavelli was in Europe. Historians such as Nag, however, implied that Chanakya was actually the end of a line, given that *arthashastra* fell into abeyance soon afterward. Indologist V. R. Ramchandra Dikshitar, while agreeing with Sarkar that Chanakya *niti* remained a living tradition in India at least until the coming of colonialism, was also skeptical of accepting Chanakya as a philosopher. The *Arthashastra*, Dikshitar said, inherited a long tradition of political thinking, invoking no fewer than ten theoreticians in its introductory verses.[19] It was therefore not an original or originary text as must be an authoritative sample of philosophy.

Note how the terms of the debate appear here as a disciplinary face-off between history and philosophy. Benoy Sarkar was impatient with the historians' debate, preoccupied as it was with figuring out the date, place, and context of Chanakya and the actual authorship of the *Arthashastra*. Because ancient Indian treatises were often written in the form of *sutras* and *shlokas* (aphorisms and couplets), "Hegelians mistook them for poetry."[20] But Indic intellectual traditions articulated philosophical insights in the form of condensed statements, meant for future elaboration in assemblies. They were not ready-made, finished products of solitary ratiocination, Sarkar insisted.[21] In other words, Indian philosophy had less stake in establishing the philosopher as an originary, contemplative, and solitary figure, and was instead interested in inviting interlocution by future commentators into the act of philosophizing itself. For that very reason, contextualist or historicist readings of early Indian texts were, according to Sarkar, both impossible and useless: "It must never be forgotten, be it repeated, that the authors of the Kautilya cycle were philosophers. They were dealing with the theory of the state, the ideals of statesmanship, the knowledge as to the ways and means of *prithivya labhe palane* (the acquisition and maintenance of the earth). As theorists, idealists, logicians of *rajarsi* [renunciate king] and of 'world conquest' they were not necessarily bound to take their inspiration from their own environment."[22] Hence, it is erroneous to consider history as a mode of intellectual apprehension with regard to Chanakya *niti* as a tradition of thought.

Sarkar had a particularly bitter debate with the Calcutta University historian U. N. Ghoshal on whether Chanakya had any modern relevance. Sarkar insisted that empiricist historians, who read ancient texts instrumentally as mere "sources," would find in the *Arthashastra* an archaic political form, namely, kingship. Their empiricism blinded them to the philosophical fact that in *arthashastra* the king was only one component of the *saptanga* (seven limbs) of the state. In India, kingship was not sovereignty in a medieval European sense. Kingship was not the source of law. *Dandaniti*, or justice/punishment, was a principle antecedent to royal decree, prior to even the concrete institution of kingship. In other words, *arthashastra* constituted a universal theoretical principle and was not predicated on a historical political form such as monarchy or democracy.[23] Ghoshal, on the other hand, argued that the *saptanga* idea itself was archaic because it placed jurisprudence, political economy, diplomacy, and international relations within the same framework, unmindful that these were separate academic disciplines. Ghoshal then went on, as befitted an honest positivist historian, to argue that theory—being abstract, speculative, acontextual—was a lesser mode of knowledge than intellectual history, that is, the study of thought "immanent" to life as "vital action."[24] Consequently, Ghoshal, who had initially called his own book *Hindu Political Theories*, renamed it *Indian Political Ideas* in the 1950s,[25] thus abandoning any universal philosophical claim for ancient Indian political traditions.

What difference did it make to read Chanakya as a philosopher rather than as a historical character? In truth, the actual text of *Arthashastra* was not of the nature of a philosophical treatise. It was an abstract technical treatise about statecraft, although early in the text Kautilya mentions philosophy or rather "critical inquiry" (*anvikshiki*) as one of the skills an efficacious ruler must cultivate. But Sarkar was desperate to prove that the *Arthashastra* was indeed a philosophical treatise. It seemed to him that the only way to ensure the freedom of a political subject from particular religious, social, or moral constraints was to set him up as a philosopher, an orientation he thought was always already extracontextual and transcendental. Being learned in German as well as Italian languages and philosophies, Sarkar was greatly influenced by continental traditions of political thinking and desired a similar philosophical tradition for India. His historian interlocutors, however, were concerned that attributing such philosophical autonomy to the political man might be an unwitting affirmation of the dangerous antisocial and amoral propensities inherent in realpolitik. In other words, the issue here was really about stabilizing the ground of politics. After all, what prevented the realpolitiker from taking flight into potential anarchy and canny opportunism? Could it be the self-consistency of the philosophical form, which politics must wear in order to protect itself against its own vicissitudes? Or was it normative regulation—social, religious, and moral? Or was it simply historicism that served to limit Chanakya and the *Arthashastra* to an archaic, Hindu, kingly past, so that the threat of unregulated realpolitik might not spill over and contaminate the modern present?

The Drama of Realpolitik

The dangerous freedom of the realpolitiker was perhaps best dramatized by twentieth-century Indian theater. The rendering of Chanakya into a dramatic character already had a precolonial moment. Vishakhadatta's *Mudrarakshasa*, placed by historians around the seventh or eighth century CE, was a play about intricate moves and countermoves by Chanakya and Rakshasa, the latter a minister of the Nandas who were deposed by Chanakya in alliance with King Chandragupta Maurya. H. H. Wilson featured the play in his 1827 Orientalist collection of Sanskrit drama, and it was later incorporated in the English collection of translated Sanskrit plays by P. Lal.[26] *Mudrarakshasa* had a renewed life in colonial and postcolonial times. Vijaya Mehta of the theater group Rangayan and later a well-known film director produced *Mudrarakshasa* in 1975 for the Sahitya Sangh, an eminent literary academy; B. V. Karanth, the doyen of the Kannada stage, did the same in 1978.

I, however, find it most interesting that the leftist theater legend Habib Tanvir—with his militant Marxism and Indian People's Theatre Association links, expressed interest in Bertolt Brecht and Henrik Ibsen, and experiments with folk forms—would direct a classical Sanskrit play such as *Mudrarakshasa*, as he indeed did in 1964. Talking about his choice of the play, Tanvir said that *Mudrarakshasa* was remarkable in being a purely political play, thick with intricate machinations by diverse political agents and urbane subjects, so much so that he had to read it many times over and even use visual insignia to disaggregate its characters' complex web of identity and allegiance. He also said, in more general terms, that his choice of Sanskrit plays was an attempt at reviving their theatrical nature. In traditional scholarly convention, such plays were read as *kavya* or poetry, within the framework of classical *rasa* (effect/affect) theory, which he considered inadequate to the thematization of politics.[27] *Mudrarakshasa*, another critic remarked, was an exceptional play because its purely political nature resisted *rasa* analysis in classical aesthetic terms, as if the political was a peculiarly modern affect or emotion that exceeded the classical list of known human emotions.[28]

The classical dramaturgical treatise *Bharatanatyashastra* lists eight *rasas* (emotions) and their corresponding *bhavas* (expressions) for *abhinaya* (enactment)—*shringar* (love/beauty) and *rati* (delight); *hasya* (mirth) and *hasa* (laughter); *karuna* (pathos) and *shoka* (sorrow); *raudra* (terrible) and *krodha* (anger); *veera* (heroic) and *utsaha* (energy); *bhayanaka* (fearsome) and *bhaya* (terror); *bibhatsa* (grotesque) and *jugupsa* (disgust); and *adbhuta* (wondrous) and *vismaya* (astonishment). In later times, some critics added to the list a ninth *rasa*—namely, *shanta rasa*, a state of emotionlessness proper to the moment of cessation, resolution, equilibrium, even peace. Many modern critics felt that this range of *rasas* could not quite depict the affective state of a political subject, even though classical plays did mobilize to great effect *rasas* like the heroic, the pathetic, the terrifying, and even the calm (most famously in the epic Mahabharata) as aspects of political being. And yet, despite modern skepticism of classical aesthetics, theater practitioners seemed inexorably attracted to the ancient figure of Chanakya and the classical play *Mudrarakshasa* as the most expressive enactment of the affective state of absolute and pure political being. (Intriguingly, Rabindranath Tagore said that the *aitihasik*, or the historical, should be added to the list of *rasas* for modern times, confirming that what was at stake here was indeed the question of the self and its affections.)[29] I return to the *rasa* question in chapter 8.

Aside from older Sanskrit plays, there also emerged a new theatrical life to Chanakya in the twentieth century, through a series of Indian-language plays, beginning with Dwijendralal Roy's Bengali play *Chandragupta* (1911) and followed by multiple plays in Marathi, Hindi, Oriya, Malayalam, and so on.[30] There were novels and poems too.[31] In fact it is believed that the first novel in Kannada, Kempu Narayan's *Mudramanjusa* (1823), was inspired by *Mudrarakshasa* and had Chanakya as a central protagonist.[32] Yet plays seemed by far the most popular genre vis-à-vis Chanakya. Or so they remained until a number of films came to be made, beginning with a cinematic rendition of Roy's play in 1939. Interestingly, the career of the famous Bengali stage actor Sisir Kumar Bhaduri took off when he played the larger-than-life role of Chanakya in Roy's play; he then went on to act and direct the 1939 film. And N. T. Rama Rao, charismatic political leader and chief minister of Andhra Pradesh for almost a decade, also played Chanakya in the 1977 box office hit *Chanakya Chandragupta*.³³ With the coming of television, we have had Chandraprakash Dwivedi directing (and playing) *Chanakya* (1991) for the mass audience. Some years ago, Manoj Joshi, a film and theater actor, staged his Chanakya play across cities in India, dedicating his January 2009 production in Mumbai to Tukaram Ombale, the police constable who died on duty during the November 26, 2008, terror attack.

Chanakya thus seemed particularly amenable to theatrical rendition, though somewhat differently from the standard tradition of historical plays and novels that became so important in India in colonial times. Starting in the late nineteenth century, there emerged in Bengal a powerful theatrical and literary tradition around past kingly figures—from Girish Ghosh's *Siraj-ud-daula* (1905), about the Bengal nawab who lost out to the British in the 1757 Battle of Palasi; to D. L. Roy's *Shahjahan* (1910); to, somewhat differently, Rabindranath Tagore's *Raktakarabi* (*Red Oleander*, 1926). On one level, these novels and plays were meant to produce a sense of national history for the masses. On another level and more pertinent for us, these kingly stories put on display the instability and the implosion of the purely political self before a mass audience. This was not just a Bengali tradition—numerous adaptations of Shakespeare's *King Lear* and *Macbeth* across India and contemporary Indian plays such as Girish Karnad's *Tuglaq* (1964) come to mind. Thus, as historians and political scientists struggled to find a nonmonarchical, quasi-democratic tradition in India's past,³⁴ it was the monarch who was repeatedly invoked in theater in order to stage the political, because the kingly figure answered better than anything else the democratic demand of presenting the political subject for mass viewing and evaluation.

What is distinctive about the Chanakya plays, however, is the interesting dispersal of political being across the two loci of king and minister—through which social questions of caste and gender come to the fore. For it is less Chanakya per se and more the Chanakya-Chandragupta pair that becomes important in modern theater—because this pairing allows the thematization of the lowborn king and the political Brahmin together. Roy's 1911 play was not titled *Chanakya* but *Chandragupta*, and a later editor of the play dwelled at great length on the complicated relationship between Chandragupta as "hero" of the play and Chanakya as its "central character."³⁵ Also note the contrast with Jayashankar Prasad's Hindi play, known to be otherwise influenced by Roy's, in which the playwright goes to great lengths to prove that Chandragupta was indeed a Kshatriya and that it was anti-Buddhists of early India who, to avenge Asoka's rejection of Vedic sacrificial religion in favor of Buddhism, accused his ancestor of being a low-caste Shudra.[36] That it was this Brahmin-Shudra couple that was meant to encompass the question of political subjectivity is also clear in another way, for unlike in *Mudrarakshasa*, in the modern-day plays of D. L. Roy and G. P. Deshpande, there were far fewer characters. The flower seller, the spies in disguise, the snake charmer, the servants, and so forth of *Mudrarakshasa*, who peopled the play world through the use of Prakrit linguistic registers,[37] as well as the technique of sociological mimesis, are palpable by their absence in the modern plays, which are centered on the Chanakya-Chandragupta pair. Not that there are no other characters in the later plays, but the more recent plays are overdetermined by this central binary framing.

Let me refer the Chanakya of theater back to the Chanakya of history and philosophy, with whom I started. Roy was writing precisely around the time that the scholarly debate around a rediscovered *Arthashastra* was intensifying. In his play we find a clear resonance of the philosophy question, and for that reason the presence of the Greeks is so marked in the plot. Chanakya here is presented as the one who, through a perfect combination of Shudra power and Brahminical intellectual acumen, brings about a marriage between Helen, the daughter of Seleucus, and King Chandragupta—a union that explicitly stands for the joining of Greek and Indic philosophy. To the altar of this philosophical union is almost sacrificed the other possible union, between Chandragupta and Chhaya, the innocent, selfless woman of the hills, who loves Chandragupta, even though he has eyes only for the philosophically erudite Helen. Chhaya's brother—created in the image of the dark, valorous aborigine of Bengali imagination—sacrifices himself, despite being spurned by Chandragupta, in an act of pure friendship, fraternity, and extrapolitical affect.

Thus in Roy's play, the extrapolitical—enunciated as the intimate and the immediate—appears distributed across the characters: the "primitive" hill tribe unconditionally extrapolitical; Chandragupta, the Shudra king, torn between the political and the extrapolitical; Chanakya, the Brahmin, epitome of realpolitik freedom and philosophical detachment, purely cerebral and unqualifiedly political. And yet, in his monologues, Chanakya reveals his secret self, traumatized by the loss of his wife and daughter, moved to tears by songs of wandering mendicants. Chanakya, in a weak moment, invokes the virtue of affection—intimacy, friendship, loyalty, motherhood, the obliteration of the self in unconditional love—as he evokes, in a powerful soliloquy delivered to a Bengali audience deeply familiar with Bhakti traditions of love and music, the relentless and compelling flow of the river of devotion. Pure political cunning thus stands circumscribed by the extrapolitical imperative of irresistible intimacy, not only embodied in the quintessential figures of alterity—the simple, valorous hill man and woman—but also tenuously held back in the heart of the realpolitiker!

Roy's play sets up a high-strung tension between Chandragupta and Chanakya—engaged in a relentless struggle over who ultimately is the source of political power, the king or the philosopher, actual political power or the political principle, the accidental Shudra king or the realpolitik Brahmin, unloved, solitary, philosophical, and, most important, marked by the propertylessness of the true renouncer. Despite insults by Chandragupta, Chanakya refuses to relinquish the political game—for the sake, he says, of the political principle. But he does renounce it finally, on finding his long-lost daughter and rediscovering his own extrapolitical aspect of passionate love and fidelity.

Roy's was a commercial play, distinct from the amateur "progressive" political theater that later came to dominate the Indian scene. Presumably it was the play's mass appeal that encouraged its later translation into film. Here, then, we have Chanakya being put up for mass spectatorship—a public far more heterogeneous and indeterminate than that involved in the scholarly debate of historians and sociologists. The theatrical dynamic gives us interesting clues to the working out of Chanakya as character. Even as Chanakya gets enacted as the anarchic realpolitiker, he is also inevitably a philosopher, just as he also partakes in the somber solitude of the renouncer. But then there is also a subtext to Roy's play that makes fun of philosophy as embodied in the figure of a minister of the Nandas, whose obsession with the ancient grammarian Panini is presented as absurd and comic. And Chanakya himself, while steadfastly philosophical, verges on the manic. In his monologues, he gives vent to cruel self-irony and a perverse love for the beautiful-ugly goddess of death, destruction, and desolation—the same Kali who was the primary interlocutor of the political renouncer Vivekananda. Indeed, Chanakya is seen to frequent the cremation ground, a rather unlikely location for philosophy, in counterpoise to the city of politics and the forests of innocence. Chanakya, the canny realpolitiker, thus shades off into the classic renouncer and displays an extreme antisocial aspect symbolized by the cremation ground, a site that only the dead, untouchable Doms, deviant *tantriks*, jackals, and Chanakya dare frequent. At the same time, Roy's political narrative is repeatedly interrupted with songs—about nature, love, devotion—indexing the extrapolitical aspects of love and intimacy that even the most ruthless political man cannot escape. This mixing of genres—philosophy, theater, song, history—in effect thus reconstitutes Chanakya as a somewhat eccentric character whose purely politico-philosophical persona is really the expression of a besieged and secret self—that of a *kaliyuga* Brahmin sans traditional power and legitimacy, that of a man sans women.

G. P. Deshpande's later play *Chanakya Vishnugupta* is an interesting counterpoint to D. L. Roy's. For one, the later playwright's Marxist disposition and involvement in the by-then-established tradition of left political theater produced an aesthetic that was quite distinct from Roy's nationalist aesthetic. Amateur left theater's didactic mode of address was very different from the melodramatic address of early twentieth-century commercial mass theater. Second, the caste question in Maharashtra, the context of Deshpande and his plays, had taken a trajectory that was strikingly different from that in Bengal. In immediate precolonial times, Peshwa rule in Maharashtra took the form of an orthodox Brahminical regime based explicitly on the caste rules of the *dharmashastras*. From early colonial times onward, therefore, caste became the first political question here. Maharashtra produced two of the most sophisticated caste radicals of India—Jyotiba Phule and B. R. Ambedkar. In Bengal, despite being a palpable phenomenon, caste remained repressed in mainstream political rhetoric, overwritten as it was by the landlord-peasant and Hindu-Muslim "communal" question. Third, colonial Bengalis had a relationship of desire with Maratha history—especially its peasant warrior traditions and its history of "patriotic" face-off with the imperial Mughals of Delhi. The Maratha king from a peasant caste, Shivaji, was lionized by the Bengali middle classes. Incidentally, Benoy Kumar Sarkar, in a 1936 essay, analyzed the eighteenth-century *adjnapatra*, or ordinance, of Ramchandra Pant Amatya of Kolhapur, as an instance of the extant and functioning nature of Chanakya *niti* in early modern western India.[38]

In Deshpande's play, Chanakya is yet to finish the *Arthashastra*. He can write up his treatise only after the play ends, having to first accomplish the practical task of overthrowing the unjust Nanda dynasty—as if realpolitik was a prior moment that one must pass through before one could graduate to political philosophy. Suwasini does exactly that. Suwasini is Chandragupta's ex-lover, who first marries the Nanda king, then takes up the reins of power herself, and finally converts to Buddhism and enters a Buddhist *sangha* (monastery). In Deshpande's play, the critique of Chanakya *niti* is presented as a self-consciously philosophical critique that comes from the mouth of Suwasini. She is the true renouncer here, counterpoint and interlocutor to the realpolitiker. She speaks against the sacrifice of individual freedom to the political machine and warns of the imminent arrival of the Buddhist way of equality between castes and classes. Though he is instrumental in Suwasini's losing Chandragupta, her first and eternal love, Chanakya is forced to agree with her, even as he reminds her that as a political Brahmin, he—like the Buddha originally born to kingly lineage and like Suwasini herself—has renounced power for the sake of the ultimate task of philosophy. Once again, the realpolitiker, in his antisocial orientation, shades off into the renouncer. The play offers a philosophical resolution in the form of a dialectic between Suwasini and Chanakya, Buddhist nun and realpolitical man, with the woman here representing that extrapolitical aspect of spiritual integrity, which must in the last instance ground or at least regulate the political acumen of the canny but deeply alienated man.

Already, in the scholarly debates of the 1920s, Buddha figured alongside Chanakya. Sarkar accused Ghoshal of reducing the political philosopher Buddha to a mere moralist, just as he had reduced the political philosopher Chanakya to a mere realpolitik figure. Ghoshal in turn accused Sarkar of blindness to caste—in effect saying that Sarkar sanitized the figure of the political Brahmin by rendering him into a philosopher and glossing over his imbrication in the concrete institutions of kingship and caste. Buddha and Chanakya were incommensurable subjects, Ghoshal argued, for the Buddha and his "contract theory" of sovereign power was a minor democratic exception in the more dominant Brahminical tradition of monarchical statecraft in ancient India.[39] The imagination of the Buddha as quintessential political man did not quite take off in the scholarly debates in Bengal as it did in Maharashtra, where Ambedkar famously placed Buddha alongside not Chanakya but Karl Marx. Incidentally, contemporary "Shudra intellectual" Kancha Illiah, in *God as Political Philosopher: Buddhism's Challenge to Brahmanism*, explicitly replaces Chanakya with Buddha as India's quintessential political figure, in a final triumph of the renouncer over the realpolitiker.[40] Like in Deshpande's, in Roy's play, Buddhism figures, albeit fleetingly, in Chanakya's secret foreboding over the impending decline of Brahminical power in face of the Buddhist revolution. Roy's Chanakya presents himself as the spurned but self-aware *kaliyuga* Brahmin who, in a last dying flash of political acumen, inaugurates the rise to power of the Shudra, as was fated. He foresees and rides the Buddhist revolution rather than being passively swept away by it.

What does bringing theater into the discussion do to the problematic of the political man, whose home otherwise seems to be in history and/or philosophy? Without going into all that has been written on the productive asymmetry between the political and the aesthetic, the textual and the performative, let me simply put it this way. Staging Chanakya was a way of contemporizing him against the work of historicism. Of course, philosophy, like theater, struggled against history in order to contemporize Chanakya or, rather, render him irrespective of time—thus, despite his antiquity, Chanakya was always already seen as a "modern" political philosopher.[41] But philosophy stumbled over the philosopher's realpolitik character, as political cunning seemed to exceed philosophical reason in the case of a figure such as Chanakya. Theater, on the other hand, through the very mode of performing the figure, released Chanakya from his imbrication in history and activated the quintessential realpolitiker in the present. But precisely by virtue of this presence, the Chanakya of theater remained unstable—thematized anew across time, space, and audience. In other words, onstage Chanakya could never be rendered into an analogue of the steadfast, textually grounded Plato, that is, into a universal philosophical authority.

For onstage philosophy appeared besieged—embodied and embattled, pulled apart between abstraction and pragmatics, sexed and casted. Even more important, by holding out Chanakya, frontally and in glaring spotlight, before an unregulated mass of spectators, theater undid the solitary, safe, and interior space of philosophical operations, just as it undid the secretive space of elite political intrigue associated with the Chanakya of precolonial popular sense. This restaged Chanakya, unlike the pedagogical Chanakya of the *Arthashastra*, was destined to talk to his noncontemporaries—to Buddha, to the Shudra, and to the woman, who were meant to rise up in rebellion in *kaliyuga*. But above all, this Chanakya had to talk to that other, most threatening of his contemporaries, namely, the mass man of twentieth-century politics and the market.

Chanakya and Krishna

It is useful to end by staging a comparison between Krishna and Chanakya, rivals for the office of the classical Indian realpolitiker. Most early modern Indians were more comfortable with Krishna than with Kautilya/Chanakya. After all, Krishna, though no less amoral than Chanakya, propounded the philosophy of the Bhagavad Gita and hence was worthy of trust, following, and devotion, as if philosophy worked to stabilize and allay politics, especially when it tipped into the precarious and unpredictable dynamic of realpolitik. Ambedkar, however, preferred Kautilya over Krishna because, unlike the latter, the former seemed unconcerned with *dharma* or the caste/social order of things.[42]

Krishna was a hugely popular figure in Bengal prior to colonialism, where the devotional tradition of Gaudiya Vaishnavism, centered on worship and love of Krishna and mediated by the sixteenth-century Bhakti saint Chaitanya, was a powerful presence. As a tradition, however, Vaishnavism was heterogeneous. It produced numerous heterodox sects among the poor and often worked as the principal ground for low-caste political mobilization. It was also the site wherein popular affect, sentiment, aesthetics, and philosophies of liberation played out in complex ways. But there were socially orthodox strands in Vaishnavism as well. Vaishnavism was also a rival to the alternative devotional tradition of Kali worship.

In the late nineteenth century, Krishna was reinvented as a quintessential political figure in Bengal, Maharashtra, and elsewhere in India. For this purpose, Krishna had to be extricated from his precolonial performative and emotive contexts and relocated in the stable site of what colonial intellectuals saw as philosophy. The modern political Krishna, therefore, was laboriously set apart, by middle-class, upper-caste literate men, from the traditional infant-god, cowherd, adulterous lover, divine object of passionate desire and *bhakti*, who inspired feminine longing (rather than masculine activism) among devotees. Krishna's influence on political thinkers as diverse as the novelist Bankimchandra Chattopadhyay, the militant nationalist Bal Gangadhar Tilak, the liberal Bombay High Court judge K. T. Telang, the theoretician of nonviolence Mahatma Gandhi, and the revolutionary nationalist Aurobindo Ghosh was predicated on the modern career of the Bhagavad Gita as it came to be extricated from the epic Mahabharata and reconstituted as an autonomous, politico-philosophical text. The Gita also became India's national text par excellence in the hands of western philosophers like G. W. F. Hegel, Johann Gottfried Herder, Friedrich Schlegel, Arthur Schopenhauer, Aldous Huxley, J. Robert Oppenheimer, Ralph Emerson, Carl Jung, and Herman Hesse.[43] Krishna, as enunciator of the Gita, thus became at once the metaphysical, philosophical, and narrative font of the Indian political. Not accidentally, south Asian historiography today shows renewed interest in the Gita as a critical moment in India's modern intellectual and political history.[44]

What I want to emphasize here, however, is something slightly different from, though connected to, this process of the modern refashioning of Krishna as political philosopher and realpolitical man bundled into one. The modern political Krishna was made possible by a forgetting of the precolonial Krishna of *lila* or play, the Krishna who had been the central protagonist of popular theater, both in Bengal and in north India. Here is Girish Ghosh, the late nineteenth-century pioneer of the Bengali commercial stage, lamenting the loss of the popular *jatra* of Bengal as the loss of *Krishnalila*: "Vulgar and obscene slangs disappeared with the disappearance of the Jatras, but along with it the sweet songs of Badan Adhikary and Govinda Adhikary also were gone for good. The sweet songs of the deep emotion of the old Krishna Lila disappeared from the country. People then lost their originality and took to imitation [of western theater]."[45] In other words, the politico-philosophical life of Krishna emerged at the cost of his theatrical life. In the case of Chanakya, however, the trajectory was just the opposite, as Chanakya emerged in modern times as the most frequently renewed character of Bengali and Indian theater. In mainstream politics, however, Chanakya lost out to Krishna, because his *Arthashastra* was seen as inadequately philosophical, especially in comparison to the Bhagavad Gita of Krishna. The *arthashastra* tradition of "being politic" went into dormancy because it did not fit the schema of colonial modern disciplinary knowledges, of either history or philosophy, either practical reason or theoretical reason!

The contrast between the careers of Krishna and Chanakya may be read as a comment on the nature of modern political theater in India as much as on the respective figures themselves. But it would be a gross mistake to presume that Chanakya thrived in theater solely by virtue of his dramatic potential as character. For at stake onstage was philosophy itself. Here is what Deshpande says in the introduction to his play *Chanakya Vishnugupta*: "It would be essential, I presume, to write a couple of words about the philosophical debate referred to in the play. Indian philosophy, logic, had scaled new heights in those days. But that was rendered useless by the varna system. . . . [S]ociety was in a transitional phase, passing from the varnas to the jatis. On one level, there was a deep-rooted fear that the creativity of society itself was on the brink of death, yet there was also the possibility that the new political process would usher in a new era of creativity."[46] Chanakya's treatise was an expression of this revolutionary creativity. The connection between political movements (the rise of the Maurya Empire, the rise of Buddhism, and so on) and the production of the book was thus seen as an inherent one. Deshpande's play attempts to make a statement on that relationship. And this is the reason why Deshpande's Chanakya proclaims that his political success would not be complete until the completion of his manuscript.

But note how differently philosophy gets mobilized, indeed performed, around the two figures of Chanakya and Krishna. The Chanakya story is staged as the story of a war of philosophies (though not ideologies in our contemporary sense). Roy's 1911 play set Greek, Brahminical, Buddhist, and popular devotional and heterodox intellectual traditions to encounter. Deshpande's 1987 play made Buddhism, Vedantism, and the materialist Carvaka philosophies engage in sharply argumentative polemics. In other words, around Chanakya, philosophies themselves appeared onstage as protagonists and counterprotagonists. The Krishna story was, however, a story of philosophical synthesis rather than conflict. Krishna's Bhagavad Gita not only became India's "national" philosophical export to the global community of philosophers and a must-read in philosophy curricula of all Indian universities but also came to be, for all practical purposes, freed from the epic war narrative of the Mahabharata via mediation of German philosophy.⁴⁷ Not surprisingly, then, Sarkar would struggle against German philosophy in his attempt to reinstate Chanakya and thus implicitly dislodge the Gita of Krishna from its hegemonic philosophical position in twentieth-century India.

It is worth noting here that the scene of philosophizing in the case of the Gita is the mother of all battlefields, the Kurukshetra. And yet, Krishna's utterances therein show no signs of philosophical struggle or uncertainty. As the inimitable Marxist historian D. D. Kosambi argues, Krishna, who fills heaven, earth, and underworld and embodies time itself, appropriates and synthesizes all contemporary philosophical systems, seamlessly, within the singular discourse of divine utterance at Kurukshetra.⁴⁸ In the time of actual war, in other words, Krishna offers philosophical certainty by virtue of his godliness. In other words, even if the Gita was philosophy, Krishna was not quite a philosopher, being rendered godly, mythic, iconic (like the Spirit of Hegelian metaphysics?)—thus lending an ideality and wholeness to the Gita that would warm the hearts of idealist philosophers of totality such as Hegel.

It was this apparent unitary and "totalitarian" nature of the Gita that made Krishna amenable to nationalist politics in early twentieth-century India. Thus, Bankimchandra Chattopadhyay would argue that the Gita was "for all men": "It is the best dharma for him who believes in reincarnation just as well as for him who does not. It is the best dharma for him who is devoted to Krishna as well as for him who is not. It is the best dharma for him who believes in God, and also for him who does not."⁴⁹ Mark how different this imagination of "Indian/Hindu" philosophy is from Chanakya's dramatic location amid multiple Brahminical, Buddhist, and Carvaka philosophies, swirling around difficult questions of power, ethics, morality, atheism, and liberation. The Gita was not a philosophy contending with other possible philosophies. It was the subsumption of the partial truths of all philosophies under the sign of the One—the philosopher-god Krishna—whether Sankhya philosophy's question of the duality of *purusha* (self) and *prakriti* (matter, nature), Yoga's thesis of unity with the absolute, Mimamsa's idea of sacrifice, Tantra's harnessing of the dualistic nature of reality as an approach to the absolute, Mahayana Buddhism's ideal of the bodhisattva dedicated to universal redemption, or indeed Advaita Vedanta's imagination of nondualism.⁵⁰ In Aurobindo Ghosh's words, the Gita was a "wide, undulating, encircling movement of ideas which is the manifestation of a vast synthetic mind and a rich synthetic experience.... It does not cleave asunder, but reconciles and unifies" through a "universal comprehensiveness."⁵¹

No wonder, then, that Krishna, the dark, lower-caste, pastoral god of popular devotion and drama—who was admitted rather late and rather reluctantly into the Brahminical pantheon,[52] and who is still seen by many, such as by contemporary "backward"-caste Yadavs of Uttar Pradesh,[53] as the quintessential practical politician of India—remains curiously uninvolved in the actual action. Krishna vacillates between the roles of deus ex machina and mere menial charioteer but through the Gita solicits selfless and desireless political action from others. Of course, read on its own terms, the Mahabharata also tells us of the death and decline of Krishna and his dynasty in a final and dramatic universal event of destruction—a well-deserved ending given how he had manipulated entire nations for the sake of political efficacy. Krishna's tragic and violent end embodied the ultimate instability and pathos of realpolitik as it were. But the modern readings of Gita remain insulated from that epic denouement. The figure of Chanakya, on the other hand, remains always already particular, caste-marked, and gendered—the Shudra alienated and projected onto his other, the heroic king/conqueror, the woman always already lost to him. Chanakya also dirties his hands in acts of deceit, conquest, and political brinkmanship. He even appears schizophrenic, both in theater and in scholarly debate, torn between the imperatives of political philosophy and political action, pulled between the exercises of renunciation and technologies of power.

In other words, Krishna puts philosophy in service of politics, and for that purpose renders philosophy synthetic and whole. Krishna's philosophy—the Gita—is given the task of gathering together the community, the nation. It teeters on the verge of becoming theology. It becomes, in the name of philosophy, a theory of everything—namely, of the world and of its microcosm, the nation. Chanakya, on the other hand, embodies and exposes the politics of philosophy itself, as multiple philosophies engage each other onstage as on the battleground. Philosophy loses its seclusion from the world of work and war and becomes contaminated with practice, poetics, and prejudice—indeed, with caste and gender. Hence, apropos Chanakya, theater becomes critical, wherein competing philosophies work to frame and animate pure political being.

Perhaps it never was philosophy that was the stake here. Perhaps the stake was simply the art of being politic, of living through the vagary and contingency of politics and of cultivating the difficult skill of negotiating regimes, in peace and in war. In early India, this would go by the name of *niti*. Calling it "politics" in our times brought in the question of philosophy. And, along with it, emerged the question of whether this philosophy, indeed philosophy as such, could ever become common art—as it would necessarily have to be in the era of mass politics—or whether by virtue of being philosophy, political philosophy would forever remain segregated in a jealously guarded, quasi-Brahminical epistemic site. For the Chanakya of popular sense, however, this was never the issue. For *Chanakyasutras* taught humans to precisely be politic rather than simply moral or ethical in their everyday lives. One cannot help but feel that this was a mode of being commonly political that flew in the face of the Gita-inspired vision of the modern political man, as singular, disciplined, and normative subject.

Part II

Action

3

Karma, Freedom, and Everyday Life

> I wanted to play with my child
> in your courtyard
> but that could never be,
> in this world of war and revolution.
> so I take leave, my friend. . . .
>
> I wanted to drown in life, up to my neck.
> Live my share of life
> My friend, live my share.
> —Avatar Singh Sandhu Pash,
> "Main Ab Vida Leta Hun" (Now I take leave)

Politics, most would agree, is action, and nothing if not action. Hence, we call politics *activism* and political beings *activists*. Historically derived from ancient Greek drama and rhetoric, which valorized the *vita activa* of tragic heroes and free citizens, this imagination of politics was reinvented many times over in Europe—in the Renaissance, the French Revolution, nineteenth-century anarchism, and Narodnism; in twentieth-century decisionism and voluntarism; and in the radical philosophies of Friedrich Nietzsche, Hannah Arendt, Carl Schmitt, and Vladimir Lenin. Nietzsche famously posited Dionysian activism against Apollonian order, Socratic contemplation, and Christian asceticism, conceptualizing action as the deployment of force on the world and glossing *force* as *will*.[1]

Force, a basic concept of Newtonian mechanics (alongside mass, distance, and time), is the acting of one body on another, causing a directional and/or substantial change in the latter's state of being. Posited in opposition to inertia, force became, in the early modern scientific imagination of multiple bodies acting on and reacting to each other, a model for mobility and change—and, by that logic, politically salient. Newtonian physics imaged the world as stable—as much in motion as in rest. It was only the play of forces that subverted this stasis. Concomitantly, modern political philosophy posited life and living as a state of routine and repetition—a kind of pre- or nonpolitical passivity that awaited the eruptive force of political action. The human condition seemed to mirror Newtonian nature, involving a constant dialectic of inertia and force, passivity and activity, an image further confirmed by conventions of (Indo-European) languages, which displayed a syntactical duality of active and passive voices. Arendt provided the clearest statement of this position, by contrasting politics not just to the quiet life of contemplation but also to labor and work, activities of quotidian life driven by necessity rather than freedom.[2] This imagination has come to assume an axiomatic form in modern times, disallowing—as if by common sense—the possibility that there can be practices that fall somewhere in between or even outside the alternatives of action and inaction.

This modern imagination of politics as willed action—as application of force on the world—had two long-lasting implications. In the first place, it produced "life" as an intractable philosophical problem. Life, after the invention of the modern political, appeared as that calm domain of the normal, the customary, the habitual, the structural, on which politics came to bear (hence the structure/agency problematic in sociology and political science and the event/everyday problematic in anthropology, as well as the twentieth-century philosophical attempts to return "vitalism" to life by those like Henri Bergson and Gilles Deleuze). The philosophical question that followed was about the relationship of politics with life, a relationship that appeared in proxy forms as disciplinary relationships between politics and economics, politics and culture, politics and religion, politics and society, and so on. Many, like James Scott and Michel de Certeau, worked to return politics to everyday life.[3] Yet they ended up replacing the notion of spectacular and historic action with notions of strategy and tactics, actions still, though relatively more minor and stealthy. Asef Bayat offers a critique of this imagination of life as always already tactical. And yet, in rendering "life as politics" in the Middle East, he bolsters the supremacy of the political, always already holding sway over the conceptually secondary domain of life as such.[4]

Second, the modern imagination of politics as action also resulted in an overdetermination of politics by the violence question. Most twentieth-century political forms—renunciation, revolutionism, Narodnism, syndicalism, decisionism, voluntarism, *satyagraha*, passive resistance, and the general strike—shared, along with the imagination of politics as uninhibited action, an intense preoccupation with the problem of violence. Earlier, such as in the Mahabharata, violence, both within and between species, was seen as constitutive of life, not exceptional to it. War and revolution only dramatized this otherwise commonplace fact. In this tradition, there were two ways of engaging life's inherent violence—through noncruelty or *anrsamsata* in everyday social life and through nonviolence or *ahimsa* via a renunciation of social life (including renunciation of cooking or, in a later Jain reinterpretation, a modulation of breathing lest one harm microorganisms).[5] In contrast, the modern political absorbed the entire violence problematic within itself—because violence came to be, with the rise of politics as action, a metaphor for both efficacy, action's measure, and event, action's manifest form. Even Gandhi imagined nonviolent politics as the application of "soul-force," except here force did not appear in the image of colliding bodies as much as "action at a distance," as potential held in reserve.

The Travails of Karma

With colonialism, the imagination of politics as action came to be globalized. The colonized were recast as lacking valid modes of practice and thus lacking politics. Evangelists criticized Hinduism for being otherworldly; contemplative; plagued by superstitious, idolatrous, and uncivil customs; and lacking the ethos of philanthropic activism.[6] Colonial historians and ethnographers criticized the colonized for lacking in historical acumen and living in an uneventful, changeless social continuity.[7] Rammohan Roy craved a dose of New Testament ethics for Hinduism, Bankimchandra Chattopadhyay lamented the lack of worldliness among Indians, and Rabindranath Tagore admitted that Indians were temperamentally restful and reposed whereas Europeans were restless and active.[8]

This denial of practice to the colonized was, paradoxically, tied to a denial of theory itself. Hegel and Edmund Husserl famously argued that non-Europeans lacked universal theory that could be abstracted from immediate practical considerations and therefore lacked norms that could adjudicate on the world of practice.[9] No wonder colonial and postcolonial philosophers spent a lot of energy trying to prove Indian philosophy's status as pure theory, as opposed to being imbricated in ordinary questions of life and living.[10] This strange predicament—of lacking both theory and practice—complicated the theory/practice relationship in the colony. In order to recover practical virtuosity, the colonized had to henceforth negotiate a form of universal theory that was in mismatch with their own practices and that, instead of appearing irrelevant for that reason, drew legitimacy from just such a mismatch.[11] The colonized thus experienced the knowledge/practice binary not merely as a generic distinction between thought and action but as a special kind of alienation of indigenous practice from political philosophy itself.

This proposition that non-Europeans lacked theories of action was of course untrue. In fact, the concept of action was central to early Indian intellectual traditions.[12] Highly contested philosophies of *karma*, which initially denoted the sacred ritual of Vedic sacrifice but later came to mean human activity in general, thematized action as the very essence of being human. Life was understood as always already determined by fruits of action, and action and its consequence formed an infinite chain of causality in time, binding humans to the world. Practical, ethical, spiritual, and epistemological questions were at stake in these theories of action, which worked without any a priori distinction between pure and practical reason (even knowledge was predicated on prior practices of *askēsis*, which rendered the self open to enlightenment). Note the range of questions at stake here: Can consequences of individual action be transferred to others?[13] Is collective action conceivable?[14] How can responsibility of action be precisely assigned, and how can the efficacy of action be measured when actions have deferred consequences?[15] What is the relationship between natural causes and *karmic* causes? Does action distinguish life from lifeless matter? Do plants and animals have *karma*? What kind of action enables the acquisition of knowledge?[16] Is the meaning of a word or sentence also an injunction to act?[17]

Karma was also central to early Indian social theory. *Dharmashastras* codified the entire range of life's activities—from ritual to politics to social practices like interdining and marriage to intimate practices like bathing and sex—according to an individual's caste, gender, stage in life, profession, and country (*desh*). The effort was to regulate action according to an individual's social profile and to preempt the perils of unauthorized innovation and antisocial action by the likes of sexual deviants, renouncers, and rebels.[18] In this register of social theory, politics was not a conceptually distinct activity. It was simply activity authorized for kings and warriors as distinct from activities authorized for, say, wives, students, blacksmiths, and chariot makers. However, the fact that middle- and lower-caste individuals could become kings and assume Kshatriyahood tells us that politics often defied the social regulation of practice. Indeed, as we have seen in the previous chapter, politics claimed its own science—the *arthashastra*—which taught people how to be canny (rather than just lawful) in the business of life.[19] Politics in precolonial times was thus about *being* politic rather than *doing* politics. Interestingly, early Chinese military and courtly thinking, François Jullien tells us, also frowned on the notion of political action as agentive intervention or application of force. It was believed that to act on a situation—that is, to apply theoretical models or normative ideals on the world—was an external imposition, producing friction and resistance and thus diminishing efficacy. It was far wiser to appear not to act at all and to insinuate oneself into a situation such that one was able to turn the very "propensity of things" to one's advantage. In this processual paradigm, it was the indiscernible tweaking of reality—by way of what I am calling *being* politic—rather than action or *doing* politics that was at stake.[20]

This is not to say that there was no notion of exemplary action in early Indian traditions. One needs only to look at great narratives of "deeds" in *purana*, *itihasa*, and *kavya*—histories, legends, epics, poetry, and drama.[21] Often ascribed to heroic figures—gods, antigods, kings, and renouncers—deeds were actions that were in excess of or contravention to preexisting prescriptive schemes. In the Mahabharata, for instance, deeds became significant precisely when there was a crisis of *dharma* or social norm. This led to the concept of *apaddharma* or action in times of exception or emergency.[22] No wonder that the Mahabharata became, in time, the most consulted political tradition of India. Abu al-Fazl regarded the Mahabharata, the Ramayana, and the *Harivamsa*, the Puranic biography of Krishna, as histories with political lessons. Akbar titled the Persian translation of the Mahabharata the *Razmnamah*, or *The Book of War*. Akbar's scribe, Tahir Muhammad Sabzawari, made abridged prose translations in 1602-3 of the *Bhagavata Purana*, the Mahabharata, and the *Harivamsa*. He also wrote a Persian world history called *Rawzat al-tahirin*, or *The Garden of the Pure*, with a separate section on Sanskrit epics. A number of Indo-Persian dynastic histories placed the later Mughals in a series of the kings of India beginning with the heroes of the Mahabharata. Firishta (d. ca. 1633) prefaced his famous history of Indo-Muslim dynasties by interweaving the Mahabharata with the heroic cycles of the Persian Book of Kings. There was even a rumor, noted by the European traveler Oranus, that Akbar was the tenth incarnation of Vishnu or Krishna![23] Not surprisingly, the colonized would return to the Mahabharata in order to refashion, for modern times, a concept of political action.

Karma, Yoga, and Politics

Central to this refashioning was the Bhagavad Gita.[24] Composed between the sixth and second centuries BCE, the Gita—a dialogue between the charioteer-god Krishna and the warrior Arjuna—was part of the much longer Mahabharata story of a "world war" between the royal lineages of the Pandhavas and Kauravas. Standing in the no-man's-land between enemy lines, in a momentary pause between war cries, Krishna and Arjuna hold a philosophical discourse on "what is to be done." As much as the content and form of the discourse, it is the mise-en-scène that is crucial here. It demonstrates that political philosophy arises neither in a purely theoretical context, away from the scene of action, nor directly out of the logic of action. It arises at the edgy moment of suspended action as it were, when one falters in the midst of the act, in the face of the failure of existing codes of conduct.

Arjuna, on the brink of war, is overwhelmed on seeing that his enemies are none other than his friends, relatives, and teachers—an adversarial context very different from Carl Schmitt's friend-enemy face-off. Arjuna is arrested by conflicting senses of duty. He cannot fulfill his duty to family and lineage (*kuladharma*) without violating his social duty as warrior for justice (*varnadharma*) or his eternal duties (*sanatana* or *parama dharma*) of nonviolence and noncruelty. The very concept of duty is in jeopardy. In response to Arjuna's dysfunction, Krishna launches into a lengthy discourse on *karmayoga* or the "practice of practice."

In the 1880s, Bankimchandra Chattopadhyay wrote three interpretations of the Gita: *Krishnacharitra* (The persona of Krishna), *Dharmatattva* (The concept of dharma), and *Srimadbhagavadgita* (The Gita)[25]—and posited *nishkama karma* as the model action for modern times. *Nishkama karma*—action without the desire for fruits—was an imagination of "inaction at the very heart of action" (*karme akarmata*), a combination of realpolitik and renunciation imaged after the cunning god Krishna.[26] Note how this formulation conceptually brings together rather than opposes activity and passivity. *Nishkama karma* drew on precolonial concepts of *moksha*, *nirvana*, and *kaivalya*—imaginations of an absolute freedom that was possible only when one escaped predetermination by past actions—while refuting the position that freedom from causal determination necessarily required a renunciation of worldly life. Evidently, Bankim was struggling with the most intractable problem at the heart of the modern political—namely, how to imagine political action as distinct from ordinary activities of life without having to disavow, like the renouncer, ordinary life itself.

Bankim argued that practical efficacy depended on *anushilan*, the equal and proportional cultivation of theory, action, and aesthesis. Clearly, he was influenced by the post-Kantian trend of distinguishing theoretical reason from practical reason and aesthetic intuition or perhaps more directly by Auguste Comte's identification of the three human impulses of theory, action, and feeling. And, yet, he spoke of these competences as *shakti* or force and *vritti*, a term drawn from Patanjali's *Yogasutras*, denoting "whirlpools" or "turbulences" produced in the self by encounter with the world—thus putting a different gloss to the otherwise mentalist category of human faculty. He also glossed theory, practice, and aesthesis as equivalent to the Gita's three *yogas* or technologies of the self—namely, *jnyanayoga*, *karmayoga*, and *bhaktiyoga* (knowledge, practice, and devotion)—geared toward attaining identity with the absolute.

As expected, Bankim prioritized the discipline of action or *karmayoga*—partaking in a long-standing debate among precolonial philosophers about the relative weightage of the three human competencies.[27] Acquisition of knowledge, however abstract, depended on prior disciplines of both mind and body, he said. Also, knowledge was an elite principle, while action was available to all. For these two reasons, *karmayoga* was primary.[28] Most religions of the world, Bankim added, imagined heaven and hell, domains of pleasure and pain, respectively, as sites of experience rather than action.[29] Only Hinduism saw humans as ceaselessly active, in this life and the next, propelled by an infinite chain of cause, action, and consequence, whether immediate, potential, or deferred.[30] Hence *anushilan* was above all an action-oriented principle.[31]

Bankim used the term *anushilan*—practice, culture, discipline[32]—as proximate to the traditional term *yoga*. *Yoga* literally meant "to yoke," such as bulls to a wagon or horses to a chariot. *Yoga* was a technique of sensory restraint, based on bodily as well as psychological disciplines, analogous to the charioteer's control of his horses.[33] (Not surprisingly, Krishna acted as Arjuna's charioteer in the Mahabharata in a clear reference to *yoga*.) But *anushilan*, unlike classical *yoga*, Bankim added, did not require the annihilation of negative or banal aspects of the self, such as anger or erotics—for anger quickened justice and erotics prompted aesthesis.[34] *Anushilan*, in other words, was action meant for ordinary mortals and not just the initiated, the adept, the spiritual virtuoso. Even a "primitive Hottentot," subject to *anushilan*, could match the most advanced European in practical competence, Bankim believed. Indeed, *anushilan* short-circuited civilizational disadvantage.[35] It was efficacy even in abjection—in poverty, hunger, homelessness, disease, and colonialism.[36]

While *anushilan* was the honing of ordinary human competencies, Bankim said, it was extraordinary in being shot through with the force of desirelessness. Action without desire for fruits—an ascetic disposition in the midst of worldly engagement—produced equanimity (*samatva, samatā, sāmya*) and enabled free and just action. It allowed impartiality and equal regard for all creatures, friend, enemy, stranger, kin. It enabled poise in the face of chance and contingency. It freed the agent from the debilitating fear of failed or incomplete action and of unintended consequence. Above all, it made possible truly voluntary and undetermined action.³⁷ Incidentally, Abhinavagupta—an eleventh-century aesthetician, philosopher, and Saiva *tantric*, who wrote a small commentary on the Gita and developed a notion of *svatantravada*, or voluntarism—argued that *svatantra iccha* or free will, perfected by *yoga*, could indeed simulate the power of *iśitritva* or lordship (*isvara* also denoted god).³⁸ Note the very different genealogy here of the concept of will—as product of discipline and askēsis—from that in modern European political philosophy. Like Abhinavagupta, Bankim argued that *anushilan* could make ordinary humans approximate god and undertake free action, without compulsions of either desire or duty (which like desire was self-regarding).³⁹ Efficacious action, in other words, was akin to divine action in its absolute and perfected freedom.

Free action, however, could slide into tyranny, anarchy, or both. Bankim's emphasis on *bhakti*, or devotion, was meant to hedge this risk. Bankim moved away from the traditional *bhakti* ideal of adoration of god to the political ideal of emulation of god. Also for Bankim, *bhakti* stood for aesthesis, inflecting in modern ways the traditional dramaturgical sensibilities of *rasa* and *bhava* (emotion and expressivity) as ways of experiencing the absolute. Bankim cautioned that neither morality nor rationalism could adequately moderate the potential hyperactivism and anarchism of divine impostures.⁴⁰ It was only *bhakti*—the surrender of the fruits of actions to god—that could do so. The term *anushilan*, one should add, was drawn from the medieval Bhakti tradition. Rupa Gosvami, a fifteenth-century theoretician of Bengal Vaishnavism, in his *Bhakti-Rasamrta-Sindhu*, defined *anushilana*—a combination of *chesta* (effort, action), *sadhana* (discipline, contemplation), and *anubhava* (experience, emotion)—as synonymous with *bhakti*.⁴¹

Interestingly, the concept of surrender was critical to this imagination of action, even though surrender—seemingly implying the abdication of agency and responsibility—appears incompatible with any principle of activism. Surrender as a concept, however, becomes legible when put in the context of precolonial commentators of the Gita who, through centuries, debated this notion. Some commentators understood surrender as an admission of the fact that the agent was a necessary but not sufficient cause for action, which depended on myriad other factors, including other agencies. Others understood surrender as a conscious disidentification of the agent with the finite embodied self, so as to overcome the limiting conditions within which one must necessarily act. Yet others understood surrender as a way of emptying the active self of ego and pride. Others still understood it as a way of identifying with god's own mode of desireless and disinterested action.⁴² God acted not out of desire or duty (he did not need to act in the first place) but only for the sake of *lokasamgraha*—

"protection of the world (*loka*)" and "gathering of the people (*loka*)"—Bankim said, playing with the double connotation of *loka*.⁴³ Surrender or *bhakti* was a way of simulating this mode of divine activism by investing the fruits of one's action in family, society, nation, and humanity, all intermediate steps toward the ultimate destination of god. With *bhakti*, the agent's sphere of concern expanded exponentially—via *priti* (affection/friendship) and *daya* (compassion).⁴⁴ Indeed, Bankim argued, *daya* was etymologically linked with *dana* or gift—the ultimate gift being the gift of one's own life. Bhakti thus was the font of ethical public action, which refused to turn coercive or tyrannical despite its absolute freedom.⁴⁵

What Is Political about Political Action?

Bankim appears to be talking of human activities generically. Even patriotism appears in his writings as a projection of everyday love for one's kin.⁴⁶ Yet, when offering examples to be emulated, Bankim unfailingly invokes kings and warriors—Rama, Yudisthira, Bhishma—and contrasts them with ascetic figures like Christ and Buddha.⁴⁷ Bankim seems to want to specify political action without quite naming it, as if it was conceptually difficult to isolate political action as a unit from the generic notion of action as such. But things change in his novels. In a footnote in *Dharmatattva*, Bankim says that his fiction, especially the novel *Debi Chaudhurani*, concretely illustrates the concept of *nishkama karma*.⁴⁸

In this novel, young Prafulla is banished from home by her father-in-law, on suspicion of being a low-caste Bagdi. Abandoned and hungry, she is exiled to a forest—an image of utter helplessness and despair. From here, Prafulla picks herself up and, under the tutelage of the Brahmin social bandit Bhavani Pathak, becomes a political leader. She robs the rich, redistributes wealth among the poor, and holds a people's court. She, in effect, runs a parallel righteous regime, but she does so reluctantly, preferring memories of her lost love to politics, as Bankim says with gentle irony. She remains morally uncertain about her own political methods. She acts but does so without stakes or desire. The transformation of Prafulla from a powerless woman to a powerful political leader happens through *anushilan*. Her training is a five-year-long project—she studies arithmetic, grammar, logic, the poetry of Kalidasa, and *Bhattikavya*, the classic seventh-century instructional textbook; learns the philosophies of Nyaya and Vedanta; and moves on to *yogashastra* and, finally, to the Bhagavad Gita. Her food is sparse and her clothing minimal; she sleeps on bare ground and shaves off her hair. Her body is exposed to sun, rain, dust, and grime; she learns wrestling, despite initial inhibitions. Eventually she regains her right to the ordinary comforts of life, which she now deserves but no longer needs. She can now transgress boundaries of gender, caste, and domesticity with ease and aplomb.[49]

Bankim's more famous novel *Anandamath* (Monastery of bliss), mentioned in chapter 1, is also set in a context of abjection, the terrible famine of 1770. Here a group of *sannyasis* wages war against the puppet Bengal nawab. The militant ascetics worship a new goddess, the motherland.[50] But in an unprecedented fusion of erstwhile rival schools of devotion, Shakta and Vaishnava Bhakti, they also worship Krishna—the Krishna who overthrew oppressors and liberated the earth, not the Krishna of popular lore who preached love, played the flute, and bantered with village women.[51] Central to *Anandamath* is the story of Mahendra, an impoverished ordinary householder who leaves with his wife and baby girl for the city. On the way, they face various misfortunes and are rescued by the warrior monks. Mahendra joins them in their fight, giving up household life, undergoing ascetic disciplines, and pledging to fight until death.[52] From a victim of the famine, Mahendra is transformed into an empowered political activist.

Contrast *Debi Chaudhurani* and *Anandamath* to Bankim's other novel, *Rajsingha*, where everyday life appears pervaded by politics. Set in the context of Aurangzeb's reign, the story is driven by the actions of a Rajput princess who refuses to marry into the Mughal dynasty and approaches King Rajsingha for protection. A series of battles follows. But the real drama of the novel lies in the young princess's canny activities navigating the world of power. She epitomizes the art of being politic, in the classical ideal of *arthashastra*. The men, both Hindu and Muslim, demonstrate valor and a penchant for self-sacrifice. Yet even the battleground—a hilly and forested terrain—seems more a scene of strategy, acuity, and cunning rather than pitched battles. The other settings in the novel are the Mughal court, the women's quarters of the palace, the road to the palace, the marketplace of Chandni Chowk, and indeed the city of Delhi itself—all teeming with characters, noblemen, fortune-tellers, spies, maids-in-waiting, palace guards, queens and princesses, flower and fragrance sellers, all engaged in realpolitik maneuvers.[53]

Rajsingha appears closer to the domain of *artha* and *niti*—of politics as the everyday art of exercising and subverting power—than to an imagination of politics as action. Starting in the early nineteenth century, the English term *politics* was used, often transcribed in Indian languages, to denote regular activities that were oriented, directly or indirectly, toward engaging rulers. Bankim used this English term routinely to denote practices ranging from associational activities, journalistic writing, and public oratory to lobbying, petitioning, spying, alliance making, power broking, and so on. This ordinary notion of politics—of being politic, worldly, and artful—was obviously distinct from the notion of politics as action, because it was not founded on an opposition between ordinary and extraordinary, everyday and exceptional. In Bankim's novels thus the notion of politics as action is accompanied rather than displaced by the more everyday notion of politics as simply being politic.

In *Anandamath* political action appears balanced precariously in a tenuous relationship with everyday life. Mahendra becomes political by pledging to give up ordinary social life. He would return to normal life, it was understood, once his political commitments were fulfilled. But the twists in the story tell us that there is no easy exit from the everyday. Mahendra's wife tries to poison herself to free him for the cause. His daughter falls fatally ill. They both eventually live. But Mahendra must not know it. He must believe that he has no social life left in order to commit to politics. His compatriot Jibananda's lover, unlike Mahendra's wife, refuses to accept that politics calls for renunciation. She disguises herself as a man and fights side by side with him, but again, Jibananda must not know it. In the literary register, thus, the theory of desireless action plays out differently, as the everyday throws its long and poignant shadow over the political moment, as common and minor instances of generous though not disinterested practice, primarily by women, rival the great instances of self-sacrificing political action by ascetic men.

In the way that gender jeopardizes the action/everyday division, caste appears as a complicating factor in Bankim's novels. The Bhagavad Gita, despite its abstract rendering, does invoke *varna* and *jati*—the social register of *dharma* as it were—in its exposition of *nishkama karma*. Bankim must engage with this fact. There are moments in his texts when Bankim expresses acute discomfort with the implicit caste references in the Gita, but he is not able to disavow caste entirely.[54] In an appendix to *Dharmatattva*, Bankim tries exploring the relationship between *anushilan* and caste and labor practices. If *anushilan* is the cultivation of the universal human competencies of theory, practice, and aesthesis, what of *svadharma* or activities proper to one's social station? Bankim believed that *anushilan* would make each caste more efficient in its ascribed task, while simultaneously enabling individuals to disidentify with their given caste attributes. This presumably would loosen the hold of caste over self-aware individuals. It is through this reconstituted relationship with social roles that the contemporary political subject would emerge, who would be contingently caste-marked but fundamentally caste-indifferent![55] In his novels, Bankim describes possible scenarios where caste is rendered irrelevant by the political turn. In

Anandamath, as Mahendra takes the vow of *karmayoga*, he also pledges to renounce caste, including his caste right as a Brahmin, to the service of menials. Here Bankim minces no words. *Karmayogis* are nothing if not renouncers—of family, society, household, and property. Ironically, thus, the caste question returns Bankim to the place that he had initially shunned, namely, the place of renunciation.

Is Bankim then saying, like Vivekananda, that renunciation is a necessary precondition to political action? It is no such simple matter. In *Anandamath*, Mahendra is to return to household life, and he indeed does so, at the end of the story. But this is an arbitrary closure, not a resolution, for the focus now shifts from Mahendra to Satyananda, the leader of the monks, who even as he defeats the tyrannical Bengal nawab, must now reconcile to foreign rule and deal with the unavoidable fact of interrupted, incomplete action. He returns to study, as befits his station as a Brahmin, and his followers return to labor and cultivation. But Satyananda is distraught.[56] Does Mahendra feel the same? If he does, then has he really returned to everyday life? His home had been turned into a commune and a battle station earlier in the story. How does he reclaim his household, property, and caste right to servants? How does he return to Kalyani, who had once tried to kill herself to enable his political activism? More difficult than the question of exiting the everyday is the question of how to return to it after the moment of the political. The novel ends with a strange formulation—"bisharjan ashiya protistha ke loyia gelo." The mother goddess, who had been brought to life by the *nishkama karma* of warrior monks, is borne away by the running waters. The idol is always immersed after worship. But everyone knows that she will return. Does one await that return, or does one act to provoke it?

Action and Insurrection

The question that Bankim poses but evades is whether an exit from the everyday is necessarily insurrectionary action. Twentieth-century nationalist revolutionaries thought so, regardless of Bankim's authorial intention. They combined his concepts of *yoga*, *nishkama karma*, and *anushilan* with cognate categories like *sadhana* (attentive practice leading to *siddhi*, or final accomplishment) and *unmadana* (madness, a condition of ecstasy displayed by rural ascetics like *fakirs* and *sannyasis*).[57] The implication was clear. If the everyday was about prepolitical normalcy, then it was only madness that made the political leap of faith possible. Political madness, however, was a cultivated condition produced through asceticism, the study of spiritual and philosophical texts, arms training, endurance exercises, eating nutritious and uncommon food regardless of caste, and intense love for family, friend, and country.[58] At stake here was *character*,[59] a word bringing together the literary sense of being a narrative protagonist and the political sense of being an exemplar. Unsurprisingly, Bankim's writings, alongside the Mahabharata, the Gita, and the writings of Mikhail Bakunin, Peter Kropotkin, Giuseppe Mazzini, Thomas Carlyle, and later Vladimir Lenin, became foundational texts for radical action in India, a form of action that persisted alongside and sometimes even bolstered Gandhian and communist mass action through the latter's ebb and flow.[60]

Aurobindo Ghosh's *Essays on the Gita*, like Bankim's essays, talks of action generically and of political action only by implication. His Bengali essays, however, completely erase the line between political and spiritual action. He speaks of the "political purpose of Krishna's incarnation" and the Mahabharata as a story of political revolution at the cusp of the two epochs of *dvapar* and *kali*. Earlier, Aurobindo argued, political power was based on lineage, valor, or both. With Krishna, however, political power comes to rest on canny action. Krishna ensures imperial unity through a series of tactical moves leading to the ultimate destruction of all political rivals and of Kshatriyas as a *varna*.[61] It is out of this epochal act of universal destruction—involving the killing not just of teachers and kin but of the entire political class—that a new political form emerges, in defiance of both caste and lineage principles.[62]

Aurobindo criticized Bankim for attempting to "rationalize" the Gita for the modern mind. He felt that one should read the Gita not as abstract political philosophy but as part of the great mythology of the Mahabharata. Nor should one be concerned, like Bankim, with the Gita's historicity. Nor indeed should one read the Gita allegorically like Gandhi,[63] in order to gloss over the violence intrinsic to the text.[64] One should take the Gita at face value, as a thesis on life, death, violence, and spirituality. Aurobindo insisted that, unlike what Bankim and Gandhi proposed, the Kurukshetra was not a battle between righteous and unrighteous forces. In war, no one is right or wrong, for war is precisely when such ethical judgments become impossible. A theory of pure action becomes necessary precisely at such moments of normative crisis. But, then, the Gita is also not a philosophy of war in the strict sense. War here is not a moment of exception or emergency but a metaphor for life, "in which by every step forward, whether we will it or not, something is crushed and broken, in which every breath of life is a breath too of death."[65] To ascribe violence to an evil out there, to an enemy or an outsider, is therefore disingenuous. Violence is part of our own selves, which is why early Indian traditions saw the world as driven by hunger and social hierarchy as a dynamic between eaters and eaten.[66]

To act, therefore, is not merely to "survive death." It is to proactively engage with the "law of Life by Death."[67] The only way to acquire this competence, according to Aurobindo, was by living "as the spirit and in the Spirit."[68] Writing from his ashram at Pondicherry to his brother and ex-revolutionary Barin Ghosh, Aurobindo said that while Gandhi tried to spiritualize politics, he was still unable to work out the full implications of spirituality. In the name of *dharma*, Gandhi merely offered a disappointing version of Indianized Tolstoyism. Aurobindo was writing in 1920, responding both to Gandhi's *satyagraha* and to Hindu identitarian politics.[69] He argued that to act decisively was to act spiritually, that is, to act on an assumption of durability, immortality, and infinity, all characteristics of the indestructible *atman*. But to act was not to assume a godly disposition. On the contrary, it was to own up to the sheer smallness and contingency of one's agency. Aurobindo said, echoing Bankim, that the individual agent was mere *nimitta*—medium, occasion, pretext—of action.[70] Hence the Gita's injunction to act without any desire for fruits of action.

Standing in the battlefield, Krishna declares that the self is not a subject. It is a mere conduit for the cosmic forces that propel the rise and fall of worlds. He then goes on to display his *viswarupa*—his indescribable cosmic persona in which he assumes the form of the world itself—before the bedazzled eyes of his devotee Arjuna, just as he had done earlier when his mother, Yashoda, scolded him for his pranks. Aurobindo, unsurprisingly, spent many pages discussing early Indian theories of the self.[71] The human is never self-identical, he said, split as she or he is between the active self, the experiencing self, the knowing self, the inactive witness self, and indeed the universal self. Note how this theory of the self is different from a theory of the subject. Even though the universal and the ultimate self are often thought of as god, Brahman is actually continuous to embodied selves (*jiva*). Divinity thus is not an absolute other of the human, which is why it is possible for humans to partake in the immortality and universality of the divine. In other words, it is not the identity but the constitutive nonidentity of the human self that allows the individual agent to exceed body and ego, overcome fear, invest fruits of action in god and society, and act freely. This form of action, according to Aurobindo, was neither competitive self-interested action (liberal politics) nor selfless sacrificial action (revolutionary politics)—because it was not about a self in the first place.[72]

Here, then, is an effort at imagining pure action—action that speaks for itself without reference to an intending agential subject. This returns us to the perplexed question we encountered in chapter 1. What is the political after all? Is it the political self regardless of his action/inaction, or is it the self-expressive political act regardless of its agent? To Aurobindo, *nishkama karma* is not what we conventionally understand as selfless action—humanitarianism, charity, philanthropy, moral duty, even sacrifice.[73] For sacrifice, he says, is predicated on a heightened sense of the self and duty on a stable network of familial and social relationships in which the self is embedded.[74] When social relationships come into crisis or when relationships are forged outside authorized social networks, duty no longer suffices as a normative compass.[75] In any case, duty, like other ordinary activities of life, is embroiled in *prakriti*—that restless and changeful materiality of Sankhya imagination, which determines not just the senses but also intellect (*buddhi*) and mind (*manas*). Note that in the tradition Aurobindo invokes, mind and body are not seen as opposites; instead, mind and body together stand in opposition to the witness self (*purusha*), the universal self (*atman*), or both. *Prakriti* is of the order of experience—Aurobindo reminds us—and experience generates determined rather than free action.[76] Experience works by producing propensities or *gunas*—*tamas* or inertia, *rajas* or kinesis, and *sattva* or clarity.[77] These three *gunas* combine differentially in the case of each individual and produce a particular *svabhava* (disposition) and *dharma* (predilection). But *nishkama karma* requires perfect equipoise and equanimity, not a disposition or propensity, even if it is of the highest order of *sattva*.[78] *Nishkama karma*, in other words, requires a nonself.

Aurobindo, like Bankim, repeatedly invokes *shakti*, a term approximating "force" but distinct in its figuration from the force of mechanics. Force here is god. I am careful to not say, as one ordinarily would, that this is a metaphor or a superficial religious gloss on the secular scientific fact of force. Instead, taking *shakti* at face value, I reckon seriously with the proposition that force here is indeed god. Force here is a nonhuman or extrahuman phenomenon, which is impossible to harness as an instrument of human action. It is precisely this resistance to instrumentalization that makes force politically efficacious. This force works by calling on an empty and hospitable self that facilitates its conduct or passage. And because of its cosmic and divine nature, this force remains in an unresolved relationship to the flow of human life—putting the very notion of life at stake.

As we have already seen, this force could be the goddess Kali, a naked, wild, ferocious feminine force, operating out of the margins of the social, out of cremation grounds and dark jungles. Or it could be Krishna, crossing in a jiffy the immense distance between being a cute little prankster to being a morally suspect player of realpolitik to being a universal self. Or it could be Thakur, the god of the tribe of Santals, calling the *hor* or humans to insurgent action against colonial officials and moneylenders—a god made famous by Dipesh Chakrabarty as the intractable political protagonist who always already exceeded the logic of secular histories, however sensitive to "minority" ontologies such histories might be.[79] In other words, godly force acquired its political quality by exceeding the human subject, by holding the subject in its grip, by instrumentalizing the subject rather than the subject instrumentalizing it, as she or he would the forces of nature and of machines.

Yet this force, in its very godliness, also subsists in precarious kin relations with humans. Thus, Kali's intensity derives not just from her cosmic aspect but also from the fact that she exists, paradoxically, as mother to humans. But she is an atypical mother who devours her own children. The eighteenth-century poet and *tantric* adept Ramaprasad Sen, in his role as Kali's son, thus turned on the death-dealing mother and said, "Ebar Kali tomae khabo," in a song that remains popular in Bengal to this day: "This time, Kali, I'm going to eat You up / I'll eat You. / . . . Either You eat me / or I eat You /we must decide on one."[80]

Could one then argue that establishing a kin relation to forceful gods or godly forces was indeed to resignify kinship as the locus of commonplace life? So, when twentieth-century revolutionaries claimed to act in the name of mother Kali and motherland, thus politically charging preexisting kinship idioms, were they making a double move—simultaneously making intimate, unreasonable claims on cosmic forces, as son to mother, while offering unconditional submission to them, as human to god?[81] In the process, revolutionary rhetoric dramatized an utterly quotidian dynamic—in this instance, mother-son banter—so as to turn it into an insurgent force, as if through a deconstruction of assumptions behind everyday sociabilities and kinships. (Recall Vivekananda's own complicated relationship to Kali.)

Aurobindo imagined a relationship of *sakhya* (friendship) between Krishna and the human—friendship being, he said, other than kin relations and yet productive of a wide range of social, kinship, and romantic affects.[82] Friendship between god and human thus encompassed but exceeded sociality. The structure of friendship both played out and dangerously disrupted norms of common life. We know that Krishna's popular persona—as disobedient son and adulterous lover—was that of ironic participation in quotidian work and play. Krishna simultaneously partook in and obliquely challenged the mores of everyday social life, allowing possible breaching of caste and gender divides.

One should note that social life here is primarily figured as household life—*garhastha*—involving an extended network of birth, marriage, and patronage and located in a network of "graded inequalities" (to use Ambedkar's term) involving kings, priests, servants, menials, teachers, neighbors, and nonkin proximates like students and the sheltered. The household is the locus of desire and obligation as well as of social norms and hierarchies. To admit to cosmic forces, therefore, is also to expose the household for what it is—contingent, ephemeral, and in the grip of larger forces beyond the control of even the most powerful patriarch. To engage these larger forces, then, is to both inhabit and refute household life, that is, to admit to both life's animation (in love, devotion, power, and desire) and its limits (in death, suffering, and meaninglessness). After all, on encountering the four canonical antilife moments—age, disease, destitution, and death—Siddhartha felt compelled to leave his royal household, including his wife and newborn son, in order to become the Buddha. Perhaps this explains the centrality of the household, both common and royal, in Bankim's political novels. It is as if life becomes a question before thought via a political deconstruction of household and lineage, making the self productively vulnerable to extrasocial cosmic forces that enable revolutionary action.

Action and Time

Cosmic force, the driver of pure, undetermined action, was often figured as time in early twentieth-century India. Time works here as the extrapolitical supplement animating—in fact, making possible—political action. Aurobindo invoked *kala* (time) as the true name of god, in the face of which the intending agential subject was but a flicker of imagination. In this telling, human action unfolded not in biographical or historical time but in a time that moved relentlessly, crushingly, in absolute indifference to particular lives and particular deaths. Sacrifice, Aurobindo argued, trying to reclaim the term from its earlier Vedic associations, was thus neither killing nor the courting of death but the dissolution of the acting self in the movement of time—a formulation once again rendering fuzzy the line between activity and passivity. Only thus could one act without fear of interruption, incompletion, contingency, or unintended consequence.[83] In other words, free action was possible only in simulation of the work of time because time moved freely, regardless of lives, traditions, and histories.

Time, we know, was a popular concern during colonial times. The idiom of *kaliyuga*—the final epoch of the Puranic cosmic cycle, marked by social and moral inversions—was widespread in the late nineteenth and early twentieth centuries, as what helped make sense of the novelty of the colonial experience. *Kaliyuga* enabled unprecedented practices against preexisting social norms, such as the remarriage of upper-caste widows, crossing the seas without loss of caste, or the rise of untouchables to political power. Imaginations of women ruling men and lower-caste insurgency indexed the arrival of Kali, as was often depicted in social satires of the time.[84] When the forest Santals rebelled in 1855, they too invoked time as the true "cause" of their actions.[85] Aurobindo's formulation about the force of time was thus no philosophical idiosyncrasy.

Muhammad Iqbal, poet, philosopher, and political thinker, also shared this intense investment in the concept of time. Iqbal said that God—who was both eternity and change (not in linear succession but in contemporaneous differentiation)—held time as an unceasing vibration within his own being. Creation was God's activism. But creation was not a onetime act. The universe was still in the process of becoming and the realm of human possibilities infinitely expanding—he argued in criticism of the paradigm of natural laws as given for all times to come:[86] "Shut ye not then, the way to Action, alleging the 'exigencies of nature'"![87] In Iqbal's masterpiece *Javednama*, Zurban or Time addresses the poet. Time promises that if the poet is able to envision cosmic time, he will not only see incredible emergent things but also attain *sultan* or divine/political force. He can then wield time as a sword to cut asunder the veil of destiny (*dahr*) and undertake undetermined creative action.[88]

Rabindranath Tagore, in his well-known critique of historicism,[89] said that creative action emanated out of the resonance, the twang, of human life with cosmic time (he uses the metaphor of musical chords here).[90] In his play *Kaler Jatra* (The journey of time), Tagore figures time as a great chariot that rolls on like a behemoth and sets off one epoch after the other. One day the chariot gets stuck, obstructed by the inequities of human society. Time stands still. Those who boasted of driving the chariot—priests, soldiers, merchants—all give up. Finally, Shudras get time's chariot moving again. But Tagore does not stay with the Shudra either, as final political subject. For him, it is the rope of the time chariot that is at stake, not the historical subject who pulls it. In Tagore's telling, like Iqbal's, the one who truly senses this critical work of time is none other than the poet, who sets temporality to rhyme and partakes in god's own creativity. In the play—otherwise peopled by sociological entities like priests, kings, soldiers, merchants, Shudras, and women—the poet stands apart, by virtue of his ability to play with time, with a lightness of touch at once more nimble and more modest than the labors of those who claim to be subjects of history, seeking in vain to shift the weight of the ultimate sovereign, time itself![91]

The Everyday and the Paradox of Practice

In this rendering, then, political action is that which partakes in the creative and destructive force of time while quotidian social activities are those that play out in the everyday temporality of calendars, almanacs, and chronologies.

Or so it appears in the writings of Bankim and Aurobindo, who were the earliest to engage with the modern definition of politics as action and consequently deal with the perplexed question, If life is an unceasing flow of cause, action, and consequence, how does one even isolate and identify action as sui generis political? Bankim tried to formulate *karmayoga* as common practice for common householders. But when he tried to describe *karmayoga* as a concrete set of practices, as he did in his novels, *karmayoga* unwittingly turned into exceptional political action based on a necessary disavowal, if temporary, of everyday common life. And Aurobindo, in his own telling, experienced absolute freedom precisely at the moment of his physical incarceration and imposed passivity. In his prison memoirs, *Kara Kahini*, Aurobindo writes how physical bondage, material deprivation, and social isolation—a parody of voluntary renunciation, as it were—helped him realize true spiritual freedom for the first time. In solitary confinement, he did not even have books to read or paper to write on. It was then that he learned to take repose in and mobilize the power of his inner self, which brought him back from the edge of madness.

And yet, Aurobindo also admitted to the experience of a new sociality inside the prison walls. He noticed for first time the collective behavior of ants. He also enjoyed hitherto unimaginable proximity to sweepers, scavengers, and other untouchables who serviced the prisoners and promised antisocial prohibited friendships. He also rubbed shoulders with common criminals. Above all, through living with his own feces and smell and washing, drinking, and eating with just one utensil that was allowed by authorities, eating whatever came his way—all anathema in a caste society based on notions of purity and pollution—he learned the meaninglessness of caste conventions.[92] True equipoise thus became possible only in segregation from social life, though prison experience ultimately pushed Aurobindo to the side of formal renunciation.

The everyday thus stealthily reenters the conceptual domain of *nishkama karma*—most vividly by way of caste. In his *Doctrine of Passive Resistance*—a mode of political action that exerted effective force without directly causing violence—Aurobindo invoked social boycott and social ostracism as practices that could compel people to act but without physical coercion.[93] In other words, one way to make people act politically was to make everyday life impossible. Indeed, social boycott was used extensively during the 1905 Swadeshi movement in Bengal as a way of forcing people to renounce British products.[94] Ironically, social boycott was one of the traditional ways in which caste transgressors were punished without direct recourse to brute force. In the space between the political and the everyday, then, the question of caste would repeatedly raise its grotesque head.

It is, then, but natural to end with Ambedkar. Ambedkar read the Bhagavad Gita as a text of counterrevolution, by which Brahminical orthodoxy reestablished its power by co-opting and neutralizing Buddhist criticism. He also interpreted the Hindu notion of *karma* as nothing but an ideology of caste dominance, which proposed that everyone deserved their present station in life by virtue of bad actions in a previous life. Far from accepting *karma* as a model of political action, Ambedkar argued that the theory of *karma* was exactly what disabled emancipatory political action. His mode of reading the Gita was the opposite of Bankim's and Aurobindo's. Instead of distilling a pure concept of *karma* from entangled theoretical and empirical propositions in the Gita, Ambedkar showed the concept itself to be nothing more than a reification of the everyday and empirical fact of caste. He also read the Mahabharata as the literal stage setting for the Gita, arguing that the Gita was an elaborate justification of fratricidal violence in the name of political action. *Nishkama karma* was simply another name for war. (He was responding here, we know, to Gandhi's interpretation that the war of Kurukshetra was a metaphor for the inner struggle within the human heart between righteous and unrighteous forces.)[95]

And yet, tellingly, Ambedkar did not abandon the *karma* concept entirely. In his theological text *The Buddha and His Dhamma*, Ambedkar posited an alternative notion of *karma* as a model not for political but for everyday social action, as it indeed was in earlier times. Ambedkar said that the Buddhist law of *karma* simply meant "reap as you sow;" it was a basic principle of social responsibility and accountability. Hinduism and Christianity saw the self and the individual, respectively, as the locus of spirituality. But Buddha taught us that *dhamma* arose only when there were at least two people engaged in face-to-face interaction. *Dhamma* was irrelevant to the solitary individual. Buddha's *dhamma* thus was nothing if not a code of social conduct, a mode of ethical sociability. In other words, in the Buddhist paradigm, *karma* was a model of everyday action and *dhamma* simply a theory of common life.[96] Ambedkar, unlike Aurobindo and Bankim, clearly had little stake in proving the distinctiveness of political action as that which followed a crisis in social norms. For him, social norms in caste-ridden India were always already in crisis and quotidian life beset by routine and spectacular violence. If the choice was between political action and everyday sociability, Ambedkar chose to stay with the latter as the primary object of his concern.

4

Labor, Hunger, and Struggle

> Through labor, a teleological positing is realized within material being, as the rise of a new objectivity. The first consequence of this is that labor becomes the model for any social practice.
> —Georg Lukács, *The Ontology of Social Being*, vol. 3, *Labor*

With the rise of mass politics in 1920s India, political action came to be recast around questions of labor and hunger. These were questions that resided in the everyday, yet they lent themselves, apparently seamlessly, to politicization—under the sign of "struggle," a common but warlike disposition incited by, it was believed, experiences of everyday hardship. Contrary to expectations, however, this did not mean that the political simply returned to its rightful place, to everyday life. Rather, political action came to be staged as a way of alternately reiterating and suspending quotidian life—so, too, with work and the striking of work, eating and fasting.

Both Gandhi and the communists brought the question of labor to the fore. While this is a well-known fact and a logical corollary to the entry of the working classes into national politics, its implications are not always fully worked out. I propose in this chapter that the modern imagination of politics as action was made possible by the twentieth-century production of a homology between the practice of labor and the practice of politics. In a sense, *karma* as desireless activity transmuted into *karma* as productive or creative activity—a mutation made easy by the fact that the same term, *karma* and its vernacular derivatives *kam* and *kaj* lexically meant both. Not accidentally, political activists came to be called "workers" or *karmis*. This recasting of political action after the image of labor, however, stumbled on an irresoluble split in the concept of labor itself—between the sui generis understanding of labor as innate transformative drive and the figuration of the laborer as common subject—returning us once more to the persistent question: Is the political to be understood in terms of the subject of politics, regardless of his or her actions, or in terms of the nature of action, regardless of who performs it?

Labor as Such

Gandhi talked of labor as a generic substance since his days in South Africa. In 1910, discussing his Phoenix and Tolstoy farm experiments, Gandhi said that daily manual labor helped one overcome moral and practical errors brought on by too much thinking: "The body is like an ox or donkey and should therefore be made to carry a load."[1] Gandhi was criticizing the intellectualism of middle-class politics in India, implying that "intellectual labor"—a term communists used routinely—was an oxymoron.[2] To Gandhi labor was by definition manual and menial and was part of the problematic of human corporeality. The modern-day hegemony of scientific knowledge and the consequent social privilege of the intelligentsia had resulted in a general deprecation of labor worldwide. Labor, therefore, needed to be reinstated as concept and practice. Further, modernity both indulged and instrumentalized the human body. To remedy this civilizational pathology and regain moral value and political efficacy for the body, humans must self-consciously engage in agricultural and artisanal labor as well as in fasting, celibacy, and other bodily disciplines.[3] After all, unlike other species that grazed on what nature offered, humans were meant to labor for food, clothing, and shelter. Anyone who consumed without putting in proportionate labor was thus a thief. The crux of social inequality lay in the simple fact that some people lived off the labor of others.[4] Clearly, at stake for Gandhi was not so much the working classes as the non-working classes, whose members had to be returned to their share of socially necessary labor as part of the nation-building process.

To Gandhi the political valence of labor derived from its moral aspect, which encompassed its economic, social, and aesthetic dimensions. This comes through in his choice of the *charkha* as a political symbol. Gandhi believed that spinning could help all classes identify with the common Indian artisan. Spinning was also sound economics because it gave supplementary employment to peasants in the lean season.[5] It also denoted a move forward from the earlier

Swadeshi days, when leaders called for a boycott of British textiles without attending to the question of indigenous productivity. Further, the *charkha* symbolized resistance to capital-intensive production, which deindustrialized traditional societies and deskilled human labor. The *charkha* also inspired national pride in India's premium handloom tradition. Additionally, in Bhakti and Sufi metaphysics, the *charkha* worked as a poetic metaphor and a philosophical concept and was a symbol dear to Hindus, Muslims, and Sikhs. Also, spinning was an act of clean labor (unlike sweeping and scavenging), involved less physical hardship than farming and factory work, and could be done privately, making possible its quiet insertion into the domestic routine of nonlaboring classes. Above all, spinning made possible thinking and contemplation in the very act of labor, producing patience, discipline, and nonviolence in political actors. No wonder Gandhi sought to make Indian National Congress membership conditional on the labor of spinning yarn. In the 1934 Congress session, Gandhi proposed that the four-*anna* subscription be replaced by "labor franchise"; that is, every member would annually contribute a certain length of yarn to Congress as a membership fee. In his opinion, this was the closest one could get to universal adult franchise in colonial times, that is, franchise for all those who labored for the country and thereby deserved the vote.[6]

If Gandhi pitched labor as a moral question, communists pitched it as an economic question. From the 1920s, Marx's labor theory of value was explicated in simple Bengali in various communist periodicals.[7] Labor was the mode by which each individual contributed to and received from society.[8] Labor was the only force that could generate value by itself. Because labor time was the basic unit for calculating the value of all goods and services, the working classes were the primary driver of politics. Society did not realize this generative potential of labor and therefore oppressed workers.[9] And so on.

And yet, despite their formal obeisance to economic theory, communists seemed to deploy the concept of labor more widely in aesthetic terms. In communist fiction, poetry, and song, labor was directly figured as a metaphor for political action. Thus, Ansar, the hero of Kazi Nazrul Islam's novel *Mrityukhuda* (Hunger for death/Death by hunger), on being arrested by the police, exhorts the assembled crowd to use the tools of labor as "weapons" of transformation:

> "How can I say you have no weapons? Coachman, you have your whip to tame wild horses. Can you not tame humans? Mason, you build majestic palaces with your tools . . . can you not build heaven on earth for the exploited? My sweeper, scavenger brothers, you make yourselves untouchable by breathing the toxic air and give us life by purifying the atmosphere. Can

you not use your brooms to sweep away the filth and poison in our minds? My peasant brother, your plow makes the earth bloom, can you not make fertile the sterile hearts of inhuman humans?"[10]

To Nazrul, as for his compatriots, labor was a force of both resistance and creation. It held exploiters at bay just as it built the world anew. Hemanga Biswas's "Harvest Song" went:

> O peasant brother, whet your sickle
> > Whet your sickle sharp
> Cut the golden crop at harvest time
> If the looters come cut them up too
> > Whet your sickle sharp.[11]

His "Song of the Railway Workers" described working with boilers and engines as driving the nation toward freedom.[12]

This seamless move from labor to political action must not be read as simply a duplication of Soviet-style "productivism," though the ideal of indigenous productivity did have a nationalist charge of its own. Rather, for communists, the equation between labor and action derived from an aesthetics of the body, such that the body's comportment and mobilization came to be imagined as continuous between labor and politics. This becomes evident if we look closely at visual images of the time. As an illustration, I present here some well-known photographs of Gandhi at work and walking, alongside the leftist photographer Sunil Janah's images of laboring and marching bodies.[13]

In the photographs, note Gandhi's deployment of his body in labor—his emaciation, solitude, repose, even contemplativeness, in the midst of work and politics. He is still and self-contained at work. In the Dandi march, he is alone and self-absorbed even in a crowd, walking with eyes downcast. In the communist images, on the other hand, muscles ripple through skeletal frames. There is a choreographed mobility to the bodies, a collective surging forward. The tools of labor—*charkha*, broom, and spade for Gandhi; sickle, rope, and plowshare for the communist subject—are wielded differently. The loincloth and the stick are, however, common, telling us perhaps that we are seeing a contest between Gandhi and the communists over the same political body. Contra the disembodied self of revolutionary *nishkama karma*, we have here in the name of the mass political a "kinetics" of the body that shares a common stance across the everyday act of labor and the forceful act of politics, though the body's stance is differently designed for Gandhi and the communists. I should add here that Janah's images are not entirely idiosyncratic. I might have used other images,

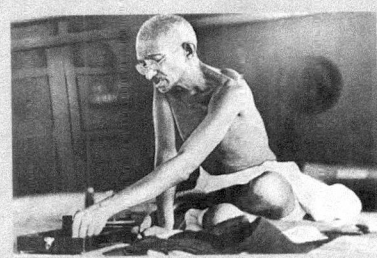

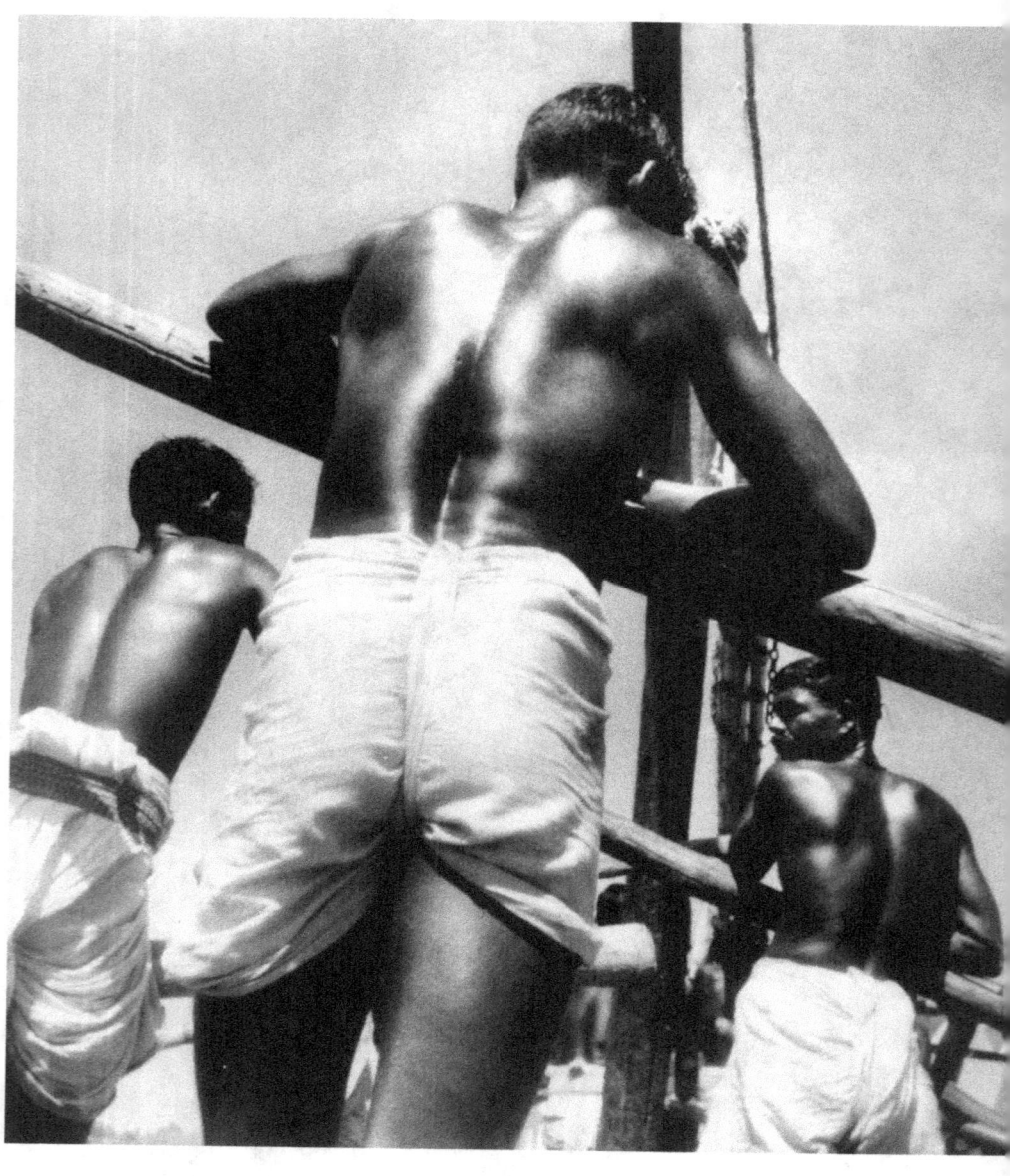

such as by the painters Chittaprasad or Somenath Hore, whose sketches of laboring and political bodies were routinely published in the communist periodicals *People's Age* and *People's War* and evoked the same kinesis that Janah's images display.

That labor was salient because of its aesthetic aspect was confirmed by the greatest Indian aesthetician of the time. Tagore, even as he disputed Gandhi's valorization of labor for its own sake, spoke of labor in ways not dissimilar to the communists. As he said in his 1923 preface to the inaugural issue of *Sanhati* (Solidarity), a periodical covering trade union movements in Bengal, labor was the force that drove the world.[14] In his poem "Ora Kaaj Kore" (They work), Tagore contrasted the ceaseless labor of commoners in field and factory to the ephemeral actions of kings and merchants who "traversed the sky" without leaving a trace on the horizon of everyday life.[15]

Tagore disputed Gandhi's choice of the *charkha* as universal symbol of labor and politics. Laziness, Tagore wrote in 1921, was not just when "man fatten[ed] on another's toil" but also when he fell into mindless "drift."[16] Freedom called for innovation, not routine labor. If freedom was the end, then spinning at the wheel could never be a means to achieve it. The Gandhian motto "Spin and weave, spin and weave" smacked of the "narrow life [of] the [bee]hive." It led to "self-atrophy," as did work in European military camps and factories: "The charkha in its proper place can do no harm . . . [but in the wrong place] thread can only be spun at the cost of a great deal of the mind itself."[17] Tagore was uneasy with Gandhi's moral rendering of labor. He felt that the rhetoric of purity and impurity with respect to national and foreign products overlapped with the traditional language of caste. "The contagion of untouchability" now threatened to spread from society to economics and politics, he said.[18] When Gandhi argued that the classical terms *karma* and *yajna* (ritual sacrifice) actually connoted the basic act of human labor and that "to a people famishing and idle, the only acceptable form in which God can dare appear is work,"[19] Tagore retorted that Hindu scriptures prescribed rigid duties to each caste, made labor into drudgery, and killed the "mind of man who is a doer, whose work is creation."[20] Traditional conceptions of caste labor created an "abject state of passivity" in the very midst of work.

To Tagore, the wheel—the weaver's wheel, the potter's wheel—was beautiful because it was laborsaving rather than labor-inducing, and helped make time for human creativity.[21] The nation, Tagore argued, was a work of art and not "heaps of thread, and piles of cloth."[22] Labor did have an economic logic, but this logic was useful only when it helped enhance labor's aesthetic potential. Hence Tagore emphasized arts and crafts and the cooperative movement (like Gandhi, he was a critic of modern mechanized labor). After all, he argued, poverty was a complex condition of impoverishment that needed both economic and aesthetic redress.[23] Spinning, Tagore added, was an individualistic act of labor. Even when masses of people simultaneously worked at the *charkha*, they all chose to be alone and hence sans political potential.[24] Labor became political only when it brought people, Hindus and Muslims, together in cooperation, in a way that neither religion nor morality could.[25]

Though antagonists in the field of literary and aesthetic theory, Tagore and the communists thus shared the understanding that labor was really about the aesthesis of everyday life, displaying in their discourses a counterintuitive coming together of the economic and the aesthetic, the productive and the creative. Hemanga Biswas put it in literal terms. In his study of popular musical genres and their organic connection to art-house music, Biswas stated that melody and rhythm emerged out of the patterning and cadence of labor, out of the coordinated and resonant movements of bodies in the act of working the field, rowing the boat, wielding the tool.[26] Labor made dance and music possible, and dance and music in turn made possible the political march, the demonstration, the rally. Biswas's own songs were meant to capture this kinesis of bodies in coordinated action, in work as in politics. Gandhi, for his part, admitted that the imagination of labor as aesthesis was opposed to his moral rendering of labor. To him, labor was necessity (for the poor) and sacrifice (for the prince). Labor indexed the ultimate nonduality of the world, where rich and poor were but the same body racked by hunger and need.[27] In contrast to the poet's world of novelties and wonders, in his own world of "old and worn-out things," he said, economics was ethics and just that![28]

In conventional rendering, labor becomes political through its suspension, through the striking of labor. Thus it is the withdrawal of necessary labor, rather than labor itself, that becomes action. The preceding discussion, however, tells us that while the strike did become a popular mode of political action in modern India, the salience of labor went beyond merely asserting the power of labor to either maintain or disrupt the logic of the everyday. Labor became a model for political action. But for labor to become a modular form of (mass) political action, it had to simultaneously index the political and the everyday. Gandhi, the communists, and Tagore tried to ensure this by supplementing labor with ethics, economics, and aesthetics, respectively. These so-called nonpolitical imperatives thus appeared necessary to augment the common and unremarkable act of labor politically. And yet, in the final instance, neither ethics nor economics nor aesthetics seemed to suffice, as the extrapolitical and extradiscursive aspect of bodily kinesis came to be invoked to make plausible the labor/action homology.

Labor and Hunger

Hunger brings out the perplexed question of everyday life with even greater clarity. In a manner of speaking, hunger is the opposite of labor. If labor denotes the dynamics of the body in creative and productive action, hunger is that vital imperative that calls for labor, in a primordial need to feed the body—though it is also potentially that which drains the body of the capacity to labor. Hunger, like labor, became a mode of political action in the age of mass politics by way of the hunger strike, which drew political charge not only from the fact that it entailed a suspension of the daily activity of eating but also from exactly the opposite fact that not getting to eat was a daily experience of the laboring classes. Like labor, hunger thus held in tenuous suspension, at the precise moment of the political, the everyday and the exceptional, the ordinary and the extraordinary. I offer as illustration two iconic political images of hunger from twentieth-century India—a photograph of Gandhi on a fast and Zainul Abedin's sketch of a hungry, passive body in the "man-made" Bengal famine of 1943.

For Gandhi, fasting was a regular everyday practice as well as an exceptional political act. His ashram routine consisted of study, penance, charity, practices of sensory restraint, fasting, vegetarianism, labor, celibacy, and silence.[29] This was his vision of an ethical everyday, counterpoised to the pathologies of the modern everyday, which made the body indolent, indulgent, and dependent on external props such as machines and medicine.[30] The suspension of eating, among other disciplines, was thus a way of bringing back reflexivity into everyday habits. Fasting for Gandhi clearly was not a stand-alone act. It had to be accompanied, he insisted, by the rigorous spiritual practice of *satyagraha*, truth and nonanger.[31]

Gandhi distinguished fasting from the hunger strike. Passive resistance and the hunger strike, he said, were "weapons of the weak"—strategic political acts when the other side had clinching force at its disposal. But the *satyagrahi* fast was never "passive." It entailed "intense activity" and superordinate force. Also, *satyagraha* was not a purely political or exceptional act. It arose out of practices of quotidian living: "Father and son, man and wife are perpetually resorting to satyagraha, one towards the other."[32] It was a way of facing up to injustice not by retribution but by love, suffering, and moral exposure of the other. Inaugurating the Rowlatt Satyagraha in 1919 with a day's fast, Gandhi explained: "I have regarded this movement as a purely religious movement and fast is an ancient institution amongst us. You will not mistake it for a hunger strike."[33] In Gandhi's formulation, the *satyagrahi* fast uniquely straddled the two registers of routine discipline and exceptional protest/regret. Thus Gandhi's June 1913 fast was in penance for some students and teachers misbehaving at the Phoenix Farm, his May–June 1914 fast an atonement for a young boy's breaching of his vow against gluttony, his June 1915 fast was against lying by some ashram boys, his September 1915 fast was against ashram members resisting an untouchable family's entry into the community, and so on. Gandhi also fasted in public protest—in 1913 against the three-pound tax on Indians in South Africa, in 1918 in support of the Ahmedabad textile mill workers' strike, in 1919 to launch the Rowlatt Satyagraha, in 1921 against riots in Bombay, in 1922 against mob violence at Chauri Chaura, in 1924 for Hindu-Muslim unity, in 1932 against separate electorates for untouchables, in 1933 demanding the right to do scavenging work in prison, in 1934 for self-purification, and so on and on, in 1939, 1940, 1941, 1943, 1944, 1946, 1947, and finally, in 1948, against post-Partition Hindu-Muslim riots.

But even though the *satyagrahi* fast was derived from practices of common life, it was not, Gandhi paradoxically insisted, an appropriate mode of mass action.[34] One had to earn the right to fast, he said as he exhorted others not to join him in fasting. Gandhi claimed that through his everyday practices of fasting, he had "reduced [the fast] to a science." Fasting as political action, in other words, required a virtuosity, honed through practices of a reformed everyday life.[35] Not just the masses but even other national leaders must desist from following his example because fasting was an extraordinarily forceful political act and dangerously close to psychological coercion unless morally perfected.[36]

Significantly, Gandhi's first political fast in India was in the context of the 1918 Ahmedabad mill workers' strike for a 30 percent wage hike. Gandhi saw the workers' demand as fair. But the burden of his communication to workers was to insist that a labor strike did not entail a cessation of labor. Workers must give up their social prejudices, take on whatever manual or menial jobs they could get, and continue to earn their living without awaiting resolution or relief. Striking must not cause idleness.[37] Despite Gandhi's exhortations, some workers, under threat of starvation, returned to work at lower pay. It was then that Gandhi started his fast—not against mill owners but against workers "break[ing] their pledge out of fear."[38] Gandhi claimed that his fast was not a hunger strike. It was to demonstrate to workers that *satyagraha* entailed suffering and to persuade them to join him in menial work. Hunger, he implied, was

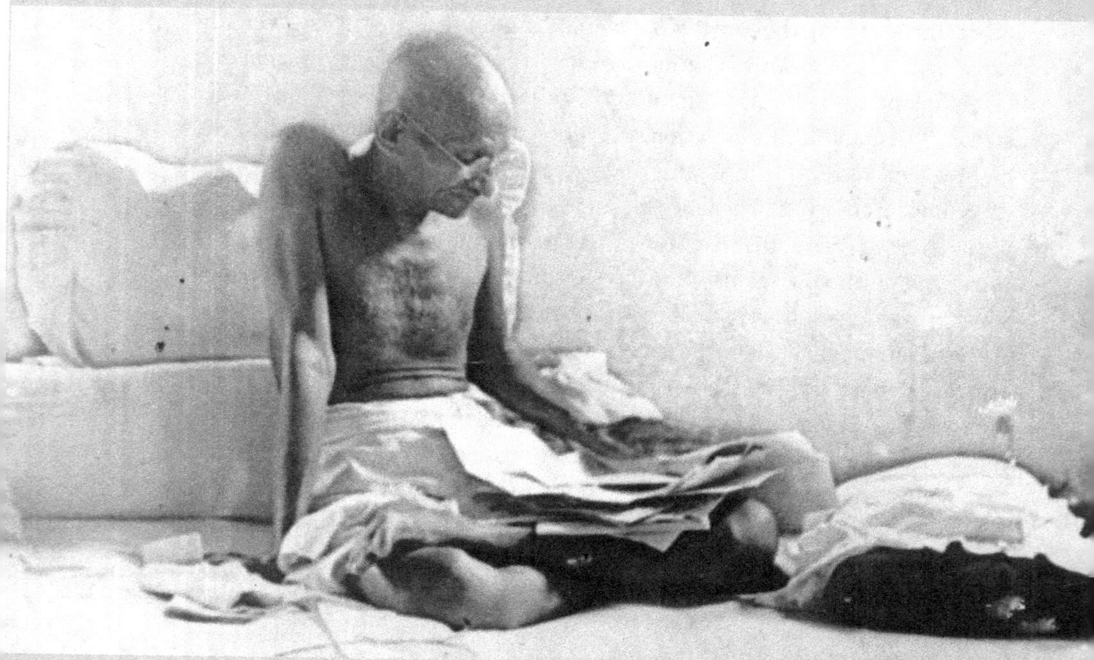

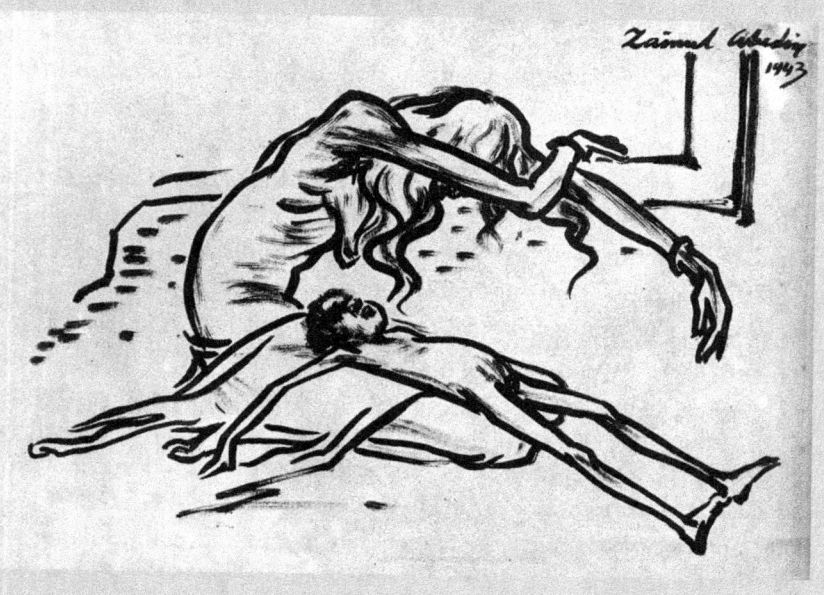

fair punishment for those who refused to take up "degraded" labor because of caste prejudice.[39] Gandhi thus fasted less to show solidarity with workers in their own condition of starvation and more to reinforce his argument about the universality of labor across all professions. To Gandhi, thus the strike and the fast, the labor question and the hunger question, were conjoined.

The question of hunger acquired great intensity in Bengal and India in the 1940s.[40] Consider the young communist poet Sukanta Bhattacharya's (1926–47) iconic lines from "He Mahajiban" (O great life):

proyojon nei kobitar snigdhota,
kobita tomay aajke dilam chhuti,
kshudhar rajye prithibi godyomoy,
purnima chaand jeno jholsano ruti.

No need here for the mellowness of poetry,
Poetry, I give you leave today,
In the kingdom of hunger, the world turns to prose,
And the full moon is like a charred bread.[41]

Colonial Bengal had a long history of famines—from the famous 1770 famine that wiped out a third of the population (and generated debates on land and property among British officials, leading to the famous Permanent Settlement) to the wartime famine of 1943 that was crucial to the consolidation of both communist politics and communist realist aesthetics in the region. (Incidentally, *famine* in Bengali is *manvantar* or "change of epochs.") The 1943 famine killed more than three million people in Bengal, and the Calcutta streets became littered with dead bodies and crowded with destitute people from the countryside. But the food crisis did not end with the end of the famine. Food scarcity, price increases, hoarding, black marketing, starvation deaths, and even suicides became everyday facts for the next few decades.[42] Communists set up "food committees," smoked out black marketers, looted food from hoarders and redistributed it, and agitated for price control, a fair public distribution system, laws against speculation, and, above all, the confiscation of surplus land from landlords and its redistribution among poorer peasants. Communists scoffed at Gandhian *satyagrahis* and their ritualized fasts and "hunger processions."[43] Death by hunger was very different from death by sacrifice, they said. It was slow, unspectacular, and without honor. It was not even counted statistically, blamed as it often was on poor health and unsanitary habits.[44] In the face of mass starvation, communists argued, fasting as political action had lost moral authority. Incidentally, 1946 and 1947 were also years of intense

Hindu-Muslim bloodletting, another kind of macabre dance of death that Bengal witnessed right after the famine. It was at this time that Gandhi held his iconic fast in Noakhali in East Bengal—a place reporting many deaths from starvation at the time. Clearly, starvation and fasting carried on side by side, each claiming a greater degree of political visibility and political efficacy.

Communists' 1940s food activism later resulted in militant food movements in Bengal—first in 1959 and then in 1966—transforming communists from being fringe radicals to being the dominant political force in the region for decades to come. Writing of the consequences of hunger, the Bengal provincial committee of the Communist Party explicitly stated that the food crisis must be understood above all as a crisis of labor: "It is not merely that thousands are dying of hunger today.... The food crisis is destroying the invaluable labor potential of Bengal. If we cannot save labor, then soon our land will lay fallow and unworked, the food crisis will herald an unprecedented labor crisis."[45]

Subhas Mukhopadhyay (1919–2003), journalist, poet, and Communist Party member, put together the questions of labor and hunger in his political prose.[46] In 1973, Subhas—until then known for his reportage and poetry—wrote his first novel, *Hungras*. This novel commemorated the 1949 hunger strike by communist prisoners that stretched for forty-seven long days. Subhas borrowed the title from the peasants of Midnapur, who called hunger strike *hungras* in their local lingo.[47] Incidentally, Subhas dedicated the novel to Satyajit Ray, whose acclaimed Oscar-winning film *Pather Panchali* (Song of the road), based on the eponymous novel by Bibhutibhushan Bandopadhyay (1929), depicted poignant scenes of hunger and want in the Bengal countryside—a mother scrounging for food for her children, empty utensils in the kitchen, a daughter being humiliated for stealing fruit, a doddering old aunt drooling over scraps and crumbs.

Hungras is written in the narrative voice of two political prisoners—Aurobindo, a middle-class writer, who nurses a guilty love for Tagore's "idealist" poetry, and Badshah, a Muslim factory worker. Both are in jail for being communists and there participate in a hunger strike. Tellingly, there is hardly anything in the novel about the specific cause and context of the hunger strike, which here appears as the default mode of politically inhabiting the prison, a way of resuming vicarious control over the incarcerated body. Unlike Gandhi, the communist protagonist writes candidly about his experience of unendurable hunger: "Today is the fourth day of our hunger strike. No four days and three nights. My counting's gone haywire! Usually it is only in the first seventy-two hours that you feel the pangs. But this time it is the reverse. Hunger intensifies each day. I keep gulping water. And licking at salt. I try holding down hunger. But the pangs return."⁴⁸ Aurobindo had been told not to speak of food during a hunger strike—"Hunger strike is war and you are a soldier!" But he envies those who can brave humiliation and break their fast. Aurobindo records his hungry days in a journal. There is war in jail—teargassing, shooting, throwing stones, sloganeering, deaths, and arbitrary occasions of force-feeding by the authorities. Aurobindo secretly waits for these occasions of force-feeding, but the prison officials know when not to oblige. In marked contrast to Gandhi's take on the spiritual merits of the fast, Aurobindo writes: "I don't care about the spirit. I am happy with my body. The form, essence, sound, feel and flavor of this world—I sense these with my body. My senses protect me from impending threats. . . . there is nothing more I love than this body."⁴⁹ Aurobindo tries reading *Das Kapital* but finds his hunger too distracting. He cannot play chess either, for intelligence fails on an empty stomach. Instead, Aurobindo passes time by holding a daily *karkhana* (factory) with Badshah. Badshah narrates his life story, which Aurobindo records for a future novel.

Badshah talks of his boyhood. He left home to work in a ship factory. Working at the blazing furnace was like staring death in the face, he said. He spent his life moving from one job to another. When he joined a bone factory, he lost social status for having befriended untouchable Chamars. He began his political career with the Muslim League. He rooted for Mohammedan Sporting, the football club favored by Muslims, and avidly followed news from Egypt and Turkey. But then he came into contact with the Revolutionary Socialist Party and later the Communist Party and became a trade unionist. He also became obsessed with *jatra* (popular theater). Badshah secretly wonders if his middle-class comrade, who has never known starvation, can actually last through a hunger strike. But he also complains that the middle classes have it easy because they have smaller bellies. It is tougher for workers who are used to eating heartily after a hard day's labor.⁵⁰ Aurobindo wonders why, if the poor are already used to starving, a hunger strike is difficult for them.⁵¹ Unlike in the Gandhian paradigm, here the struggle seems to be over who can fast rather than who is entitled to fast.

Not surprisingly, much of the conversation between Aurobindo and Badshah revolves around the question of labor. Badshah describes in detail the nitty-gritty of various kinds of factory work. He misses his welding machine. "My welding machine and your pen are similar," he says, "except that you can keep your tool always with you, even in sleep, and your machine does not emit sparks, blind you."⁵² The trade union and the party are tools too, Badshah adds, making the labor/politics homology explicit:

My welding machine is not my only tool. The party, the union—these are machines too. Machines can do good but also evil, depending on how they are wielded. You need a lot of skill.

Dad's problem was that he knew only one machine—his tool of labor. He left it behind in the factory. But my hands are never empty. I hold in my fist this other machine that drives humans, the party. There is a great high in this work, comrade.[53]

"There is pride in labor," Badshah states happily. "You know the world needs you."[54] Aurobindo envies Badshah. Workers know how to marry "will to purpose," he muses. Hard work focuses, channels the mind! Aurobindo wonders whether writing is also not a form of labor. If labor is what fills a lack—the emptiness in the belly—then literature must be labor too, for it also fills a void, "making happen, making real, what is not yet there."[55] Unlike Gandhi, who simply defines labor as that which is not study, the communist seeks to turn labor into a metacategory, subsuming all forms of human activity, including thought, under it.

Laborer and Labor

The question of labor, however, was not the same as the question of the laborer. Even though communists came to designate workers of the world by catchall terms such as *proletariat*, *mazdoor* (in Hindi/Urdu), and *sarvahara* ("one who has lost all" in Bengali), early communist writing in India focused less on labor and more on laborers as embodied and socially identifiable subjects. Thus the essay "Dharmaghater Siksha" (Lesson of the strike; 1921) mentioned the coolie, wageworker, peasant, fisherman, boatman, sailor, and palanquin bearer.[56] Another simply referred to working people by their caste names: Hadi, Muchi, Dom. The essay "Chhotor Aparadh" (Crimes of small people; 1923) invoked peasants, oil pressers, jute growers, utensil makers, washermen, and barbers.[57] An essay from 1924 claimed that in early Islam, spiritual leaders (*alims*) were cultivators, masons, carpenters, tailors, and weavers and lived by "working their hands."[58] Clearly, there was no single term such as *labor* to designate working people. Some used the colonial term *coolie*, and others simply used the ancient *dharmashastric* name Shudra to denote the servile classes. Evidently, before labor could emerge as a universal category, a great diversity of peoples engaged in different kinds of work had to be first recognized and accounted for. Manik Bandopadhyay's novel *Padma Nadir Majhi* (1936), a highly textured narrative about the boatmen of eastern Bengal, which later became a Marxist classic, starts with a long description of the activities of sailing boats, catching fish, and selling the fish in wholesale markets on the riverside.[59] The narrative detailing of empirical work practices that concretized particular laboring communities thus conceptually preceded their recasting as abstract and generic labor.

Gandhi contrasted labor not only with thought but also with work, that is, diverse occupations with differential skills and social value. When he argued that one should not abandon one's traditional vocation even if lowly, when he did sweeping and cleaning to symbolize the "dignity of labor," when he made spinning the center of his nationalism, he was doing precisely this—namely, denying the difference between work and work, by reifying the thing called labor as such.[60] In his address to the striking mill hands of Ahmedabad in 1918, Gandhi argued against modern-day specialization, which prevented workers from moving between different kinds of work.[61]

Ambedkar argued strongly against this articulation of labor as a generic activity. He challenged both Gandhi's moral rendering and the Marxists' economic rendering of labor, and he did this precisely by bringing to center stage the question of the laborer. Ambedkar disputed the modern opinion that caste was a local variant of the universal division of labor—a formulation that allowed one to talk of labor as an abstract category across a social hierarchy of callings, such as study, war, production, commerce, and servile work. The caste system, he argued, was a division not of labor but of laborers.[62] Writing in 1935, Gandhian and anthropologist Nirmal Kumar Bose argued along similar lines. He said that in India, *adivasis* or "first peoples" traditionally engaged in a great variety of occupations, from cultivation to craft to hunting. Hinduism integrated them into mainstream society by turning them into castes and assigned them fixed vocations, freezing their social and economic destiny for all time to come. Bose was one of those who used the name Shudra to denote working classes as a whole.[63]

In 1929, Ambedkar refused support to the striking Ahmedabad Mill-Workers' Union. Untouchables were not allowed to work in cotton mills because touchable workers refused to associate with them.[64] Thus, even when they gave up untouchable work for mainstream factory work, untouchables continued to carry on their person the trace of degraded labor. Labor was thus clearly inalienable from the laborer, and so it was erroneous to talk of labor as a universal category and workers as a universal class. In India, Ambedkar argued, the caste system prevented the rise of labor as a reckonable concept. Caste destroyed labor power, created a disconnect between labor and aptitude, "devitalized" laborers, and prevented their political mobilization. It enclosed groups of workers into impermeable compartments, preventing them from coming together in equality and solidarity. Caste enclosures also prevented mobility between occupations, which might have encouraged the experience of labor as a common activity across vocations. There was also in the caste system an unbreachable division between one kind of work and another. Some forms of labor were stigmatized as untouchable and provoked evasion in the worker and aversion in others.[65]

Yet Ambedkar established a labor party of his own in 1936. His Independent Labour Party campaigned for state-sponsored industrialization, fair labor laws, workers' education, abolition of the *jagirdari* and *khot* systems that kept low-caste individuals tied to servile labor in rural areas, and the inclusion of untouchables at all levels of industrial work. He was criticized by communists for breaking up the unity of the workers' movement, and his party fared badly in the 1937 provincial elections. Soon after, he gave up on the idea of a labor party and set up the Scheduled Castes Federation. His experiment with labor qua labor thus seemed to have failed.

Stating that the *homo economicus* was nowhere to be found in the world, including in the capitalist West, Ambedkar criticized both nationalists and communists for their economism. They expected workers to participate in trade unions as labor, that is, as a purely economic subject, but in the national movement as a potential citizen, that is, as a socially and culturally unmarked political subject. They refused to set up a labor party, which would have turned labor from an economic into a political force, or acknowledge that the politicization of labor could never just be a class activity. Labor in India, Ambedkar added, had to fight not just capitalism but also Brahminism. For if capitalism was the exploitation of labor, Brahminism was the degradation of laborers. Both elites and workers were under the spell of Brahminism. "I say that it is the primary concern of the laboring class to bring about a reconstruction of society," Ambedkar said, in an implicit critique of the Gandhian version of "social reconstruction" based on an absolutist imagination of the dignity of labor.[66]

Though Ambedkar is known predominantly as a theorist and critic of caste, the labor question (and his engagement with Gandhi and the communists on the same) was critical to the development of his thought. While his experiments with a labor party might have been partly pragmatic—an effort at widening his political base beyond untouchables in the absence of universal franchise or separate electorates for Depressed Classes[67]—they cannot be read only as strategic. By cast(e)ing the labor question, Ambedkar showed the difficulty—even the impossibility—of glossing the everyday activity of labor as political action, despite contemporary efforts at universalizing labor through its recasting as economic necessity, aesthetic creativity, or moral value. As Ambedkar poignantly argued, labor as pure and universal action was always already haunted by the shadow of the laborer as a particular subject.

Labor and Struggle

This brings us to *struggle*, the other term that came to stand in for both the everyday fact of labor and political action in the twentieth century. Gandhi's propagation of nonviolence and his unceasing criticism not only of revolutionaries and communists but also of the disorderly masses have caused the "violence question" to appear determining of modern Indian politics. This ethical focus on violence per se, however, takes away from what was at the time a more widely debated question—that of struggle and force. Violence, of course, is one form that struggle can take. But a conceptual collapse of struggle and violence prevents us from grasping the full complexity of the question of action as it emerged in twentieth-century politics—involving issues of labor, hunger, and war with respect to the ontology of common life.

Gandhi recognized the centrality of struggle in human life. His practices of fasting and celibacy were nothing if not struggles with the desires and cravings of the self as much as against the temptations of modern society. Gandhi also acknowledged with empathy the everyday struggles of people against poverty and hunger. His theory of capitalist trusteeship—the principle that the rich held their wealth not as owners but as trustees of the public—was, however, geared toward a sublation of the question of struggle.[68] Equally, by saying that enlightened politics required that erstwhile masters learn to serve the servile classes, Gandhi transformed labor—especially untouchable labor—into a principle of *seva* (public service).[69] It was by inverting struggle into service that Gandhi elaborated his framework of nonviolence, turning labor from being an acutely agonistic everyday experience to being a moral discipline. To communists, on the other hand, the laboring body was political not because it was moral but because it could turn, seamlessly and quickly, into a retributive and forceful body by virtue of its inherent kinesis.

Zainul Abedin's sketches of man and beast in heavy, physical labor, are titled *Struggle*. In his essay on *sanhati* (solidarity), quoted earlier, Tagore described working people of the world as *vahan*—draft animals who dragged and drove the world forward—reiterating the image of power and struggle in the sketches that follow.[70]

Communists in Bengal wrote profusely in order to establish struggle as a valid mode of political action for the masses. In more didactic writings, struggle was posited as the way in which the philosophical principle of dialectics

translated into common experience. Conflict and contradiction were critical to the movement of not only thought but also life, as Jagajjit Sarkar explained in a 1931 essay—whence our experience of the world as a set of antinomies: life/death, light/darkness, rich/poor.[71] Many of these essays on struggle and dialectics illustrate the novel ways in which dialectics were concretized and popularized in vernacular Marxist traditions. More relevant for us, however, are writings that sought to establish struggle as an everyday fact of life. Human labor, after all, was a struggle against the vagaries of nature, scarcity, hunger, and ultimately the appropriation of fruits of labor by those who did not labor.[72] In other words, struggle was a priori constitutive of the act and experience of labor and not a cultivated skill. The task was simply to politicize this commonplace fact of struggle.

The catch, however, lay in what exactly politicization meant. At one level, struggle could too easily shade into war. The metaphor of war, we know, was central to modern political imagination. We have already mentioned Aurobindo's staging of the Kurukshetra War as representative of those moments in life when *dharma* or existing codes of social and moral conduct came into crisis. Communist discourse, unsurprisingly, was also full of idioms of war. Subhas Mukhopadhyay published his first volume of poems in 1940 and named it *Padatik*, after the figure of the foot soldier. Even Gandhi described *satyagraha* as a "battle" for truth—*dharmayuddha*.[73] And Ambedkar incessantly talked of "class war."

What work does the metaphor of war do in these debates around labor and politics? War, incidentally, did not always signify a moment of exception, a decisionist and founding moment of sovereign violence à la Carl Schmitt. Even Aurobindo, who might be read as suggesting this by virtue of his crisis-of-*dharma* thesis, insisted that ordinary life itself was full of warlike moments. Ambedkar, like the communists, also argued that the everyday life of the oppressed was unceasing class war. War was therefore a permanent condition of being rather than a momentous political event. This "normalizing" of war might not seem surprising with regard to the communists, given Marx's famous formulation that "all human history is a history of class struggle." It is, however, worth staying a bit longer with Ambedkar.

In his comparative text "Buddha or Karl Marx," Ambedkar argued that while Marx's theses on the economic determination of history and the inevitability of socialism were no longer valid, his theses regarding private property and class war were still indisputable. Even the Buddha, epitome of nonviolence, who said that possession was at the heart of avarice and instructed the monk to practice nonpossession, acknowledged the eternal reality of class conflict based on private property.[74] In his "Philosophy of Hinduism," Ambedkar argued against those who criticized Marxists for propagating war. Indian history was full of instances of caste and class war, Ambedkar said, especially war between Brahmins and Kshatriyas. During Maratha rule, there was war between Brahmins and Shudras. Even today, class war was a persistent condition: "It must not be supposed that these class wars were like ordinary wars which are momentary phenomena which come and go and which leave no permanent chasms to divide the peoples of the different nations. In India the class war is a permanent phenomenon, which is silently but surely working its way. It is a grain in the life and it has become genius of the Hindus."[75]

Ambedkar argued that the study of war was a useful meditation on the nature of action. In a review of Bertrand Russell's *Principles of Social Reconstruction*, he said that though Russell's was a thesis against war, it must not be read—as Indians were prone to do, under the influence of the dogma of nonviolence—as a pacifist or quietist text. Russell argued, according to Ambedkar, that many of the constituent elements of war—adventure, contingency, contest, solidarity, resistance and its overcoming—were essential to human action.[76] Elsewhere, Ambedkar added that the Buddha was not an absolutist regarding nonviolence in the way that Mahavira, the founder of Jainism (and perhaps by implication Gandhi), was.[77] He even argued that Hinduism was able to impose the grossly unjust caste system on people because it had perfected the strategy of preventing "direct action" by Shudras, by prohibiting castes other than Kshatriyas from carrying arms. Like the denial of knowledge, the denial of arms to the poor was crucial to the institution of inequality.[78] Thus, despite his trenchant critique of the fratricidal violence of the Mahabharata, Ambedkar insisted that struggle, indeed armed struggle, was a valid mode of political action for the oppressed.

Gandhi's theory of nonviolent action was based on his famous means-end thesis. Gandhi argued that the righteousness of an end did not justify the violence of the means. Means had to be morally accounted for on their own terms. Ambedkar gave a profound twist to this means-end problematic. He argued that Shudras in India were unable to act politically because they themselves were the means of other people's actions. Hindu lawbooks defined Shudras and untouchables as those who were meant to serve other castes. Servitude denied them autonomy of labor and freedom of action. The oppressed—like slaves of Plato's time—were instrumentalized by others.[79] Clearly, if Gandhi referenced war as grounds for his means-end thesis, Ambedkar referenced labor as a counterpoint in order to rethink the very same means-end problematic.

War and labor inflect the means-end problematic in very different ways. It is not just that war is a means of destruction and labor a means of production. Rather, war and labor entail differently configured means-end relationships. In war (as in sports), despite stable rules of engagement, contingency, innovation, and improvisation decide the end. It is because of this shifting and unpredictable nature of actions—surprise and chance elements as they are often called—that, in war, the means always already remains under dispute. The means of war turns into a gray gambit zone beyond the domain of plan, strategy, decision, and even tactics. The end of war—victory or validation—therefore stands apart, somewhat autonomously, from the means of war, in the sense of being causally underdetermined by the means. Thus, in evaluating the conduct of war, the question of morality tends to supersede that of efficacy. In labor, however, the efficacy of the means is of supreme concern. In labor, questions of skill, competence, plan, and experience become technical and poetic, in the archaic senses of the terms.[80] Labor oriented toward the production or creation of an end product involves a combination of innovative artfulness (*poiesis*) and appropriate technicality (*techne*) in the acts of making or doing. The product of labor is thus the manifest form of the means of labor. In labor, unlike in war, the question of the rightness of means thus cannot be displaced entirely into the moral realm. Political action in colonial India appeared suspended between these two distinct connotations of the means-end problematic, mobilized, respectively, by Gandhi and Ambedkar. It is this ambiguity that is captured by the term *struggle*. Struggle is a mode of action that draws on both war and labor but in the end is neither. It embodies an in-between moment, framed by the moral-social, on the one hand, and the technical-aesthetic, on the other.

Ambedkar disagreed with the Gandhian proposition that the end did not justify the means. If the end did not justify the means, what else did, he wondered, after his mentor, John Dewey.[81] Ambedkar stated:

> Buddha would have probably admitted that it is only the end which could justify the means. What else could? And he would have said that if the end justified violence, violence was a legitimate means for the end in view. He certainly would not have exempted property owners from force if force was the only means for that end. . . .
>
> As to Dictatorship the Buddha would have none of it.[82]

Ambedkar was criticizing communists not for their espousal of violence as Gandhi did but for another reason altogether. The communists saw the state as their primary means of action. Ambedkar not only objected to the idea of the "dictatorship of the proletariat,"[83] but he also questioned the communist promise that once the task of the state was done, it would automatically "wither away" like a redundant and obsolete tool. Communists, Ambedkar argued, failed to offer any alternative means of political action in the absence of the state. Will politics itself disappear in a perfectly equal society? he asked.[84]

Dictatorship, perhaps, was also a veiled reference to Gandhi and his attempts at the strict regulation of mass political action. Ambedkar implied that Gandhi turned the means question into a fetish. Hinduism did precisely that, he added. It prescribed a plethora of rules and rituals, which were in effect the means for instituting a structure of "graded inequality" across classes. But instead of admitting these rules as mere means to an end, Hinduism represented them as ends in themselves. "These customs are essentially of the nature of means, though they are represented as ideals. . . . One might safely say that idealization of means is necessary and in this particular case was perhaps motivated to endow them with greater efficacy."[85] By dissimulating the means as ends—that is, through their idealization and absolutization—Hinduism not only "sacralized" social order but also sacralized "economic relationships between workman and workman." "Nowhere has society consecrated its occupations—the way of getting a living. Economic activity has always remained outside the sanctity of religion. . . . The Hindus are the only people in the world whose economic order—the relation of workman to workman—is consecrated by religion and made sacred, eternal and inviolate."[86] Thus, particular forms of labor in India—in actuality the means of production—were made into ends in themselves and therefore turned into absolute caste destiny for laborers.

It was here that Ambedkar's famous distinction between rules and principles came into play. Rules were prescriptive; they decreed and regulated action. Principles, however, did not engender action by themselves. They were materialized in action via diverse acts of interpretation.[87] Rules produced compliant and obedient bodies; principles produced autonomous and imaginative agency. Rules were of the status of mere means—they could be rendered into religious law as did Hinduism, but that did not change their true nature. Principles, on the other hand, were ends that called for a creative fashioning of appropriate means according to the contingencies of time and place. Hinduism was a religion of rules, Buddhism of principles. They enjoined different modes and mechanisms of action.

The open-endedness of means was critical to Ambedkar. Actors do not always have full control over means, he said: "For a means once employed liberates many ends—a fact scarcely recognized—and not the only one we wish it to produce."[88] Even though, in practical terms, we put absolute value on a single end, we must remain alert to the other potential results that might follow from our action. We must remain wary that other ends unleashed in the course of an action are not sacrificed to one singular end (so therefore freedom must not

Labor, Hunger, and Struggle 113

be sacrificed at the altar of equality and vice versa). The analogy with labor is evident. Labor intended toward one product creates multiple by-products of no less value than the product itself. The force, contingency, and unpredictability of means, as epitomized in war, is thus mitigated in Ambedkar by the image of the many-pronged productivity of means, as epitomized in labor. (Note that Ambedkar is not talking here of unintended consequences as much as of the infinite and unregulated potentiality of action as such.)

We return to labor once more. Ambedkar dwelled on the Buddhist precept of "nonpossession" and critiqued the institution of private property. However, in response to the Gandhian criticism that modernity promoted acquisitive and possessive instincts, Ambedkar argued that the notion of ownership must be differently understood with regard to haves and have-nots. For the laboring classes, ownership was about the right to the fruits of one's own labor (mark the contrast with the *nishkama karma* notion), while for the capitalist, ownership was about the expropriation of fruits of other people's labor. Referring to industrial disputes in modern times, Ambedkar argued that labor was prone to greater militancy, even violent action, not because workers lacked civility but because they lacked ownership over their own labor. The only way to mitigate violence, then, was to return to the working classes ownership over labor and the products of labor. For labor undertaken with a sense of ownership and responsibility was an ideal combination of creative and possessive human instincts.[89] Ambedkar quoted the Buddha's advice to his disciple Anathapindika—that believers must be encouraged to "acquire wealth justly and lawfully through industry and to delight in gifts and sharing."[90] In this idealized ancient yet postcapitalist form, labor was indeed model human action—unlike in an unequal society, where labor became a subsidiary instrument, merely a means, toward other people's property and accumulation.

Conclusion

In the tradition of European political theory, Hannah Arendt and Karl Marx proposed two distinct ways in which to think the politics of labor. Arendt saw labor, the moment of private necessity rather than collective freedom, as the opposite of public political action. Conversely, Marx saw labor as potentially the freest of political agencies because it was productive, futural, and without stakes in the capitalist present. Instead of following either Arendt or Marx, however, I offer here a rereading of the history of labor in order to interrogate the assumed self-evidence of the modern concept of political action. After all, in and by itself, action means nothing in a world where, we now know, nothing is inactive, even matter. The significance of action as we know it today derives from a fairly recent conceptual collapsing of action with politics. *Action*—otherwise an empty and unremarkable term—in order to become sui generis political had to be qualified as alternatively sacrifice, labor, and war, and made to simultaneously index politics and life. The term *struggle* was meant to subsume all three moments of *karma*, labor, and war without becoming identical to any of them. The twentieth-century global symbol of the sickle—tool of labor, weapon of war, crescent moon of poetry—embodied this projected multivalence of struggle as productive, creative, everyday, and, if need be, spectacularly violent action.

Part III

Idea

5

Equality and Spirituality

> Men are born unequal.
> —B. R. Ambedkar, *The Buddha and His Dhamma*

Norm and ideology are the two forms in which we recognize the political being of an idea. As norm, an idea adjudicates on empirical politics, as if from outside and above. As ideology, an idea drives empirical politics from within. While a norm works by displaying its ideality, which politics aspires to but never fully achieves, an ideology works by making the idea indistinguishable from the real, the true, the ordinary—that is, by extinguishing any imaginable gap between idea and experience. In this chapter (and in chapter 6), I ask, What is the place of ideas in politics? How does an idea come to be qualified as a political idea? Do political ideas always operate as norm or ideology, or do they also operate in more underdetermined ways, for example, as a frame or a horizon that renders politics legible in the first place? Are ideas free-floating, abstract entities that necessarily travel light across borders, or are they predicated on particular forms of embodiment, modes of address, and what Deleuze and Guattari call conceptual "personae," which limit their mobility and purity?[1] Above all, how does an idea, in the process of its politicization, define and delimit the political as such?

I take the idea of equality as an example. Equality has been known since there has been inequality, that is, from the beginning of history. Equality "happens" every time a subaltern speaks back to power, suspending—sometimes momentarily, sometimes for longer—the hierarchical order of things. In that sense, equality always already accompanies inequality as its shadow and its specter. But equality as an idea—whether self-standing or flanked by liberty and fraternity—is an eminently modern phenomenon. In modernity, equality transitions from being a stance or an intimation to being an idea par excellence. I want to explore how equality comes to be conceived of as an idea in the first place and as a quintessential political idea at that. Needless to say, equality emerges from experiences of inequality. Hence, the first step in the career of equality as a political idea is the detailed depiction of inequalities. And yet, it is never an easy move—from thinking inequality to thinking equality as such. This chapter focuses the conceptual difficulties faced by modern politics in making a transition from a critique of inequality to equality as a positive idea.

Unequal Differences and Different Inequalities

Bankimchandra Chattopadhyay's essay "Samya," written between 1873 and 1875, is justly famous for being one of the earliest theoretical considerations of equality in modern India. Like others before and after, Bankim dedicated most of this essay to detailed description of inequalities. But unlike most others, he tried to make a self-conscious transition from describing inequality to positing equality as a positive idea.

Bankim's primary theoretical move was to juxtapose the concepts of equality and difference. He used the same term, *baishamya*, for both because inequalities were often organized and experienced as difference, and differences as inequality, he said.[2] Hence, the first analytical step in the thinking of equality had to be a query into the distinct but overlapping provenances of the two terms, *inequality* and *difference*. Humans were born unequal, Bankim said. Natural inequalities, such as of appearance and aptitude, one had to live with. But created inequalities—of caste, class, race, and gender—demanded analysis and intervention, especially because they were often passed off as innate differences between people.[3] Having described in detail class, caste, race, and gender inequalities in India, Bankim then declared that not all inequalities were equal. Caste, class, and gender were not just different grounds for the same phenomenon called inequality. They were incommensurable inequalities—differently structured, differently experienced, differently tied to the fact of difference, and indeed, differently amenable to politicization. Inequality of wealth, as between landlord and peasant, was the most obviously arbitrary and the easiest to expose and remedy. Indeed, the longest sections of "Samya" were descriptions of economic inequality. Caste inequality, on the other hand, was more difficult to overcome because it was founded not on an externality like wealth but on centuries-long denial of freedom of thought to the Shudra and the outcastes, causing caste to appear as just another instance of the quintessential difference between intellectual and manual work.[4] And gender inequality, Bankim added, was the most difficult to politicize because it played on the purportedly real differences in the natures of men and women.[5] Taking gender inequality as the paradigmatic moment in his argument, Bankim proclaimed that if difference were indeed a ground for inequality, then we could not have criticized the racially unequal treatment of Englishmen and Indians in colonial India, for who could deny that they were as different from each other as women from men?[6]

In Bankim's work equality and difference appear as continuous concepts. Thus, unlike our a textbook understanding of the history of liberalism, it was not as if (political) equality was thought first and (social) difference thought post facto, in order to expand and nuance the idea of equality. It was not as if equality as an idea, as embodied in the event of the French Revolution, was logically and chronologically prior to difference as an idea, as embodied in the Haitian Revolution and in Mary Wollstonecraft's *A Vindication of the Rights of Woman*. Equality, as examples from the colony show even more starkly, was unthinkable, from the very beginning, without a simultaneous thinking of difference. In the colony, the novel facts of colonial and racial difference reanimated the older facts of gender and caste difference, creating a matrix of different inequalities and unequal differences within which equality had to be thought. Just as equality is unthinkable without engaging difference, difference too is unthinkable except in association with equality, Bankim implied. For difference can be grasped in its pure form, as difference per se, only when we can assume that two or more entities are otherwise equal and equivalent and therefore only different. Bankim thus painstakingly ran through a comparison of women and men in Indian society and evaluated each instance of difference in terms of whether it was an index of inequality, or shorn of all inequalities, of actual difference (as did Tarabai Shinde in Maharashtra, in her 1882 tract *Stripurush Tulana*[7]).

Equality in Bankim thus appears not merely as the other of inequality but as the logical implication of different kinds of inequalities "thought together." Equality cannot be gleaned, Bankim seems to be saying, simply out of the logical negation of any single instance of inequality, for the undoing of one inequality does nothing for another. Equality can be gleaned only from thinking together diverse asymmetrical inequalities. The common criterion that allows a conceptual equivalence across diverse inequalities was equality itself— equality in its unqualified, absolute mode of being as absence. In other words, if equality must be thought via a negation of inequalities, then it seems as if equal-

Equality and Spirituality   21

ity is thinkable only as an absence that acquires body and presence in so many iterations of inequality. In Bankim, thus, equality emerges as an abstraction—a pure theoretical construct thought into existence from within the delineation of myriad inequalities. In that equality as concept cannot be gleaned from a direct experience of actually existing equality, it seems to assume, in Bankim, the ontology of an idea par excellence.

This early thinking of equality in Bengal can be seen as a moment of fashioning a certain language of thought that would be adequate to equality as an idea. Bankim serialized "Samya" in his journal *Bangadarshan*, surrounded by other essays on diverse topics such as history, evolution, causality, and consciousness. Evidently, equality here was part of a more general effort at fashioning a language of thought, at testing out the "thinkability" of equality as well as other concepts and quasi concepts. *Bangadarshan* was a forum for the fashioning of modern Bengali prose. It showcased experiments with the essay form, in an open-ended effort at rendering the world at large into thought. The critical terms of discourse were yet to be settled. The term *samya* itself, in contemporary Bengali, had various shades of meaning, such as similarity, equivalence, balance, calmness, consistency, unity, assurance, equanimity, and equilibrium. The term *baishamya* could mean both inequality and difference but also disunity, inconsistency, imbalance, conflict, and indeed, a state of misfortune. The thinking through of equality thus was also a thinking through of a language adequate to giving equality the ontology of an idea.

In Bankim, therefore, equality is not yet a political utopia. Even as Bankim discussed, alongside John Stuart Mill, nineteenth-century utopian socialists—Robert Owen, Louis Blanqui, Charles Fourier, Henri de Saint-Simon, Pierre-Joseph Proudhon—and their experiments in communal living and property sharing, he barely partook in any utopian passions. He agreed that there should be a general sharing of property, especially of land—he called it *sadharanikaran*, or generalization (and not nationalization as in later socialist discourse)—and mentioned the superiority of Islamic *sharia* laws of inheritance over both Hindu joint family customs and European systems of primogeniture.[8] Bankim discussed European utopian socialism as if it were only a matter of finding the right institutional and legal mechanism for setting up a more egalitarian inheritance and property regime.

And yet, there are passages in "Samya" that stand out. These are passages in which Bankim tries to imagine equality as a positive concept, that is, as more than the negation or absence of inequality. Of the many thinkers of equality, Bankim said, the most important were Buddha, Christ, and Jean-Jacques Rousseau, whom he called avatars of equality.[9] Each imagined equality in the context of a particular historico-empirical form of inequality—casteism and Brahminism in India, slavery and tyranny in the Roman Empire, and aristocratic privilege and rack-renting in ancien régime France. But Buddha and Christ were different from Rousseau in that they posited equality as a sacred and timeless idea and hence came to be worshipped as gods. Rousseau, on the other hand, was more narrowly political and context bound, and hence not entirely free of errors. He thought that society was a voluntary contract among individuals—Bankim exclaimed with incredulity.[10] Buddha's and Christ's theories of equality did have profound political impact—Buddhism led to the rise of the great Maurya Empire headed by a Shudra king, and Christianity gave dignity and rights to the poor—but the significance of their ideas went far beyond their local secular expressions. Indeed, if Rousseau's theory of equality had far-reaching implications—not just the French Revolution but communism and the Communist International were direct results of Rousseau's writings, Bankim said—it was because Rousseau shared in, even if partially, this imagination of equality as eternal and sacred truth.

Bankim prefaces "Samya" by saying that he conceptualized equality differently from his European contemporaries.[11] Is it here, in this gesture toward spirituality, that Bankim locates his difference? Even though early Bankim is seen as a rational and liberal thinker and often contrasted with a later Bankim, more invested in religion and culture and hence a favorite of Hindu nationalists, it is clear that in "Samya" (the text quoted most often as proof of his early liberalism) Bankim is already working on two registers. When he describes and critiques existing inequalities, he takes on a historico-political perspective—as does, for example, his contemporary Jyotiba Phule in western India, historicizing the enslavement of lower-caste peoples as caused by Aryan subjugation of indigenes.[12] But when trying to think of equality as such—that is, equality as more than the absence of inequality—Bankim moves to a spiritual register, a move that Ambedkar will also make half a century later. It seems, then, that the theoretical move from inequality to equality, in the late nineteenth to early twentieth centuries, was crucially predicated on a certain mobilization of spirituality, not just in canonical thinkers such as Gandhi and Ambedkar but also, as we shall see, among many liberal, socialist, and communist ones.

The Spirituality Question

It is commonly assumed that equality is a spiritual question only in premodern times, until it gets secularized, with the French Revolution, into being a purely political idea. It is also assumed that before modernity equality was imagined as and only as equality in the eyes of God—as in popular Christianity and in devotional Bhakti and Sufi traditions. To conceive of equality, one had to invoke what Ajay Skaria calls a sovereign "third party"[13]—who, by mediating empirical difference, equalized two beings facing each other across a hierarchy. Equality-in-difference, thus, could only be a triangulated condition of being. You and I are never equal by ourselves. We are equal only when we appear in the eyes of God or, in the secularized theology of the modern state, in the eyes of law. Many believe that with the rise of Marxism equality came to be imagined as a phenomenon immanent to human society. As equality came to be an economic concept, it assumed the form of an unmediated bilateral relationship between two individuals or two classes facing each other directly and agonistically.

The centrality of the state in socialism and communism, however, belies this claim of Marxism as able to imagine equality as an immanent phenomenon. Ambedkar pointed this out when he set up a comparison between Buddha and Marx, stating that while Buddhism imagined equality as the mutual orientation of two social subjects, Marxism, in the name of the "dictatorship of the proletariat," privileged the superordinate state as mediator, arbitrator, and enforcer.[14] No doubt the rise of the economic as a measure of inequality was a deeply transformative historical moment. And yet, I believe that Marxism, in order to cross the threshold between critique and affirmation, had to borrow a certain spiritual orientation from other traditions of thought—hence, liberation theology, Christian socialism, Islamic socialism, and so on. In chapter 6, where I explore the rise of the economic conception of equality via the work of vernacular Marxisms, I show how many early twentieth-century Bengali thinkers felt compelled to rethink the very nature of the economic—by mobilizing sociology and literature—in order to affirm equality as a positive idea, so much so that the economic would come to share some features of what I call the spiritual in this chapter. In this chapter, I stay with the spirituality question.

The modern-day secularist reading of all precolonial spiritual traditions as necessarily having to do with the figure of God as judge and arbitrator is incorrect. All spiritual traditions of the world did not work in the same way. This is something that we forget because modernity forces all spiritual traditions into the rather narrow and inhospitable category of religion, with its inescapable identitarian and civilizational connotations. Instead of religion, I use the term *spirituality* here, though it too is problematic because all traditions of the world did not subscribe to the notion of a spirit either, Buddhism again being a case in point. So I use the term *spirituality* merely as a placeholder, denoting the whole complex of philosophy, theology, ethics, performance, and practice that constitutes what we today understand as the domain of the nonsecular. I intend to show, through a close reading of late nineteenth-century and early twentieth-century writings, how equality comes to be staged on a spiritual register in modern times—in terms of an intersubjective, interpersonal, often interspecies orientation, with or without God. I explore three spiritualist takes on equality—Advaita Vedanta, Islam, and Buddhism

Equality and Nondualism

We have encountered Advaita Vedanta already in chapter 1, in the context of Vivekananda. A philosophy of nondualism (imperfectly translated as *monism* or *oneness*) associated with the eighth-century thinker Shankara, Advaita Vedanta proposed that individual beings had no separate existence from the universal self or Brahman. Brahman was pure consciousness, in which embodied and experiencing selves dissolved not just in death but also in life, once true knowledge of nondifference or indifference was achieved. The experiencing and embodied self related to this ultimate undifferentiated consciousness in the way that the space within a container related to space as such (as undifferentiated in reality though arbitrarily separated by the contingency of form, or *rupa*) or in the way that a mirror reflection related to the body (in terms of a false doubling necessary for self-recognition). Hence, we have the famous nondualist aphorisms that are often invoked in modern times—*ahambrahmasmi* (I am Brahman) and *tat tvamasi* (you are that)—and the nondualist promise that it is indeed possible to overcome alterity or otherness.

Four aspects of Advaita Vedanta lent themselves to re-citation in modern times as grounds for equality. First, in this tradition, Brahman was not God but pure consciousness. Hence, in nondualist terms, one was equal to another not because both were equal in the eyes of God, but because the self, the other, and Brahman were continuous with each other—being, in the final instance, made of the same substance or element. Not surprisingly, detractors often accused nondualists of being atheists and even crypto-Buddhists!

Second, in this tradition, difference was understood as the default condition of being. Worlding was understood as a ceaseless movement of differentiation of primal consciousness, via the work of creative energy or *maya*. Equality was therefore not the point of departure of thought in nondualism, unlike in liberalism, where thought begins from the axiom that all humans are born equal, or in Marxism, where thought begins from the quasi-historical moment of primitive communism and arrives at the historical moment of transcendence to future communism. In nondualism, equality can be thought only out of experiences of immitigable worldly difference, rather than as a return to or a reiteration of any originary, extrahistorical, undifferentiated state of being. One had to *arrive* at equality, as it were, against the grain and push of everyday experience, marked by *avidya*, the limited or partial cognition proper to the second-order reality of practical (*vyavaharik*) life. By that logic, in nondualism, difference was anterior to equality and equality an insight predicated on a prior experience of empirical multiplicity.

Third, according to this tradition, to arrive at equality one needed only knowledge of the true nature of the self (*atman*) as continuous with other selves. By implication, equality happened not in a distant, utopian future of either communism or moksha but at the very instant of personal enlightenment. For once the knowledge of equality was achieved, one could not but act equitably toward all creatures, high and low. Hence, there is an overlap among the terms *samya*, *samata*, and *samabhava*—equality, equanimity, and equilibrium—and hence also equality is imagined as consciousness or, more correctly, "enlightenment."

Fourth, even though classical Advaita was a highly abstract, asocial, and disengaged philosophy—which argued that the world was an illusion—medieval and early modern nondualists transformed this tradition substantially by bringing other spiritual traditions like Yoga and Bhakti to bear on it.[15] Matthew Lederle talks about "vernacular" nondualisms, involving devotional hagiographies and hymns, which questioned Brahminical high scriptures (*shastras*) and posited experience or *anubhava* as a valid condition of knowledge (*pramana*). The thirteenth-century Varakari saint Jnaneshwar, famous for his critique of the caste system and for being the first vernacular commentator on the Bhagavad Gita, was just such a radical nondualist and would become popular in modern times as an exemplar of equality.[16]

Vivekananda, as we have already seen, invoked nondualism as the basis for his own allegiance to socialism. He characterized the modern age as the global age of Shudra power.[17] Other anticaste theorists in turn invoked Vivekananda—Kuvempu in Karnataka (who wrote a biography of Vivekananda and a play on a Shudra renouncer called *Shudra Tapaswi*) and the poet Kumaran Asan in Kerala (who is said to have named the Ezhava movement's periodical *Vivekodayam* following Vivekananda's visit to Kerala and memorialized the legend that Vivekananda had boldly called out Kerala as a "madhouse" of caste conflict). Many nationalist revolutionaries turned communists too were inspired by Vivekananda. Vivekananda can thus be situated in a longer precolonial tradition of transformation of classical Advaita Vedanta in the name of worldly equality. As Madaio shows, Vivekananda frequently drew on the text *Vivekachuda-*

moni, which qualified nondualism in light of human experience. Vivekananda also cited precolonial *nirguna* philosophers (who believed that the divine had no form or quality, very much like the Brahman of Advaita)—such as Kabir, Nanak, and Dadu Dayal, who, he said, were "reformers" laboring to "raise the lower classes of India."[18]

No less influential than Vivekananda was Sree Narayana Guru's re-citation of Advaita Vedanta in late nineteenth-century Kerala. Like Vivekananda, Narayana Guru dealt in later versions of nondualism mixed with Saiva Siddhanta devotional principles. As Udaya Kumar shows, Narayana Guru's philosophical works—such as *Atmopadesa Sataka* and *Arivu*—proposed that primal differentiation was integral to the manifestation of knowledge (*arivu*). Difference thus was not illusory (as Shankara might have said in an earlier time) but a positive condition of the world and of knowledge of the world. The point was to distinguish between valid (gender) and invalid (caste) principles of differentiation and thus develop a critique of contemporary social hierarchy. Humans were marked by a special creaturely predicament. Unlike other animals, they failed to recognize themselves as a species being, living in the midst of other species. Humans were divided by false concepts such as caste. Narayana Guru exhorted the low-caste Ezhavas to give up castemarks and form a collective (*samudayam*), which could act simultaneously as community and as species, that is, as Ezhavas and as humanity.[19]

Interestingly, Narayana Guru, at the end of his life, consecrated mirrors as deities in temples to facilitate the recognition and worship of the self as Brahman. As Udaya Kumar explains, because the eye cannot see itself seeing, the mirror is necessary to enable self-recognition. And yet because the mirror image is passive and does not look back, there remains a need for a second-order self, which helps perceive the first person, the I, in the intimate of act of self-recognition.[20] This doubled consciousness is Brahma-*jnyan*, the ultimate experience of equality-in-difference, made possible not just by seeing oneself but also by overseeing the very act of seeing oneself—a theory of recognition very different from identitarian philosophies of recognition popular today.

Writing in the 1920s and 1930s, the Muslim communist poet Kazi Nazrul Islam also invoked nondualism. As a child, Nazrul earned his keep as a muezzin calling prayers at the local mosque and studied at a *maktab*, learning the essentials of Islamic theology. Gifted with a beautiful voice, he then joined a wandering *leto* troupe—where he became familiar with popular drama that performed stories from the Puranas and the epics. Later he joined the Bengal Forty-Ninth Regiment and got posted in Karachi, developing further connections with Arabic and Persian traditions. He returned to Bengal as a poet and a communist, who nevertheless continued to write on Hindu and Muslim spiritual traditions. Nazrul translated the Islamic concept of *tawhid* or the oneness of Allah as Advaitic nondualism. This was not entirely idiosyncratic. As Jonardon Ganeri shows, the seventeenth-century Mughal prince Dara Shukoh had undertaken a mutual adaptation of Upanishadic and Islamic philosophies in what he called the *Majma ul Bahrain* (the meeting of the oceans).[21] Nazrul in a different way was doing the same. Addressing a political assembly of Muslim students, he declared that global humanity was poised to come together in nondualism. Only if we could awaken this insight within us, would the poor and the exploited be liberated.[22]

In a long poem titled "Abhedam" (Nondifference), Nazrul plays with the nondualistic concepts of *nama* and *rupa*—name and form—the distinguishing mechanisms by which the universal self appears as differentiated in the world. Combining Vedantic metaphors with metaphors from the popular tradition of devotion to Kali, Nazrul writes of impending equality:

> I will sorrow, suffering, and disease into being—I am the exploiter
> Who takes from others—and I am also the god who punishes such sins
> There is no anger in me, it is just a game
> I make inequality—and I abolish it too
> I play, I chance upon myself,
> What an ugly, unfitting shadow am I
> I want to kill it too
> —there is no difference here, between myself and others
> No thirst for fame, no anger
> No fear of violence, no division
> No war, no peace, only supreme equality [*samya*]
> No politics, no fear, only the name *abhedam*[23]

Three points are worth noting with respect to this nondualistic mode of thinking equality. First, the locus of equality here is the first person—the I—and not figures of alterity, such as a you or a they, even though Shudras and the working classes do animate the sense of that I. Second, the ground of equality here is nondualism and not unity, community, indivisibility, or identity. Third, nondualism emerges not entirely via the activity of argumentation, as in the Bankim moment, but through exhortation and performance—not just in Vivekananda and Narayana Guru, who primarily worked through public appearance and public address, but also in Nazrul, whose poetic diction was fashioned in an exhortative and mobilizing mode.

Islam and the Mundane Facts of Life

Nazrul was accused by many of being a bad Muslim—because he used metaphors from Hindu devotional traditions, because he was too steeped in music, and because he was a self-proclaimed communist. And yet, Nazrul was not exceptional in his interest in spirituality and equality. Many other Muslim writers wrote copiously on equality in spiritual terms, but there was a crucial difference between Advaitic and Islamic ways of theorizing equality that we must note.

Vedantic nondualism engaged with the human condition in its presocial creaturely aspect, wherein both difference and indifference appeared as anterior to the historical institution of hierarchies such as of caste, race, and nationality. Islam, in early twentieth-century Bengal and India, theorized equality differently—by claiming to bring into the ambit of spirituality the mundane sociological facts of human life and livelihood. This was done on the grounds that Islam was a worldly tradition. Worldliness, however, did not imply a division between religious and secular pursuits of life or between theological and political discourse (in fact, many Muslim political thinkers of this period were *maulavis* and ulema, especially those mobilized during the noncooperation and Khilafat movements of 1920–22). Worldliness here was a critique of the ruling philosophical binary of the times—namely, the binary between idealism and materialism.

Abul Hashim, an important leader in the Bengal Provincial Muslim League sympathetic to the Left, argued that *deen*, originally an Arabic term meaning "way of life" that became indigenized in both Persian and the Indian vernaculars, was not religion. Religion was a western European concept that reduced spirituality to private contemplation and faith, leaving vast aspects of life out of its purview. *Deen* combined philosophy, law, and intuition and was therefore more encompassing of life. As a philosophy, *deen* was a matter of rational intellection and knowledge. As law, it was a matter of regulating ordinary, everyday aspects of life—economic activities as much as worship and prayer. And as intuition, it was an opening toward the transcendental and the futural, that is, toward matters as yet unknown. *Deen*, therefore, was neither pure idealism, like Advaita Vedanta, nor pure materialism, like scientific Marxism.[24] Already by this time, Marxism-Leninism had taken root in India, and with it the binary between idealism and materialism had become common sense. In the context of everyday politics in India, the idealism/materialism binary translated directly into the binary between the spiritual and the economic. Muslim thinkers of equality resisted this binary.

The philosopher-poet Muhammad Iqbal, in his 1930 magnum opus *The Reconstruction of Religious Thought in Islam*, argued that the Islamic notion of the oneness of God's creation denied the dichotomy between nature and society. In Islamic thought, nature was not dead matter, devoid of intent, purpose, and action, an object world to be conquered and harnessed by humans under the spell of a purely economic logic. God's creation was imbued with animation and movement; difference—as among humans, animals, and objects—was merely a difference of degree rather than of quality, a neomaterialist statement if any! Some humans simply had a more developed self or ego (*khudi*) than other creatures. Iqbal, as mentioned in chapter 4, disagreed with the theological position that there was a strict division between God and his creation, and that creation was a finished and finalized entity, a once-and-for-all act by God, subject to a regime of fixed natural laws, which could be studied by pure science sans spirituality. Creation was the mode of being of Allah, dynamic and ongoing—full of surprises, contingencies, and openness toward the not-yet—and from it were derived human freedom and human futures. A poet above all, Iqbal saw an analogy between poetic creativity and the creativity of God—making Iqbal's God quite distinct from that of both deists and pantheists of earlier times. It was precisely the underdetermined and unfinished nature of the world, the unpredictable movement of its becoming, that produced revolutionary potentialities and what Iqbal called the capacious and integrated "now" of transformation—the duration of poetic/divine creativity, wherein the past, present, and future became simultaneous.[25]

Abul Hashim also insisted that humans must live in communion with nature and not by dominating or objectifying it, as dialectical materialism would have us do, because both *qudrat* (nature, the universe, forces immanent to the world) and *fitrat* (the nature of a thing or person) were aspects of God. The universe was not a sum of isolated fragments and identities—a set of fixed differences—but a differentiated whole in which every genus and species was interdependent, defining and supplementing one another. Obviously familiar with Vedantic nondualism and Vivekananda, Hashim implied that both the idealism of Advaita Vedanta and the dialectical materialism of Soviet Communism were inadequate to the thinking of equality precisely because both divided the unity of Allah's creation into a subject world and an object world.[26]

Khalifa Abdul Hakim, who taught philosophy at Osmania University, Hyderabad, spoke similarly about the nature of matter: "The materialism of Marx suffered the same contradiction as the evolutionary materialism of Herbert Spencer. Spencer's unconscious, blind, mechanistic matter somehow takes care to preserve and advance the life-values it creates, so does the presumably unspiritual matter of Marx which advances towards a proletarian revolution steadily with a logic and method which could emerge only with a goal-seeking spirit."[27] Marxism is secretly founded on a spiritual principle, Hakim implied, which generated a spirit of sacrifice in political actors and a deep faith in the inevitability of communism. But its imagination of matter as inert/objective produced a determinism that, paradoxically, left no space for precisely such revolutionary faith. Hence, Marxism introduced, through the backdoor as it were, a sensibility of spiritual freedom and moral obligation, while loudly decrying religion. Islam, being invested in the sustenance of life on earth, however, proposed that diverse domains of life—economics, sexuality, and politics— were equally shot through with intent, sense, and animation. What we call morality and spirituality today is nothing other than the sensibility that "adjudicates between the competing claims of our physical, sexual, economic and political existence."[28] That was the meaning of *tawhid*—namely, the understanding that economics, politics, culture, and morality were not separate spheres of life, following different laws and different disciplines, but a mutually articulated whole.

This spiritual paradigm based on *tawhid*—which brought matter, nature, livelihood, and worship within the same framework[29]—resonated with the history of popular Islamic piety in Bengal. As Richard Eaton has shown, the spread of Islam in eastern and frontier Bengal, led in medieval times by Sufi and Pir vanguards, happened via activities of forest clearance, land reclamation, agricultural settlement, and the consequent admission of low-caste and aboriginal elements into an Islamic civilizational world.[30] A particular relationship to nature, in both its dangerous/wild and its domesticated/bountiful aspects, was therefore constitutive of the East Bengali experience of Islamic life. This was also true of what came to be seen, by the late nineteenth and early twentieth centuries, as the specifically Islamic virtues of industrious labor, personal thrift, austerity, economic self-dependence, charity, and indeed, a reformed, unostentatious piety—all of which were invoked by spiritual leaders of the time in terms of Koranic injunctions about hard work, compulsory *zakat* (contributions to a common fund for the needy), and prohibition against usury.[31]

Add to this the living memory of the Faraizi rebellion and Wahabi reformism in East Bengal. Abul Mansur Ahmed, one of the early leaders of the Krishak Praja Party who started *raiyat samitis* (peasant committees) when he was only a teen, introduces himself in his memoirs as a descendent of Gazi Ashequllah, son of Asraddin Faraizi, and mujahedin of Syed Ahmed Barelvi. Known as the great jihadi of the area, Ashequllah spent his old age—after his return to Bengal from the northwest frontier—teaching martial arts to the village youth and discussing issues of jihad and martyrdom with peers. Those who participated in these discussions were, according to Ahmed, mostly peasant smallholders.[32] Interestingly, when the poet Nazrul contested elections for the upper house of the Central Legislative Council in 1926, Badshah Pir, grandson and spiritual successor of the Faraizi leader Dudu Miya, canvassed for him.[33] In Bangladeshi writer Akhteruzzaman Elias's remarkable novel *Khoabnama* (The saga of dreams), peasant insurgency—electoral mobilization led by the Muslim League and the Krishak Praja Party as well as the sharecroppers' Tebhaga movement led by communists—appears always already haunted by the ghost of Faraizi warrior Munshi Barkatullah Shah, who was martyred fighting the East India Company soldiers.[34]

An insurgent popular discourse about the oneness of Allah and the equality of men thus accompanied the articulation of spiritual and economic issues in the wider agrarian world of Bengal, where the majority of peasants were Muslims. The Bengali periodical *Samyabadi* (The egalitarian), which was run, between 1922 and 1925, mostly by Muslims, is a good example of this phenomenon. Neilesh Bose discusses this periodical's career extensively in his study East Bengal's regional sensibility, marked as it was by a strong Muslim cultural presence, both elite and subaltern. The periodical's frontispiece displayed quotations such as "All humans belong to one community"; "May he who is one and without varna grant us insight"; and "He who is abstract, he who has no race, color, caste, creed show us the way to enlightenment." Maulvi Huq Selbarshi wrote in the first issue of *Samyabadi* that Islam was the religion of equality par excellence. It was only because of contingent historical reasons, such as proximity to Hinduism, that Muslims had fallen prey to caste distinctions. Mohammad Sanaullah wrote that Islam was the historical refuge of oppressed low-caste Hindus. Another essay argued that all religions develop hierarchies in time, such as race in Christianity, high culture/low culture (*ashraf/altaf*) in Islam, and *jati* and *varna* in Hinduism. But it was also religion that ultimately abolished hierarchies. Mohammad Barkatullah argued that inequality was the way in which Allah tested humans and their capacity for self-transformation.[35] Theological differences—such as between reformist ulema of the Anjuman e Ulema e Bangla, like Muhammad Akram Khan, who ran the periodicals *Al Islam* and *Mohammadi* and wrote the important text "Sud Samasya" (The problem of interest) on the issue of peasant indebtedness,[36] and the Pir Abu Bakr of Furfura, who represented an unreformed variety of popular worship involving discipleship, magic and healing—did not seem to trouble the general agreement over the equation between Islam and equality. Abul Hossain, in fact, described Bengal peasants as *banglar balshi* (the Bolsheviks of Bengal) and anticipated an impending peasant revolution.[37] More self-consciously communist periodicals of the time—such as *Dhumketu* (The comet) and *Langal* (The plow)—were also dominated by Muslim authors and editors, including the poet Nazrul and one of the earliest of Indian communists, Muzaffar Ahmed.[38] The first issue of *Langal* ran an essay titled "Samyabad Ki" (What is egalitarianism?), which directly translated *Islam* into *egalitarianism*: "Some Muslim leaders have alleged that Samyavad is the enemy of Islam. Quite to the contrary, Islam is a greater critique of Dhaniktantra [capitalism] than Samyavad [socialism]. . . . Taking interest on loans is forbidden among Muslims. Because earnings from interest is earning without undertaking labor, Islam does not tolerate those who make money from usury. Communism has also said that taking interest is illegal."[39]

In other words, popular Islamic discourses of equality threw a shadow over thinkers both self-avowedly communist and anti-communist. Abul Hashim's *The Creed of Islam* argued that Islam was more socialistic than socialism itself. He summarized Islam in terms of the principle of absolute and exclusive sovereignty of God, which, he said, logically denied sovereignty to man. Man was not meant to rule over other men or over nature. Hence, the revolutionary *kalima* of the Koran was against the master-slave hierarchy. Even though historically there were slaves in Muslim lands, slaves could achieve great glory in Islam. The paradigmatic story was that of the black slave Bilal, appointed by the Prophet Muhammad as the first muezzin, who refused allegiance to Abu Bakr after Muhammad's death, on the grounds that he bowed only before Allah. In Muslim India, slaves had been sultans in medieval times. *Bandagi*, a term that meant both service and worship, thus denoted one's obeisance exclusively to God and, by implication, the universal equality of men, in their common condition of being nonsovereigns unto themselves.[40] This image—of slave kings—was frequently invoked in Muslim discourse of the times, such as in the speeches of Azizul Haq and Mohammad Rampuri, as was the image of the untouchable Dom and Chandal praying side by side with the elite *ashraf* in the mosque.[41] And from the fact that the slave Bilal was a man of color, Abul Hashim further concluded—as did many of his contemporaries—that Islam denied racial and national distinctions, for in Islam humanity (and nature) was one and universal.[42] Hence Pan-Islamism and socialist internationalism were frequently combined by contemporary Muslim authors, such as by Mushir Kidwai.[43]

In an interesting gloss on the concept of God being the sole sovereign, Abul Hashim argued, clearly in response to the communist promise of the withering away of the state, that an ideal Islamic society was the only imaginable instance of true anarchy or statelessness. Deeply involved though he was in electoral politics in Bengal in the 1930s and 1940s, Hashim argued that despite what European political philosophy might say, there was really no such thing as popular will. Society was an artificial construct, a matrix of differences and inequalities, and by no means an organic whole that could operate as *a* people. The modern representational state therefore did not actually represent the people, not even the majority of people. The state was just an instrument of domination—a symbol of inequality if any. In contrast to the modern state, Hashim held up the ideal of the Khilafat (caliphate), which he said was a regime without state machinery and monopoly of violence, wherein order emanated from within the moral social order rather than from outside and above.[44] Abdul Hakim quoted Arnold Toynbee to say that in modern times God had been replaced not by man but by the racial state. We must study the history of religion, lately displaced by the study of purely political and economic history, in order to be able to imagine human society as an immanent form, that is, as more than being simply the conceptual other of the state.[45] A significant resonance appears here with Ambedkar's formulation in "Buddha or Karl Marx," where he criticized communism precisely for its state-centricity and propagated Buddha's way of realizing equality via the immanent morality of interpersonal conduct.

Many of these Islamic texts, significantly, were self-consciously theological. The elaboration of equality was thus intended as theological elaborations, complete with Koranic exegesis. And yet, these texts operated side by side with poetry—perhaps illustrating Hamid Dabashi's reading of the Persianate intellectual world, including south Asia, as above all a "humanistic" world, wherein the poet—often figured as the marginal, the vagabond, the ungovernable being, mad with love/passion/oneness with God—operated as the most intractable critic, speaking back to both theological and political power, a characterization that, by the way, fits quite well with the persona of Kazi Nazrul Islam.[46] But I am more interested here in how the poetic form enabled a particular embodiment of the contemporary Islamic critique of the idealism/materialism binary and thus allowed the embedding of mundane economic facts within a spiritualist narrative. Poetry, one could say, became a place in-between the didactic aspects of communism and Islam. A good example is Iqbal's poem "Lenin," in which Lenin encounters Allah and apologizes for his cognitive limitations. How could a human know whether God existed or not—"trapped [as she or he is] in nights routinely following days / While You create ages and preside over moments?" But then the human must also ask of God the challenging question, which remains "like a thorn stuck to the heart": "What is this apparent wealth that is nothing but speculation / which is millions in usury for some and untimely death for others? / What is this new knowledge that drinks blood and preaches equality?"

> Tū qādir o aadil hai magar tere jahāñ meñ
> Haiñ talkh bahut banda-e-mazdūr
>
> Kab Dūbegā sarmāya-parastī kā safina
> Duniyā hai tirī muntazir-e-roz-e-mukāfāt⁴⁷
>
> You are powerful and just, but in your world
> bitter is the place of the working man.
>
> When will the ship of capital sink?
> The world awaits the day of your retribution.

Kazi Nazrul Islam wrote of the day of revolution as the moment when Israfel, the burning one, blows his trumpet, announcing the Day of Judgment. Note how he renders *zakat* poetically:

> The bandit moon rises in the sky to take zakat.
> The poor, the wretched open your palms, the rich secure your granary.
> The moon of Id is the rosy smile of Belal.
> Standing on the scales of justice in the blue sky, calling out *azan*,
> I have brought the message from the moon of Id of Allah.
> After Ramzan, we shall break our fast with their hoards.
> All shall get food, Id will be a happy day.
> Plunder what is given to you by Allah; none of you will be a sinner
>   for that.⁴⁸

Elias, in his *Khoabnama*, creates the persona of the wandering poet-renouncer, the *fakir* who sings ballads of revolutionary war as well as of farming activities, through the unfolding of the story of equality in the East Bengal countryside.

Buddhism and Equality without God

It is appropriate to end with Ambedkar—not only because he "returned" to spirituality as the last great expressive act of a life dedicated to the cause of caste equality but also because, even as he sought to fashion a particular religion of equality, he tried to account for the phenomenon of religion as such. In his "Philosophy of Hinduism," Ambedkar said that religion was constitutive of the human condition because it dealt with elemental questions of life such as birth and death, nourishment and disease. But this is not to say, as Gandhi did, that all religions were true at heart. There were indeed true and false as well as good and bad religions. The history of religion was one of change and revolution. Ambedkar did not go by the conventional narrative of modernity. The rise of science and the alleged triumph of secular reason over religion was not really the defining event of his story. To Ambedkar, the most important revolution in the history of religion was the invention of God![49]

Through an anthropological study of "primitive" religions, Ambedkar argued that early forms of religion did not have conceptions of either God or morality. Religion—concerned as it was with death, disease, birth, growth, food, scarcity, and other such struggles of material life—propitiated productive and destructive forces of nature, such as sun, rain, wind, and pestilence. These forces were neither good nor evil. They were amoral, simply there to be fought, harnessed, and placated. In other words, religion was simply about life in its exigencies, dangers, and flourishing. The concept of God had extrareligious origins. It emerged out of deference to great and powerful men—heroes and kings—or out of pure speculation about an author-architect of the world. God came to be integrated with religion only in later times.

The invention of God was followed by a second major revolution—namely, the subsumption of morality under religion. In early times, the relationship between gods and humans was imagined as a form of kinship—hence the familiar image of god as a father or mother figure. "Political society"—Ambedkar's term—was thus composed of descendants and worshippers of a common progenitor god; consequently, competing polities had competing gods. Later, once society came to be imagined as composed only of humans and gods became transcendental figures beyond political society, the God-human relationship changed from being that of kinship to that of faith, belief, and adoration. Instead of watching over the public and civic life of the community, God now appeared to watch over the individual and regulate his or her personal conscience. Lineage loyalties came to be replaced by moral injunctions. Consequently, it became possible to imagine a single polity composed of people worshipping different gods (e.g., the Indian nation), just as it became possible to imagine a single universal God watching over a humanity otherwise divided into different polities (e.g., modern-day Islam or Christianity).[50]

Ambedkar's was not the standard story of secularization but was instead a more complex story of the changing constitution of both politics and religion and of their changing relationship. One could say that Ambedkar was enunciating what we today call "political theology" (though the term *theology* is a tad inappropriate for traditions like Hinduism and Buddhism, which, unlike Abrahamic traditions, were more practice based than scripturally driven). Ambedkar's reconstruction of Buddhism as a religion of equality must be placed in the context of this longer narrative of the changing nature of political theology through time. To Ambedkar, Hinduism was a particular political-theological formation, in which religion was law and law was religion. It was an elaborate set of social proscriptions and punishments, posited as sacred, timeless, and scriptural. Its gods were amoral (Krishna of Bhagavad Gita even encouraged fratricide for the sake of political power). Its defining concepts—*atman*, *karma*, and rebirth—implied that people were born to inferior castes owing to bad *karma* in their previous lives. Hinduism thus was not only an elaborately sanctified justification of inequality but also a religion of status quo, obedience, and conformity. It was, most importantly, an antisocial religion because it prevented sociability ("fraternity," Ambedkar said)—such as eating together and intermarrying—across peoples born to different castes. It was in defiance of Hinduism as political theology that Buddhism emerged as a religion of equality in ancient India. The rise of Buddha was nothing short of a revolution—for Buddha promulgated a supremely moral religion, which did not discriminate on grounds of caste, gender, or species. It admitted low-castes and women into the *sangha* and critiqued the sacrifice of mute animals in the Vedic fire.

Ambedkar, however, was making a far more complex move here than just valorizing one religion over another based on superior morality. Even though Ambedkar did say, apropos Buddhism, that religion was morality and morality religion, he also said, in *Annihilation of Caste*, that morality by itself was never a sufficient condition for equality. What was needed was religion, no less—because it was only when equality was sacralized as an idea that it became truly inviolable.[51] So Ambedkar offered his followers Buddhism. While he called his Buddhism *navayana* or the new path, he did not invent a new religion, a civil religion in the Rousseauian sense. Instead, he self-consciously enacted a return to religion in its most primordial, purest, and barest form—that is, to a religion without God.

In *The Buddha and His Dhamma*, written just before his death, Ambedkar proposed a conception of religion without the mediation of gods and prophets and without grounding in any notion of an eternal inner being, such as soul or *atman*.[52] To Ambedkar, the religious subject and the subject of religion was the ordinary, mortal, finite human being in his or her everyday life—with no guarantee of God, soul, scripture, or heaven. Buddha, he said, never claimed to be God or prophet or avatar. Nor did he offer revelation or miracle. He even refused to comment on questions that had no answers—such as "What is the self?," "What happens after death?," and "Is the world finite or infinite?"[53] For such questions had no bearing on everyday life.[54] Buddhism, in Ambedkar's telling, was thus simply a set of meditations on the finite human condition, no more and no less—and for precisely that reason religion in its truest and most originary sense. It was *dhamma*—a vision of everyday social behavior—based on *prajnya* (insight, as opposed to Brahminical knowledge or *jnyan*), *sila* (proper conduct), *karuna* (compassion), and *maitri* (friendship), in precisely that order of ascension.[55]

Buddhism proposed that *dukka* (suffering or sorrow) was an "incontrovertible fact" of life. *Dukka* was the result of the universal fact of conflict. While in Ambedkar, conflict and suffering were indexed as caste oppression, they were not reducible to that. Suffering could result from conflict between kings, between nations, and between mother and son, husband and wife, friend and friend. Buddhism, however, did not see suffering as a precondition to enlightenment, as did many ascetic and hermetic traditions in early India and elsewhere. *Dukka* was there to be overcome. And this was possible because of the nature of existence as *shunyata*. *Shunyata*—often translated as "the void," "nothingness," or "emptiness," translations that Ambedkar disputed because it seemed to deny the materiality of the world—simply meant "impermanence." The Buddhist conception of *shunyata* was therefore an insight into the ultimate ephemerality and inconstancy of the world—which proposed change itself as the proper ontology of being. Referring to the Buddhist epistemological principle of "dependent origination" (which held that an entity was itself only by virtue of its relation to other entities), Ambedkar argued that Buddhism was an antifoundationalist philosophy.[56] Hence, it had no need for God or a soul or any other form of essence or identity. It allowed escape from all given identities, however ancient, including caste. Buddhism was by nature a revolutionary doctrine, a doctrine of change.[57]

Ambedkar was a master of the long essay form. His *Annihilation of Caste*—originally written as a speech that could never be delivered—was an inimitable example of how to properly set up a structure of disputation, complete with thesis and counterthesis, scale changes from particular to general, and a systematic movement toward resolution, which, in this case, was to arrive at religion as the ultimate issue at stake with respect to equality. But Ambedkar intended *The Buddha and His Dhamma* as a scripture, a Buddhist Bible. The book followed the life and travels of Buddha in his quest for enlightenment. Ideas were staged as dialogues and disputations between Buddha and his interlocutors, both disciples and opponents. The conversion of diverse figures—from king to untouchable to courtesan—to Buddhism was recorded, and teachings were set out as aphorisms, even as many passages reappeared in the text in the familiar form of the Ambedkarite long essay. The point to note is that, as far as Ambedkar was concerned, equality ultimately emerged as embedded in scripture.

It bears mentioning that Ambedkar was not the only one who co-theorized Buddhism and equality. So did Iyothee Thass in Tamil Nadu, Rahul Sankrityayan in north India, Dharmanand Kosambi in west India, Anagarika Dharmapala in Sri Lanka, and Haraprasad Shastri in Bengal. Haraprasad Shastri was as different a figure as possible from Ambedkar. A Brahmin scholar of purely academic orientation, Shastri spent most of his life searching for old manuscripts and trying to reconstruct the history of Bengal as the original land of Buddhists. In his essay "Jatibhed" (Caste division), he argued that Bengal was originally inhabited by Shudras, untouchables, and aborigines—the name Banga or Bengal apparently derived from the caste name of the untouchable Bagdis.[58] The history of Bengal was really a history of caste, he said.[59] Brahmins came late to Bengal, appropriated popular religious forms, battled Buddhism, and finally, consolidated their caste supremacy during Muslim rule through anti-Muslim rhetoric.[60]

One of Shastri's greatest concerns was to understand how and why Buddhism vanished from Bengal and whether Buddhism could have survived among the poor and the outcaste in transformed ways. In a series of essays published in nationalist leader Bipin Chandra Pal's periodical *Narayana* in the mid-1910s, Shastri blamed Brahminical appropriation of the tenets of Buddhism for the loss of the Buddhist way (along with, he added, local Buddhism's turn toward secret *tantric* practices, which involved, significantly, touching "polluting" substances such as female genitalia, urine, and excreta). Through extensive fieldwork in various parts of Bengal, Shastri reconstructed the tradition of *dharmapuja*, which he argued was the modern surviving form of Buddhism in Bengal. By legend, the untouchable Kalu Dom was the initiator of this form of *dhamma* devotion. In this tradition, *shunya-murti* (the figure of the zero, symbolized often by an opaque black stone) was the object of worship. Priests were almost always low-castes and outcastes (Shastri found one case of a Dom woman priest), and iconic texts were pitched against Brahmin oppressors of the poor. Ramai Pandit's *Shunya Purana*, also known as *Dharma Puja Bidhan*, written most likely in the eleventh century, recounted how when Brahmin oppression became unbearable, Dharma took the form of Muslims and defeated them. Bhim Bhoi's *Kali Bhagavad* recounted the setting up of a neo-*bhikshu* or neomonastic way of life, with great similarities to *Vinayapitaka* (an early Buddhist text of monastic governmentality), in which begging for alms from Shudra households was mandatory.[61] Not just Brahmins but even powerful kings were put in their

Equality and Spirituality

place by Buddhists in earlier times, Shastri added. As the Buddhist philosopher Chandrakirti had said already in the fifth century, there was no pride in being a king—the king, after all, was a servant of the people, whose salary was but one-sixth of what peasants produced.[62] Buddhism in Bengal was thus a lost religion of equality. Hence, Haraprasad Shastri lamented the loss of Buddhism: "Shunyabad, Bigyanbad, Karunabad bhule gelo, Darshan bhule gelo, shila, binay bhule gelo" (The doctrines of shunyata, rationality, and compassion were forgotten; philosophy, codes of moral conduct, and conscience were forgotten).[63]

Conclusion

In modern times, thus, diverse spiritual traditions have been critical in rendering the idea of equality thinkable as a positive concept. Different spiritual traditions did this differently, and we must remain wary of lumping them together simply by virtue of their being "religious" and not "secular." But three common elements should be flagged here in order to clarify the nature of the phenomenon we are studying. First, all the spiritual traditions I discuss had an intense relationship with Marxism, even as they were often critical of it. By the same logic, all these spiritual traditions, especially Islam, sought to resignify the economic itself as part of the spirituality question. Second, all these traditions offered additional concepts to supplement the concept of equality—such as non-duality, *tawhid*, *maitri*, and *dhamma*. These were concepts meant to engage the fact and concept of difference, without which equality remained unthinkable, just as difference remained unthinkable without equality. These were by no means concepts signifying community or unity or indivisibility—such as of the poor or the proletariat or the people—bearers of equality, as it were. In fact, Marxism-Leninism made this move—of displacing the question of equality onto the question of (class) unity or community, thus postponing with undue analytical haste, the preliminary question of What is equality? in favor of a very different question, Who is equal? True, the thinkers I discuss here invoke particular subaltern figures as signifying the thinkability of equality—Bankim's woman, Vivekananda and Narayana Guru's Shudra, Nazrul and Abul Hashim's Muslim peasant, and Ambedkar's untouchable. And yet in place of identity, which denies difference within and exacerbates difference without, what we have in these thinkers is the imagination of "encounter." What the spiritual traditions seek to do, in other words, is imagine equality as that which emerges out of an encounter of unequals. Whether Iqbal's Lenin encountering Allah or Narayana Guru's worshipper encountering herself in the mirror, it was encounter as a form—encounter across unequal differences and different inequalities—that was resignified as moments of nonduality, *tawhid*/oneness, and *maitri*/friendship. In fact, even as Marxism-Leninism sought to imagine equality as universal equivalence, via the transvaluating work of the economic, in the concept of class struggle, it too mobilized the form of the encounter—a very different, warlike, agonistic encounter—as the precise moment of equality.

What then of equality as idea and as political idea? Needless to say, an idea becomes an idea by fighting free of its imbrication in diverse moments of encounter—acquiring in the process the autonomy, abstraction, lightness, and mobility that are properties of an idea qua idea. Equality becomes an idea just so—by traveling out of liberal political philosophy and the historical stage of the French Revolution and passing through not just economic but also spiritual and aesthetic registers of enunciation in diverse languages. As important, it becomes an idea by becoming amenable to diverse forms of embodiment—essay, exegesis, exhortation, poetry, and indeed scripture.

But equality, I propose, does not quite become a political idea. Like the economic fact, as I argue in chapter 6, spirituality remains in the last instance an extrapolitical imperative—as being both before and beyond the moment of politics. By that logic, the spiritual, like the economic, appears as both the condition of possibility of the political and its limit. It promises to stabilize and regulate the political against its own immediacies—and it continues to remain efficacious when politics fails or goes into abeyance. Can the moment of Ambedkar's conversion to Buddhism and his final writing of *The Buddha and His Dhamma*—after the cessation of his long political career and his resignation from the first government of independent India—be seen as an index of precisely this extrapolitical prospect of equality?

6

Equality and Economic Reason

> The English bring the economic and the political together. But in their case the contradiction sometimes becomes apparent. Brahmins, however, perfected a way of bringing together the economic and the spiritual. This they did by valorizing not the commodity but the gift!
>
> —Shibram Chakraborty, *Moscow Banam Pondicherry*

Colonialism subtly transformed the relationship between politics and economics. If earlier, as we have seen in chapter 2, the term *artha* implied a co-constitution of economic and political power, now the company state fashioned its primary technology of rule via a discursive and material separation of political and economic rights among its subjects.[1] As Sudipta Sen shows, the East India Company undertook, in the name of free trade, a rigorous "settling" of markets, so as to turn markets into purely economic sites, indifferent to the political, religious, and cultural networks in which they were earlier embedded.[2] Indigenous rulers were denied their traditional political, military, and commercial powers and, through new revenue arrangements, were "pacified" into being pure economic subjects—that is, rentiers, whose mandate as landlords (rather than kings) was to revert land from being territory to being resource, and peasants and artisans from being subjects to a polity to being tenants and workers. As I have argued elsewhere, colonialism enforced market exchange as the only permissible civil interface between diverse peoples—such as forest tribes and settled cultivators—on the grounds that unmediated political interaction across social heterogeneity was bound to degenerate into violence.[3]

The argument behind this novel separation of the political and the economic was Kantian—namely, the spirit of commerce converted nations to "perpetual peace," cosmopolitanism, and economic productivity.[4] The implication, however, was recognizably Marxian—namely, modern power was "rule by the economic," an autonomous force that no longer needed the help of political or cultural power (as in feudal or despotic times) in order to extract value. In Marx's telling, the economic became the main operative force in modernity because capitalism dispossessed peasants and artisans of access to the means of production and thus forced them to sell their labor power in the market of their own accord, driven by no other logic except the purely economic logic of survival.[5] Marx did not notice, however, that "primitive accumulation" was not just a process of alienating subjects from their economic means but also a process of instituting an unprecedented separation between economic rights and political rights.

Horace William Clift, the earliest writer of a political economy textbook in India, expressed in 1835 this emergent sensibility of the economic as an autonomous and automatic force (best illustrated by Adam Smith's "invisible hand"). "Every young man will be controlled by its principles," Clift said, "whether he learns them or not."[6] As Iman Mitra shows, political economy texts were now copiously translated into Bengali and David Ricardo, Thomas Malthus, and John Stuart Mill frequently invoked, as economics came to be pitched as a foundational imperative, derived from basic livelihood practices common to all peoples, irrespective of their particular cultural and political predilections.

Benoy Kumar Sarkar translated *Sukraniti*, a medieval *arthashastric* text, in 1914 to demonstrate the "economic basis" of state power in precolonial India. He also translated Friedrich Engels's *The Origin of the Family, Private Property and State*, Paul Lafargue's *The Evolution of Property from Savagery to Civilization* in 1928, and Friedrich List's *Das nationale System der politischen Ökonomie* in 1932. He frequently spoke about Marxism, started the first economic periodical in Bengali (*Arthik Unnati*), and set up the Bengal Economic Association. Sarkar saw himself as a kind of economic activist, advising Bengali businessmen, associating with the Bengal National Chamber of Commerce, and educating the public in the intricacies of insurance and banking.[7] In his two-volume book *Economic Development*, he argued that economic relations among nations could be represented as statistically measurable parities and inequalities, enabling economic actors to predict and plan for a nation's future by comparing it with the economic trajectories of other nations.[8] Sarkar even believed the Permanent Settlement of Bengal to be equivalent to the English enclosures, both leading to capitalism. To him *zamindars* were India's first capitalists, who operated as bankers to the peasant—an unpopular political view at a time when Bengal landlordism was widely criticized as the primary cause of peasant poverty. But Sarkar insisted that economic thinking must be a nonpolitical and nonparty affair![9]

I mention Sarkar as a typical example of how colonial subjects experienced the new principle of unconditional universality and autonomy of the economic, as it came to ground the political inequality of nations. Unsurprisingly, the earliest anticolonial critique emerged in India in the form of economic nationalism in the hands of liberals and constitutionalists (though peasant revolts could be seen as an earlier form of economic criticism among those not educated in political economy).[10] The first nationalist mobilization against colonial rule in 1905 centrally involved economic activities—boycott and picketing of British goods, *swadeshi* (or self-sufficiency in manufacture, banking, and insurance), and refusal of colonial jobs and education.[11] Even the spiritually oriented Gandhi organized his political activities around familiar economic symbols—the spinning wheel, handloom, and salt. The striking of work was as important to Gandhian *satyagraha* as it was to communist class struggle, and even Ambedkar, who accused communists of narrow economism, considered the "general strike" as the epitome of political action.[12]

The rise of economic reason in India was thus predicated not just on liberal discourses of free trade and colonial technologies of rule but also on an emergent politics of equality. It was not just that equality came to be imagined in modern times primarily as economic equality à la Marxism-Leninism, but that equality, in the course of its constitution as political idea par excellence, helped entrench the modern sensibility that the economic was the most valid mode of reasoning in life and politics. And yet, even as economic reason became crucial to the critique of inequality, it never quite sufficed as the language of equality as a positive idea, that is, as more than the mere absence of inequality. For that purpose, the economic had to be resignified. In Bengal, I argue, sociology and literature overwrote the economic in ways that both echoed and rivaled spiritualist imaginations of equality, bringing me back to the proposition that equality becomes a political idea in modern times through a dialectic between the spiritual and the economic, each claiming to best embody the universal human condition and thus be the ultimate ground of politics.

The Exemplarity of the Peasant

Even prior to the systematization of economic nationalism, many were writing about the economic abjection of peasants in India. In addition to Bankim's "Samya" and "Bangadesher Krishak," there was Peary Chand Mitra's "The Zemindar and the Ryot" (1846) in the *Calcutta Review*; Dinabandhu Mitra's controversial play *Neel Darpan* (1860), on the exploitation of Bengali peasants by British indigo planters; Sanjibchandra Chattopadhyay's *Bengal Ryots* (1864), on issues of property and tenancy; R. C. Dutt's *The Peasantry of Bengal* (1874), on the history of peasant impoverishment; Lal Behari Dey's *Govinda Samanta* or *Bengal Peasant Life* (1874); Mir Mosharraf Hossain's play *Zamindar Darpan* (Mirror of Landlords, 1873); and the extraordinary reportage of *kangal* (destitute) Harinath Majumdar, in *Grambarta Prakashika* (The publication of rural news).[13]

The peasant's political potential was variously judged.[14] To a liberal such as Nehru, the peasant was a symbol of backwardness and had to be educated into modern nationalism; to Gandhi and the Congress socialists, the peasant was a symbol of national authenticity; to Ambedkar, peasant society was the den of casteism, which untouchables had to escape through education and migration to cities; to communists, peasants were a conservative force except when they were landless and thereby equivalent to the industrial proletariat; and to Maoists, peasants were a strategic force that would surround the city and help take over the state. Academic writing in India remained preoccupied with the peasant until at least the 1980s—economists discussed agrarian modes of production and the intricacies of rural class structure, sociology discussed tradition and change in rural caste and kinship systems, and historians (most recently of the subaltern studies school) wrote of peasant insurgency and everyday resistance. Despite ideological and disciplinary divisions, there was thus a general agreement about the centrality of the peasant in modern Indian politics.

And yet, it was never quite clear who or what the peasant was. Defined as a purely economic subject—as worker of the land—the peasant in Bengal, as recent scholarship shows, always already appeared as either a Muslim or an ex-untouchable Namashudra. The peasant had many names—*krishak*, or plowman; *chasha*, or a rustic; *chhotolok*, or small people (as opposed to *borolok*, the rich, and *bhadralok*, the genteel); *jotedar*, or middle peasant, who rented land from a bigger landlord; *kamia*, or landless, often bonded labor; *bargadar/adhiar*, or sharecropper; and *raiyat*, a term of Arabic origin meaning a herd or populace subject to a leader. As often, the peasant was known as Namashudra, Paundra Kshatriya, and Mahishya (new respectable names assumed by erstwhile low-caste Chandalas, Pods, and Kaivartas) and Hadi, Muchi, Dom, Kamar, Napit,

Tanti, and so forth (artisanal and service castes of fishermen, weavers, smiths, cobblers, leatherworkers, barbers, and scavengers, who often worked land part-time without entirely being peasants). But the name that became the most politically efficacious in Bengal was the ancient term *praja*, meaning subject to a king, later glossed as tenant to a *zamindar*, or landlord.

Clearly, a political overlay animated the term *praja* in ways that exceeded what would have otherwise been a purely economic term for a peasant, even though communists tried hard to popularize the term *krishak* (of the *krishak-mazdoor*, or peasant-worker duo) in place of the term *praja*, which they felt stood for smallholding peasantry rather than true revolutionary subjects, the rural proletariat.[15] And yet, in East Bengal, the peasant came to be so commonly identified as a Muslim that, as Ananya Dasgupta shows, born-Hindu communists felt compelled to assume Muslim names when campaigning there.[16] Even Pakistan came to represent the promise of a peasant utopia.[17] As important, Jogendranath Mandal, leader of the Namashudras, Ambedkar's main ally in Bengal and head of the Bengal Scheduled Castes Federation, called himself *praja-bandhu* (friend of peasants) and negotiated political alliances alternatively with the Muslim-dominated Krishak Praja Party (KPP) and the Muslim League. Even though he insisted that untouchables were a separate political entity, Dwaipayan Sen shows, Mandal believed that untouchables and Muslims had "identical economic interests" and hence were politically equivalent.[18]

Unlike earlier scholarship, which saw Namashudra and Muslim politics as class politics by another name, new scholarship on Bengal has effectively deconstructed the economism of earlier thinking. It shows that economic reason functions not in terms of any abstract universal logic but in terms of culturally specific meanings, subjectivities, and indeed proper names. While I agree with this important corrective, I feel that it is not enough to culturize or localize the economic or simply to collapse the economic into politics. To do so would be to overlook the power of the modern-day separation of the economic and the political and the very real ways in which the economic comes to be operative in our times, under the sign of equality, as both ground and limit of politics.

This becomes clear when we pay attention to the language of political claim making among Muslim and Namashudra leaders in Bengal during the 1930s and 1940s. Mandal, as Sen shows, fought land dispute cases on behalf of poor tenants of Barisal; debated amendments to the Bengal Tenancy Reform Act; demanded the representation of Scheduled Castes in the official positions of cooperative officers and debt settlement officers; used classically communist jargon such as *proletariat*, *class struggle*, and *exploitation*; and advocated for *zamindari* abolition and land redistribution among landless Dalits.[19] Like Ambedkar, labor minister in the viceroy's executive council and law minister in Nehru's cabinet, Mandal was cooperatives minister in the provincial Bengal government and law and labor minister in the first Pakistan government—demonstrating a preoccupation with the economic on the part of both Dalit leaders. (Ambedkar's PhD thesis was also on economics.)

The Muslim-dominated KPP also made *zamindari* abolition its top demand, contra the upper-caste and upper-class-dominated Congress, which prioritized the release of political prisoners from colonial jails.[20] In *praja* discourse, the Islamic injunction against usury was reformulated as a rational economic principle—shared by Gandhians and communists—namely, that real wealth was generated out of the productive labor of peasants and workers and not out of speculation, usury, rent seeking, and inheritance.[21] Mahishya political militancy in southwest Bengal was also based on similar claims by Kaivarta peasants and fishermen to productivity. Not surprisingly, the famous Mahishya leader of Midnapur, Birendranath Sashmal, came to be known as "friend of the Muslims" (unlike other Bengal Congress leaders, who were explicitly upper caste and Hindu) owing to the rhetoric he shared with Muslim and Namashudra leadership, of the poor embodying the productive potential of the nation.[22]

Clearly the language of economic justice had become common currency—such that even as the Bengal peasant remained a deeply caste- and religion-marked figure, her political presence came to be thematized in terms of her economic potential. Even the question of political representation had at its heart economic reasoning. This had to do not just with governmental categories—majority, minority, Depressed Classes, Scheduled Caste, Scheduled Tribe, labor, and so forth—which mobilized demographics as it came to be thematized, post-Malthus, as an essential part of political economy and in turn inspired subaltern demands for proportionate representation in education and employment as a form of economic justice. This had also to do with the very meaning of the vote. If limited franchise gave the vote to those who earned participatory rights in the state by paying taxes, it was now argued that peasants and workers deserved the vote even more because of their greater contribution to the gross national product. In 1935 politicians debated the issue of separate electorates for both Muslims and the industrious low-caste peasants, who were socially marginalized yet economically central to the nation.[23] Thus while the Bengal peasant never emerged as a class identity, she did emerge as an indisputably economic subject—wielding, in the name of equality, a new mode of reasoning, namely, pure economic reasoning.

Economic Reason and Its Limits

The power of economic reason did not lie in its ability to produce a universal class subject, despite the ongoing romance of working-class internationalism (and socialist pan-Islamism). It lay in its three other functions: the critique of political reason, the measure of social equivalence, and the supreme diagnostic of the age of masses.

We know that equality—a liberal coinage popularized via the global circulation of the French Revolutionary slogan "Liberty, Equality, Fraternity"—appeared first as political equality, the equality of the rich and the poor in the eyes of the state. Political reason thus appeared as autonomous of and indifferent to economic reason. If the political was the domain of equality, then the economic was the domain of liberty—of the free pursuit of security and property by individuals, unconstrained by the "reason of the state." Equality had no particular purchase here, except in the minimalist sense of the "equality of opportunity." Marxism inverted this liberal arrangement. By exposing how the liberal ideal of political equality disguised and deferred the question of economic equality, Marxism showed up the limits of political reason. Marxism proposed that political form, including that of the nation, was derivative of existing economic relations. That is, while maintaining the liberal separation between the economic and the political, Marxism inverted their valence—the economic became autonomous of and prior to the political rather than vice versa. By the same logic of inversion, Marxism replaced the liberal rhetoric of equality by a powerful rhetoric of inequality.

Early Indian communists M. N. Roy and Abani Mukherjee criticized the Indian National Congress, at the height of Gandhian mass mobilization, for putting political unity before economic equality: "Non-cooperation cannot unify the nation. . . . It is bound to fail because it does not take economic laws into consideration. . . . [T]he boycott is doomed to failure, because it does not correspond, nay it is positively contrary, to the economic condition of the vast majority of the population."[24] Other Marxism-influenced writers often reiterated this politics/economics binary—stating that political sovereignty was a tired and futile idea, already "tested out in Europe fifty years ago."[25] In other words, economic reason worked by exposing the ruse and limits of pure political reason.

The power of economic reason also lay in its institution of a common measure—money in liberalism, labor time in Marxism, and number in the newly regnant discipline of statistics. Common measure rendered inequalities calculable, comparable, and thereby amenable to compensation and restitution.

The sociologist-economist Radhakamal Mukerjee, with the help of working-class students of his night school, surveyed the economic worth of diverse rural households in Bengal in ways that sought to measure and thereby render economically thinkable all aspects of everyday life. Along with listing conventional economic indices—such as area of landholding, number of plows, and distance to markets—he evaluated women's housework and other informal activities; children's contributions in selling milk, grazing cows, and catching birds; the worth of household items (jewelry, utensils and umbrellas); and even social and ritual costs.[26] Mukerjee meticulously recorded the religion and caste of each household, setting up an equivalence, via economic intermediation, across diverse social identities—a move that founded the promising though temporary Hindu-Muslim alliance in 1930s peasant politics in Bengal, without the collapse of one identity into another in the name of class.

Especially after the Bolshevik Revolution of 1917, innumerable tracts came to be published in Indian languages describing economic abjection as the common condition of diverse social groups: Muslim and Hindu peasant, untouchable, and Negro; "worker, peasant, fisherfolk, luggage carrier, coolie, boatman, sailor, ship-hand, cobbler, scavenger, cook, valet"; and indeed, women.[27] This proliferation of occupational and caste names thus worked not to disassemble the economic but to stage the economic as a mediatory moment allowing heterogeneous inequalities to be thought together. Achintya Kumar Sengupta (1903–76)—who was influenced by Marx and Freud, began his career by writing under a woman's name, and edited the infamously brash literary periodical *Kallol*—called himself a "poet of the shoe-makers, carpenters and sweepers."[28] And communists, while very much sticking to class rhetoric, organized the famous Calcutta sweepers' strike of 1928 in which, in an obvious case of caste action, women strikers threw polluting substances like human excreta at policemen.[29]

The power of economic reason also lay in its function as the supreme diagnostic of the times. The current historical moment was the epoch of *Vaishya-shakti*, the power of money or capital, wrote Upendranath Bandopadhyay in 1920. Economic criticism was necessary in pointing out that the wealth of the Vaishya derived from the backbreaking labor of workers and peasants.[30] Novelist and satirist Shibram Chakraborty said that inequality, and not Marxism, imposed economic reductionism on life and thought. Under capitalism, people were so preoccupied with economic survival that they had no time left for moral, intellectual, and aesthetic pursuits.[31] It was communism that promised a future beyond the economic. Many writers, including those who were formally academically trained (e.g., the Gandhian sociologist Nirmal Kumar Bose and civil servant and littérateur Annada Shankar Ray), now redeployed the caste label Shudra for "workers of the world" and pitted global Shudra power as a counter to regnant Vaishya power.[32]

This widespread use of the economic as diagnostic of the times signaled the rise of the masses—an immeasurable entity made conceivable by precisely the economic concept of measure. Derived from the ontology of number—an infinite series without cessation or closure—it was the unbounded mass that henceforth became the bearer of equality in the popular imagination, as opposed to the strictly defined class, the enumerated but closed community of caste/religion, and the individuated domain of national civil society. Already in the late nineteenth century, Jyotiba Phule had invented the term *bahujan* (the many) as counterpoint to the power of the *bhatji-shetji* (the Brahmin and the moneylender).[33] And in "Sanhati" (Solidarity), Rabindranath Tagore, himself a critic of cultural nationalism, accounted for the uncountable masses, the "teeming millions" of the world, in terms of their economic indispensability and power.[34]

Yet despite the indisputable power of the economic—as language of political criticism, framework of mutual recognition, and index of mass politics—a purely economic rendering of the idea of equality seemed impossible. This becomes apparent when we look at early Bengali translations of terms associated with Marxism and Leninism. The first Bengali translation of *The Communist Manifesto* (by Soumendranath Tagore, 1929) translated *communism* as *sadharan svattvabad*, or "the ideal of generalized property ownership"; the *bourgeoisie* as *parasrambhogi*, or "the consumer of others' labor"; and the *proletariat* as *atmotpanna banchita sampraday*, or "those deprived of their own produce"—clumsy neologisms all.[35] We saw earlier how Bankim translated the utopian socialist ideal of the commune as *sampatti sadharanikaran*, or property "generalization." Other contemporary translations of *communism* were *samuhavad* (collectivism), *samanadhikarbad* (equal rights), *svadhin sattvadhikarbad* (free property holding), *sarvasattvabad* (property for all), *samabayabad* (cooperativism), and *samaj samyabad* (social egalitarianism).[36]

A 1932 translation by Krishna Goswami rendered *The Communist Manifesto* as *Samyabadir Fatwa* (Egalitarian's declaration), as did a 1938 translation by Brajabihari Barman. *Class* was initially translated as *sampraday*, a term earlier used to denote religious communities or sects such as Vaishnav and Saiva, and then later became *sreni*, a term used to denote commercial and occupational guilds.[37] Rajarshi Dasgupta tells the story of how Subhas Mukhopadhyay's translation of the term *labor power* as *gatar* created great controversy in communist circles, because in Bengali the term had an intensely sensuous connotation, used colloquially for a woman's body in the context of domestic and sexual chores and was thus seen as not abstract or economic enough![38] These moments of intranslability showed up the inadequacy of the purely economic as a language of political equality.

A Spiritual Detour

Economic reason, to become adequate to the thinking of equality, thus needed to be resignified, and at times this involved a cross-referencing of the economic and the spiritual. Consider the example of two early communists. Shibram Chakraborty did not deny the spiritual antecedents of the modern idea of equality. In his polemic *Moscow Banam Pondicherry*, he invoked Buddhism and Islam against those who called communism a foreign and irreligious ideal.[39] He saw the epic battlefield of Kurukshetra and the modern battlefield of class struggle, the Bhagavad Gita and *Das Kapital* as analogous. He even called class struggle *mahati vinashti*—the "profound destruction"—that, according to the Upanishads, preceded cosmic creative action.[40] But he was also fully committed to economic reason.

Chakraborty said that spiritual discourses valorize ascetic, elite, and exemplary political selves, of the nature of the Nietzschean Übermensch.[41] Such selves can never be the subject of equality because by definition the exemplary presumes the average and the ordinary. Economic reason, on the other hand, works with quotidian selves of the poor and the uncultivated, selves that are outward-looking and expressive. Because the economic is an inherently shared condition, needing no labor of interpretation, the ordinary economic man always already recognizes himself in others and consequently pulls others into his own ambit. His political efficacy lies in this outward projection of the self rather than in any refined interiority. After all, "It is sunlight, and not the sun itself, which makes life possible on earth"![42]

The spiritual virtuoso is the one who renders others zero. The common economic self, however, is the (non)number infinity.[43] (Note the play on number and measure here.) This infinity, however, is not a metaphysical principle. It is the infinity that we experience in our immersion in the materiality of the world.[44] Spiritualists, who say that the Bolshevik mass man has only materiality and no "personality," forget that unlike in the market, in nature no two entities are ever the same.[45] Spiritualists see wealth as a function of desire and possession. They are guilty of this misconception because they believe that politics necessarily entails the sacrifice of self and property—a cruel joke on the poor who have hardly anything to sacrifice in the first place. The communist, however, knows that wealth becomes generative not in possession and accumulation but in circulation, distribution, and socialization. It is a modern economic insight that like "economic capital," "capital I-s" too must "flow unobstructed through society," Chakraborty said, playing with the double entendre of *capital* as a term, denoting productive wealth, on the one hand, and the first-person pronoun, on the other![46]

Equality thus is neither sacrifice nor exchange, as spiritualists and bourgeois liberals, respectively, would have us believe. Equality is a kiss, for in the kiss, one takes as one gives. The way to future equality, then, is not just the externality of touch, as Gandhi implied in his criticism of untouchability, but the intimacy of sexual encounters and the intermixing of blood, especially regarding the Shudra and the Muslim.[47] A highly unorthodox interpretation of economic reason, if any! Chakraborty then turned to the literary.[48] For literature, or *sahitya*, literally meaning "to be with," inspires *sahridayata* or "oneheartedness." Clearly, to Chakraborty, the mode of coming together in the face of sublime art, like coming together in erotic pleasure, was proper to the experience of equality.[49] Harking back to India's literary traditions, he said that while Brahmins wrote legal treatises, non-Brahmins like Valmiki and Vyasa (the authors of Ramayana and Mahabharata, respectively) wrote epic poetry. He exclaimed, "The creator of India is the Shudra, its natives are Shudra, this is a Shudra civilization."[50]

If Chakraborty invoked the Shudra as his preferred figure of equality, M. N. Roy invoked the Muslim. And if Chakraborty invoked the literary as metaphor of the economic, Roy invoked sociology. To Roy, Islam was the "ideology of a new social relation."[51] Equality was unknown before Islam. The great civilizations of Greece, Rome, Persia, India, and China oppressed servile classes with impunity until the first caliph, in a primitive formulation of economic reason, declared that surplus in the hands of producers inspired trade and prosperity. It was the mobile and minimalist life of the Arabs—and the attendant social virtues of hard work and piety—that made this economic insight possible at a time when only worship and war were recognized as glorious vocations. In early Islam, labor for the first time became a source of freedom.[52] Islamic equality was subsequently reforged in the equality of the battlefield. War is intimately connected to trade, Roy argued, for if commerce is about competition, then annihilation of the competitor in war is its primordial or elemental form. So, Roy claimed, warrior-like characteristics and commercial acumen were native to Arabs.[53]

In their encounter with distant lands, strange peoples, and unfamiliar customs, traders develop tolerance and sympathy, keen powers of observation, and an empirical orientation. They also acquire the power of abstraction, for "profit is an idea abstracted from concrete commodities."⁵⁴ Roy then devoted an entire chapter to Islamic rationalist philosophy, discussing Al Farabi, Al Gazzali, Ibn Rushd, Ibn Sina, and others, to demonstrate how the European Enlightenment would have been impossible without mediation by Arab theoretical acumen. He also dwelled at length on the cosmopolitan nature of Islamic empires, which gave political asylum to heretics from Christian Europe and Zoroastrian Persia. Islam permitted freedom of worship within the empire, on condition of political fidelity and economic tribute, encompassing difference within the capacious idea of one abstract God. For the same reason, Shudras and untouchables in India converted en masse to Islam in order to escape caste oppression.⁵⁵

Roy argued that Islam produced the only true monotheism of the world and that monotheism was the ideal best suited for equality. Whereas Christianity, with its Trinitarian doctrine, turned idolatrous, Islam perfected the most abstract and absolute concept of God—singular, underived, and inscrutable. Muhammad's, unlike Voltaire's, however, was not a "civil religion" in service of economic exchange and political unity. He invented the very idea of God in the most foundational sense, in that he proposed the fundamentally unthinkable principle of *creatio ab nihilo*, or creation out of nothingness. Rationalist religions—such as paganism in Greece, Hinduism in India, and eventually Christianity in Europe—could never imagine God in such perfect alterity. They remained anthropomorphic or animistic and ultimately fell back into some sort of pantheism. Pantheism saw God as pervasive of the world and therefore gave a theological overlay to "natural laws." Islam, on the other hand, being committed to the absolute otherness of God, placed him so far above the world that it opened up the "possibility of doing without him entirely."⁵⁶ Herein lay the "subversive" paradox of Islam. While being the "highest form of religion," Islamic monotheism inaugurated an age of materialism, Roy said, quoting the neo-Kantian socialist Friedrich Albert Lange. Hence Islam as a religion was not much more than a set of ordinary rules for everyday life (the parallel is obvious with Ambedkar's account of Buddhism in *The Buddha and His Dhamma*). It enjoined political sense, community sensibility, and personal virtues like cleanliness, sobriety, fasting, prayer, charity, and almsgiving. Its imagination of paradise was purely worldly, being a place of affluence and pleasure denied to most in this world. This is what makes Islam the most attractive religion for the poor and the unequal, Roy argued.⁵⁷ If only Hindus understood this, they would overcome their animosity toward Muslims.

Evidently, the positing of economic reason as proper to a politics of equality required, in early twentieth-century India, unusual retellings of the relationship between the spiritual and the economic. Neither Chakraborty nor Roy posited a clear-cut dichotomy between the two. On the contrary, in their writings the economic appears to come into its own via a detour through religion—a necessary detour that makes the economic, like the spiritual, signal the universal creaturely condition that was human life. (The Gandhian economist J. C. Kumarappa was not such an exception after all, when he proposed an economics shot through with spiritual commitment to truth and nonviolence.)[58]

Economic Reason and Sociology

Radhakamal Mukerjee, founder and member of the Lucknow school of economics and sociology, recalled that his interest in economics arose from his daily contact with poverty and squalor in the Calcutta slums. Around the time of the Swadeshi movement, long before the rise of Marxism and Leninism in India, Mukerjee and his friends embarked on a "declassing" enterprise, calling themselves "ministers of the poor" and "giving up shirts, coats and shoes."[59] Mukerjee's intellectual project was to reinvent economics, a "static science" with no sense of either "energy kinesis" or social dynamics, on an "ethosociological plane."[60] He proposed a double movement of thought—of descent into the physiognomic, biological, and environmental and of ascent into the psychological, sociological, and spiritual.[61] Accordingly, he proposed a revision of economic concepts, including well-established ones such as demand, supply, price, value, and utility. For example, disputing the theory that price was a universal measure of equivalence, Mukerjee argued that market price was but a social convention, temporarily agreed on by people for the convenience of economic exchange. Classical economics suffered from category confusion when it mistook such a popular and contingent "rule of thumb" measure as an eternal scientific principle.[62]

Mukerjee argued that economic value was determined by neither price (classical economics) nor labor (Marxist economics) but by the net result of energy expended and energy recouped in any economic activity. Progress and efficiency therefore had to do with not just productivity but also the net measure of energy use, loss, and waste. There was thus an element of justice, a calculus of repair and restoration, involved in every economic formation. Classical economics recognized only the "irreducible minimum" of human life—subsistence and need—and was blind to the question of "physiological justice," which was synonymous to "the principle of work."[63] "Arithmetical and mechanical" measures of utility, even the so-called Benthamite qualitative turn toward "pleasure and pain," failed to grasp this basic fact of economic justice.[64]

The fundamental error of classical economics lay in its imagination of the economic subject as an interest-maximizing rational individual—"chronically conscious," with only "external relations" to social life.⁶⁵ Such asocial, ceaselessly calculative beings existed nowhere in reality. Humans were driven not only by social customs but also by their unconscious as well as by the "multiplicatory and intensifying" logic of numbers, "multitude, mass, crowd and folk" being animated by the "resonance and reverberatory effects" of "sympathy, imitation, suggestion, play."⁶⁶ In any case, there was no universal human interest (or will) that was indifferent to time and place.⁶⁷ Worse still, classical economics failed to do justice even to its own fiction of the individual. Economics produced a "hypostasis of functions," disassembling the individual into "mutually exclusive and repellent fragments" via the popular concept of "factors of production"—such as "landlord-man, laborer-man, capitalist-man"—as if "the differential productivity of each factor" (land, capital, and labor à la Ricardo) could be neatly separated and precisely measured, without any reference to each other. In real life, however, humans always functioned as "mixed" economic subjects, such as "artisan-cultivator or landlord-capitalist."⁶⁸

Mukerjee proposed an alternative wage theory. Fair wage was determined by five factors, he said: one, the energy use, waste, and recovery involved in the transformation of matter (contra the "productivity theory of wages"); two, the optimal recoupment of labor power (contra the "subsistence theory of wages"); three, socially mediated demand and supply of labor, involving "custom, interest, need, expectation, desire" and not just abstract market mechanisms; four, "social and regional values" that ascribe differential worth to different kinds of labor (an obvious reference to caste); and five, a measure of "cooperative productivity." Classical economics denied the basic fact that wage, rent, and profit contained "apart from the share due to specific productivity of individual agents and factors, certain elements which they claim in virtue of being partners in a joint concern." Wages therefore must index not only individual need and productivity but also the "scale and structure" of cooperation, in which each member is taken as "equal and interchangeable" with others. In other words, the "restoration of land, labor and capital as a whole" cannot be founded on "the classical version of individual justice" but on "a new scheme of socialistic justice."⁶⁹

Mukerjee declared that "communalism" was the universal economic form of the future.⁷⁰ The resonance with communism is obvious. Mukerjee drew "lessons from nature"—from examples of "accumulation" of water and food by desert species and of "interspecies cooperation."⁷¹ Humanity, too, was evolving toward this universal end. In early stages, communalism was mechanical and instinctive, as among herds and swarms. In the second stage, that of slavery and serfdom, communalism took the form of "polymorphism," such as among bees and ants, demonstrating elaborate specialization, zero competition, a thwarting of class struggle, and complete suppression of individuality. In the third stage, a medieval "particulate system" came into existence, involving semi-independent guilds and corporations, loosely owing allegiance to a sovereign. The fourth stage was of absolutism and centralism, resulting in a dialectic between statism and militant-competitive individualism, causing "anarchism, class struggle, sex strife and incessant strikes." Contemporary capitalism, with its monopolies and cartels, and state socialism both exemplified this current moment. The future and final stage would be "communalism," when central command would become redundant and humans would work on the principle of immanent and voluntary social cooperation. Contemporary socialism and communism, despite their current state-centricity, intimated this imminent future.[72]

As must be obvious, Mukerjee's critique of classical economics was not of universalism as such but of its antisocial assumptions. He believed that economics was indeed universally grounded in "energetics" and "vitalities," but he insisted that vital life processes acquired distinct "value patterns" in different regions of the world. A meticulous comparison of "regional" economic formations was therefore essential, which would show up homologies, but not homogeneity, of global life-forms.[73] An unthinking imposition of foreign economic principles on a society was therefore both economically unsound and politically unjust. Even the seemingly universal socialist principle—of the eight-hour workday—did not apply to humid, tropical contexts such as India, where longer work hours, with intermittent rest periods, and a steady rather than intense pace of work was more worker friendly.[74] Similarly, private property rights on land, as introduced in Bengal by the Permanent Settlement, were a foreign principle derived from Roman demesne law and led to grave distortions in Indian economy, causing ceaseless state intervention in rural life via the litigation work of civil courts.[75]

Dhurjati Prasad Mukerjee—a younger member of the Lucknow school and a maverick thinker who called himself a "Marxologist" (rather than an ideologically committed Marxist)[76]—wrote a short outline of the history of value.[77] In political economy, he began, value was initially imagined as both use value and exchange value. But the concept of use, in the absence of any sensitivity toward concrete life-forms, soon became unthinkable. It became mere "datum" and was "politely dismissed" from the academy. Only exchange value remained conceivable as an economic fact because it could be measured numerically as price. Price, an unstable and free-floating abstraction, was subsequently rationalized by tying it to the concept of utility. Economists then invented a "psychological law" to accompany the abstract concept of utility, by forging the "marvelous" tool of the "margin" and of utility's diminishing returns. But the old problem returned. Margin—the limit beyond which value addition slowed down or turned negative—could be measured no better than could the earlier concepts of need or use. And yet, the concept of marginality was not discarded. Economists merely replaced cardinal analysis by ordinal analysis, as relative ranking of commodity values with respect to each other began to substitute all imaginations of value as a quality inherent in things and people. The result: a "general equilibrium theory," a self-referential framework in which markets interacted with each other via pricing mechanisms, without any reference whatsoever to people and their lives. Economic thinking now took to hypermathematization and "cold conceptualization" and produced a division between economy and society that became impossible to breach, either conceptually or practically.[78]

Dhurjati Prasad Mukerjee's stake lay in a sociological rendering of economic categories. Class, he said, was a sociological category, which included "the economic concept of surplus value"; the political aspect of "movement through conflict"; the philosophical aspect of dialectical thinking; and the interpersonal aspect of "social distance," the affective and psychological way in which social division, be it class or caste, was articulated in real life.[79] His remarkable Bengali essay "Amra o Tahara" (Us and them) set up a conversation between a bookish middle-class intellectual and a group of nine-to-five clerks (Mukerjee stated that pretending to dialogue with the working classes was an unforgivable conceit). The purpose was to try to imagine the everyday ways in which economic division, between thinkers and workers, came to be expressed in society. A fascinating exercise, showing up moments of utter transparency as well as funny misrecognitions, this dialogue dwelled on a range of topics—from music and literature to conflict and revolution. Responding to petty clerks who claimed that the "masses" were inherently revolutionary, Mukherjee said that revolution was a middle-class obsession. Peasants wanted bigger land; workers wanted better wages, better working hours, and dignity in the workplace. In other words, economic reason was a mass sensibility, while politics was an intellectual orientation![80] No wonder the communist leader P. C. Joshi took the work of the Mukerjees seriously, even though neither could strictly be called a Marxist.[81]

Economic Reason and the Literary

Most of Dhurjati Prasad Mukerjee's Bengali writings were on art, literature, and music, while his English writings were more discipline-based. He ended his Bengali essay "The Sorry State of Economics" with an appeal—that the essay never be translated into English.[82] Clearly, he saw his native tongue as a language of candor, allowing a certain literary affordance to his critique (he in fact believed that societies had "personalities," thus ascribing a literary aspect to a social scientific category).[83] Mukerjee also wrote a trilogy—*Antashila* (The flow within), *Abarta* (Whirlpool), and *Mohana* (Delta), novels referencing the journeying of rivers—in which the hero, an introspective and intellectualized middle-class man, moves from failed domesticity to spirituality and eventually, in a moment of final resolution, to working-class politics in Kanpur.[84] Radhakamal Mukerjee also saw it fit to write of poverty and inequality in the genres of novels and plays. His novel *Sasvata Bhikhari* (The eternal beggar) echoed Tolstoy's "back to the people" slogan, *Nidrita Narayan* (The sleeping god) provided an account of slum children, and *Manimekhala* depicted the goddess Parvati impersonating a temple dancer and taking on her poverty and disease.[85]

At one place in "Amra o Tahara," Dhurjati Prasad Mukerjee asks, whether women can be considered part of the "masses." He continues: "Women's work does not cease even at home—cooking, looking after children. . . . The condition of today's women is worse than that of medieval slave women."[86] This off-the-cuff statement gives us a clue to the literary resignification of the economic in Bengal in the early through middle twentieth century. It seems to me that women's lives and labor were critical to the overwriting of economics in ways that exceeded politics and signified the problem of life as such, as is apparent in the work of the most well-known communist writer of the times, Manik Bandopadhyay (1908–56). Dhurjati Prasad Mukerjee, incidentally, was one of the first to review this upcoming novelist. Curiously, he found Bandopadhyay's writing somewhat "feminine," a counterintuitive reading, if any, of self-consciously male, revolutionary, "realist" prose.[87]

Most relevant for our purposes is Bandopadhyay's novel *Janani* (Mother; 1935). Like all communists of his time, Manik had read and been inspired by the novel *Mother* by Maxim Gorky.[88] And yet nothing could be as different from *Mother* as *Janani*. Gorky's novel presents the story of a woman, with an alcoholic husband, who brings up her son to be a revolutionary and joins him in his political work. Bandopadhyay's Shyama, too, has a failure of a husband who, when he cannot provide for his family, runs away for days at a time and begs, borrows, and steals, dragging his family down with him. Shyama brings up her children on her own, with ad hoc help from relatives and neighbors. She is obsessed with money and breathless with household chores, care work, and renovating her house over and over again. She saves and scrounges, keeps a close watch on property and inheritance, jealously eyes the wealth of relatives and friends, rents out rooms, and engages in incessant petty politics around debts and charities, all for the future of her children. At one point, ironically, her husband, now ill and at home, accuses her of being petty, miserly, and money-minded. Despite all her efforts, however, Shyama ends up losing her house and living on the charity of, first, a relative and then her own son, who eventually has to leave his studies to take up a petty clerk's job, breaking Shyama's heart.[89]

Bandopadhyay's *Janani* is the story of a woman driven by a highly personalized economic logic and embodying its ultimate collapse. An overly rational, calculative, managerial woman, Shyama ends up on the verge of madness when all her schemes fail. She eventually lapses into a tragic muteness in a final failure of motherhood. The narrative unfolds as a series of domestic situations, in a way not quite expected from a revolutionary author. Yet even as the story is indisputably a woman's story, wherein tedious domestic details seem to tire out readers as much as the characters, the real protagonist here is the economy as such, as it unfolds in everyday, intimate life.

Bandopadhyay makes explicit the impossible economy of women's lives and labor in an eerie short story titled "The Hand." The story's main character, Mahamaya, has beautiful, strong hands, even though her body has shriveled from a childhood mishap. Her hands, however, have taken on a life of their own—they work ceaselessly. When they don't find work, they destroy—tearing up saris, uprooting saplings, even hurting others. Mahamaya worries that some night her hands might even strangle her sleeping husband. Mahamaya finally cuts off her hands on a paper-cutting machine—screaming that she wants to live but without her hands.[90] Incidentally, both Shyama and Mahamaya are other names for Kali. One wonders if Bandopadhyay makes a deliberate ironic move in his choice of names for these hyperactive, industrious, yet lost economic subjects. He might have, given that in his most famous novel, *Boatman of the River Padma*, he calls his impoverished fisherman hero Kuber, after the god of wealth!

In a remarkable series of short stories on the topic of wives, Bandopadhyay creates a strange mirroring of men's and women's work, with women's work acting as a mode of exposure of men's professional and economic reason. The wife in "The Shopkeeper's Wife" amplifies her husband's commercial instinct to such an impossible extent that she ends up hoarding her husband's hard-earned capital, leading to a collapse of his business.[91] The wife in "The Clerk's

Wife" takes on her husband's disempowerment at his workplace and becomes a pathologically obedient and disciplined subject—fearing even to step out onto the terrace of their home without permission.[92] And the wife in "The Littérateur's Wife" tries to literally enact the lives of her husband's women protagonists, demanding from the writer such perfect fidelity to his own fiction that he eventually stops writing![93]

I am not suggesting that Bandopadhyay deliberately intends to use women's work as a strategy to overwrite conventional economic logic. But there is no denying that women's lives become, in his writing, a crucial site for staging the dramatic aporia of pure economic reason. Bandopadhyay's reflections on his own vocation are critical in this regard. Like many other communists of his time, Bandopadhyay imagined an equivalence across factory labor, intellectual and artistic labor, agrarian labor, untouchable degraded labor, and women's work— in effect denaturalizing the "division of labor" and "comparative advantage" arguments that undergirded classical economics, on the one hand, and shored up modern justifications of caste and gender inequalities, on the other. Writing literature is not an act of genius, Bandopadhyay said; it is labor, like any other form of labor.[94] Those who say that writers should never write for money and that art should be for art's sake are bluffing. It is like saying that wageworkers are complicit in capitalist profiteering simply because they accept wages. Littérateurs selling their labor in the market do not necessarily compromise their art—for what is the market, after all, if not the reading public? The masses, it is true, are used to sentimental literature. But isn't it the communist writer's calling to revolutionize popular taste, a political task no different from the economic task of creating a new market for new commodities?[95]

In the context of modern Britain, Mary Poovey argues that the rise of political economy as a genre of writing, independent of and different from fiction, rested on a conceptual distinction between economic value, which could be priced, and aesthetic value, which was priceless, invaluable, and eternal.[96] Bandopadhyay argues precisely against this division of values when he pitches artistic labor as just another kind of labor, with its inherent economic logic bolstering, rather than undercutting, its political and aesthetic logics. In the powerful short story "Shilpi" (Artist), Bandopadhyay depicts weavers striking work because cloth traders are supplying cheap thread for the mass manufacture of low-cost *gamchhas* (towels). Madan leads the strike, because he is an artist, who would never weave anything less than elegant saris. Weavers are starving; looms are silent; Madan's famished, pregnant wife is on the verge of collapse; and his mother pleads and prays for him to resume work. But Madan is a proud artist. Despite being a low-caste Tanti, he would not weave low-quality textiles. Nor would he touch the feet of the Brahmin middleman, even when the latter tries to cajole him into resuming work, massaging Madan's aching feet in an embarrassing reversal of caste roles. At the end, Madan is heard running his loom deep in the night. Neighbors fear that he has broken the strike. But Madan has taken to running an empty loom. His body aches without work, he says. Everyone feels vindicated. After all, "the day Madan weaves a *gamchha*, the sun will rise in the west."[97]

And yet Bandopadhyay does make a slip, inadvertently calling the activity of writing *sadhana* (and not merely *sram* or labor). *Sadhana*, a classical Indian term, has the double connotation of disciplined work and spiritual self-cultivation.[98] Women's household work has a similar double valence, denoting both disciplined industry and committed service and care—which is perhaps why Bandopadhyay repeatedly falls back into a depiction of women's household labor so as to stage the economic as a kind of "artfulness," involving sentiment, affection, contingency, failure, and above all, human relationships, a far cry from the economic as an abstract measure of equivalence.

Sabitri Roy's 1950s novel on the Tebhaga movement—*Paka Dhaner Gan* (The song of the ripened paddy), translated into English as *Harvest Song*—does the same.[99] A communist dissident whose novel *Swaralipi* was censored by the Communist Party, Roy chooses in this narrative to move around economic issues: agriculture, landlordism, forced labor, the grain market, speculation, black marketing, famine, war finance, industrial wages, strikes, prices, and unemployment; the vagaries of diverse professions such as spinning, weaving, basket-making, nursing, schoolteaching, singing, performing, and begging; and, most important, household work. Yet these issues pan out via women's lives, casting global and national economic forces into personal and intimate ones. When the low-caste, college-educated peasant leader Partha Das presents a copy of Gorky's *Mother* to Debaki, an overworked, abandoned young wife in the village, he thinks to himself:

> She was the one to whom he wanted to reach out, *because she was the world.* Her sorrows, her poverty, her privations were what the great world suffered too. He saw her everywhere.
>
> The ground seemed to turn to stone with cold. A Muslim household was frying *dal* nearby—the strong smell wafted through the air.[100]

The communist leader experiences the economic subject as embodied in the common, domesticated woman and as materialized through kitchen smells. Partha feels that ringing through the world is "a great choral harmony of suffering, sung only in women's voices."[101]

At the end of the novel a conversation is staged around the kitchen stove. The men urge the women to give up household chores. Women are meant for revolutionary tasks, they say. The women insist that there is something both necessary and ethical involved in domestic work, so widely denigrated in radical circles because no value or price is put on it in the formal discourse of economics.[102] But domestic work is a way of owning up to the wider world, owning up to apparently impersonal global forces. Women's lives thus end up becoming a restatement of public economic reason.

Conclusion

We often believe that the economic and the spiritual are antagonistic imperatives, the former attending to number and measure, the latter to the incalculable and immeasurable aspects of life. With respect to equality as a political idea, however, the economic and the spiritual, I have tried to show, always already appear locked in a dialectic without resolution. The economic and the spiritual both seek to index the shared, if not universal, creaturely predicament of humans in the world. Both dwell on presocial aspects of human life in its animality, mortality, desire, and intimacy, wherein humans reappear as a species being rather than divided by names and identities. Or, as in the case of literary overwriting of economics, humans appear as women. Most important, the spiritual and the economic both claim to continue their transformative work before the institution and after the abeyance of politics, in personal, domestic, intimate, and inner spaces. In other words, both claim to be extrapolitical forces that simultaneously drive and delimit the political—catapulting the very idea of equality itself to a register beyond politics, even as politics necessarily carries on in its name. Perhaps one can then say that equality never really becomes a political idea, let alone a norm and ideology, even though it operates as a frame of reference within which politics becomes legible and cognizable in the first place.

Part IV

People

7

People as Party

> Every party is totalitarian, potentially and by aspiration. If one party is not actually totalitarian, it is simply because those parties that surround it are no less so.
> —Simone Weil, *On the Abolition of Political Parties*

The word *party* derives from the common term *part*. As Giovanni Sartori reminds us in his classic textbook of political science, the party simply denotes part of a whole, a subgroup within a larger group, such as Whigs and Tories in the early modern British Parliament or Girondins and Montagnards in the post-revolution French National Assembly.[1] This chapter, however, presents a somewhat different story of the party from the perspective of colonial India, which helps us rethink this conventional part/whole imagination of the political party.

Modern politics is defined as the exercise of popular will, as opposed to the exercise of virtuosity in public life as in classical times. Yet there is really nothing called the people. There are monads and communities, classes and identities, friends and enemies, strangers and neighbors—but no one people as such. In other words, there is nothing called the people until a people is named into being. In modern times, the people has had various names—humanity, nation, *Volk*, crowd, mob, public, mass, proletariat, and multitude. Of these, the nation, perpetually crisis-ridden as it is, has been perhaps the most stable, simply because the nation came to be concretized as a state form (as opposed to, say, the proletariat or the mass, which never really produced adequate institutional complexes except as utopias like "dictatorship of the proletariat" or "direct democracy").

We now know a great deal about how the people came to be staged as the nation in modern times, in terms of both an imaginary and a governmental apparatus. The story of the political party, however, is a relatively unthought aspect of that narrative. I propose in this chapter that while the nation claims to be a natural or organic mode of being of the people, in actuality the nation has had to be staged rather laboriously, via the party form, even before it could be materialized as the nation-state. In fact, the political party has been the primary mode of staging the people in modern times, the term *staging* here implying the sense of artifice and assemblage involved in aesthetic production.

Antonio Gramsci famously called the political party the "modern prince" who "neither rules nor governs" but is still the "de facto power" of our times. Gramsci believed that the political party assumed hegemonic power in the twentieth century by simulating a "reabsorption of political society into civil society"—that is, by standing simultaneously for the state and the people.[2] We miss out on this aspect of the modern political when we restrict our reading of the nation form, as historians tend to do, to the story of either ascendant culturalism or governmentalization of society. But we also do so when we reduce the political party, as political scientists tend to do, to merely a technique or instrument of state making, simply a shadow or a double of the modern state.

The history of the party is a history of staging the people as a "mass," as opposed to other modes of being of the people, like assembly, population, crowd, or multitude. Here I tease out this story from the larger story of anticolonialism in India, which was also the fraught story of making a nation out of incommensurable identities and mobilizations. I set up a contrast between the Indian National Congress and the Communist Party of India in their formative years. Though not the only parties in colonial India, these two were paradigmatic formations in that they embodied two opposing principles. While the Congress sought to encompass the people as a whole in its very structure, the communists saw themselves as a vanguard leading the people from the front. Each claimed to speak for the people as a whole and called the other sectarian. And yet each appeared bound in an inextricable relationship of desire and intimacy with the other. I believe that it is in this complicated relationship between the two party forms, the mass and the vanguard, that the paradox of people comes through with some clarity—the paradox being that the people is that which always already tends toward a whole (e.g., the nation, the Communist International, humanity) and yet is thinkable only in the form of a part (e.g., a class or a caste).

When our story begins, people in India appeared thinkable in three possible forms. In the face of colonial demographics—census, surveys, and the codification of civil laws—the people appeared as enumerated populations of castes, tribes, and communities. In this mode, the people were disaggregated, for purposes of not just administration but also political mobilization and combination—hence the ubiquity of caste and denominational associations in India at this time.[3] The people also appeared as a crowd, a fortuitous and random form of "egalitarian discharge"[4]—in peasant insurgencies, in Hindu-Muslim riots, in urban marches, and indeed, in theaters, causing the colonial state to pass the censorious Dramatic Performances Act in 1876. In this form the people appeared volatile, unpredictable, dangerous, even totalitarian.[5] Finally, people appeared as society, the national mode of being of a people, as in Indian society, French society, and so on. In this form, the people were anything but a whole, divided as they were among classes, castes, genders, and ethnicities. The rise of the political party, I argue, was a tedious process of working through these three modes of being of the people—population, crowd, and society—in order to produce a "mass," an infinite and unbounded form of the people, which could become a quintessentially modern political community.[6]

Party and Association

The Indian National Congress was set up in 1885 not as a political party but as an association. The 1887 Congress session received delegates and messages from vastly incommensurate bodies—the Indian Association, chambers of commerce, Arya Samaj, the Mombadevi Oriental Society, Anjumani Reayah, the Society for the Prevention of Crime, the Mohammedan Association, Sunbeam Library and Reading Room, the Working Men's Club, and, indeed, caste and occupational guilds—producing a rather amorphous assembly.[7] The constitution of 1899 formalized this omnibus form by proposing that Congress delegates be elected by "political associations" and "public meetings."[8] The 1908 constitution further specified the "component parts" of the party as members of the Congress; Congress committees at provincial, district, and *taluka* levels; "associations affiliated with" Congress committees at each level; and any "political association or public body of more than three years' standing" that accepted in its general body the objective of the Congress (which at this time was achieving by constitutional means the status of a self-governing member of the empire).[9] The Congress, in other words, was to be "an association of associations."

At this point, one must distinguish between the associational form and the party form. An association, however large and inclusive, always implies an outside, a set of those who do not belong to that association. The modern-day political party, on the other hand, however small, aspires to stand in for the people as a whole, for in a modern political party there is no one who is not a potential member. This is true even for parties that represent specific social constituencies. Thus the Communist Party claims to be a party of the working classes, but it posits the working class not as a specific socioeconomic group but as a universal class that conceptually stands in for the people as a whole. (One wonders how we might have to revise Jürgen Habermas's conception of the modern public sphere, if we take the party form rather than the associational form as central to political society.)

The conception of the Indian National Congress as an association of associations continued to animate the party's career for a long time, with rather paradoxical results. The paradox was as follows: in trying to encompass all possible associations with no remainder and become coterminous to the nation, the Congress expanded exponentially and became stretched to its limits by all sorts of groups demanding accommodation. By the same logic, however, it also mutated into a mass political party, canceling out its claim to be an association of associations. Poised to take over the Congress, Gandhi stated in 1920 that he did not consider it to be a party at all. The Congress "contained" all parties, and even though one party or the other might exercise dominance over the Congress for a time, that did not quite make the Congress a party. Gandhi released his manifesto to counter Bal Ganghadar Tilak's proposal for setting up a Congress Democratic Party within the Indian National Congress.[10] Yet it was Gandhi himself who took the lead in revising the constitution in the same year—introducing for the first time a four-anna individual membership, open to everyone over twenty-one years of age, thus undoing its erstwhile associational structure and turning the Congress into a recognizable political party with mass subscription.[11]

The noncooperation movement of 1920–22, by far the most widespread and intense mass movement that the Congress had ever led, was undertaken by this reconstituted Congress. The example of Bengal illustrates how in the course of the movement the Congress burgeoned, often in unintended ways, through the two contrary impulses of association and massification. The 1920 constitution incorporated Bengal for the first time into a countrywide network of regional language-based Provincial Congress Committees (PCCs). This was also when the All India Congress Committee (AICC) and its executive wing, the Congress Working Committee (CWC), were set up, to supervise PCCs, which in turn were to supervise Congress committees at district and *taluka* levels. Lower-level committees elected members to upper-level committees. It was thus that the Congress simulated being both a nation and a (shadow) state—its linguistic configuration indexed its being as a "nation of nations" (with the motto of "unity in diversity") and its internal electoral structuring indexed its being a representative government (contra the colonial bureaucratic state). The PCCs also had the freedom to devise their own constitutions and affiliate with any non-Congress association that shared the Congress creed of "swaraj by peaceful and legitimate means," while also encouraging preexisting organizations to dissolve into the Congress.

During noncooperation, this formal network of Congress committees (and its nodal assembly points like nationalist schools, *charkha* ashrams, and village *samitis*) came to be superimposed on a great diversity of preexisting political, social, and religious organizations. There was the All Bengal Khilafat Committee at the head of the movement, formed in protest against the dismantling of the caliphate by the Allied powers after the First World War, which aligned with the Congress but remained distinct in both constituency and idiom. Then there were the Sufi institutions of Furfura and Faridpur; the Deoband theological school; the Anjuman-i-Ulema-i-Bangla, which produced important nationalist theologians like Maniruzzaman Islamabadi and Muhammad Akram Khan; the New Mohammedan Revolutionary Party of Bengal, started by Maulana Abul Kalam Azad, who later joined the Congress and eventually became the first education minister of independent India; the Wahabis, led by Abdullahel Banqui of Dinajpur; revolutionary secret societies like Anushilan Samiti and Jugantar, whose members came above ground as noncooperation activists; the Swadesh Bandhab Samiti of Ashwini Dutt of Barisal, the rural units of Surendranath Banerjee's Indian Association; and so on.[12] While these organizations worked with and as the Congress in 1920–21, their distinctiveness as Muslim networks, revolutionary groups, and social work institutions resurfaced soon after the movement was called off.

Gandhi withdrew the noncooperation movement after the 1922 incident of mob violence against the police at Chauri Chaura. An intense debate ensued in the Congress between "no-changers" and "pro-changers," supporters and detractors of Gandhi, respectively, about two things: what to do with the masses who had shown themselves to be volatile and violent, and what to do with organized political dissent within the party. The Civil Disobedience Enquiry Committee reported that the country was not yet ready for mass civil disobedience because the masses had not yet internalized the truth-seeking and nonviolent spirit of *satyagraha*. The committee proposed that civil disobedience be henceforth allowed only in exceptional circumstances and in the form of "limited mass civil disobedience" (i.e., breaking a particular law, not all laws, or nonpayment of particular taxes, like the *chowkidari* tax in Bengal, not all taxes). Or it had to be "individual civil disobedience." Provincial Congress Committees could organize limited disobedience, under guarantee of nonviolence and on their own responsibility, without involving the central bodies of the Congress.[13] The AICC split a lot of hairs in trying to distinguish mass and non-mass civil disobedience. Thus, "a prohibited public meeting where admission is regulated by tickets and to which no unauthorised admission is allowed is an instance of individual civil disobedience, whereas a prohibited public meeting to which the general public is admitted without any restriction is an instance of mass civil disobedience. Such a civil disobedience is defensive, when a prohibited public meeting is held for conducting a normal activity, although it might result in arrest. It would be aggressive if it is held not for any normal activity but for arrest and imprisonment."[14] What was really being debated here was whether and how far the masses could be structured and stabilized into the party form and prevented from turning into a crowd or a mob.

In the heavily charged AICC meeting of November 1922, some members proposed the oxymoronic form of "mass-scale individual civil disobedience," which simulated the scale of mass action without actually generating a mass. Gandhi, for his part, had turned to "social reconstruction" activities after "betrayal" by the masses at Chauri Chaura. Others, however, insisted that social reconstruction also had a mass aspect. Activities such as the boycott of foreign cloth, the promotion of spinning, and the prohibition of alcohol called for picketing within the "constructive" rather than the protest paradigm. Some felt that picketing was a good rehearsal for future civil disobedience; others thought that it was not a "civil" enough action and might cause mass disorder, and that nonpayment of taxes was a relatively safer form of mass activity, though that too could tip over into nonpayment of rent (to Indian landlords), leading to peasant rebellion and a breaking up of national unity. Sarojini Naidu argued, against others like J. M. Sengupta of the Bengal Provincial Congress Committee (BPCC), that noncooperation was not really suitable as a "prolonged battle for the masses" and should be rethought as a form of minority exemplary or vanguard action.[15]

On the other side were those like C. R. Das, J. M. Sengupta, and Motilal Nehru who argued that participating in the election of colonial legislative bodies, so far boycotted by the Congress as part of general noncooperation, could become an alternative mass strategy. V. J. Patel, a member of the Civil Disobedience Enquiry Committee, said that noncooperation by an elected representative was equivalent to noncooperation by twenty thousand agitators in the street, despite limited franchise.[16] Representation harnessed mass energy in economical ways, without inciting mass disorder. But the debate between "council entry" and "social reconstruction," that is, between Das and Gandhi, could not be easily resolved. C. R. Das resigned, and the BPCC threatened to secede from the Congress. After lengthy negotiations, a deal was struck. Das and friends formed a separate political party called the Swarajya Party for electioneering purposes. In return, they accepted Gandhi's proposal to change Congress membership from the annual payment of a subscription fee—a typical mass form—to an annual spinning of two thousand yards of cloth by each member.[17] The Swarajya Party was to be a party "within and integral" to the Congress, and its creed the same as the latter's creed of nonviolent noncooperation. But its membership was eight annas annually, double the Congress subscription, because it was not to be a mass party. It was to be run by a general council consisting of all members of the party in the central legislative assembly, one-sixth of party members in each provincial council, and one-fourth of Swarajist members of the AICC elected by Swarajya Party members in each province from among themselves.[18]

This complex constitution of the Swarajya Party was meant to ensure that it was both inside and outside, regulated by and yet autonomous from the Congress. In its election manifesto, the party called itself a "department" of the Congress. But it also stated that non-Congress individuals, who adhered to "swaraj by peaceful means" but not to "noncooperation" as a political principle, could join the "Council section of the Party [Congress] without identifying with the noncooperators outside the Council." That is, they could be Swarajya Party members without being Congress members.[19] The Swarajya Party forged a Hindu-Muslim pact on its own and formulated an independent Asiatic and foreign affairs policy, but it also promised to undertake a drive to increase Congress membership.[20] In the long run, there would be much dispute over the ways in which the Swarajya Party, especially Bengal leaders like Sarat Bose, Subhas Bose, and Bidhan Chandra Roy, forged unregulated "coalitions" with non-Congress elements, of both the Left and the Right.[21]

Agitation and representation stage the masses differently. Agitation mobilizes the masses as one body, tending toward becoming a crowd. Representation mobilizes the masses as serialized—based on the disaggregative formula of one person, one vote—tending toward becoming a population. To resolve the antinomy between representation and agitation, the Congress reconstituted itself, by virtue of its preexisting associational form, as two parties in one, the *satyagrahi* party and the Swarajya Party, defying the standard typological division between parties of movement and parties of representation. Henceforth, despite its adherence to the principle of noncooperation, the Congress would participate in elections to colonial bodies—first through the Swarajya Party, then through an autonomous parliamentary board, and eventually as a mass party itself. In addition to Gandhi's yarn franchise, which was meant to stabilize a potentially volatile crowd through the discipline of patient labor, representational politics helped Congress, or so it was hoped, achieve a mean—a point of equilibrium where the masses remained poised, between being a crowd and becoming simply a demographic fact.

Party and Society

In his pioneering work on the party system in India, Rajni Kothari argued that political parties in India did not quite conform to Max Weber's narrative of the universal evolution of the party form from aristocratic cliques to organizations of notables to modern mass parties. In India, the anticolonial imperative required the Congress to present a mass face from the very beginning.[22] Writing in 1893 from Baroda, Aurobindo Ghosh exhorted the Congress—still an association of western-educated, upper-caste, upper-class males, petitioning for their fair share in colonial education and bureaucracy—to shun the British model of party politics (marked by elite networks, elections, and dry proceduralism) and adopt the French (marked apparently by the *élan vital* of people in assembly).[23] Even in the earliest years, annual Congress meetings adopted techniques of mass mobilization, with delegates chosen by show of hands and voice vote in public meetings. In 1887, the Madras presidency saw the circulation of a Tamil "Congress catechism" for the purpose of enlightening ordinary people about the party form.[24] Bernard Bate describes how oratory in mass meetings accompanied Congress sessions, decades before the onset of mass politics in the 1920s.[25] The 1888 Congress session at Allahabad had as delegates, alongside the usual lawyers, journalists, bankers, landlords and traders, commoners like "102 inferior landholders, 17 peasants, 2 artisans, 7 shopkeepers."[26]

To present itself as coterminous with the nation, thus, the Congress was compelled from the beginning to exceed the classical party form—of being a part of the whole. Instead, it sought to be the whole. For that purpose it became an all-encompassing "association of associations," such that even dissenting and opposing parties could be kept inside rather than expelled. This resulted in what Kothari called the "Congress system"—with dominant parties and opposition parties both functioning within the Congress or at least within the general zone of efficacy of the Congress. I, however, differ with Kothari's picture in two ways. I believe that the mass party principle and the association of associations principle could and did function in antagonistic ways, as evident in the intense debates around mass participation in the 1920s. I also believe that Kothari reads too neat a correspondence between parties within the Congress and the social constituencies they claimed to represent—proposing a picture of the Congress as being able to accommodate all contrary social forces within itself, as if mirroring without surplus the Indian nation as a whole.[27]

But then staging the people as a party could never be a direct translation of the nation's social map into the party's political form, because the party was predicated on an intense struggle with the mode of being of people as society. One of the earliest organizational moves of the Congress was the institution of a strict separation between itself and the Indian National Social Conference. The Social Conference, initially operating at the same time and out of the same venue as the Congress, was a forum for the discussion of social reform issues. It was started in 1887, two years after the Congress was set up, under pressure from those who felt that political freedom had no meaning without the social and economic emancipation of common people, particularly women and low castes. The conference set up subcommittees to deal with different kinds of social disadvantages and even considered a system of social sanctions to enforce adherence. However, the Congress was to formally remain uninvolved in these social deliberations, being an exclusively political forum,[28] unaffected by what P. Ananda Charlu called in the 1891 Nagpur session the "inseparable accidents" of social customs and sexual and commensality norms.[29]

It seemed as if a sociologically fractured people could become a single whole only when its purely political form could be distilled out of diverse social modes of being. The party was meant to be that purely political form. But this separation between the social and the political was a greatly contentious process. The debate was heated, and those who felt that criticism of Indian society and custom went against political consolidation of the people as a nation eventually won out. In his long evidentiary essay of 1945 titled *What Congress and Gandhi Have Done to the Untouchables*, Ambedkar remembered how in the 1895 Poona Congress, the "anti–Social Reform Party," led by the ultranationalist Tilak, threatened to burn down the Congress venue if the Social Conference was held there![30]

And yet, from the early years, decades before the rise of the "two-nations theory" leading to the India-Pakistan partition of 1947, the Congress acknowledged religious-communitarian identities as politically salient. A resolution, passed as early as 1888 and carried over into the 1908 and the 1920 Congress constitutions, clearly stated that no subject would be discussed at any Congress meeting to which "the Hindu or Mahommedan Delegates, as a body, objected by a majority of three-fourth of their number."[31] This was not because religious-communitarian issues were social issues and so outside the purview of the Congress, but because Hindus and Muslims were nations by default, whose integrity as a political form was a priori assumed. Much later, in the 1930s, discussions in the AICC explicitly acknowledged that the religion question was really a national question.[32] And when the Congress called "all-party meetings," religious organizations—and not just the two big ones, namely, the Muslim League and the Hindu Mahasabha—were always invited in significant numbers. Unlike caste or gender, therefore, religious identity was seen as amenable to the party form.

Ambedkar criticized this conception of the political party, which treated the political salience of caste and religion unequally. We know that Ambedkar was stopped from reading out his "Annihilation of Caste" speech to the Jatpat Todak Mandal (a social reform organization against the caste system based in Lahore) not because he criticized caste but because in criticizing caste he criticized the Hindu religion. It seemed that caste and religion could not be put in the same framework of analysis.[33] In his rebuttal of Ambedkar, Gandhi insisted that while untouchability was a social practice that must be abolished, Hinduism was an inalienable constituent of the people.[34] Gandhi, we know, also disagreed with religious conversion on the grounds that the religion one was born into was one's destiny, much like the nation one was born into.[35]

The Round Table Conferences held in London for the purpose of discussing the future constitution of India, however, acknowledged the Depressed Classes as a separate "party," which had the right to participate on its own terms in the making of the constitution, alongside the Muslim League and the Congress. But despite Ambedkar's presence in the second Round Table Conference of 1931, Gandhi insisted that he would represent untouchables, in his own person and as Congressman, undercutting Ambedkar's claim that Dalits were a separate political party requiring separate representation.[36] The face-off between Gandhi and Ambedkar in the minorities committee as well as in the federal structure committee of the Round Table Conference is well known. Gandhi made it clear that while separate electorates for religious communities were acceptable, it was not so for the Depressed Classes. He negotiated the "minority question" in conversation exclusively with Hindu, Muslim, and Sikh representatives, cutting off Ambedkar from the discussions and effectively denying that untouchables were a minority too. When the British eventually offered separate electorates for the Depressed Classes—putting them on a par with religious minorities—Gandhi started a fast unto death, forcing Ambedkar to back off under tremendous emotional pressure.

Gandhi's argument was that unlike Hindus, Muslims and Sikhs, untouchables were not a political entity. They lacked political consciousness and organization and had to be "save[d] from themselves." To allow them the status of a separate political party not only exposed them to upper-caste persecution but also preserved them as untouchables in perpetuity. Just as women and workers never asked for separate electorates in Europe, neither should untouchables in India. They should be content with universal adult suffrage and fundamental rights ensured by a constitution.[37] In other words, politically, untouchables—and, in Gandhi's view, women and workers—were individual citizens to be addressed as voters and bearers of rights, even though socially they were indeed a collectivity to be addressed by rural reconstruction and Harijan (Gandhi's term for untouchables) betterment programs. Hindus, Muslims, and Sikhs, however, were political bodies unto themselves and not social identities of the order of caste, class, and gender; therefore, they could be addressed as distinct parties.

Part and Whole

Workers and peasants, however, put a very different spin on this relationship between political form and social being. Having participated in large numbers in anticolonial agitation, workers and peasants now began to make explicit claims on the Congress's organization. In the 1930s, Kisan Sabhas, or peasant leagues, sprang up across north and east India, quite autonomously of the Congress, though alongside socialists and communists, many Congress members were also active in them. With membership fees of "not more than 1 anna," Kisan Sabhas worked for "political power to the masses" and "complete freedom from economic exploitation," "through active participation in the National Struggle... in alliance with other exploited classes."[38] The Kisan Sabha's self-presentation as a stakeholder in nationalism provoked debates about its relationship to the Congress. Despite some views to the contrary, the All India Kisan Sabha (AIKS) resolved that peasant leagues (unlike the Swarajya Party) should remain organizationally distinct from the nationalist party. Such peasant leagues that were composed exclusively of Congress members would be disaffiliated from the AIKS.[39] The AIKS, however, requested the Congress Parliamentary Board and the AICC to incorporate the demands of the All India Kisan Sabha program into its party agenda and "pledge" every Congress member to the peasant cause.[40]

The mass question clearly had come to a head and was now pushing against the Congress's association of associations format. We know that with the adoption of Gandhi's "yarn franchise" by the Belgaum Congress of 1924, labor had become a nationalist symbol and was no longer predicated on the figures of peasants, workers, or any other sociologically identifiable group. In its 1925 Patna meeting, however, the AICC modified this clause by making a yarn franchise optional to the four-anna membership—a step that potentially returned Congress members to their unmarked mass character and labor to its identity with laborers.[41] Gandhi was beginning to be challenged. While declaring *purna swaraj* (complete freedom) as the party's goal in its 1929 Lahore session, the Congress did not pass Gandhi's proposed change in the first article of the Congress's constitution—from "swaraj by peaceful and legitimate means" to "swaraj by truthful and nonviolent means." Socialists and communists insinuated that Gandhi's nonviolence was a ruse to prevent "direct action" by peasants and workers. Gandhi complained that Congress members were nonviolent only by "policy" and not by "faith." In 1921 the Congress had lowered the membership age from twenty-one to eighteen in order to broaden the organization. Gandhi now wanted to reverse that move to make the Congress smaller and more closely regulated. He also wanted to make the Foreign Cloth Boycott Committee, the Prohibition Committee, and the Committee for the Removal of Untouchability—all social causes by his reckoning—autonomous of the Congress, on a par with the All India Spinning Association, so as protect his "social reconstruction" agenda from "political vicissitudes." This too did not pass in the Congress at that time, and when Gandhi wanted to set up the Village Industries Association as autonomous of the Congress, that also was met with strong criticism. Subhas Bose and Srinivasa Iyengar announced the formation of a Congress Democratic Party within the Congress; pushed for abolition of landlordism, liquidation of agricultural debt, and nationalization of industry to be made part of the Congress's agenda; and demanded that the CWC should henceforth be an elected body (rather than nominated by the AICC).[42] Gandhi formally resigned from the Congress in 1934, making known his discomfort with the rise of socialism among younger members, including Nehru and Bose.

In 1935, communists and socialists proposed that the Congress's constitution, which had been amended substantially in 1934, should once again be amended so as to make provision for "direct representation" in the Congress of "organized" workers and peasants.[43] This came to be known as the question of "functional representation." While workers and peasants could become individual members of the party via mass subscription, peasant and worker associations now demanded "corporate" membership. A Mass Contact Committee was set up to consider the matter.[44] The committee was a complete failure, but it did issue to each district congress committee a printed questionnaire to elicit local opinion. Bengal sent back a response that was forty pages long! Reading the questionnaire in Bengali is instructive. The district congress committees were asked to return a vast amount of information—the character of local soil, the configuration of classes in the region, lists of social customs with bearing on peasant productivity, short histories of unions and movements in the area, names and addresses of local leaders, local techniques of mobilization, and above all, the reason why peasants felt the need for an organization separate from the Congress.[45] The questionnaire ended with the caveat "Peasants are ignorant." The task of the party was to translate peasant-speak into party language.[46] Responses varied vastly in volume and opinion. While E. M. S. Namboodiripad, who led the world's first elected communist government in Kerala (brought down in 1959 by the Congress's central government) and who was at the time the secretary of the Walluvanad Taluk congress committee, N. G. Ranga of the South Indian Federation of Agricultural Workers and Peasants, and Swami Sahajanand Saraswati of Bihar Kisan Sabha strongly supported the move for "functional representation," two-thirds of Bengal responses were against it.[47]

The Congress refused to make peasant and worker organizations group members. It argued that since the majority of Indians were peasants and workers anyway, a general drive to recruit more individual members would effectively mean more peasants and workers in the party. It also argued, unsurprisingly, that a duplication of membership would occur if peasants and workers were enrolled both individually and organizationally, leading to disproportionate weight for the laboring classes in the party. But the biggest fear was that by including peasants and workers in groups, the general political interest of the nation would be overtaken by "sectional" socioeconomic interests. Instead of functional representation, then, the Congress decided to make the village committee the smallest unit of the Congress, reduce the cost of Congress membership from four to two annas, and create a category of nonsubscribing "associate members" to draw every Indian into the fold of the party.[48] In other words, the Congress decided to suspend the association of associations principle and foreground the mass subscription principle for peasants and workers. The mass contact question henceforth stood reduced to the question of "Muslim mass contact,"[49] bringing the situation back full circle to where it started—namely, that while religious-communitarian identity was seen as admissible as a legitimate political form, class and caste remained relegated to the social domain.

And yet, when the Congress Socialist Party (CSP)—many of whose members spearheaded the campaign for functional membership—was established in 1935, it was set up as a party within the party. Unlike the Kisan Sabhas, the CSP's constitution clearly stated that only members of the Congress could be members of the CSP, and its provenance was to work within the Congress to secure the latter's acceptance of a socialist program. There was some debate about what it meant to be within yet distinct from the Congress. The CSP resolved not to contest elections or participate in any way in the colonial state apparatus. It relentlessly criticized the Swarajya Party's strategic electoral compromises with landlords and capitalists. And yet the Bengal Congress Socialists' Conference of September 21, 1936, went along with the Congress's decision to contest elections, though with the qualification that it would prevent elected congressmen and congresswomen from accepting ministerial offices in colonial government. Jayprakash Narayan, debating his comrade Sampurnanand, argued against Left "isolationism" and suggested that the CSP should recruit members for the Congress, while working as a "guerrilla organization" within the nationalist party.[50] In 1936, seven right-wing members of the CWC, including Rajendra Prasad (Nehru's chosen successor as prime minister of independent India), Vallabhbai Patel (Nehru's home minister), J. B. Kripalani (a Gandhian socialist), and C. Rajagopalachari (again, Congress home minister turned rabid anti-Congressite and founder of the Swatantra Party), resigned owing to the "preaching of socialism" on the floor of the Congress.[51]

How could the CSP (and for a while Subhas Bose's Forward Bloc, after he resigned from the Congress under pressure from Gandhi), assume the form of a party within the party, while Kisan Sabhas and trade unions could not, even though they shared a common agenda and perhaps even a common constituency and leadership? The answer, I believe, lay in the form and figuration of the people. The CSP rendered the people into a party—"socialism," after all, was an ideological sublimation of the "social," its transference from the register of the nonpolitical to that of the political. Trade unions and peasant leagues, however, stayed with the people in their social being and hence could not be accommodated within the party form.

The socialists and communists who campaigned for functional representation of peasants and workers in the Congress were themselves not free of this binary thinking with respect to social being and political form. In 1933, N. Datta Mazumdar and others formed the Bengal Labor Party, which criticized the Communist Party of India (CPI) for its essentially middle-class character, keeping it socially and psychologically tied to the Congress. Datta Mazumdar argued that a communist party should be an autonomous labor party, consisting of workers and only workers. So far, communists had engaged with the working classes in trade unions. What they must do now is set up a political party of and for labor. Only thus could the working classes be transformed from being a particular social subject—a sectional rather than a national interest—to being a universal political force.[52] (Ambedkar, as we saw in chapter 4, similarly criticized communists for expecting workers to participate in trade unions as workers but in party politics as nationalists!) By 1936, Datta Mazumdar and others had become a secessionist group inside the CPI, pushing for the latter's absolute separation from the Congress and the CSP. Eventually, the group was expelled because the CPI felt that a communist party could not be reduced to any social constituency, even if it were the working classes. On the contrary, a communist party should enable the working classes to transcend their social station and graduate to a universalist ontology, that of the people as such.[53]

The story of the Worker and Peasant Party (WPP) best demonstrates this communist dilemma—of having to represent workers qua workers and yet sublimate them into people as such. The WPP, founded by Kazi Nazrul Islam, Hemanta Sarkar, Qutubuddin Ahmad, Shamsuddin Hussain, and others, emerged out of a series of *praja* conferences in the districts of Bengal in the mid-1920s. Initially called the Labour Swaraj Party—much to the disappointment of Muzaffar Ahmed, because it sounded too nationalist and too Gandhian—the party was meant to be an integral part of the Congress. It was later renamed the Peasants and Workers Party—again disappointing the communists, who felt that correct class analysis required that workers precede peasants. Finally, the name was changed to the Worker and Peasant Party in English, though in Bengali the *krishak* retained its precedence, if only for idiomatic reasons.[54]

The WPP was imagined as a political party, consisting exclusively of peasants and workers, but categorically different from peasant leagues and trade unions. The latter were organizations of peasants and workers in their role as particular socioeconomic subjects. The WPP, on the other hand, was to be a party of peasants and workers in their universal political aspect. Communists were to become WPP members and work on peasants and workers, so that their social and economic, caste and class, sensibilities were transformed into pure political consciousness. (Some communists such as Bhupendranath Datta chose to work in the WPP without ever becoming a Communist Party member, refusing the vanguard role.) The communists were as concerned about the economism of trade unions and peasant leagues as they were about the caste and religious sensibilities of Indian workers, which kept them divided and prevented their emergence as a people. But even though communists successfully led labor strikes and no-rent movements in their role as WPP members, they did not always succeed in making peasants and workers Communist Party members. When they did transcend their social particularities at the height of the anticolonial upsurge, peasants and workers seemed to more easily flock to the Congress. Not surprisingly, the WPP was a short-lived experiment and demonstrated the difficulty of achieving a mass form that was not the nation, while being equivalent to the nation in its assumed wholeness.

To put it otherwise, the question before the communists was about how to play out a part (the part being the working classes of the country) in the form of the whole (the whole being the people as such). In effect, this question translated into the question of the relationship of the vanguard party with the mass party, of the communists with the Congress.

Vanguards and Volunteers

One task of the modern party is representation. The mass party represents the masses by simulating their scale and diversity. The communist party represents the masses by distilling from this diversity the essence of people as workers. The second task of the political party is to structure the masses into an ordered formation and, by claiming to transcend social particularities in favor of pure political form, attributing to them unity, solidity, and totality. The third task of the modern party, I should add, is to capture the restlessness and rupture proper to the crowd. The vanguardist aspect of the party does precisely this, that is, harness the crowd's evanescence into a permanent state of agitational readiness, whence the oxymoronic term "professional revolutionary," who embodies the spirit of the crowd without being the crowd, at the crunch moment of political insurrection. Both the mass party and the communist party perform all three roles—in different strategic combinations.

The Congress, despite being a mass party, was not without its own vanguardist aspect. Young people were invited to join the National Volunteer Corps, pledging, "with God as witness," commitment to nonviolence, *swadeshi*, Hindu-Muslim unity, and service to untouchables. They had to vow, "I shall carry out the instructions of my superior officers . . . am prepared to suffer imprisonment, assault or even death for the sake of my religion and my country without resentment. . . . In the event of my imprisonment I shall not claim from the Congress any support for my family or my dependents."[55] A military pledge, if any. Congress *swayamsevaks* were required to study history, economics, and political science and train in physical combat, first aid, crowd control, slogans, songs, cracking encrypted messages, emergency management (including cooking!), punctuality, precision, and espionage.[56]

In 1921, the BPCC started the National Service Workers Union, with former political prisoners Satyen Mitra, Pulin Behari Das, Pravash Lahiri, Shamsuddin Ahmed, and Subhas Bose. District and subdivision corps of this service consisted of salaried captains and vice captains, with paid service clearly following the army recruitment model. Local volunteer groups, such as in Rangpur, actually called themselves army (*sena*), leaders (*nayak*), and workers (*habildars*)—all military offices.[57] During the Quit India Movement, when the local Congress committee declared Tamluk in Midnapur a free zone under national government, Congress-run arbitration courts punished and fined individuals for party indiscipline. *Thanas* (neighborhood police stations) were organized under "dictators," who included women like Lakshmimani Hazra and Indumati Devi.[58]

In other words, a militarist and vanguardist imagination was critical to even a mass party like the Congress. Phanishwar Nath Renu's *Maila Anchal*, an epic novel about the immediate pre- and postindependence years, describes how, at the village level, the *volteer* (volunteer) was the real face of the Congress.[59] The communist thus was not the only vanguard in modern Indian politics. In fact, the communist and the *satyagrahi* were two competing models of the disposition and demeanor proper to vanguardism—the difference being that while *satyagraha* was the vanguardism of an exemplary ethical personhood, communism was a form of theoretical and professional vanguardism. During the 1930 civil disobedience against colonial salt laws, Gandhi insisted that the movement should be initiated by neither the masses nor the Congress party but only by a select group of ashram inmates who had "submitted to the discipline [of *satyagraha*] and assimilated the spirit of its method."[60] Gandhi, in a typical vanguardist role, planned every step of the agitation, such as the exact moment when civil disobedience must turn from "passive" to "active," when and where "social boycott" and picketing were to be undertaken, forms of courtesy to be observed in adversarial contexts, and strategic arrangement of women and men in the field.[61]

Shahid Amin's study of how Gandhi came to be perceived by north Indian peasants as a saintly and godly figure complicates the idea of vanguardism.[62] But this devotional mode of political following must not be seen simply as a premodern misapprehension of the modern idea of party leadership. Instead, it is a sign of the constitutive duality of the party form itself, in that the party both represents and embodies the people and appears in a relationship of alterity and exemplarity vis-à-vis them.[63] Hence Gandhi had a paradoxical persona as a mass leader and a vanguard rolled into one—on the one hand, simulating the Indian peasant in sparse clothing and famished body, spinning wheel, and walking stick, and on the other, appearing as an exemplary *satyagrahi* in a disciplinarian and didactic relationship with that very same peasant.

Particularly insightful in this regard is Satinath Bhaduri's novel *Dhorai Charit Manas*—a story that follows the narrative structure of *Ram Charit Ma-*

nas, a popular rendering of the Ramayana by medieval Bhakti saint Tulsidas and Gandhi's favorite read. The hero of Bhaduri's novel is not Prince Ram but the low-caste Tatma boy, Dhorai, abandoned by his parents and brought up by a local mendicant. Dhorai, through various accidents of life, becomes a Congress volunteer. The Tatmas have never seen Gandhi in person but know him as the saintly Mahatma who will usher in Ramrajya, the age of righteous rule. One morning, an image of Gandhi's face appears carved into a pumpkin hanging from the creeper, drawing people from far and wide for *darshan* (the haptic act of "viewing" or experiencing the deity). The Tatmas, like Gandhi himself, were a committed audience of Tulsidas's narrative, their conversations sprinkled with verses from the *Ram Charit Manas* as everyday ethical citations. Dhorai's transfer of devotion from Tulsidas's Ram to Congress's Gandhi thus appears seamless. Yet *Dhorai Charit Manas* is really about how Dhorai's life as a party volunteer fails to find an epic resolution in freedom and insight. While Dhorai, as a self-perceived vanguard, begins to disidentify with his own people in the name of the nation of the future, the vanguardist leader Gandhi remains to him far more inscrutable and alien than Lord Rama himself![64]

The vanguard, we must note here, is a military usage, denoting the advanced phalanx of an army, which leads from the front and takes the first bullet in a privileged act of sacrifice. In India, the Marxist idea of class war translated seamlessly into the language of vanguardism,[65] in combination with the revolutionary "philosophy of the bomb" and the modern reinvention of jihad as political action (many communists were ex-muhajirs who left India for central Asia, as already mentioned, after the British dismantled the caliphate, to return as Bolsheviks).[66] Accordingly, communist party members called themselves cadres.

The military and the parliament are two contrary mass formations. The parliament—a deliberative body, with a bottom-up chain of command—imagines people as authorizing representatives to legislate in their name. The military—a body of action, with a top-down chain of command—imagines people as following a leader who decides strategies of engagement and leads from the front. The political party combines both forms in one, bringing together the imperatives of deliberation and action, representation, and leadership. The Leninist term "democratic centralism," usually applied only to the communist party, signifies this twinning of military and representational imperatives in the party form in general.

The Communist Party of India was very different from the Congress model of proliferating and overlapping sets. It was and remained small, went through numerous splits over time in an attempt to remain ideologically pure, and pitched itself as a vanguard rather than a mass formation. Unlike the Congress, the CPI did not start up at one place or at one time. Nor did it have an identifiable center. Small groups from diverse backgrounds—such as literary activism, trade unionism, revolutionary terrorism, and noncooperation—came together independently of each other in Calcutta, Bombay, Madras, and Lahore to form communist parties. What was common to them was commitment to a singular idea, Leninism, which brought with it a new political concept, that of vanguardism.

Communists saw themselves as not just a military but also an intellectual vanguard. This intellectual vanguardism was made up of multiple elements. The first was internationalism,[67] involving not only a critique of cultural nationalism but also, for many, ideological loyalty to the Communist International and the Soviet Union. Communists refused to call their party the Indian Communist Party for fear of sounding too nationalist and instead went with the Communist Party of India.[68] They even dissociated from the Quit India Movement, the popular nationalist uprising of 1942, alienating a large number of members and sympathizers. The Communist Party leadership wanted to suspend all anticolonial activities that might draw the British away from their war effort, because in their imagination, the world war was a people's war against Fascism, colonialism notwithstanding. Not surprisingly, the organizational growth of the CPI in the 1930s and 1940s largely happened by way of an intellectual network of study circles and party classes, and a consecration of "scientific socialism" as the theoretical foundation of party identity.[69]

The second element of communist vanguardism was the exile experience, not unlike Lenin's own. Indian communists were mostly erstwhile nationalist revolutionaries fleeing the law or Muslim muhajirs escaping British India. They often nurtured an existential disconnect with Indian society, as befitted persons of the future. M. N. Roy's personal trajectory—traveling from India to Europe to Mexico to start the Mexican Communist Party, then to Tashkent to start the Communist Party of India, and eventually Moscow to meet Lenin—is a good example of a communist, cut loose from his roots, following the trajectory of world rather than national history.[70]

The third element constitutive of communist vanguardism was the experience of being outlawed. The CPI remained a proscribed organization for most of its existence, except briefly around 1942 when it was rewarded with legitimacy by the colonial state for having opposed the Congress-led agitation against what Congress called an "imperialist world war." Most communists spent long periods in jail,[71] cut off from everyday life and politics outside, reading and debating communist literature.[72] (Bengal communists jokingly called the jail the university.) Intellectualism and messianic fervor, combined with widespread suspicion and paranoia proper to those forced to live life underground, thus made the communists an exclusive group of "professional revolutionaries," who claimed to lead the masses more than represent them.[73]

And yet, the CPI, despite its vanguardist orientation, struggled to assume a mass aspect and eyed the Congress with envy. While being suspicious of "bourgeois nationalism," communists faced a people already given to them as a nation and staged as a mass party. At the same time, the communist attempt to stage the people otherwise, that is, as the Communist International, was thwarted by the geopolitical interests of yet another nation, the Soviet Union. Despite paying lip service to the ideal of national self-determination, the Communist Party of the Soviet Union repeatedly misread the dynamics of the anticolonial movement in India, leading to disenchantment among many communist activists with the idea of a global organization of "workers of the world." It seemed as if the nationalist paradigm was impossible to escape while adhering to the imagination of the people as party. The nation and the party seemed to be mutually implicated, whence the Indian communists' agonistic relationship with both the Congress and the Comintern, the nation and the International—leading to their infamous political schizophrenia, now supporting the Congress, now against it, while trying to follow contradictory signals from the Comintern, on the one hand, and the Indian masses, on the other.[74]

The communists called the Congress not a party but a "front"—mass front, national front, joint front, united front, and so on. The front, once again a military derivative, denotes the edge or the threshold where two combative forces meet. For the communists, the front was where the vanguards encountered, and stage-managed, the masses. The front also had a second meaning, implying a face or facade. The mass front, in this second sense, was not only the legal and legitimate face of an otherwise proscribed organization but also a kind of disguise for the vanguard. The communists related to the Congress in both these senses.

Unlike the CSP, which saw itself as a party within the party, the communists saw themselves as outsiders to the Congress. To them, the Congress was "sectarian," that is, subordinate to the interests of the upper classes, despite its claim to being a party of the nation. Hence there was a need to transform the Congress from within. Communists "infiltrated" the Congress, often in the guise of CSP membership, to try to weld together an internal "Left unity." The idea was that various shades of socialists and communists would combine into a critical mass and eventually take over the Congress, and the masses along with it. That Left unity of course remained a chimera. Smaller and more puritanical communist groups, like the Indian Bolshevik Party and the Revolutionary Socialist Party, argued for a sharp divorce from bourgeois nationalists, while the CSP toed the Congress line uncritically. The CPI remained strung between these two extremes but could never shake itself free of the dream of inheriting from the Congress a ready-made mass, which could be potentially converted from nationalism to communism.

The other side of the story was the rise of socialism as hegemonic opinion within the Congress—spearheaded by, among others, Nehru, who would become the first prime minister of free India, raising hopes, though dashed soon after, of the nation graduating into a socialist future after independence. The Congress continued to use socialist rhetoric well into the twentieth century. When India's second prime minister and Nehru's daughter, Indira Gandhi, suspended civil and democratic rights and declared a national emergency in 1976, it too was in the name of socialism and in the wake of a face-off with the Indian judiciary, which refused to support, in the name of the constitutional right to property, the government's proposed law for the abolition of landlordism.[75] Ironically, the only other political party that supported this dictatorial move by the Congress was the CPI.

In other words, a nationalist party seemingly tilting toward socialism and a communist party tilting toward nationalism created a general zone of political practice in India in which the people came to be sublated into the party form. The imagination of the people as a totality remained a shared imagination between mass activists and vanguards, as was the belief that such a totality was achievable only in the form of a party. Formally, the internal structures of the two parties were not very different, both combining a military chain of command with a representational configuration of committees. Both set up student, youth, women, peasant, and workers' wings, keeping these so-called social units separate from yet attached to the purely political form of the party. Their strategies, though, were rather different. The Congress as a mass party sought to co-opt communist and socialist opinions via the expansionist logic of an association of associations. The CPI as a vanguard party sought to take over and instrumentalize the Congress for its own purpose via the logic of the mass front. Neither strategy was entirely successful, for the masses, in their social aspects, stubbornly exceeded and returned to haunt the party form.

It bears mentioning here that communists eventually came to power in the state of West Bengal in 1977 by defeating the Congress Party. They ruled uninterrupted for the next thirty years, by instituting what Dwaipayan Bhattarcharyya calls "party society" (as opposed to "political society"). This was a new form of political sociability, with the party as sole mediator in all social, cultural, intellectual, and even domestic interactions, overwriting, without abolishing, preexisting forms of ethnic, caste, and community sociabilities.[76] It was thus that the Communist Party resolved the binary between social being and political form, at least for a while, until peasant revolts against industrial land acquisition brought down the Left government in 2009, releasing once more myriad caste and religious energies in Bengal politics.

Conclusion

In his novel *Jagori* (1945), Satinath Bhaduri thematizes the problematic of social being versus political form. The story is of a single night, the year 1942 or 1943, the place a colonial prison. Three out of four members of a family, belonging to different political parties, are in jail. The older son is a socialist and a nationalist, a member of the CSP, charged with leading the masses in violent "direct action" in 1942. He is to be hanged by the end of the night, having been sentenced based on his younger brother's testimony. The younger brother is a communist. The CPI's People's War line required him to support the British in its war against Nazi Germany, even though the Congress and the CSP, taking advantage of the war situation, had called for an all-out movement against the British. The younger brother sees the Quit India movement as a wasteful expenditure of mass energy, with misplaced nationalist passions undercutting unity among international workers. Hence his testimony against Congress socialists, including his own brother. He is not in jail (because the Communist Party is now legalized as a reward for its support of the colonial war effort) but sits out the night in front of the prison gate, waiting to receive his brother's body. The father is an old Gandhian, a member of the Congress party, also in the same jail. The mother, who has spent her life managing her husband's ashram, out of deference to him more than her own political conviction, is in the women's wing of the same jail. *Jagori* is an account of the night of wakefulness of this family as they wait for the son's execution.

The jail is a microcosm of the modern state, with an elaborate bureaucracy; a hierarchy of powers of violence, from petty disciplining to execution; a juridical gradation of various "classes" of prisoners into common criminals, "security prisoners" (charged under the state's special security and emergency laws), and political prisoners (belonging to legally recognized political parties such as the Congress and so possessing greater rights in prison); daily routines and rituals like marches, counting of heads, regimented labor, and physical exercise; institutionalized corruption; and unexpected acts of benevolence. At the same time, the jail is a microcosm of society, with affiliations of caste, class, and gender cutting through the mechanical functioning of prison bureaucracy. Untouchable prisoners are forced into cleaning and sanitation duties, lower-caste and lower-class inmates serve upper-class and upper-caste inmates, as if in continuity of "normal" social life. Just as often, unexpected intermixing and miscegenation also occur, unimaginable outside prison and in society. Political prisoners function on both registers, simultaneously participating in and defying state routines and social rules.

But political prisoners also operate on a third register—that of political parties. Gandhians, socialists, and communists—now forced into unwelcome proximity, even intimacy—band together by ideological predilections and stay away from each other. Gandhians pray, sing devotional songs, fast, and spin. Socialists and communists run study circles, debate Marxism and Leninism, ceaselessly quarrel with the prison authorities, smoke, and sing revolutionary songs. They also make fun of the Gandhians and their spiritual rituals. But unlike the more "civil" Gandhians, who refuse to retort to communist taunts, they breach caste, class, and generational barriers with greater aplomb. In the women's quarters, party divisions are less marked, but caste, class, and generational hierarchies prevail, though they too are often set aside unceremoniously in domestic chores and care. It is as if the political party rivals society as a mode of being together.

And, then, there is family and household—another register of sociability that operates quietly in the prison but is, as Bhaduri shows, torn asunder as kinspeople transfer their love and loyalty to political parties. *Jagori* is the story of alienation of sons from father (whose ascetic Gandhian disposition prevents him from expressing affection toward his own progeny), of brother from brother (whose respective party lines force a choice between fraternal love and political commitment), and of husband from wife (who resents the sacrifice of her household at the altar of party affiliations). All four are distraught, as they wait for the hanging. The father tries to calm his mind by following the Gandhian method of patient, mindful spinning. The mother has taken to bed, overwhelmed by unrelenting memories of her sons as children. The younger son, as he awaits his brother's execution, struggles to convince himself that political principle must outweigh brotherly affection. And the older son, at the very edge of madness, simply wonders: How could the political party replace family, not just in the utopic future of universal humanity but in this very present?[77] G. Arunima shows in her reading of Thoppil Bhasi's Malayalam novel *You Made Me a Communist*, how becoming a communist party member was often mediated by comrades literally "falling in" (romantic) love with each other.[78] And yet, as Bhaduri's novel poignantly shows, belonging to a political party, living a purely political mode of being, required just as often a proactive disavowal of relationships of affection. For the political party the people could only be imagined in antinomy to social and filial forms.

8

People as Fiction

> So we have the greatest people's theatre but no people.
> —Stefan Grossmann, review of Max Reihardt's "Ortesia," *Vossische Zeitung*, December 29–30, 1919

When the Indian People's Theatre Association (IPTA) was set up in 1943, its structure mirrored that of the classical political party. In its first all-India conference, held in Bombay, it adopted a constitution and mapped itself, as did the Congress and the communist parties, horizontally across linguistic provinces—hence its Bengal, Bombay, and Andhra "squads"—and vertically across a representational hierarchy, local to regional to national.[1] Clearly, there was an imagined overlap between people as party and people as culture. In this last chapter, I explore how, in counterpoise to the structure and solidity of the party, the people come to be staged in modernity as an aesthetic formation, fictional and fantastic.

We know that the rise of the nation in modern times as the hegemonic form of political community was predicated on a notion of culture as the "way of life" of a people. The story I explore here, however, is not that of modern-day "culturalism," on which there is already a rich scholarship. Here I am interested in how aesthetics, rather than the broader category of culture, came to be mobilized in the twentieth century, as that which gave form to an otherwise inchoate entity called the people. I have in mind the rise, around the time of the two world wars, of political novels, political theater, political poetry, and so forth, as well as the general spread of the idea of "cultural revolution" across

Europe and Asia. The rise of aesthetics as a ground of politics was, I argue, a departure from nineteenth-century culturist imaginations.

I think of the distinction between culture and aesthetics in the following terms: if culture is about what the people are, habitually and organically, aesthetics is about what the people can become, consciously and politically; if culture is about community and identity, aesthetics is about the reorientation of experience and sense perception in ways that transform community and identity. Mine, however, is not the well-known "aesthetics of power" argument à la Walter Benjamin that sees the aestheticization of politics as salient only to extreme and pathological forms of "total mobilization," such as fascism and Nazism, which seek to produce, like a sublime work of art, an "aura" around the people and the leader who embodies them.[2] Instead, I propose that modern politics per se—being the paradoxical enterprise of naming a people into being while invoking people as prior guarantee—demands a certain aesthetic orientation of and from the people.

Literature and Ethnography

Culturalism is predicated on the act of "finding" the people, which is usually a middle-class quasi-ethnographic project. In India, as in Europe, this search for the people as an authentic and organic community took the form of a modern "rediscovery" of folk traditions.[3] In Bengal, a number of committed, even obsessive, intellectuals took to this search from the mid-nineteenth century onward—researching, collecting, recording, printing, and disseminating folk artistic genres from remote corners of the region: Lal Behari Dey (1824–92), who became a Christian missionary and in that capacity came into contact with common people; Sarat Chandra Mitra (1863–1968), who worked as lawyer in Bihar and published innumerable essays on north Indian tales and riddles; Dinesh Chandra Sen (1866–1939), a Calcutta University professor famous for his comparison of Shakespeare and Kalidas and his collection of ballads from East Bengal; Dakshinaranjan Mitra Mazumdar (1877–1957), known to children for his two folklore collections, *Grandma's Bagful* and *Grandpa's Bagful*; Gurusaday Dutt (1882–1941), who wrote on folk art and dance and initiated the *bratachari* movement (*brata* [vow], also a popular ritual among rural Bengali women) for national regeneration; indeed Rabindranath Tagore himself, who, given his interest in *swadeshi samaj* (national society), encouraged the publication of folk songs and verses in the journal of the Bangiya Sahitya Parishat (Bengal Academy of Literature) and in 1907 wrote a much-discussed essay on folk literature.[4]

By the 1920s, however, this culturalist imagination of the people came to be criticized by younger littérateurs. They complained that Bengali literature was confined to narrating genteel, middle-class lives and national historical stories. It did not stage common people as protagonists, thus abandoning them to the work of ethnography. The implication was clear—it was not enough to simply know the people in their default cultural being; the people had to be "rendered into literature," *sahityabhata* (turned literary, the poet Bishnu Dey's term) and *rupayita* (given form).⁵ This distinction—between people as an anthropological object and people as a literary subject—thus became critical to the imagination of people as political community.

But what exactly did "rendering into literature" mean? In the 1920s, a number of new literary periodicals were established in Bengal, most famously *Kallol* and *Kali Kalam*, which published stories about the lives of peasants, mine workers, factory laborers, slum dwellers, untouchables, and women. Tagore was their literary bête noire because he allegedly wrote on idealist themes like nature, spirituality, and love rather than about real lives of real people.⁶ Tagore—a Nobel Prize winner, global icon, and big *zamindar*, who witnessed firsthand the plight of his peasant-tenants and ran his own version of rural reconstruction through his Shantiniketan ashram—was acutely aware of the need to depict common lives and sought to do so in his *Galpaguchha* (Bouquet of short stories) and *Chhinnapatrabali* (Epistolary snippets). His protégé Pramatha Choudhury started a literary periodical called *Sabuj Patra* (Green leaf)—to "shock" readers into newness—which encouraged literature in *chalti bhasha* or colloquial Bengali. (Tagore had earlier used colloquial Bengali only in letters and diaries and not in literary works.)⁷

And yet, on reading Jagadish Gupta's novel *Laghu Guru* (1931), depicting the sexual encounters of a destitute woman, Tagore felt that Gupta's reality was an "alien country."⁸ It sensationalized misery and denied the basic impulse of aesthetics—which, in Tagore's telling, was to depict the inherent vitality and beauty of life from within even the most crushing poverty and squalor. Gupta was associated with *Kallol*, and his famous short story "Radhasati" depicted a Brahmin touching the feet of an untouchable woman in a shocking inversion of moral hierarchy. Younger authors, influenced as much by Marx as by Freud,⁹ in turn accused Tagore of being an elite and a traditionalist, who reified aesthetics in the name of abstruse spiritual principles, like truth, beauty, and beatitude. The 1920s literary scene was thus marked by bitter polemic—especially between *Kallol* and *Shanibarer Chithi* (The Saturday letter), led by Sajanikanta Das, around what were seen as the obscene sexuality and faddish nonconformity of new literature.¹⁰

Realism was the buzzword of the times.[11] On the face of it, then, it would appear that the issue at stake was representation—fidelity to the actual details of common lives, a form of anthropological veracity that could posit the people as a recognizable and credible cultural fact. In truth, however, the debate was about something else altogether, namely, how best to stage the people such that everyday lives became politically expressive, a task for which ethnographic narratives seemed grossly inadequate. The question at stake was how best to capture not the being but the becoming of the people—hence the emphasis on the fictionality of realist fiction, on the work of imagination rather than representation.[12]

Rasa and Realism

Tagore and his allies often invoked classical Indian aesthetic concepts like *rasa* and *bhava*. *Rasa*—a term approximating emotion, mood, relish, or taste—was the defining quality of any aesthetic experience and was seen as the shared effect produced in the mutual vibes between performer and spectator, poet and audience. *Bhava*—literally meaning "to become"—was understood as the aesthetic means and expressive strategies mobilized to accomplish or "bring into being" the right *rasa*. Interestingly, the basic problematic in this tradition was to distinguish aesthetic effect from both representation and experience. The argument went as follows. If fear appeared as the representation of fear, it appeared as the fear of another person (e.g., of the actor or the character onstage) and thus failed to move the spectator. But if fear appeared real as in experience, then the spectator herself was gripped by fear, and thus aesthetic enjoyment was hampered. In neither case did fear (*bhaya*) transition from being a mundane emotion to being *rasa* proper.

Aesthetic rendering thus was about neither representation nor experience—both of which were in fact aesthetic failures—but about a third effect, namely, the production of *rasa* through a process of *sadharanikaran* (generalization). *Rasa* appeared only when mundane emotions were liberated from the locus of the individual and became emotions that were neither of the self nor of the other—neither mine nor yours, as it were—but everyone's.[13] A successful work of art, in other words, was that which made possible *sahridayata* (one-heartedness) or a common mode of being across singular selves. In the *rasa* paradigm, however, this common world was not real but "more than real," to use David Shulman's felicitous phrase describing aesthetic traditions of early modern southern India, because it involved those worlds of imagination that awaited "bringing into being" by the poet, often against the grain of reality.[14]

Tagore believed that depictions of suffering and despair, as in realist fiction, should generate an aesthetically shared sense of enjoyment and not an intensely individualizing experience of suffering in the reader or audience.[15] In that sense the truth of fiction had to be distinct from both a faithful representation of lives and a personal or intimate experience of such lives. New authors disagreed on Tagore's idea of enjoyment or pleasure (*ananda*) as aesthetic purpose. They argued, as radical Dalit writing would do even more sharply in western India in the 1960s and 1970s, that realist depiction should shock and agitate the reader—so that the passive consumption of art became difficult and readers and viewers were forced into awakening and animation.[16] Thus, despite their differences, new authors shared with Tagore, without quite acknowledging it, the sense that realist fiction must exceed its representational intent and produce an emotional effect that brought people together in community, whether in pleasure or in outrage. New literature, in other words, must achieve a properly realist *rasa*, to propose a rather oxymoronic phrase.

Sudipta Kaviraj, in arguing that modernity in India was debated much more elaborately and subtly in literature than in discursive writings, proposes the idea of a "rasa of modernity,"[17] which exceeded the classical list of nine *rasas* but nevertheless called out for an unavoidably literary articulation. One could in fact propose, on the same lines, a "*rasa* of the political" that twentieth-century radical literature was striving for. A recent book on early novels shows how in India the unfolding of the protagonist's inner self, the defining aspect of the novel as an aesthetic form, assumed the unmistakable nature of political becoming, unlike, say, in a novel by Jane Austen or George Eliot.[18] In other words, in colonial times, the world of desire and emotion appeared always already mediated by politics just as politics appeared as charged with desire and emotion, breaching the public/private or inner/outer binary of modern political philosophy and positing politics itself as an intimate experience, perhaps even a psychological drive.

Communist criticism against noncommunist realist writing, such as of the *Kallol* group, was precisely along these lines. They felt that the *Kallol* writers' realism generated emotions of despair and alienation, political dead ends as it were.[19] However squalid life might be in reality, communist critics argued, literature must generate hope and struggle, a sense of the imminent future, a possibility of dialectical overcoming: "Realism gives form [*rupayita*] to the movement of life in such a way that it renders literary [*sahityabhata*] the underlying truth. At the root of this truth lies the worldview of dialectical materialism."[20]

Realist literature in that sense must indeed be "more than real"—a position no different from Tagore's on the point that aesthetic effect must necessarily exceed the veracity effect. To the distinction made by Abu Sayyid Ayub—between politically motivated "applied" literature and "eternal" or "ultimate" literature—Amarendraprasad Mitra insisted, almost in Tagorean terms, that true communist literature too was ultimate, eternal, and generative of *ananda* or bliss.[21] The issue at stake thus was not the representation of reality but the correct *rasa* and *bhava* of people as political community, in their everyday lives as well as in their inner travails.

Tarashankar Bandopadhyay (1898–1971), perhaps the most popular Bengali novelist after Rabindranath Tagore and Saratchandra Chattopadhyay, was a committed Gandhian and a Congress activist, who turned to literature full-time in 1931. In his literary memoirs, Tarashanka recollected how his political travels familiarized him with the intricacies of local subaltern lives. He cross-referenced his fictional characters with real-life figures whom he met in various parts of Bengal—revealing his sources as informants almost in an ethnographic mode of evidentiary veracity.[22] His 1951 novel and perhaps his best, *Hansulibanker Upakatha* (The tale of the village at the river bend)—rendered into film in 1962—was, however, accused of being ethnographic by communist critics.[23] The implication was that the novel was indeed an *upakatha*, of the nature of a folktale or a fairy tale, and belonged to the culturalist paradigm. It invoked feelings of wonder and delight rather than struggle and *Aufhebung*, despite the novel's indisputable narrative realism and the fact that Tarashankar gathered inspiration for his plots and protagonists in the course of political campaigns and not folklore forays. Achintya Kumar Sengupta (1903–76), of the *Kallol* group, too was as realist a writer as any—as evinced by the provocative titles of his short-story collections, *Hadi, Muchi, Dom*, names of three untouchable castes of Bengal, and *Kath, Khar, Kerosene* (wood, straw, kerosene), types of everyday household fuel. But he, too, was accused by communists of writing in an ethnographic mode—drawing facts from Kisan Sabha reports and local court documents, without any sense of the drama of dialectics.[24]

Clearly, the realism question was far more complicated than appears on the surface. Communist writers made a fine distinction between realism and dialectical materialism, on the grounds that while the former depicted only present reality, the latter sensed the historical movement toward the future that subtly animated that reality. In other words, at stake was the fictionality rather than the reality of realist fiction, wherein futural elements, elements of becoming, when not present as already accomplished facts accessible to empirical ethnographic knowledge, appeared as a striving, an atmosphere charged with potentiality. Paradoxically, the question of affect and effect exceeded the question of facticity and veracity with respect to the realism debate.

Theater and Drama

The question of affect and effect brings me to the question of theater and drama. Interestingly, the origins of both the *rasa* theory of the ancients and the affect theory of today can be traced back to theater. The concepts of *rasa* and *bhava* were first posited in the classical text *Bharata's Natyashastra* (The science of performance).[25] Over time, these concepts traveled from the domain of performance to the domain of *kavya* or literature, and from the domain of the poet's or actor's recital to the domain of the readers' or spectators' emotional experience. Accordingly, *kavya* came to be distinguished from other textual forms, on the grounds that while religious texts (such as the Vedas) worked through injunction and command and historical texts (*itihasa-purana*) through friendly counsel and teaching, *kavya* worked through the production of a generalized *rasa* or shared emotional experience in the audience. Sheldon Pollock shows how in early modern times, *rasa* once against returned from literariness to theatricality in Bhakti and Sufi devotional traditions, with devotees enacting various affective states before the deity of desire.[26]

Affect theory, for its part, was initiated by the psychologist Silvan Tomkins, who began his academic training as a student of drama at the University of Pennsylvania between 1927 and 1930. He also wrote plays intended to dramatize various forms of "human motivation" onstage.[27] Tomkins developed, in a surprising overlap with classical *rasa* theory, a list of nine primary or basic emotions and their corresponding expressions.[28] Based on his study of the extralinguistic force of facial expressions and bodily movements, Tomkins argued for a dramaturgical model for understanding why and how people acted. He even proposed a "script theory" of human cognition and volition in which he argued that "scenes" were the basic unit of the unfolding of ordinary, everyday lives.[29]

It seems, therefore, that twentieth-century debates about realism and representation, especially with respect to political community, were tacitly animated by questions of theater and drama—not as a particular performative or textual form but as an aesthetic orientation shared across genres, from poetry to novels to short stories. Theatricality, it appears from the frequent use of idioms of *rasa* and affect/effect, was understood as that which animated common life and made routines of the everyday politically expressive rather than merely culturally identifiable.

Here Gernot Böhme's concept of "atmospherics" is useful. New writing in Bengal between the 1920s and 1950s was very much about "atmospherics." Even when the subject of a novel or a short story was a particular subaltern community or caste, as was often the case, the narrative was framed not in terms of sociological or cultural identity, as in ethnographic telling, but in terms of a particular mode of staging that appeared shared across communities. This stage or mise-en-scène was the *anchal* or what can be called the "locality," the "ecology," or, better still, the locus of being. The *anchal* was fleshed out—through intensive use of local dialects and community idioms; intricate descriptions of landscapes; ethnological detailing, almost in the visual mode of set construction; attention to the complex dynamics of caste names and proper names as part of character development; invocation of local festive, work, and erotic traditions; and attention to the minutiae of ordinary household lives, which dramatized the apparently uneventful and the routine—all in order to produce a thick atmosphere that was irreducible to either social structure or cultural identity. Shailajananda Mukhopadhyay's depiction of Birbhum coal mines, Premendra Mitra's writings on urban slums, Satinath Bhaduri's depiction of tribal life in Purnea, Narayan Gangopadhyay's depiction of life in the delta and tidal flats of Sundarbans—all created an atmosphere that effected the real but also spilled beyond it. A self-consciously nationalist author such as Tarashankar Bandopadhyay and a self-consciously communist author such as Manik Bandopadhyay, seen as literary adversaries by their contemporaries, shared this investment in the *anchal* and the atmospherics that it made possible and plausible.

In a critique of Kant, who theorized aesthetics as a form of "judgment," that is, as a cerebral or an analytical orientation, and of classical mimetic theories of art, which raised the irresoluble problem of representation in terms of the relationship between an object and its copy, Böhme argues that aesthetic power is best understood as the production of an atmosphere, which inheres neither in an object (the people, in our case) nor in its subjective representation (in literary genres) but enfolds both as a borderless, nonlocalizable, sensory, and affective ambience. It was precisely this sense of atmospherics that came to be rendered as the *anchal*, or what I am calling "the locus of being," in Bengali writings of the time, indexing the ontology of the people as such. As Böhme reminds us, it is in theater and performance that atmospherics become most significant, as they indeed do in the classical Indian dramaturgy of the *Natyashastra* in the form of a generalized or generalizable *rasa*.[30] As Erika Fischer-Lichte says, the production of the right atmosphere produces an aesthetic effect, which is beyond meaning and message, semiotics and ideology, and is "shared" rather than "translated" across languages and groups.[31] New writing in Bengal tried to produce atmospherics in this sense, in order to render people as a unity—irrespective of cultural and social incommensurabilities—which is why the literature of this period is perhaps better understood as "staging" rather than "saying."

This is best demonstrated by Tarashankar's novel *Aranya Banhi* (Forest fire), a fictionalized account of the 1855 rebellion by the Santal tribe against colonial officials and Bengali moneylenders. The event is staged amid the hills and forests of Birbhum in the best mode of "atmospheric" novels of the time, with the associated ambience of haunting, light and shadow effects, dark tactile bodies, and declamatory dialogue flavored with local idioms. The novel ends with a classical dramatic denouement—with fire, analogous to the fire of sacrifice, spreading across the forest and consuming the insurgents themselves. But even more important, the event is re-created via a deliberate setting up of a contrast—between colonial accounts of the rebellion and ethnographic studies of the Santal tribe, on the one hand, genres that claimed representational veracity and are quoted ironically by Tarashankar, and folk memories and visuals of the past, on the other. Tarashankar's narrative faithfully follows the recital of a local low-caste *patua* (painter), Nayan Pal (the term *nayan*, incidentally, means the eye), as the latter unfurls one *pat* or painting after another, creating a sequence of pictures for the author, frame by frame, depicting the unfolding of the event of insurgency. "Right before my mind's eye," Tarashankar wrote in explicitly visual terms, "the curtain over the stage [*rangamancha*] of history was drawn back."[32] Notably, many of Tarashankar's novels and short stories were produced as plays, confirming the fact that a certain adaptability to theater was inherent in his literary prose. He also wrote twelve plays, some of which, like *Arogya Niketan*, were major hits. In fact, it was from theater that he earned his meager livelihood. Many of his works—including *Hansuli Banker Upakatha*, *Agun*, *Rai Kamal*, and *Kabi*—were also rendered into film and included *Manjari Opera*, which was itself a story about popular theater.

Jacques Rancière, in his *Politics of Literature*, defines modernity as a transition from the theater to the novel. Classical Greek theater was a mode of calling on the people to follow the exemplary action and the rhetorical speech of heroes onstage. It was an authoritative mode of address to the public assembly. In contrast, the late eighteenth-century and nineteenth-century realist novel offered, in place of theatrical exhortation, a thick description of objects, peoples, and landscapes, "mute signs" inscribed on the world that invited competing interpretations by now empowered readers. Realism was thus a process of aesthetic "democratization," Rancière says, as it came to rest on autonomous reading and hermeneutic practices rather than on the injunctive force of dramatic speech and demonstrative action delivered from elsewhere.[33]

Reading the same texts as Rancière, Baidik Bhattacharya shows how European realist descriptions and the reading practices they elicited were predicated on colonial classificatory knowledge systems, like comparative philology, ethnography, and Hegelian world history. This militates against Rancière's claim of realism as a democratic form, because realist reading practices produced a racialized author-reader compact from which the Orient and Africa were excluded, even as the Orient and Africa were staged, both explicitly and allusively, as "objects" in these narratives.[34] It was precisely against this mode of description modeled on ethnography, and the forms of facticity it generated, that the littérateurs I discuss here argued. They tried to proffer in its place a literature charged with the theatricality of becoming, which mobilized and yet exceeded the narrative's realist intent.

In any case, the story of so-called realism in colonial India was very different from that in Rancière's telling. In Bengal, modernism, if we indeed want to call it that, emerged riding on poetry rather than the novel. This newfangled poetry addressed the nation and its people, through a reframing of ancient myths on the one hand and lyrical descriptions of nature and people on the other.[35] Something like realism also emerged simultaneously, but not in association with modernism as such. The poet Ishwar Chandra Gupta (1912–59) wrote poems on the everyday nitty-gritty of colonial urban life that were as often performed as read, in street corner impromptu poetry competitions before mass audiences.[36] Kaliprasanna Sinha (1840–70) wrote an intricately detailed exposé of Bengali elite life and hybrid everyday customs in the colonial city. But while these texts were prima facie "realistic," in the simple sense of being about everyday mundane life, their semantic and allusive reach far exceeded realist conventions. As Sambudha Sen shows, Sinha's *Hootum Pyanchar Nakhsa* (Portrait by the barn owl) worked by mixing up different languages, idioms, and imageries, juxtaposing incommensurable registers of description, derision, and critique, and, I would add, displaying an unmistakable performative address and diction.[37] As poetry turned more lyrical by the second half of the nineteenth century, under the influence of English and German Romanticism, and novels turned more self-consciously realistic, the expressive strategies fashioned by Gupta and Sinha came to reside in plays, especially those that satirized everyday social mores of colonial India. These plays were both staged and read in the form of cheap printed chapbooks sold at Battala, Bengal's Grub Street. "Realism" in other words arose performatively rather than purely textually in colonial Bengal, creating a relationship between text and theater very different from what Rancière imagines. But perhaps realism does not accurately describe this expressive strategy as does an inelegant neologism such as "mundane-ism"—a mode of staging common life so as to expose the conflict, drama, and even absurdity at the very heart of the mundane.

The People's Poet

The matter of ethnographic rendering versus aesthetic rendering, facticity versus fictionality, representation versus imagination, and realism versus theater came to a head around questions of music and performance—artistic forms that expressed with particular poignancy issues of staging and atmospherics. Hemanga Biswas, who was a singer, composer, and musicologist in addition to being a communist leader, debated with compatriots the subtle distinctions between folk music (*lok sangeet*), people's music (*gana sangeet*), class music (*sreni sangeet*), and patriotic music (*deshattvabodhak sangeet*). Folk music was authentic and real, Biswas said, as was vouched for by many ethnographers, both foreign and Indian. It resonated directly with the people. Yet folk music was not necessarily generative of political community because it preexisted the mobilization and consolidation of the people. Class music authentically expressed peasant and worker lives, but it too fell short of capturing the people as a universal category. Patriotic songs, especially popular ones by Tagore and D. L. Roy, were undoubtedly about political community but did not stage the people as such. Rather, they staged the nation—as landscape, as mother, as goddess, or simply as an abstract ideal. People's music on the other hand was generated out of the dynamics of political struggle and captured people in the process of becoming. It could be written by communist leaders or by the people themselves and could be set to preexisting folk tunes, or not. It belonged to the people not because they authored it or because it represented the people truthfully but because it captured them in the dramatic moment of insurgency and awakening. People's music was thus of and for the people even though it was not always by the people.[38]

While Biswas and his colleagues in the IPTA composed many people's songs, they also encountered a number of poets and performers from among the people themselves. The people's poet became a critical figure in the staging of people as political community. Many such people's poets, or *lok kavis*, are mentioned in Communist Party and IPTA documents: Ramesh Seal, son of a barber from Chittagong, who wrote on the Khilafat movement and revolutionary nationalism, then became a devotee of the *pir* of Majhbandar Sarif and eventually joined the Communist Party; Sheikh Gumhani Dewan of Murshidabad, who performed episodes from the Ramayana and the Mahabharata and later versified tracts written by the communist leader Bhavani Sen; Nibaran Pandit of Mymensingh, who moved from writing about Radha and Krishna's amorous adventures to Hindu Muslim riots to the great Bengal famine of 1943, going on to become an important officeholder of the Kisan Sabha; Suren Naskar, a jute mill worker who seamlessly incorporated images of ongoing working-class struggles into older compositions dedicated to the god Ghentu Raja; and Gurudas Pal, alias Sanatan Pandit, a factory worker from Metiaburuz, who went on to become one of the front-ranking composers of IPTA.[39] Most of these poets reworked existing folk forms and folk melodies, stuff of contemporary ethnographic delight—*baul* (songs of an itinerant dissident sect involving both erstwhile Hindus and Muslims), *bhatiali* (boatmen's songs from East Bengal), *jari* (Muslim folk songs sung during Muharram), *gambhira* (songs of Lord Shiva sung during the *gajan* festival), *chaad petanor gaan* (songs sung during construction of roofs), *kavi gan* (songs sung during extempore poetic competitions), and so on—the difference being that they inflected these preexisting genres by self-consciously turning them political.

Nibaran Pandit became a close friend to Hemanga Biswas, but they fell out over what or who exactly was a people's poet. Unsurprisingly, the debate was about the relationship between politics and aesthetics. Should the people's poet faithfully follow the ideological and political agenda of the Communist Party? (Ironically, Pandit believed that he or she should and accused Biswas of being a middle-class aesthete.) Or should his or her first commitment be to the aesthetic integrity of an art form, as Biswas insisted?—a familiar debate across the world in the times of political art. Pandit stated with pungent sarcasm that he was never sure of how to properly perform the role of the people's poet, because he was not an educated city man![40] For his part, Biswas was clear about the proper stage that the people's poet must inhabit, as can be seen in his description of Nibaran Pandit's performance during the 1945 peasant conference at Netrokona, Mymensingh:

> Just as a lotus flower is best appreciated in the middle of the lake, the people's poet is best seen at large among the people. This soft, polite man had disappointed many in the literary connoisseurs' conference in Calcutta. Besides Nibaran-*babu* is not exactly a virtuoso singer. But in Netrokona, when he appeared amid the Muslim peasant *jari* dancers—bare-bodied, muscular, with a *gamchha* tied around his waist—I immediately recognized the spell that he could cast over people's minds. . . . The pledge to create a new society spread like contagion [from his body to other bodies].[41]

It was as if the people's poet was an actor/protagonist onstage. Biswas strongly believed, like his contemporary littérateurs, that the right stage and set for the people's poet was the *anchal*—hence the need to conserve local diction of both language and melody. He was impatient with the way in which the

Communist Party cannibalized folk music for immediate political purposes. Biswas once asked Ramesh Seal why his recent music failed to produce the same charge as the wistful (*maramiya*) songs he used to sing earlier in his own village. Seal replied that his new songs came from the "outside" impulse of politics and not "from the heart." Biswas felt vindicated that the people's poet was lost on the urban stage, even if it was the stage of the Indian People's Theatre Association.[42]

Biswas argued that more than distinctions of form and content, it was the distinction in stage and setting that separated people's music from *marga* or virtuoso music. He had no patience for the form/content debate that preoccupied many of his communist friends.[43] Quoting Bengali musicologists of his time, Biswas argued that there were recognizable formal continuities between folk music and art house music, and indeed the latter might have historically originated from the former. The distinction between the two lay elsewhere—namely, in the fact that while virtuoso music was performed indoors, in courts, drawing rooms, and auditoriums, and was transmitted through closed networks of lineage and succession (*gharana*), folk music was performed under the open sky and spread from mouth to mouth (*bahiriana*). Folk music was thus by nature a "movement" and animated everyday, outdoor activities of life and labor, unlike leisure music, which was an "enclosed" and "interrupted" art form.[44]

Contemporary fiction too found it important to stage the people's poet as a central character. By the late nineteenth century, the *baul* (often called a "wandering minstrel") came to be a highly celebrated figure in Bengal, especially because *bauls* advocated a form of philosophical spirituality that cut across Hindus and Muslims, upper castes and lower castes. *Kangal* Harinath Majumdar, whom I mentioned in chapter 6 as the rural journalist and radical critic of peasant exploitation, popularized the songs of the late eighteenth-century *baul* Lalan Fakir and, indeed, considered himself an amateur *baul*, performing his own songs as Fikir Chand. When Tagore published a book of patriotic songs in 1905, inaugurating the Swadeshi movement against the partition of Bengal, he called it the *Baul*. Later, in association with Kshitimohan Sen, he began publishing *baul* songs, especially by Lalan and Gagan, in the periodical *Pravasi*. Most interestingly, Tagore himself played the part of a blind *baul*, a figure of social conscience, in his dance-drama *Phalguni*.[45] Abanindranath Tagore, front-ranking member of the Bengal school of art, immortalized this image of the poet Tagore as a *baul* in his 1916 painting.

The irony of the most elite and idealist of all poets posing onstage as a people's poet was not lost on later generations. New writing, therefore, tried staging the people's poet differently. Tarashankar Bandopadhyay, Manik Bandopadhyay, and Achintya Kumar Sengupta all narrativized, in rather different ways, this figure of the *lok kavi*. In fact, Manik and Achintya became embroiled in a rather bitter debate regarding this. Achintya wrote a story titled "Muchi Bayen"—about a musical contest between two low-caste performers, which is settled when the wife of one bribes the other with sexual favors, causing the latter to withdraw from the contest.[46] Manik Bandopadhyay, in turn, wrote the story "Gayen"—once again about a musical contest between an older and a younger *kavi*, where the latter trumps the former because he sings of protest and struggle and not, like the older man, about hunger and suffering. The older *kavi* defers to the younger because he now realizes that people were no longer satisfied with *karuna rasa* (the emotions of grief and sorrow) and were rearing to rebel. He then offers his daughter in marriage to the younger poet![47] Communist critics felt that while Achintya Sengupta individualized the figure of the people's poet by highlighting the contentious aspect of poetic competition, charging it unnecessarily with sexuality, Manik Bandopadhyay captured the crux of what it meant to be a true people's poet—namely, the ability to sense when the people stood transformed, from erstwhile victimhood to political community[48]—even though the question of sexual transaction was a shadowy presence here as well.

Tarashankar's novel, simply called *Kavi* (Poet), was about the unlikely ambition of an untouchable Dom, who is made fun of by the local Brahmin for even dreaming of being a poet. But he cannot stop himself from composing, singing, and participating in local poetry contests. Nor can he stop himself from falling in love with the local milkman's wife—like Radha in the Vaishnava devotional tradition, the wife of a middle-caste Ahir, whom Lord Krishna loved and played the flute for (though instead of Krishna, the dark god, here it is the woman, the Radha equivalent, who is dark-skinned, inspiring the Dom to write verse after verse in praise of black skin, black hair, black clouds, and the black god Krishna!). The poet tries to flee his love, wandering away with a *jhumur* band, peopled by gypsy women who sing, dance, act, and drink and are part-time sex workers. He learns to compose and sing raucous poetry, but his heart lies in writing devotional and love poems. He even tries to become an ascetic and leave for the mountains, but the landscape and language of his home region draw him back inexorably. Even though his lover dies of heartbreak, he must return to his *anchal*, where no one awaits him any longer but which makes his poetry possible and credible in the first place.

Tarashankar's *kavi* is not an obvious political figure, unlike Manik Bandopadhyay's *gayen*. Nor is he just a driven poet, who desires fame and success even at the cost of personal loss, like Achintya Sengupta's *muchi bayen*. He is a poet, a lover, a devotee—but political in that he stubbornly steps out of line and into unauthorized social roles. He is an untouchable who refuses menial labor because he is a poet and seeks to earn his living by performing poetry. He is an adulterous lover, who desires one who is not his either by lineage or by caste. And he is a devotee and an artiste of eroticism among those who seek pornographic pleasure.[49] Rancière, in his thesis on "nights of labor," depicts mid-nineteenth-century French workers burning midnight oil writing poetry and reading philosophy. In Rancière's telling, the figure of the worker-poet appears more intractable than the figure of the worker-revolutionary because the worker-poet upsets the division of places and roles in the established order of things.[50] Tarashankar's *kavi* resonates with Rancière's worker-poets.

And yet, there is a crucial aspect that all three authors seem to share—namely, the importance of the stage. All three write of people's poets who do not simply compose poetry but also perform their poetry before a live audience, exhorting the people into being. In that sense, the people's poet is a very different figure from the middle-class littérateur who writes in solitude and approaches his readers via the mediation of the market and the printing press. It is the theatrical immediacy of the persona of the people's poet that gives it, as Hemanga Biswas insisted, its radical charge.

Onstage and Offstage

It is worthwhile, then, to dwell briefly on twentieth-century debates concerning theater, to try to further understand the salience of theatricality to people as political community. The middle classes of India saw theater as an antisocial institution, a site of class miscegenation and transgression of social boundaries. Theater was identified with low-caste performers, men dressing as women, and from the nineteenth century onward, women actors of "suspect morals."[51] Despite middle-class demands for a respectable, European-inspired theater,[52] however, the commercial stage in Bengal continued to flourish and be feared as a dangerous and liminal space, symbolized above all by the figure of the public woman, likely of low-caste origin, such as *nati* Binodini Dasi, who impersonated onstage the most sublime and sacred figures of history, like the Bhakti saint Chaitanya.[53] But then theater was also widely seen as potentially a site of mobilization. "The country is my stage, the people actors"—the Assam People's Theatre Association propagated, blurring the boundary between actor and spectator, people and performer.[54] And discussing theater in Shakespeare's England, the communist playwright, director, and actor Utpal Dutt (1929–93) celebrated the fact that in early modern playhouses, spectators of antagonistic classes faced each other directly, often leading to political confrontation.[55]

In India, interestingly, the origin myth of theater reflected this very sensibility. When the gods staged a play about their victory over the antigods (*dvaityas*), the latter entered the playhouse and violently disrupted the performance. The gods then called on the sage Bharata to frame a regulatory scheme for theater, including a division of spectators into their "proper" places, which eventually would become the science of performance.[56] Colonial authorities also recognized native theater's potential for disorder, in the context of political plays such as *Neel Darpan* (1860, 1872, on the exploitation of peasants by British indigo planters); *Surendra Binodini* (1876, on a colonial magistrate's assault on a servant woman); *Gaikwar Darpan* (1875, on the deposition of a Maratha king by the British); *Gajananda Prahasan* (1875, a satire on the Prince of Wales); and *Chakar Darpan* (1875, on tea plantation labor), which was why the Dramatic Performances Act was passed in 1876.[57]

When people's theater was inaugurated in India in the 1940s, it mobilized both an avant-gardist sensibility of theater as a radical political institution and a modernist criticism of commercial mass theater as marked by "petty conventions," "sobstuff," melodrama, "bad history," and "senseless mythology"—to quote Hiren Mukherjee's speech at the first conference of IPTA in 1943.[58] The 1944 staging of *Nabanna* (New harvest), codirected by playwright Bijon Bhattacharya and the future doyen of the Bengali stage Sombhu Mitra, is usually seen as the inaugural moment of people's theater in India. The play depicted the travails of a rural family in the great famine of 1943, as the family migrates to the city and to utter destitution, and finally returns to the village to organize a peasants' collective. A celebratory review of the play explained that theater was, by definition, a collective art and taught people conventions of collaboration.[59] It was also the most immediate art form in its interface with common people. *Nabanna* successfully captured this essence of theater. Until recently, plays were structured around virtuoso performances by individual actor-heroes. Theater was synonymous with star names—Girish Ghosh, Manoranjan Bhattacharya, and Sisir Kumar Bhaduri, who both directed and acted in plays. It was the first time that *Nabanna* staged the people as a collective protagonist and expressed the principle of the choral unity of human action. The play was utterly realistic, the review added, and dispensed with theatrical artifices such as romance, melodrama, stunt, fantasy, emotion, comic relief, and sets and scenes (there was only a tattered burlap cloth hung in the background). The reviewer hoped that *Nabanna* would henceforth be staged outdoors, so that even the bare walls dividing people in the theater from people on the street would disappear.⁶⁰ This was very much in the spirit of IPTA's slogan in 1943—"People's Theatre Stars the People" (note, however, the continuing use of the term *star* with regard to the people onstage).⁶¹

Needless to say, *Nabanna* was played not by actual peasants but by middle-class IPTA activists, including four Communist Party members. This choice was an act of conscious dissimulation, in that the figures onstage were neither the people nor theater professionals. As a posture of unmediated presence, *Nabanna* seemed to artfully conceal its own theatricality, its aesthetic artifice, in a way that would be impossible for a novel or a painting. Reviewers registered this fact of dissimulation. Writing about *Jabanbandi* (The testimony), another "realistic" play by Bijon Bhattacharya, a reviewer marveled at the fact that communist activists played peasants better than peasants themselves—reminding him of the legendary nineteenth-century actor Ardhendu Shekhar Mustafi, who played a nasty colonial indigo planter in *Neel Darpan* to such effect that the famous social reformer Ishwarchandra Vidyasagar threw a shoe at him in sheer revulsion.⁶² The point of theater, it appears, was not so much to represent reality faithfully as to effect a productive confusion between reality and art. Hence perhaps *impersonation* would be a better term to use here than *representation*. By that logic playacting was indisputably a political skill—enabling middle-class communists to "declass" more effectively onstage than in life!⁶³

A detractor, however, criticized *Nabanna* for failing as theater precisely because of its unmitigated realism. The play incorporated a long list of political issues—the Quit India Movement, the 1943 famine, black marketing of food, the colonial government indifference to people's suffering, and trafficking of destitute women—sans any aesthetic unity or narrative cohesion. *Nabanna* lacked emotional focus and character development, merely showcasing a set of discrete social roles in the name of the people. These lacks, however, were overcome by the sheer power of acting, the critic conceded, thus formulating sharply the paradox of a real that was predicated on playacting and impersonation.⁶⁴ In response, yet another reviewer pointed out that the very act of "staging the people before the people"—producing a mirror effect via techniques of impersonation—created an unprecedented atmosphere and a political charge that made technical issues of theatricality redundant.⁶⁵

Right after the success of *Nabanna*, both Bijon Bhattacharya and Sombhu Mitra disassociated from IPTA.⁶⁶ The Communist Party asked that *Nabanna* travel to various parts of rural Bengal as part of a party campaign. There was also talk of mass subscription for IPTA on the line of party recruitment. The directors refused on the grounds that theater required technical skills, regular rehearsals, and a certain professional patience, which would be jeopardized by such direct politicization.⁶⁷ The very realism of the play required, in other words, a honing of theatrical artifice, a point that was entirely missed by party leaders, who were more interested in giving people's theater an organizational form like the political party.⁶⁸ Utpal Dutt, who worked with IPTA for less than a year, was also critical of the party's understanding of people's theater. Even as he agreed that people's theater must be democratized and rescued from the tyranny of the individual actor-hero, he criticized *Nabanna* for its inattention to stagecraft. Inattention to stagecraft, Dutt said, led one to reduce theater to acting and unwittingly succumb to the traditional tyranny of the actor-hero, undercutting the task of staging the people as political community. In fact, Dutt was as impatient with the conventions of urban proscenium theater, with its flat and/or revolving stage, pictorial framing, painted scenes, and curtains and wings, as he was with the naturalistic claims of people's theater.⁶⁹

Dutt was fully committed to experimenting with sets, music, lighting, and acting. Theatrical devices were not *alankaras* (embellishments) to be taken off like ornaments from the body of the play, he said, in an implicit criticism as much of socialist realism as of the precolonial "figural" (*alankara*) school of aesthetics that was once engaged in a debate with the *rasa* school.⁷⁰ Theatrical devices were limbs of the body.⁷¹ Plays were not just about dramatic text, story, plot, or dialogue. While a play was indeed literature—*Hamlet*, Dutt said, was a visualization of thought onstage and hence literature as much as theater—its literariness was always subject to overwriting by the logic of staging. Theater was a mobilization of the entire sensorium—opening up new possibilities of vision, sound, and atmosphere. Contra Rancière, Dutt argued that stagecraft would in the near democratic future emancipate "the pen of the littérateur." Mobilizing theatrical atmospherics would enhance the expressivity of novels and short stories, far beyond literature's realist possibilities and semantic horizon.⁷² Theater would recast the literature of the future, rather than the opposite.

In a fascinating set of essays called "Steaming Hot Tea"—staged as a conversation among a philosopher, a playwright, a theater director, a linguist, and "us," the audience—Dutt tried to zero in on what exactly was unique about theater as an art form. To philosophers, theater was a means of conveying an idea; to linguists, it was a matter of semiotic and semantic intent; to playwrights, it was story, plot, and dialogue; to actors, it was a medium of self-expression (though actresses were more oriented toward politics, he added approvingly). And then there were the technicians—of light and sound—the proletariat who made stagecraft possible in the first place and who were also the theater public. But ultimately, it was the director or the dramaturge, Dutt insisted, who brought idea, meaning, story, technique, self, and community together. And, most important, the director rendered theater adequately theatrical.[73]

Theater, Dutt agreed with the Communist Party, was a powerful political tool because it breached social boundaries and brought the masses face-to-face with themselves. But, more important, he added, theater was a powerful political tool because it brought together and subsumed all art forms, transforming the very nature of worldly experience and sensory perception. Its efficacy lay in its being a meta-genre that subsumed poetry, novel, story, painting, music, and much more.[74] If in earlier times acting was the crux of theater, it was now a potent combination of sound, light, sets, and stagecraft, which took over the actor (and presumably the spectator) in such a way that she would surprise herself onstage, Dutt said, quoting Gordon Craig's description of acting as a series of "accidental confessions" and implying that the theatrical experience by definition was one that took people by surprise, leading them to become a political community when they least expected.[75]

The world of thought was chaotic, like a dream, Dutt exclaimed. The task of theater was to capture this multisensory and multidirectional nature of thought and give it unity—a unity that discursive and narrative prose achieved only at the cost of flattening out the polysemic and sensuous quality of the aesthetic moment. Theater, however, achieved this by generating an atmosphere—a total, immersive experience—mobilizing whatever aesthetic artifice and artistic genre the director saw fit. For it was atmosphere that held together the heterogeneous forces that made up both theater and life. Dutt took the example of Tagore's play *Achalayatan* (1912), which was a critique of a regimented and petrified society with a strict hierarchy between knowledge, work, and devotion. The play, according to Dutt, was held together by the ambience of relentless rains, which eventually dissolved the boundaries between the dry theoreticians, the worker drones, and the obedient public who peopled the play. Similarly, the major commercial hit *Alamgir*, about the last Mughal emperor Aurangzeb, was held together by the atmospherics of desert dryness and unquenchable thirst. We are back to atmospherics, once more, which give theater its inherent theatricality—subtly challenging and reorienting the spectators' sense perceptions and gathering them into a shared ambience.[76]

To Dutt, theater, having passed through the moment of realism, must leave it behind and strive for the hyperrealism proper to theatricality. No one demanded realism from music and dance, he exclaimed. Poetry, too, exceeded realism in its uses of rhyme, meter, and sonorous effect. In the same way, theater must also be freed from realist expectations.[77] Dutt mentioned the example of successful nationalist plays—Girish Ghosh's *Siraj ud daula* (1906) and *Mir Ka-*

sim (1907), both about Bengal nawabs deposed by the British in the late eighteenth century; D. L. Roy's *Rana Pratap* (1905), about the valorous Rajput king who fought the Mughals; and Kshirode Prasad Vidyabinode's *Alamgir* (1921) to prove the importance of heroism, romance, emotion, intrigue, and atmosphere in theater. There is "nothing called too much theatricality," he said. Theatricality by definition was a form of excess, an exaggeration and enhancement of real life.[78] Dutt was particularly impressed by *Alamgir*, a play much criticized by Bengal modernists for being melodramatic and historically fallacious. *Alamgir* was, however, a major box-office hit, not only because of its emotional intensity but also, according to Dutt, because of its efficacious use of theatrical devices. The play was structured around pairs of characters—Aurangzeb and Udipuri, Bhimsingha and Jaysingha, Rupkumari and Kambaksh—meant to express the different aspects of the medieval Mughal-Rajput political dialectic. The frisson between the characters of each pair was interrupted by the mediatory presence of a third impartial and tranquil character, an instance of *punctum indifference*. The result was a framework of politics that moved beyond both historicism and realism. Historians, both colonial and national, depicted Aurangzeb as a religious bigot and tyrant. In the play, however, Aurangzeb comes across as a self-ironic and hyper-rationalist figure. He destroys temples because they are the dens of corrupt priests who defraud common people. That such a statement could be made publicly in 1920s Bengal, by no less than the much-maligned Muslim king Aurangzeb, without it leading to Hindu-Muslim political violence was only because it was done theatrically. In other words, to Dutt, theater was political because it made possible what was impossible in reality—in this case, a political community of the future cutting across existing identitarian hostilities.[79]

Dutt, as ideologically driven a communist as any, staged plays as part of communist election campaigns. Yet instead of seeking to depict the people as a collectivity onstage, as *Nabanna* did, he favored classical theater with its larger-than-life heroes and its declamatory delivery: "The strife of the people are no less than those of any heroes of our time, any of the Greek gods. Dionysian rituals are still performed in our land, it awaits an eye to see it and to project it on the stage.... A snake charmer or a boar hunter or a boatman on the river Padma with all his troubles seems to be glorious. Project him, and he will sail down the river in Greece, even down the Clyede into the sea, yes, he can."[80] "The proletarian hero is today's Hamlet," he said, simultaneously simple and complex, subject to intense hatreds and cosmic loves. Leftists might, he added, scoff at the sacrifices of nationalist revolutionaries like Bhagat Singh or Kshudiram Bose, as individual acts of heroism and no more. But they were the ones that people made songs about, because these figures rendered themselves to theatricality.[81]

True, the real hero of today's politics is the people as collectivity. But that does not mean that theater must stage the people literally as a collective. Communist theater tends to stage a cartel of villains—the capitalist, the military, the police, the landlord, the black marketer—and then posit the people as a mirror image of that combination, hoping that the people would come through by the mere dint of inversion. But if we learn to "see the worker through the eyes of another worker," the worker too will stand individuated, as a unique combination of good and evil, strengths and weaknesses, no less than a Hamlet or a Lear. He will then appear both as a maker of history and as a plaything of destiny, and in that sense a hero like that of classical Greek tragedy.[82]

Utpal Dutt then turned to popular theater. The masses in India, he said, are "addicted" to epics, the Ramayana and the Mahabharata. In fact, the Mahabharata is itself a staged narrative. Every episode in it is structured in the form of reported speech and problematizes the spectatorial experience (for instance, through the story of the blind king Dhritarashtra witnessing the great war through the eyes of the rapporteur Sanjay). This dramatic form—of staging stories within stories[83]—creates a reflexive distance between witness and spectator, actor and narrator. Bertolt Brecht uses this epic form in a modern way in his theory of *Verfremdungseffekt*. But to the Indian people, alienation is already a familiar aspect of the theatrical experience, Dutt argued. When the *sutradhar*—the one who holds the thread of the story—comes onstage, interrupting the unfolding drama, his commentaries are precisely an occasion for reflection and analysis. In the same way, when the *kathak* (the teller of the epic) performs the double role of dramatic character and interpreter of drama, of actor and viewer, he effects a productive estrangement of the spectator from herself in the very act of spectatorship[84] and, one might add, the desired confusion between art and reality that makes political community possible.

But this does not mean, as Brecht implied, that emotions have to be eliminated from theater. Dutt insisted that the traditional dramatic form of the *jatra* survived well into the twentieth century because it was able to produce intense shared emotions—*rasa*—as the ground of political community.[85] Interestingly, the term *jatra* literally means a "procession," a term that would acquire political connotations in modern times. Scholars of this popular theatrical form trace the origins of *jatra* to religious processions, animated by song and dance, that were earlier part of Vaishnava devotional practice. *Jatras* eventually became the most popular theatrical form of Bengal.[86] Because they were traditionally staged around mythological and religious themes, they remained outside the purview of state censorship under the Dramatic Performances Act, allowing them to be more transparently political than urban commercial theater. The transformation of *jatra* to a political art form was led by the "people's poet" Mukunda Das (1878–1934). His *swadeshi jatras*—such as *Karmakshetra* (The land of karma), *Samaj* (Society), *Palliseva* (Service to the village), and *Brahmacharini* (The ascetic woman)—which combined songs, recitations and long political speeches, were powerful tools of mobilization during both the 1905–10 movement against Bengal partition and the 1920–22 noncooperation movement. His works were proscribed, and he was put in jail. Following Mukunda Das came the *jatra* of Bhushan Das (d. 1917), whose *Matripuja*, ostensibly based on a story from the *Markandeya Purana*, staged the conflict between kingly power and *praja* power, leading to the incarceration of its writer, publisher, and printer.[87] At the very time when IPTA staged *Nabanna*, Brajendrakumar De (1907–76), a school headmaster by profession, produced the *jatra Akaler Desh* (Land of famines, 1944).[88] Later, Bengal *jatra* would go on to stage plays on Marx, Lenin, Hitler, and Mao.

Utpal Dutt himself produced *jatras*. In his *Toward a Revolutionary Theatre* (1982), he said that *jatra* as a theatrical form allowed a perfect "dialectical balance" between "poetry and dramatic prose, between finiteness of each of my characters and the infinity of re-created myth."[89] Dutt often staged plays and *jatras* simultaneously and side by side, as he did with his play on Left militancy *Teer* (Arrow, 1967) and his *jatra Rifle* (1968). Recalling his production of *Rifle* under the guidance of the *jatra* actor Panchu Sen, Dutt said that the denouement of *jatra* had to be intense and exaggerated, a veritable explosion of emotions—as if in imitation of an insurrectionary moment.[90] In fact, Dutt subtly transformed some of the conventions of traditional *jatra* in order to heighten its emotional potential. Traditional *jatra* inevitably had figures like the *vivek* (the voice of conscience) and the *juri* (the singer who connects narrative episodes), who would come onstage to interrupt the flow of action with commentary and song. Dutt eliminated these elements because these ancient "Brechtian devices," he felt, belied the people's expectation of "the dramatic atmosphere getting thicker and thicker, until it became almost unbearable."[91] Theater scholar Rustom Bharucha tells us that, according to Dutt, *jatra* moves in a series of inexorable "convulsions": "Your body becomes part of a mass of bodies and your life becomes absorbed in a cluster of experiences. Just as one loses one's identity in a crowd, one tends to lose oneself in the expectations of a jatra audience. It is difficult to respond to jatra as an individual. . . . Jatra is truly the people's theatre of Bengal."[92] Dutt's statement thus echoes the classical definition of *rasa* as a collective or generalized emotional experience. Dutt even staged *Macbeth* in villages, before thousands of peasant spectators. Shakespeare was successful among rural crowds, Dutt would say, because Shakespeare's form of theatricality could be easily rendered into the form of myth, with larger-than-life figures—kings, gods, demons, cosmic forces, "blood and thunder," and "high-flown prose."[93]

In perhaps his most self-reflexive play, *Tiner Talawar* (The tin sword), Dutt played the role of Benimadhab, the tyrannical director of the nineteenth-century Great Bengal Opera. The play opens with the director's backstage encounter with a sweeper, who cleans feces and scares others by his polluting presence. He has no interest in theater but is a critical part of the cluttered backstage of commercial theater, involving dubious financial transactions and quarrels between actors, playwrights, technicians, and the director—exposing to public view the contingencies of theater as a collaborative event. Benimadhab refuses a young idealist playwright's demand that they stage *Titu Mir*, a play on the eponymous peasant leader of the Faraizi rebellion, because it might be neither commercially viable nor acceptable to colonial censors. But when Benimadhab goes onstage, acting out his role in *Sadhabar Ekadasi* (a social satire by Dinabandhu Mitra of *Neel Darpan* fame), he encounters a scornful Englishman in the audience. Benimadhab, unbeknownst to himself, slowly transforms into Titu Mir onstage. It is through the staging of a play within a play, through the internal dialectics of theater itself, that we thus see the unexpected emergence of the people before an audience of the people.[94] The people once again surprise themselves by becoming a political community without intending to do so!

It is interesting to contrast Dutt's *jatras* and plays to the play *Michil* (The procession) by Badal Sarkar (1925–2011). Sarkar, the doyen of Third Theatre or Poor Theatre, turned his back on the commercial stage and did away with sets and scenes, working only with empty space and the bodies of his actors in an explicitly realist mode, which however exceeded realism via its stylistic innovations. *Michil* is a play about the quest for the true procession, the true political assembly. *Michil* does not happen on a stage. Instead, in an empty room, bare benches are placed for the audience, with a mazelike arrangement of empty, L-shaped corridors in between. The actors move through these spaces in diverse versions of crowd formation, in changing speed and rhythm. They become a surge of travelers on a train, anonymous bodies hanging from the doors of an overcrowded bus, a jubilant procession going to the river Ganga to immerse the Durga idol at the end of the season of worship, Hindus and Muslims engaged in a bloodletting riot, political demonstrators scattering before police charge, and so on. Throughout this incessant movement, the spectators as much as the protagonists keep waiting for the true procession to emerge—for the people to materialize in purity and community.[95]

Conclusion

Theatricality and antitheatricality, Martin Puchner says, are central to modern imaginations of politics. European modernists looked with suspicion on theater—with its unruly mass audience, idiosyncratic and amoral star actors, profiteering practices, collective and itinerant life, and, above all, emotional charge and demagoguery—all of which seemed to challenge the purity and integrity of art. Modernists preferred the textual form of the drama to the performative form of theater because texts were amenable to solitary reading and aesthetic judgment, by an emotionally stable, impartial, individual reader. Consequently, the modernist practice of writing plays meant to be read "in the closet," as it were, rather than staged, by those like Samuel Beckett, Bertolt Brecht, and Stéphane Mallarmé. In opposition to modernists, avant-gardists, however, celebrated theater as a total work of art, involving all the human senses and all classes of people, artistes, audiences, workers, and businessmen, implying that theater was indeed a model of people in collectivity. Despite their "stage fright," then, modernists felt compelled to return to theater over and over again as a constant reference point.[96] And not just in theater; Puchner finds theatricality pervading diverse genres of political writing in modern times, including the manifesto and indeed political philosophy itself.[97] He argues that twentieth-century philosophers like Søren Kierkegaard, Friedrich Nietzsche, Jean-Paul Sartre, Albert Camus, and Gilles Deleuze constructed their texts in the form of a "drama of ideas," following Plato, who developed a dialogue-based dramaturgy for thought, in opposition to the Aristotelian rejection of theater as a place of sensory illusion and moral decay.[98]

I agree with Puchner's finding of widespread theatricality in diverse modern genres. Developing philosophical arguments via staged dialogues was common in colonial India as much as in Europe, as demonstrated by iconic texts like Bankim's *Dharmatattva*, which I have discussed at length, and Gandhi's *Hind Swaraj*. But the European story of modernism versus avant-gardism does not entirely sit well with the story I am trying to narrate here, even though we do see glimpses of modernist antitheatricalism and avant-gardist theatricalism in modern India as well. For unlike the modernist recasting of theater as a textual genre, to be read rather than experienced, what we see in Bengal at this time is quite the opposite tendency—namely, a heightened presence of staging and theatrical techniques in textual genres like novels and short stories and an unexpected redeployment of precolonial theatrical concepts such as of *rasa* and *bhava* in the context of modern political art. We also see a deep preoccupation with the actual performance rather than only the writing and reading of plays. So popular novels and stories of the time, such as by Tarashankar Bandopadhyay and Saratchandra Chattopadhyay, almost inevitably came to be adapted as plays and later cinema, even if they were not originally intended as such.

This was not only because the theater was a site of popular assembly and intermixing of diverse publics, which it indeed was, but also because, and this has been the intended argument of this chapter, theater seemed to be the form in which common life appeared politically expressive. This imagination of theatricality, as that which inhered in and animated common people's everyday chores, sought to neutralize the activity/passivity, event/structure, politics/life, political/nonpolitical binaries that plagued modern political philosophy. And by cannily playing with sensory experience and with reality and fantasy, theater hoped that the people would surprise themselves by becoming a political community, even when the laws of historical necessity and routines of everyday life deemed it implausible.

EPILOGUE

> Then all the nations of birds lifted together
> the huge net of the shadows of this earth
> in multitudinous dialects, twittering tongues,
> stitching and crossing it. . . .
> until
> there was no longer dusk, or season, decline,
>   or weather,
> only this passage of phantasmal light . . .
> and this season lasted one moment, like the pause
> between dusk and darkness, between fury and peace,
> but, for such as our earth is now, it lasted long.
>   —Derek Walcott, "The Season of
>   Phantasmal Peace"

This book has examined elementary aspects of the political, with Durkheim on religion and Guha on peasant insurgency as predecessors of this form. The four elementary aspects I identify, following modern common sense, are self, action, idea, and people. I investigate each of these elements in its two contrasting aspects, with the dialectical tension between them serving as a demonstration of the operations through which they become political at particular moments in history. By highlighting this tension, I question—unlike Durkheim and Guha—the claim to elementary status of each element.

I write of each element in chapter pairs, in order to put sharply the constitutive gap within the element's claim to political ontology. So in my account, the political self appears split by the tension between renunciation and realpolitik. Action appears strung between being labor and being *karma*, the former invested in and the latter indifferent to the ends of action. The idea strives to simultaneously index the mundane and the supramundane, stumbling over an antinomy internal to the ontology of the idea and hence irreducible to the conventional theory/practice binary. And the people, in whose name modern politics happens, remain split between being pure structure and pure fiction.

Through this account I make three moves. The first is to expose, by showing up what is untenable at the heart of modern politics, our contemporary assumptions about the self-evidence, universality, and primacy of the political. The second is to demonstrate that there is indeed no essence to the political. What we call the political emerges only in terms of its differentiation from the nonpolitical—variously imagined in modernity as the religious, the economic, the aesthetic, and so on—and in terms of its delimitation by the extrapolitical that always already returns to haunt it. And the third is to try to bring to the surface the diverse traditions of theory and practice that play out in the setting up of the modern political. That is why in the title of the book I signpost the global South and begin this epilogue with an homage to Derek Walcott's "nations of birds," speaking "multitudinous dialects" and defying borders, both temporal and territorial.

I want to end this book with a few words about the currently popular phrase "theory from the global South." This is an exciting time in the academy. A number of scholars in Asia, Africa, and other parts of the world are thinking about global theory, opening up diverse forgotten and unnoticed worlds of ideas, practices, and metaphors. All of us, wherever we are located, shall no doubt emerge the richer for this. And yet, there is no denying that the global South, like the erstwhile third world, is a geopolitical rather than an intellectual concept. It certainly has an unmistakable rhetorical charge and currency today, in its promise to challenge global epistemological hierarchies. It also helps us get away from narrow nationalist and "area studies" cartographies of the mind. In India, however, I must confess, this term is less often used and understood. Here I use it as a placeholder, even though I realize that there is really nothing called the global South and, indeed, there never was.

Historically, there have been crisscrossing thought circuits and thought regions (forgive the inelegant turn of phrase), where ideas have inhabited and passed through—India, Southeast Asia, and China; India, the Mediterranean, and the Arab world; and indeed India and Europe. And there have been fascinating instances of "thinking across traditions" for centuries—philosophical border crossings reminiscent of Walcott's nations of birds. After all, as philosopher of science Sundar Sarukkai says, it is only through translation across languages and traditions that words, including scientific terms, become philosophical concepts. Otherwise, they remain just words, with local meanings and contextual allusions.[1] The history of any intellectual tradition thus is a history of travel and translation. I have already mentioned some instances in the book—David Hume reading Dara Shukoh's mutual adaptation of the Upanishads and the Koran; Weber referencing Chanakya as exemplar of the vocation of politics; and everybody, from Italy to Persia, reading the *Panchatantra* for political insights via animal stories. It was only in colonial times that these intellectual circuits got obstructed and replaced by an unhelpful West/non-West organizing principle.

What we today recognize as modern European political philosophy was also very much a product of intellectual exchange across traditions, even if the histories of these exchanges were subsequently erased by discourses of modernity, race, and colonialism. So Laura Marks's study of Deleuze and new media art describes in great detail the cross-pollination of European philosophy, algorithmic imagination, Islamic art and architecture, and Arabic philosophies of atomism and illusionism.[2] Souleymane Bachir Diagne describes the cross-fertilization of traditional African art, modern African poetry, and French existentialism in the early twentieth century.[3] Murad Idris discusses the rise of the modern idea of "war for peace" in the interface of Greek, Christian, and Arab philosophies.[4] The term "global South"—based on a North/South binary—even as it seeks to liberate thought from Eurocentrism, engenders a forgetting of these histories of shifting cartographies of thought, something we must remain wary of.

Thinking across traditions, one should add, not only allows us to recover lost and forgotten intellectual cartographies but also helps us carve out thought regions anew. This is as crucial, because charting unusual philosophical routes helps us step outside of the common sense of our times. This book implicitly tries to do so. When I argue that the nonpolitical and the extrapolitical are at the very heart of the modern concept of politics, it appears highly counterintuitive to all of us who have grown up with an unshakable faith in a ubiquitous and universal political. Similarly, when I argue that it is conceptually impossible to think of politics as action, because it renders life itself into an irresoluble problem before thought, that too appears equally counterintuitive, given that we continue to call politics "activism" even today. Again, when I say that equality never really becomes a political idea in modernity, because both the economic and the spiritual grounds for the thinking of equality return as extrapolitical foundations of the political—that too appears rather strange because modern politics continues to happen in the name of equality. That I do make such arguments in this book and with some conviction is only because I am compelled to think across incommensurable temporalities and traditions, which lead me in unexpected and even surprising directions.

I am forced to think across traditions by the very nature of the materials I study. I read diverse modern texts, major and minor, in English and in the Indian languages, at the cusp of which modern imaginations of the political emerge. In this process of reading and reassembling, it becomes clear that in modern times, even as everybody cross-references European thought, something that is reducible neither to a mechanical image of European influence nor to some seamless globalism unsullied by knowledge politics, they also think with a diversity of concepts and categories drawn from noncolonial, nonmodern, and indeed nonnational traditions—vernacular, Sanskrit, Persian, and Arabic but also spiritual, theological, economic, aesthetic; and discursive, literary, visual, satirical—not all of which have to do with politics in any obvious sense. One is able to make sense of the intricacy of this material only by seriously taking at face value, and patiently working through, its excess over our given analytical frameworks, founded as they are on the European tradition of normative political theory. What emerges at the end of the project is an imagination of the modern political, and indeed of the limits of the political, very different from what we assume today.

But the project of this book is not to demonstrate theory from the global South or even global theory for that matter. Its project is merely what it states—namely, to understand the nature and limits of the modern political. To do so, the book has had to traverse multiple intellectual traditions, simply because it was demanded by the materials at hand. In other words, the implication of the book, rather than its stated remit, is global theory.

In retrospect, however, it seems to me that thinking across traditions and temporalities has an added advantage for those of us who are specifically interested in politics. It helps us approach in new ways what we experience in modern times as impossible political conundrums. The most obvious one that comes through in the context of this book is the intractability of the economy to political analysis. This intractability is usually understood in two ways. In the academy, it is understood as the product of a two-hundred-year-old disciplinary separation between politics and economics, allowing politics to borrow a certain universal language from economics while keeping the economy beyond the reach of politics and its vicissitudes. In a popular sense, it is understood in terms of an unholy alliance between politicians and powerful market forces, which keeps the economy artificially insulated from structures of political accountability. Both readings are undoubtedly correct. But there is more to the issue than this. When one studies, as I try to do in this book, economic reasoning as part of the history of equality, as it struggles to emerge as a modern political ideal, it becomes obvious that in modernity, the economic often operates on the same conceptual ground as the spiritual, both claiming to index those aspects of the human creaturely condition that resist total politicization and, for that very reason, help ground and render meaningful politics itself. This extrapolitical aspect of the economic, like that of the spiritual and more recently the ecological, marks out the limits of the political. It resists final resolution as it were in terms of purely political answers, while enabling us to recognize politics when we see it.

This brings me to the other major political conundrum of our times, which we may call "waiting for revolution" (wistfully rhyming Tracy Chapman's beautiful song "Talkin' bout a Revolution" where we forever stand in "welfare lines" straining to sense the whisper of imminent change). This is our disappointment with the so-called political apathy of ordinary people who refuse to mobilize, when by all political logic, they should and they must, or when, instead of mobilizing, they abdicate their so-called sovereignty to a powerful and populist demagogue. Pierre Rosanvallon writes of this conundrum in his critique of the modern imagination of politics as dramaturgy of the will.[5] I go over the same ground in this book when I show up the impossibility of staging popular will in terms of a permanent mobilizing structure such as the party. Rosanvallon further argues that politics, even in modern democracies, is always the preoccupation of a few. The people at large exist in an oblique relationship to politics, watching over and asking questions of the political class.[6] My sense is to go a step further and, at the risk of sounding blasphemous, admit that the people are indeed reluctant political beings who take to the streets once in a while and when absolutely cornered. Otherwise, people go about the business of life and living, and sometimes voting. But this does not mean that people are antipolitical or apolitical (Rosanvallon uses the term *unpolitical*). They appear antipolitical only in light of a very narrow definition of politics. This is the modern definition of politics as action par excellence, a definition, as I argue in this book, that places politics in an impossible dichotomy with life. It is this narrow definition of politics that compelled a number of political thinkers in modern times, such as Tagore and Gandhi, to espouse a critique of the political. They insisted—sometimes in the name of spirituality, sometimes aesthetics, sometimes even purely existential questions of desire and loss—that not all problems of life have a political resolution. But if we shed our modern imagination of politics as action and nothing but action, it becomes clear that most people are indeed acutely politic in their everyday lives—displaying the orientation, which I call "being" politic rather than "doing" politics and which has had a long intellectual history in the *arthashastra* and *nitishastra* genres of thought that I cite extensively in this book.

To put it differently, there is a quiet subtext to this book suggesting that it is no longer enough to critique Eurocentrism, though that has been an essential opening move toward decolonializing thought (I use the term *decolonial* here following the concept of decoloniality as coined by Walter Mignolo and his colleagues in Latin America as well as more recently inflected by many thinkers on the African continent).[7] Nor is it enough to merely note and celebrate the fascinating diversity of thought traditions in the world. The task at hand for us is to think "outside the box," to use a managerial cliché, the box being our modern-day political common sense. The task is also above all to think theoretically.

In an attempt to discuss our experience of teaching theory in Indian classrooms, my colleagues and I wrote a longish essay a few years ago titled "The Work of Theory: Thinking across Traditions."[8] In this quasi manifesto, we stated that decolonizing thought requires us not just to write counterhistories and elicit counterfactuals from other traditions, but also to attempt counterphilosophies, in the process redefining what theory and philosophy mean in the first place. This in turn requires us to rethink the very relationship between history and philosophy, that is, between historical events and conceptual events. The first step toward this end is to read with attention and patience details from unfamiliar histories. While Indians are used to reading in great detail about the history of Europe, they are just as unfamiliar with, say, Arab or Chinese or African history as Europeans and Americans are about Indian history, a colonial-cum-nationalist legacy with which the world, despite its claims to globalism, still struggles.

But then even as we practice fidelity to other histories, the discipline of history must also be rethought. I say this self-consciously as someone who has been a historian by disciplinary training. History as a discipline has come a long way, and yet, I believe, it is still somewhat a prisoner of transition narratives. It may no longer be the transition narrative that held us in thrall when we were young—namely, feudalism to capitalism to socialism. But it still is one or more of the following—absolutism to liberalism to neoliberalism, or print to celluloid to digital, or empire to nation to global to planetary, or god to man to the posthuman. In any case, what is modernity if not a theory of a temporal supersession of the past (despite retro music and retro fashion!), and what indeed is our current fascination with the prefix "post-" (postmodern, posthuman, postcolonial, postnational, and such like) if not a desperate attempt at escaping transition narratives?

The problem with transition narratives is that they disallow the recognition of contemporaneity, of different pasts in the present, to invoke Eelco Runia's theory of "presence" here.⁹ Thinking outside transition narratives allows us not only to pay full attention to our own times but also to sense the presence of different traditions and genealogies in our contemporary, of different futures and emergences, indeed, of different temporalities working "at the same time." Hence while engaging with other histories is absolutely necessary for a global theory, we must also strive to emancipate ourselves from history and context, that is, achieve a certain transcontextuality and transtemporality, even a certain disjointedness with our own times. It is for this reason that we must reconfigure the relationship between history and philosophy.

Finally, we must recognize that different thought traditions in the world have differently configured the relationship between the historical and the philosophical, the particular and the universal, the sociological and the cosmological, and that we must start by admitting that there is no one model or one level of abstraction that is sui generis theory. Once we do so, we shall also be able to break out of the debilitating theory/practice, philosophy/life binary, which constrains political imaginations in modern times. This book is a modest offering in that direction.

The question for me, then, is no longer whether a Marx or a Foucault or an Agamben is Eurocentric or "applicable" to southern societies or not. The question is also not whether there are universal figures of philosophy in the global South analogous to a Marx or a Hegel or a Spinoza. The question really is about what kinds of conceptual insights and conceptual personae of global salience emerge from a faithful study southern realities and materialities, if we actually pay attention to them by taking off our Marxist, Foucauldian, Agambenian, or Latourian spectacles.[10] And then we can sit back and enjoy reading Marx and Foucault and Agamben and Latour, and Partha Chatterjee and Wang Hui and Ibn Sina and Abhinavagupta and Nagarjuna and Senghor and Fanon and Ambedkar and Du Bois and C. L. R. James and Souleymane Diagne and Sylvia Wynter and so, so many more (there is indeed a poetry to lists, as some classical Indian schools of epistemology remind us). We can then embark on an adventurous time travel that makes us not just free political subjects but also free theoretical subjects!

NOTES

Introduction

1 Chakrabarty, *Provincializing Europe*, 9.
2 Kaviraj, "An Outline of a Revisionist Theory of Modernity," 497–526.
3 Chakrabarty, "A Small History of *Subaltern Studies*," 3–19.
4 Bandopadhyay, "Another History."
5 Mukhia, *The Feudalism Debate*.
6 Bayly, *Recovering Liberties*.
7 Sartori, *Liberalism in Empire*.
8 Chatterjee, *Lineages of Political Society*, 1–28.
9 Schmitt, *The Concept of the Political*.
10 Lefort, *The Political Forms of Modern Society*.
11 Nancy and Lacou-Labarthe, *Retreating the Political*, 108.
12 Badiou, *Being Singular Plural*, 47–48.
13 Marchart, *Post-foundational Political Thought*, 8–9.
14 Badiou, *Being and Event*; Rancière, *The Politics of Aesthetics*.
15 Rancière, *Hatred of Democracy*; Mazzarella, *The Mana of Mass Society*.
16 Chatterjee, *The Nation and Its Fragments*, 25–26.
17 Inston, "Inscribing the Egalitarian Event," 15–26.
18 Ajay Skaria mentions, in a private conversation, that equality is best thought of as an "intimation," perhaps even an originary intimation. This intimation can become an idea, as during the French Revolution. But equality's nature as an intimation rather than an idea or an ideal continues, as evinced by the indubitable restlessness of this quasi concept.
19 In the Indian context, the definitive statement was made by Ranajit Guha in his lecture on *An Indian Historiography for India*.
20 Schmitt, *The Concept of the Political*.
21 Ries, "Anthropology and the Everyday," 725–42.
22 Dodescu, "State versus Market," 17–32.
23 I use the term *aspects* here—and not *forms* (of religion à la Durkheim) or *structures* (of kinship à la Claude Lévi-Strauss)—for the following reason. The term *aspect*—with its connotations of direction, perspective, facade, surface—better

captures my argument that what we are dealing with here is the political at "face value," which is exactly what I am trying to deconstruct. Structure, on the other hand, is a claim of a deep, stable truth below the surface, which is not my claim at all. And I reserve the term *form* for the more active aesthetic impulse of "giving form"—e.g., the political party as an effort to give political form to the people. My *form* does not preexist historically changing modes of being political, as it does for Durkheim in his account of religion.

24 Deleuze and Guattari, *What Is Philosophy?*.
25 Guha, *Elementary Aspects of Peasant Insurgency*, 2.
26 Das, *Life and Words*.
27 Galanter, *Competing Inequalities*.

Chapter 1. Renunciation and Antisocial Being

1 Sinha, *Colonial Masculinity*; Chowdhury, *Frail Hero and Virile History*; Sarkar, *Hindu Wife, Hindu Nation*.
2 Banerjee, "The Abiding Binary."
3 I do not fully subscribe to the argument made by south Asian "early modernists" that the whole world was becoming "modern" before colonialism came and spoiled it. Subrahmanyam, "Connected Histories."
4 In precolonial times, *samaj* did not mean society. It meant the ability "to move together," the sociality of caste groups, heterodox religious communities, or even urbane cultured classes. A region had and an individual belonged to multiple *samajs* at the same time. *Samaj* was neither national society nor the conceptual other of the state.
5 Tagore, "Bharatbarsher Itihas" (1902), in *Rabindra Rachanavali*, 4:382–84.
6 Mehta, "Gandhi on Politics, Democracy and Everyday Life."
7 For the relationship between law and violence, see Kolsky, *Colonial Justice in British India*.
8 Sinha, *Specters of Mother India*; Dirks, *Castes of Mind*.
9 Sumit Sarkar and Tanika Sarkar, *Women and Social Reform in Modern India*.
10 Ambedkar, *Annihilation of Caste* (1936), in *Babasaheb Ambedkar Writings and Speeches*, 1:23–97.
11 Ambedkar, *What Congress and Gandhi Have Done to the Untouchables*, in *Babasaheb Ambedkar Writings and Speeches*, 9:78–84.
12 Ambedkar, "Philosophy of Hinduism," in *Babasaheb Ambedkar Writings and Speeches*, 3:84.
13 Nikhilananda, *Vivekananda: A Biography*; Chattopadhyay, *Swami Vivekananda in India*.
14 Vivekananda, "The Social Conference Address," in *The Complete Works of Swami Vivekananda*, 4:303–7.
15 This was the time of the "rediscovery" of Buddhism. Edwin Arnold published *The Light of Asia* in 1870; Rajendralal Mitra published *The Sanskrit Buddhist Literature of Nepal* in 1882; Aghornath Gupta published *Sakyamuni Charit o Nirvanatattva* in 1882; and Girish Ghosh's play *Buddhacharit* was commercially staged in Calcutta in 1885.

16 Vivekananda, "Religion: The True Basis of Moral Life" (excerpted from "Practical Vedanta IV"), in *The Indispensable Vivekananda*, 148.
17 Nivedita, *Master as I Saw Him*, 161.
18 Nivedita, *Master as I Saw Him*, 152.
19 Nivedita, *Master as I Saw Him*, 30.
20 Sarkar, "'Kaliyuga,' 'Chakri' and 'Bhakti'"; Chatterjee, "The Religion of Urban Domesticity."
21 Shamashastry, *Kautilya's Arthashastra*, 64–65.
22 Bandopadhyay, "Pita Putra Dvairath," 386–88.
23 Pinch, *Peasants and Monks*.
24 Pinch, *Peasants and Monks*, 4–5. See also Pinch, *Warrior Ascetics and Indian Empires*.
25 Chatterjee, *Congress Politics in Bengal*.
26 For an argument about the centrality of renunciation in Gandhi and in early twentieth-century imaginations of democracy, see Gandhi, *The Common Cause*.
27 Sahajanand, *Sahajanand on Agricultural Labour and Rural Poor*.
28 Omana, *Sree Narayana Guru*; Kumar, "Self, Body and Inner Sense."
29 Chattopadhyay, *Anandamath, or The Sacred Brotherhood*.
30 Sarkar, "Birth of a Goddess."
31 To refer to some Indian-language authors whose work I read as primary material, such as Bankimchandra Chattopadhyay and Aurobindo Ghosh, I use first names, citing them as Bankim and Aurobindo. This is because in the case of Indian names, surnames such as Chattopadhyay and Ghosh are often very common, and the first names are really the distinguishing ones. In Indian-language texts or texts using materials in Indian languages, the convention is often to use first names, especially when these are famous. In the case of secondary materials, I follow the standard convention of citing by surname.
32 Bandopadhyay, *Kabitabali*, 115–17.
33 Prabhakar, *Awara Masiha*.
34 Banerjee, "Rehearsals for a Revolution."
35 Biswas, *Ujan Gang Baiya*, 32.
36 Many popular plays and farces on *kaliyuga*, published in the middle and late nineteenth century from *battala*, or the Grub Street of Calcutta, argued along these lines. Banerjee, "Time, Space and the 'Primitive' Within," in *Politics of Time*, 40–81.
37 Vivekananda, "The Right Approach to Reform," in *The Indispensable Vivekananda*, 102.
38 Vivekananda, "Religion: The True Basis of Moral Life," 145.
39 Nivedita, *Master as I Saw Him*, 111.
40 Vivekananda, "The Right Approach to Reform," 102.
41 Nivedita, *Master as I Saw Him*, 71; Lefort, *Democracy and Political Theory*, 19.
42 Vedanta, one among six Indic philosophical systems or *darshana* (Sankhya, Yoga, Nyaya, Mimamsa, Vasheshika, Vedanta), was a reinterpretation of the Upanishads. Vedanta argued against rituals and externalities of Vedic sacrifice and posed the problematic of dualism (or otherwise) of the supreme self

(*atman*), individual selves (*jiva*), and the world. Nineteenth-century Indian intellectuals, including Rammohan Roy, recast Vedanta as a rational and progressive religion.

43 Vivekananda, "The Vedanta: Lecture Delivered at Lahore on 12th November 1897," in *Selections from the Complete Works of Swami Vivekananda*, 255.
44 Vivekananda, "Is Vedanta the Future Religion?" (talk delivered in San Francisco, April 8, 1900), in *The Complete Works of Swami Vivekananda*, 8:122–41.
45 Vivekananda, "Practical Vedanta," in *The Indispensable Vivekananda*, 176.
46 Ganeri, *The Concealed Art of the Soul*.
47 Vivekananda, "The Vedanta," 251.
48 Vivekananda, "The Vedanta," 263.
49 Sloterdjik, *The Art of Philosophy*, 3.
50 Vivekananda, "A General Introduction to Yoga," in *The Indispensable Vivekananda*, 195–97.
51 Vivekananda, "Karma Yoga: Service before the Self" (1896), in *The Indispensable Vivekananda*, 208.
52 Vivekananda, "Karma Yoga," 207.
53 Nivedita, *Master as I Saw Him*, 59. *Paramahamsa* was an epithet for spiritual adepts who achieved perfect equanimity, or *nirvikalpasamādhi*.
54 Sen, "Editor's Introduction," in *The Indispensable Vivekananda*, 18.
55 Nivedita, *Master as I Saw Him*, 59.
56 Nivedita, *Master as I Saw Him*, 131.
57 Isherwood, *Ramkrishna and His Disciples*; Gupta, *The Gospel of Sri Ramkrishna*.
58 Sen, "Editor's Introduction," 18.
59 Nivedita, *Master as I Saw Him*, 61, 73.
60 Nivedita, *Master as I Saw Him*, 118.
61 Nivedita, *Master as I Saw Him*, 115–16.
62 Odud, *Hindu-Musalmaner Birodh*.
63 Nivedita, *Master as I Saw Him*, 95.
64 Nivedita, *Master as I Saw Him*, 119.
65 Vivekananda, "Sannyasa: Its Ideal and Practice," in *Selections from the Complete Works of Swami Vivekananda*, 365.
66 Nivedita, *Master as I Saw Him*, 48.
67 Nivedita, *Master as I Saw Him*, 51. For the concept of the witness-self in early Indian philosophy, see Gupta, *The Disinterested Witness*.
68 Nivedita, *Master as I Saw Him*, 49.
69 Devi, "Swami Vivekananda" (*Bharati*, 1896), in *Saraladevi Chaudhuranir Nirbachita Prabandha Sankalan*, 60.
70 Vivekananda, letter to Alasinga Perumal, November 19, 1894, in *The Complete Works of Swami Vivekananda*, 4:368.
71 Vivekananda, "Our Duty to the Masses: Letter from Chicago to H. H. Maharaja of Mysore" (June 23, 1894), in *The Complete Works of Swami Vivekananda*, 4:362.
72 Vivekananda, "Modern India" (*Udbodhana*, March 1899), in *The Complete Works of Swami Vivekananda*, 4:438–80, 468.

73 Vivekananda, "The Future of India," in *The Complete Works of Swami Vivekananda*, 3:294.
74 Nivedita, *Master as I Saw Him*, 198–99.
75 Cited by Basu, *Religious Revivalism as Nationalist Discourse*, 162.
76 Khare, *The Untouchable as Himself*.
77 Datta, *Swami Vivekananda, Patriot Prophet*.
78 Datta, *Studies in Indian Social Polity*; Datta, *Baishnaba Sahitye Samajatattva*.
79 Chakrabarty, "Bidhi Bam? Kolkatae Marx."
80 For the ascetic self-fashioning of early Bengal communists, see Dasgupta, "Marxism and Middle-Class Intelligentsia."
81 Vivekananda, "Thoughts on the Gita—I," in *The Indispensable Vivekananda*, 151–57.
82 Basu, *Religious Revivalism as Nationalist Discourse*, 34.
83 Roy, *Indian Traffic*, 92–127.
84 Aurobindo, *Bhavani Mandir* (1905), in *Bande Mataram*, 61–74.
85 Nivedita, *Master as I Saw Him*, 96.
86 Nivedita, *Master as I Saw Him*, 114.
87 Vivekananda, "Karma Yoga," 202.
88 Vivekananda, "Vedanta in Its Application to Indian Life," in *The Complete Works of Swami Vivekananda*, 3:245–46.
89 Vivekananda, "Influence of Indian Spiritual Thought in England" (speech presented at the Star Theatre, Calcutta, March 1898), in *The Complete Works of Swami Vivekananda*, 3:445.
90 Vivekananda, "Karma Yoga," 1:27–117; Vivekananda, "'Each Is Great in His Own Place,'" in *The Complete Works of Swami Vivekananda*, 1:37.
91 Tambe, "Gandhi's 'Fallen' Sisters," 24.
92 At Chauri Chaura, a group of peasants set fire to a police station. Gandhi withdrew the noncooperation movement overnight in criticism of violent masses, even though the movement was actually reaching its peak in 1922.

Chapter 2. Philosophy, Theater, and Realpolitik

1 Olivelle, *King, Governance, and Law in Ancient India*.
2 I use *Arthashastra* to refer to Kautilya's text and *arthashastra* to refer to the general tradition of thinking about worldly efficacy, as found in myriad texts across centuries. Similarly, I use Yoga to refer to a philosophical school and *yoga* to refer disciplines and practices of the self; Bhakti to refer to a devotional tradition and *bhakti* to refer to an orientation or disposition of the self.
3 Alphonso-Karakala, "Facets of Panchatantra."
4 McClish, "Political Brahmanism and the State."
5 Rao and Subrahmanyam, "An Elegy for *Niti*."
6 Alam, *The Languages of Political Islam*.
7 Kantorowicz, *The King's Two Bodies*.
8 Singh, "Politics, Violence and War in Kamandaka's *Nitisara*."
9 Carlo Formichi, 1899, as discussed by Sarkar in "Hindu Politics in Italian: Part 1."
10 Mishra, *Evolution of Kautilya's Arthashastra*, 17–18.

11 Sarkar, "Hindu Politics in Italian: Part 2," 751–52.
12 Sarkar, "Hindu Politics in Italian: Part 3," 370–72.
13 Weber, "Politics as Vocation," in *The Vocation Lectures*, 32–94, 88.
14 Kalidas Nag, historian, archaeologist, secretary to the Asiatic Society of Bengal, and one of the first nominated members of the upper house of the Indian parliament, was well known for a number of historical books and for his correspondence with Romain Rolland.
15 Nag, "Prof. Benoy Kumar Sarkar and the 'New Machiavelli.'"
16 Mantena, "Another Realism."
17 Kangle, *The Kautilya Arthashastra*, 280–81.
18 Sarkar, "Hindu Politics in Italian: Part 3," 370.
19 Dikshitar, "Kautilya and Machiavelli."
20 Sarkar, reflecting on Carlo Formichi's 1899 lecture "Hindus and Their Political Science," in "Hindu Politics in Italian: Part 1," 532–33.
21 Sarkar, "Hindu Politics in Italian: Part 1."
22 Sarkar, "Hindu Politics in Italian: Part 2," 755.
23 Sarkar, in a long footnote critiquing U. N. Ghoshal's 1923 magnum opus *Hindu Political Theories*, in "Hindu Politics in Italian: Part 3," 359.
24 Ghoshal, "More Light on Methods and Conclusions in Hindu Politics."
25 Ghoshal, *A History of Indian Political Ideas*.
26 Wilson, *Select Specimens of the Theatre of the Hindus*; Lal, *Great Sanskrit Plays, in Modern Translation*.
27 Tanvir, "Interview," 13, 16–18.
28 Das, *A History of Indian Literature, 500–1399*, 58–59.
29 Tagore, "Aitihasik Upanyas," in *Rabindra Rachanavali*, 13:818.
30 Chanakya plays were written by N. C. Kelkar (1913, Marathi), Badrinath Bhatia (1915, Hindi), Jayashankar Prasad (1931, Hindi), Balkrishna Kar (1926, Oriya), K. Mamman (1919, Malayalam), K. Vasudevan Musatu (1927, Malayalam), V. Krishnan Thampi (1930, Malayalam), and G. P. Deshpande (1987, Marathi), and so on.
31 Harinarayan Apte's Marathi novel *Chandragupta* (1905), translated into Hindi in 1924, Vidyananda Paramhansa's Kannada novel of 1917, and P. Avittam Tirummal Tampuran's Malayalam poem *Chandragupta Vijayam* (1920) are good examples. Das, *A History of Indian Literature, 1800–1910*, 113–14.
32 George, *Modern Indian Literature: An Anthology*, 1:167.
33 Mentionable Chanakya films are *Chanakya* (Saila Barua, Oriya, 1959), *Chanakya Chandragupta* (N. T. Rama Rao, Telegu, 1977), *Chanakya Sapatham* (K. Raghavendra, Telegu, 1986), *Chanakya Soothrangal* (Somanathan, Malayalam, 1994), and *Chanakyam/Chanakyan* (Rajeev Kumar, Telegu/Malayalam, 1989). See Rajadhyaksha and Willeman, *Encyclopaedia of Indian Cinema*.
34 Thus K. P. Jayaswal would quote precisely the *Arthashastra* and mention the term *janapada* to prove the existence of republics in ancient India. Jayaswal, *Hindu Polity*.

35 Sukumar Bandopadhyay, "Editor's Introduction," in Roy, *Chandragupta*, 17–18.
36 Prasad, "Chandragupta" (1931), in *Sampurna Natak*, 51.
37 Women and the lowborn, in principle, did not have a right to speak Sanskrit, the language of gods and Brahmins. They were therefore meant to speak in either Prakrit or the vernaculars.
38 Sarkar, "The Maratha Political Ideas of the 18th Century," 93.
39 Sarkar, "Hindu Politics in Italian: Part 3," 360–61; Ghoshal, "Reply to Benoy Kumar Sarkar," 422.
40 Illiah, *God as Political Philosopher*.
41 In Deshpande's play, the *sutradhar*, who appears in a Nehruvian jacket but still wears a *dhoti*, says at the very beginning: "The tale we are about to narrate is about the man who presented *modern* political thought in the third century BC." Deshpande, *Chanakya Vishnugupta*, 1; my emphasis.
42 Ambedkar, *Who Were the Shudras?*, 117.
43 Herling, *The German Gita*.
44 See Kapila and Devji, "Bhagavad Gita and Modern Thought."
45 Dasgupta, *The Indian Theatre*, 138.
46 Deshpande, *Chanakya Vishnugupta*, xi.
47 Bayly, "India, the Bhagavad Gita and the World."
48 Kosambi, *The Culture and Civilisation of Ancient India*, 186.
49 Harder, *Bankimchandra Chattopadhyay's* Srimadbhagabadgita, 60, quoted in Sartori, "The Transfiguration of Duty in Aurobindo's Essays on the Gita," 324.
50 Sartori, "Transfiguration of Duty," 327.
51 Aurobindo, *Essays on the Gita*, 10.
52 Kosambi, *The Culture and Civilisation of Ancient India*, 83.
53 Michelutti, "We the Yadavs Are a Caste of Politicians."

Chapter 3. Karma, Freedom, and Everyday Life

1 Nietzsche, *The Birth of Tragedy*, 130; Deleuze, *Nietzsche and Philosophy*.
2 Arendt, *The Human Condition*.
3 Scott, *Weapons of the Weak*; Certeau, *The Practice of Everyday Life*.
4 Bayat, *Life as Politics*.
5 Lath, "The Concept of Anrsamsya in Mahabharata."
6 Halbfass, "Practical Vedanta."
7 Guha, *An Indian Historiography for India*.
8 Roy cited in Halbfass, "Practical Vedanta," 177; Chattopadhyay, "The Ultimate Philosophy of Brahmanism" (letter to the editor, *Statesman*, September 29, 1882), in *Bankim Rachanavali*, 3:194–200; Tagore, "Nababarsha" (April 1903), English trans., Sumita Bhattacharya and Sibesh Bhattacharya, http://ifihhome.tripod.com/articles/nababarsha.html, accessed October 10, 2018.
9 Hegel, *Lectures on the Philosophy of World History*; Husserl, *The Crisis of European Sciences*, 280–83.
10 Sinha, "Theory and Practice in Indian Thought."

11   Partha Chatterjee shows how colonialism managed "alien" practices as "deviances" and "exceptions" to universal norms. Chatterjee, *Lineages of Political Society*, 1–28.
12   Mohanty, "Theory and Practice in Indian Philosophy."
13   The family of Valmiki, author of *Ramayana* and erstwhile bandit, refused to share in his *karma* even as they lived off the fruits of his plunder.
14   Was it the king's or the subjects' karma that was responsible for famine and epidemic in a kingdom?
15   Halbfass, "Karma, *Apurva*, and 'Natural' Causes."
16   This was equally true of nonmodern European philosophies. Hadot, *Philosophy as a Way of Life*; Sloterdjik *The Art of Philosophy*.
17   Sarma, *Mīmāṁsā Theory of Meaning*.
18   Olivelle, *The Dharmasutras*.
19   Chousalkar, "Political Philosophy of Arthashastra Tradition"; Chousalkar, "Methodology of Kautilya's Arthashastra"; Olivelle, *Pancatantra*.
20   Jullien, *A Treatise on Efficacy*.
21   Singh, "Role of Good Manners as a Bridge between World Religions."
22   Chousalkar, "The Concept of Apaddharma and the Moral Dilemma of Politics"; Bowles, "The Failure of Dharma."
23   Ernst, "Muslim Studies of Hinduism?."
24   My understanding of the Gita draws from Ellen Jane Briggs's insightful doctoral dissertation, "Freedom and Desire in the *Bhagavad Gītā*."
25   The three essays were almost simultaneously serialized in the 1880s in the periodicals *Prachar*, *Navajivan*, and *Bangadarshan*. *Krishnacharitra* was published as a book in 1892. *Dharmatattva* was first published as *Dharmatattva—1: Anushilan* in 1888. A revised version titled *Dharmatattva* was published after his death in 1894. *Srimadbhagavadgita* was published as a book in 1902. All three are collected in Chattopadhyay, *Bankim Rachanavali*, vol. 2.
26   Chattopadhyay, *Srimadbhagavadgita*, in *Bankim Rachanavali*, 2:705.
27   Chattopadhyay, *Dharmatattva*, in *Bankim Rachanavali*, 2:568.
28   Chattopadhyay, *Dharmatattva*, 2:583.
29   Chattopadhyay, *Srimadbhagavadgita*, 2:638.
30   Chattopadhyay, *Srimadbhagavadgita*, 2:669.
31   Chattopadhyay, *Dharmatattva*, 2:540.
32   Chattopadhyay, *Dharmatattva*, 2:526, 2:573.
33   Balslev, "The Idea of Abhyasa."
34   Chattopadhyay, *Dharmatattva*, 2:537, 2:540.
35   Chattopadhyay, *Dharmatattva*, 2:531, 2:552.
36   Chattopadhyay, *Dharmatattva*, 2:525–26.
37   Briggs, "Freedom and Desire in the *Bhagavad Gītā*," 29.
38   Briggs, "Freedom and Desire in the *Bhagavad Gītā*," 56–57.
39   Chattopadhyay, *Krishnacharitra*, in *Bankim Rachanavali*, 2:354.
40   Chattopadhyay, *Dharmatattva*, 2:562.
41   Haberman, *Acting as a Way to Salvation*, 69.

42 Briggs, "Freedom and Desire in the *Bhagavad Gītā*," 132.
43 Chattopadhyay, *Srimadbhagavadgita*, 2:689, 2:705.
44 Chattopadhyay, *Dharmatattva*, 2:585–86.
45 Chattopadhyay, *Dharmatattva*, 2:600.
46 Chattopadhyay, *Dharmatattva*, 2:585–89.
47 Chattopadhyay, *Dharmatattva*, 2:534–35.
48 Chattopadhyay, *Dharmatattva*, 2:549n.
49 Chattopadhyay, *Debi Chaudhurani* (1884), in *Bankim Rachanavali*, 1:727–808, 1:754–55.
50 Chattopadhyay, *Anandamath* (1882), in *Bankim Rachanavali*, 1:653–726. Also see Sarkar, "Birth of a Goddess."
51 Chattopadhyay, *Anandamath*, 1:688.
52 Chattopadhyay, *Anandamath*, 1:689.
53 Chattopadhyay, *Rajsingha* (1893), in *Bankim Rachanavali*, 1:607–714.
54 Chattopadhyay, *Srimadbhagavadgita*, 2:614–15, 2:691, 2:702–3.
55 Chattopadhyay, *Srimadbhagavadgita*, 2:609–10.
56 Chattopadhyay, *Anandamath*, 1:725.
57 Samaddar, *Emergence of the Political Subject*.
58 Chattopadhyay, *Dharmatattva*, 2:548–49.
59 Samaddar, *Emergence of the Political Subject*, 127.
60 MacLean, *A Revolutionary History of Interwar India*.
61 Aurobindo, "Gitar Bhumika" (1909), in *Sri Aurobinder Mul Bangla Rachanabali*, 79–128.
62 Aurobindo, "Gitar Bhumika," 102–3.
63 Lectures delivered in February through November 1926 at the Satyagraha Ashram, Ahmedabad, reprinted as *The Bhagavad Gita according to Gandhi*.
64 First published in two series in *Arya* in August 1916 and July 1920, reprinted as Aurobindo, *Essays on the Gita*, 32–33.
65 Aurobindo, *Essays on the Gita*, 367.
66 Aurobindo, *Essays on the Gita*, 38; Smith, "Eaters, Food, and Social Hierarchy in Ancient India."
67 Aurobindo, *Essays on the Gita*, 40.
68 Aurobindo, *Essays on the Gita*, 56.
69 April 1920, in Aurobindo, "Gitar Bhumika," 79–128.
70 Aurobindo, *Mul Bangla Rachanabali*, 116–17.
71 Briggs, "Freedom and Desire in the *Bhagavad Gītā*," 22.
72 Aurobindo, "Jatiya Utthan" (1909), in *Sri Aurobiner Mul Bangla Rachanabali*, 176–79; Aurobindo, "Amader Asha" (1909), in *Sri Aurobinder Mul Bangla Rachanabali*, 180–82.
73 Aurobindo, *Essays on the Gita*, 242.
74 Aurobindo, *Essays on the Gita*, 31.
75 Aurobindo, "Gitar Bhumika."
76 Aurobindo, *Essays on the Gita*, 91–94.
77 Aurobindo, *Essays on the Gita*, 412, 413–14.

78 Aurobindo, *Essays on the Gita*, 448.
79 Dipesh Chakrabarty, "Minority Histories, Subaltern Pasts."
80 McDermott, *Singing to the Goddess*, 118.
81 Sanyal, *Revolutionary Pamphlets, Propaganda and Political Culture in Colonial Bengal*.
82 Aurbindo, "Gitar Bhumika," 75.
83 Aurobindo, *Essays on the Gita*, 242.
84 Sarkar, "Renaissance and Kaliyuga."
85 Banerjee, *Politics of Time*, 166–67.
86 Iqbal, *The Reconstruction of Religious Thought in Islam*, especially chapter 2.
87 Iqbal, *Taslim-u-Riza*, quoted by Bausani in "The Concept of Time in the Religious Philosophy of Muhammad Iqbal," 170; Majeed, *Muhammad Iqbal*.
88 Bausani, "The Concept of Time in the Religious Philosophy of Muhammad Iqbal," 170.
89 Tagore, "Sahitye Aitihasikata," cited by Guha in *History at the Limit of World History*, 75–94.
90 Tagore, "Aitihasik Upanyas" (1898), in *Rabindra Rachanavali*, 4:685–88; Tagore, "Atit Kal" (1924), in *Rabindra Rachanavali*, 7:161.
91 Tagore, "Kaler Jatra" (1922), in *Rabindra Rachanavali*, 11:249–97.
92 Published first in 1921 in *Pravartaka*; reprinted in Aurobindo, *Sri Aurobinder Bangla Rachana*, 7–48.
93 Aurobindo, *The Doctrine of Passive Resistance*, first published in the daily *Bande Mataram* in April 1907, reprinted in *Bande Mataram*, 112.
94 Guha, "Discipline and Mobilise."
95 Ambedkar, "Revolution and Counter-revolution," in *Babasaheb Ambedkar Writings and Speeches*, 3:149–439.
96 Ambedkar, *Buddha and His Dhamma*, 57–59, 178–79, 185.

Chapter 4. Labor, Hunger, and Struggle

1 Gandhi, letter to Maganlal Gandhi, Tolstoy Farm, August 21, 1910, in *Collected Works of Mahatma Gandhi*, 10:307–8.
2 Gandhi said that he did not read the Gita philosophically but for practical lessons. Only thus could the classical text become accessible to subalterns. Gandhi, *Discourses on the Gita*, lectures at the ashram in 1926–27.
3 Alter, *Gandhi's Body*.
4 Gandhi, "The Poet's Anxiety" (*Young India*, June 1, 1921), in Gandhi and Tagore, *The Mahatma and the Poet*, 65–67.
5 Gandhi, letter to R. P. Paranjapye, July 14, 1919, in *Collected Works of Mahatma Gandhi*, 15:459–60.
6 Malhotra, "The Contribution of Gandhi to the Development of the Congress Constitution," 23.
7 See, e.g., Panchugopal Bhaduri, "Marxer Arthaniti," Kolkata, date unknown; Swadeshranjan Das, "Marxio Dhanatantrik Arthaniti," date unknown; Chinmohan Sehanabis, "Mojuri o Munafa" (*Agrani*, 1939–40), in Das and Sarkar, *Bangalir Samyabad Charcha*, 254, 281–88.

8 Bijoylal Chattopadhyay, "Samyavader Marmakatha" (1938), in Das and Sarkar, *Bangalir Samyabad Charcha*, 215.
9 Muzaffar Ahmed, "Dvaipayaner Patra" (*Dhumketu*, 1922), in Das and Sarkar, *Bangalir Samyabad Charcha*, 49.
10 Kazi Nazrul Islam, *Mrityukhudha*, in Das and Sarkar, *Bangalir Samyabad Charcha*, 86–88; translation by author.
11 Published in *Bishan* in 1943, reprinted in Biswas, *Hemanga Biswas Rachana Samgraha*, 10; translation by author.
12 Biswas, *Hemanga Biswas Rachana Samgraha*, 16, 23.
13 Many more images of Gandhi are available in the photo archives held at https://www.gandhiheritageportal.org/. Thanks to Tridip Suhrud and Kinnari Bhatt for permitting me to access this source. Sunil Janah's photographs are available in Janah, *Photographing India*, 163, 185, 196. Chittaprasad's sketches and paintings can be found in Chittaprasad, *Chittaprasad: A Retrospective 1915-78*; Hore, *Tebhaga: Artist's Diary and Sketchbook*.
14 Tagore, preface to *Sanhati*, in Das and Sarkar, *Bangalir Samyabad Charcha*, 53–55.
15 Tagore, "Ora Kaaj Kore," in his collection of self-chosen poems *Sanchayita*, 829–30.
16 Tagore, "The Call of Truth," in Gandhi and Tagore, *The Mahatma and the Poet*, 68.
17 Tagore, "The Call of Truth," 81–82, 83.
18 Tagore, "Cult of the Charkha" (1925), in Gandhi and Tagore, *The Mahatma and the Poet*, 111.
19 Gandhi, "The Great Sentinel" (*Young India*, 1921), in Gandhi and Tagore, *The Mahatma and the Poet*, 89.
20 Tagore, "Cult of the Charkha," 104–5.
21 Tagore, "Cult of the Charkha," 104–5.
22 Tagore, "Striving for Swaraj" (*Prabasi*, 1925), in Gandhi and Tagore, *The Mahatma and the Poet*, 118.
23 Tagore, "Striving for Swaraj," 108–10.
24 Tagore, "Striving for Swaraj," 121.
25 Tagore, "Cult of the Charkha," 106–7.
26 Biswas, "Bangla Loksangiter Sankater Svarup" in *Hemanga Biswas Rachana Samgraha*, 244–59.
27 Gandhi, "The Poet and the Charkha" (*Young India*, 1925), in Gandhi and Tagore, *The Mahatma and the Poet*, 124.
28 Gandhi, "The Great Sentinel," 90; Gandhi, "The Poet and the Charkha," 123.
29 Gandhi, letter to Manilal Gandhi, January 18, 1913, in *Collected Works of Mahatma Gandhi*, 11:437.
30 Gandhi, *Ashram Observances in Action*; Gandhi, *From Yeravada Mandir*, especially "Control of the Palate," 22–27; Gandhi, *Key to Health*.
31 Gandhi, Id greetings (*Indian Opinion*, November 9, 1907), in *Collected Works of Mahatma Gandhi*, 7:338.
32 Gandhi, "Satyagraha Not Passive Resistance" (September 2, 1917), in *Collected Works of Mahatma Gandhi*, 13:523.

33 Gandhi, speech on Satyagraha movement, Trichinopolly, March 25, 1919, in *Collected Works of Mahatma Gandhi*, 15:154.
34 Gandhi, Satyagraha leaflet no. 17, May 7, 1919, in *Collected Works of Mahatma Gandhi*, 15:285–86.
35 Gandhi, statement to the press, September 16, 1932, in *Collected Works of Mahatma Gandhi*, 51:64; Gandhi, letter to Naraindas Gandhi, September 13, 1922, in *Collected Works of Mahatma Gandhi*, 51:53–54.
36 Gandhi, interview with the *Times of India*, September 24, 1932, in *Collected Works of Mahatma Gandhi*, 51:135–36.
37 Gandhi, speech to Ahmedabad mill hands, March 15, 1918, in *Collected Works of Mahatma Gandhi*, 14:256–57.
38 Gandhi, Ahmedabad mill hands' strike, leaflet no. 15, March 16, 1918, in *Collected Works of Mahatma Gandhi*, 14:258–59.
39 Gandhi, Ahmedabad mill hands' strike, leaflet no. 15.
40 Mukherjee, *Hungry Bengal*.
41 Bhattacharya, "He Mahahiban," in *Sukanta Samagra*, 70; translation by author.
42 "Joint Petition" submitted in 1946 by communists to the Muslim League government in the Bengal province, in Das and Bandopadhyay, *Food Movement of 1959*, 17.
43 Das and Bandopadhyay, *Food Movement of 1959*, 9.
44 *Hindustan Standard*, January 6, 1959, quoted by Basu, "The Chronicle of a Forgotten Movement."
45 Das and Bandopadhyay, *Food Movement of 1959*, 5.
46 Mukhopadhyay, "Banglar Bismrita Bandira," in *Subhas Mukhopadhyay Gadya Samgraha*, 1:621–26.
47 Mukhopadhyay, "Preface to 1st Edition of *Hungras*," in *Subhas Mukhopadhyay Gadya Samgraha* 2:472.
48 Mukhopadhyay, *Hungras*, in *Subhas Mukhopadhyay Gadya Samgraha*, 2:14; translation by author.
49 Mukhopadhyay, *Hungras*, 2:172.
50 Mukhopadhyay, *Hungras*, 2:37.
51 Mukhopadhyay, *Hungras*, 2:19.
52 Mukhopadhyay, *Hungras*, 2:172; translation by author.
53 Mukhopadhyay, *Hungras*, 2:161; translation by author.
54 Mukhopadhyay, *Hungras*, 2:151; translation by author.
55 Mukhopadhyay, *Hungras*, 2:39; translation by author.
56 "Dharmaghater Siksha" (*Prabarttak*, Jaistha, 1921), in Das and Sarkar, *Bangalir Samyabad Charcha*, 39–42.
57 "Chhotor Aparadh" (*Samyavadi*, Baisakh, 1923), in Das and Sarkar, *Bangalir Samyabad Charcha*, 49–50.
58 "Gorhae Galat" (*Samyavadi*, Ashar-Bhadra, 1924), in Das and Sarkar, *Bangalir Samyabad Charcha*, 69–70.
59 For a recent translation, see Bandopadhyay, *The Boatman of the Padma*.
60 Gandhi, "Notes—The Right Way" (*Young India*, October 10, 1929), in *Collected Works of Mahatma Gandhi*, 41:540–41.

61 Gandhi, speech to Ahmedabad mill hands, 41:257.
62 Ambedkar, *Annihilation of Caste*, in *Babasaheb Ambedkar Writings and Speeches*, 1:47.
63 "Hindu Socialism" (review of Kaliprasanna Das's book *Socialism ba Samajtantrabad*), 1942, in Das and Sarkar, *Bangalir Samyabad Charcha*, 188.
64 Presidential speech at a public meeting organized to extend support to "Parvati Satyagraha in Poona" (Bombay, October 16, 1929), in Ambedkar, *Ambedkar Speaks*, 3:67–68.
65 Ambedkar, "Philosophy of Hinduism," in *Babasaheb Ambedkar Writings and Speeches*, 3:3–92, 3:67–63.
66 Ambedkar, presidential address at the Conference of Untouchable Workers of the GIP Railway, February 13, 1938, in *Ambedkar Speaks*, 3:175.
67 This is suggested by Jaffrelot in *Dr. Ambedkar and Untouchability*, 74–75.
68 Gandhi, "Economic Equality," in *Gandhi: Selected Writings*, 133–34.
69 Srivatsan, "Concept of 'Seva' and the 'Sevak' in the Freedom Movement"; for a study of Gandhi's thoughts on caste and caste labor, see Kolge, *Gandhi against Caste*.
70 Tagore, "Sanhati," 54.
71 Jagajjit Sarkar, "Dvandamulak Bastubad" (1931), in Das and Sarkar, *Bangalir Samyabad Charcha*, 135–40; Pramatha Choudhury, "Marxer Dialectics" (*Parichay*, 1936), in Das and Sarkar, *Bangalir Samyabad Charcha*, 198–201.
72 Muzaffar Ahmed, "Srenisangram" (*Langal*, February 25, 1926), in Das and Sarkar, *Bangalir Samyabad Charcha*, 80–81.
73 Gandhi, preface to *Satyagraha in South Africa*, 6.
74 Ambedkar, "Buddha or Karl Marx," in *Babasaheb Ambedkar Writings and Speeches*, 3:441–62, 3:444.
75 Ambedkar, "Philosophy of Hinduism," 3:64.
76 Ambedkar, "Mr Russell and the Reconstruction of Society" (1918), in *Babasaheb Ambedkar Writings and Speeches*, 1:481–92.
77 Ambedkar, "Buddha or Karl Marx," 3:450–51.
78 Ambedkar, "Philosophy of Hinduism," 3:70.
79 Ambedkar, "Philosophy of Hinduism," 3:40.
80 Heidegger, "The Question Concerning Technology," 283–317.
81 Ambedkar, "Mr Russell and the Reconstruction of Society," 1:484.
82 Ambedkar, "Buddha or Karl Marx," 3:451.
83 Ambedkar, "Buddha or Karl Marx," 3:441–64, 3:452.
84 Ambedkar, "Buddha or Karl Marx," 3:459–60.
85 Ambedkar, "Castes in India" (paper presented at an anthropology seminar at Columbia University, New York, May 9, 1916), in *Babasaheb Ambedkar Writings and Speeches*, 1:3–22.
86 Ambedkar, "India and the Prerequisites of Communism," in *Babasaheb Ambedkar Writings and Speeches*, 3:128.
87 Ambedkar, *Annihilation of Caste*, 1:44–45.
88 Ambedkar, "Mr Russell and the Reconstruction of Society," 1:485.
89 Ambedkar, "Mr Russell and the Reconstruction of Society," 1:489–91.
90 Ambedkar, "Buddha or Karl Marx," 3:450–59.

Chapter 5. Equality and Spirituality

1 Deleuze and Guattari, *What Is Philosophy?*, 64.
2 Chattopadhyay, "Samya," in *Bankim Rachanavali*, 2:381–82.
3 Chattopadhyay, "Samya," 2:389.
4 Chattopadhyay, "Samya," 2:383, 2:396.
5 Chattopadhyay, "Samya," 2:406.
6 Chattopadhyay, "Samya," 2:399.
7 Shinde, *A Comparison between Women and Men*.
8 Chattopadhyay, "Samya," 2:388.
9 Chattopadhyay, "Samya," 2:383.
10 Chattopadhyay, "Samya," 2:383, 2:386.
11 Advertisement for the book edition of "Samya," put together out of the *Bangadarshan* essays "Samya" and "Bangadesher Krishak," in Chattopadhyay, *Bankim Rachanavali*, 2:1031.
12 Phule, *Gulamgiri*. Also see Rao, *The Caste Question*.
13 Skaria, *Unconditional Equality*, 79.
14 Ambedkar, "Buddha or Karl Marx," in *Babasaheb Ambedkar Writings and Speeches*, 3:451–52.
15 Minkowski, "Advaita Vedanta in Early Modern History," 138–59.
16 Lederle, *Philosophical Trends in Modern Maharashtra*.
17 Vivekananda, "Modern India" (original in Bengali, *Udbodhana*, March 1899), in *The Complete Works of Swami Vivekananda*, 4:468; Vivekananda, "The Future of India," in *The Complete Works of Swami Vivekananda*, 3:294.
18 Madaio, "Rethinking Neo-Vedanta," 101.
19 Kumar, *Writing the First Person*, 43–85.
20 Kumar, *Writing the First Person*, 64.
21 Ganeri, *The Lost Age of Reason*, 26–29.
22 Islam, address to *Bangiya Muslim Sabha* (winter 1940), in *Kazi Nazrul Islam Rachana Samagra*, 7:629.
23 Islam, "Abhedam," in *Kazi Nazrul Islam Rachana Samagra*, 5:20; translation by author. See also "Mahasamar," 1940, a poem in which Islam literally sets out the battle between *tawhid/ekatvavad* (oneness) and *bahutvavad* (manyness) as the primary battle in the times of equality, in *Kazi Nazrul Islam Rachana Samagra*, 5:68.
24 Hashim, *The Creed of Islam*, 34–35.
25 Iqbal, *The Reconstruction of Religious Thought in Islam*, 58. The overlap with Bergson is obvious, though Iqbal critiques Bergsonian vitalism for creating a dualism between will and thought, owing to a reductive view of intelligence as only a spatializing (rather than temporalizing) impulse. He quotes the Persian poet Urfi against Bergson (42).
26 Hashim, *The Creed of Islam*, 38–39.
27 Hakim, *Islam and Communism*, 16.
28 Hakim, *Islam and Communism*, 19–20, 62–63.
29 The Sufi concept of *wahdat ul wajood* (unity of being) was also an important philo-

sophical idea in precolonial times. In the context I discuss, however, *tawhid* was more routinely invoked.

30 Eaton, *The Rise of Islam on the Bengal Frontier.*
31 There is a rich scholarship on these Muslim self-improvement texts. See Datta, *Carving Blocs*, 65–67; Bose, *Recasting the Region*; Sartori, *Liberalism in Empire*; Sarkar, "Two Muslim Tracts for Peasants," 96–111; Dasgupta, "Labors of Representation."
32 Ahmed, *Amar Dekha Rajnitir Panchas Bochhor*, 3–4.
33 Downey, "Religious Revival and Peasant Activism in Bengal," quoted in Dasgupta, "Labors of Representation," 174. The Faraizis believed that while political tribute to a ruler was acceptable in Islam, rent was unlawful because the earth belonged to Allah. Also see Chowdhury, *Peasant Radicalism in Nineteenth Century Bengal*.
34 Elias, *Khoabnama*.
35 Bose, *Recasting the Region*, 65–66.
36 Khan, *Samasya o Samadhan*.
37 Hossain, *Banglar Balshi*.
38 For the relationship between Nazrul and Ahmed, see Ahmed, *Kazi Nazrul Islam Smritikatha*.
39 "Samyabad ki," quoted in De, *Nazruler Langal Patrikae Krishak o Sramik Prasanga*, 91–92.
40 Hashim, *The Creed of Islam*, 129–37.
41 Dasgupta, "Labors of Representation," 83.
42 Dasgupta, "Labors of Representation," 130.
43 Kidwai, *Islam and Socialism*. Kidwai also wrote in 1908 a book titled *Pan-Islamism*. For a study of the relationship between Pan-Islamism and early Indian communism, see Ansari, *The Emergence of Socialist Thought among North Indian Muslims*.
44 Dasgupta, "Labors of Representation," 143.
45 Hakim, *Islam and Communism*, 176.
46 Dabashi, *The World of Persian Literary Humanism*.
47 Iqbal, "Lenin (Khuda ke Hazoor Mein)"; translation by author.
48 Islam, "Zakat," in *Kazi Nazrul Islam Rachana Samagra*, 7:9–10; translation by author.
49 Ambedkar, "Philosophy of Hinduism," in *Babasaheb Ambedkar Writings and Speeches*, 3:10–12.
50 Ambedkar, "Philosophy of Hinduism," 3:19–20.
51 See Ambedkar, *Annihilation of Caste*, in *Babasaheb Ambedkar Writings and Speeches*, vol. 1, sections 22–26.
52 Ambedkar, *Buddha and His Dhamma*, 215–22.
53 Ambedkar, *Buddha and His Dhamma*, 317.
54 Ambedkar, *Buddha and His Dhamma*, 271.
55 Ambedkar, *Buddha and His Dhamma*, 295–300.
56 Ambedkar, *Buddha and His Dhamma*, 57, 75, 240–41.
57 For some recent insights into Ambedkar's rethinking of religion, see Skaria, "Ambedkar, Marx and the Buddhist Question"; Kumar, *Radical Equality*.

58 Shastri, "Jatibhed" (*Bibha*, 1887), in *Haraprasad Shastri Rachana Sangraha*, 4:86.
59 Shastri, "Banglar Samjik Itihaser Mul Sutra" (*Masik Basumati*, 1949), in *Haraprasad Shastri Rachana Sangraha*, 4:378–79.
60 Shastri, "Jatibhed," 4:92.
61 Shastri, "Ekhono Ektu Achhe" and "Orissar Jangale" (originally published in 1915), in *Bauddhadharma*, 114–37.
62 Shastri, "Raja o Manush," in *Haraprasad Shastri Rachana Sangraha*, 4:161.
63 Shastri, "Raja o Manush," 4:171; translation by author.

Chapter 6. Equality and Economic Reason

1 For a European history of how the economy came to be discursively and materially structured as a nonpolitical domain, a realm of "necessity" emptied of the vicissitudes of political negotiation—especially between the late eighteenth-century Malthus moment and the early twentieth-century Keynes moment—see Tellmann, *Life and Money*.
2 Sen, *Empire of Free Trade*.
3 Banerjee, "A Social History of Banking in Bengal"; Banerjee, "Debt, Time and Extravagance."
4 Ypi, "Commerce and Colonialism in Kant's Philosophy of History."
5 Wood, "The Separation of the Economic and the Political in Capitalism."
6 Quoted in Mitra, "Exchanging Words and Things," 510.
7 Das, *The Social and Economic Ideas of Benoy Sarkar*.
8 Sarkar, *Economic Development*; Sarkar, "The Equations of Comparative Industrialism and Culture-History" (1937), in Baneswar Das, *Social and Economic Ideas of Benoy Sarkar*, 28–40.
9 Sarkar, "Bengali Zamindars in Relation to Bengali Industry and Commerce" (*Arthik Unnati*, September 1933), in Baneswar Das, *Social and Economic Ideas of Benoy Sarkar*, 51; Sarkar, "Modernism in Land Legislation" (*Calcutta Review*, December 1937), in Das, *Social and Economic Ideas of Benoy Sarkar*, 63. For a statement on the "nonpolitical and nonparty" nature of economics, see Sarkar's reflections on money in *Social and Economic Ideas of Benoy Sarkar*, 74.
10 Chandra, *The Rise and Growth of Economic Nationalism in India*.
11 Sarkar, *Swadeshi Movement in Bengal*.
12 For Ambedkar's, along with W. E. B. Du Bois's, reformulation of Georges Sorel's notion of the "general strike," see Kumar, *Radical Equality*, 142.
13 Raha, *The Plough and the Pen*.
14 Jodhka, "Nation and Village."
15 Ahmed, *Rajnitir Panchas Bochhor*, 48.
16 Dasgupta, "Labors of Representation," 7.
17 Hashmi, *Pakistan as a Peasant's Utopia*.
18 Sen, "The Emergence and Decline of Dalit Politics in Bengal," 58, 116.
19 Sen, "The Emergence and Decline of Dalit Politics in Bengal," 90–100; also see Ray, *Barisaler Jogen Mandal* for a fictionalized but well-researched account of Mandal's life.

20 Ahmed, *Rajnitir Panchas Bochhor*, 105.
21 Dasgupta, "Labors of Representation," 22, 59.
22 Chatterjee, "Sacred Calling, Worldly Bargain," 108–15. Also see Sashmal's memoirs, *Sroter Trina*.
23 Chakrabarty, "The Communal Award of 1932 and Its Implications in Bengal"; Chatterjee, *Bengal Divided*, 18–54.
24 "Manifesto to the 36th Indian National Congress, Ahmedabad 1921," in Majumdar and Datta, *Banglar Communist Andoloner Itihas Anusandhan*, 1:133–34.
25 "Dharmaghater Siksha" (*Prabartak*, 1921), in Das and Sarkar, *Bangalir Samyebad Charcha*, 41; Abul Hossain, "Banglar Bolshi" (1921), in Das and Sarkar, *Bangalir Samyabad Charcha*, 44.
26 Mukerjee, *Daridrer Krandan*, 37–43.
27 "Dharmaghater Siksha"; also "Chhotor Aparadh" (*Sarayabadi*, 1923), in Das and Sarkar, *Bangalir Samyabad Charcha*, 50.
28 Quoted in Chakravarty, "Readers' Responses," 181.
29 Shingavi, *The Mahatma Misunderstood*, 51.
30 Upendranath Bandopadhyay, "Europe Samajbiplab," in Das and Sarkar, *Bangalir Samyabad Charcha*, 35.
31 Chakraborty, *Moscow Banam Pondicherry*, 36.
32 Ray, *Pathe Prabase*, 53–54. Disputing Kaliprasanna Das's argument in his 1935 book *Socialism ba Samajtantrabad*, that the *varna* system was an ancient kind of socialism, Bose makes this point in an essay titled "Hindu Socialism," in Das and Sarkar, *Bangalir Samyabad Charcha*, 185–90.
33 Srinivas, *Caste in Modern India*, 20.
34 Tagore, "Sanhati," in Das and Sarkar, *Bangalir Samyabad Charcha*, 53–55.
35 Bagchi, *Banglabhashae Samyabad Charcha*, 35.
36 Bagchi, *Banglabhashae Samyabad Charcha*, 21.
37 Bagchi, *Banglabhashae Samyabad Charcha*, 37–39.
38 Dasgupta, "The Ascetic Modality," 67–87.
39 Pondicherry was the ashram of ex-revolutionary Aurobindo Ghosh.
40 Chakraborty, *Moscow Banam Pondicherry*, 32.
41 Chakraborty, *Moscow Banam Pondicherry*, 23–24, 41.
42 Chakraborty, *Moscow Banam Pondicherry*, 29; translation by author.
43 Chakraborty, *Moscow Banam Pondicherry*, 103.
44 Chakraborty, *Moscow Banam Pondicherry*, 90, 97.
45 Chakraborty, *Moscow Banam Pondicherry*, 105.
46 Chakraborty, *Moscow Banam Pondicherry*, 39, 98–101.
47 Chakraborty, "Harijan Andoloner Naba Adarshya," in *Moscow Banam Pondicherry*, 139.
48 Chakraborty, *Moscow Banam Pondicherry*, 83, 92.
49 Chakraborty, *Moscow Banam Pondicherry*, 117.
50 Chakraborty, *Moscow Banam Pondicherry*, 147; translation by author.
51 Roy, *Historical Role of Islam*, 24.
52 Roy, *Historical Role of Islam*, 17, 20.

53 Roy, *Historical Role of Islam*, 51.
54 Roy, *Historical Role of Islam*, 21–24.
55 Roy, *Historical Role of Islam*, 43–50, 53.
56 Roy, *Historical Role of Islam*, 63–64.
57 Roy, *Historical Role of Islam*, 68.
58 Govindu and Malghan, *The Web of Freedom*.
59 Mukerjee, "Faiths and Influences," 4–45.
60 Mukerjee, *Principles of Comparative Economics*, 38.
61 Mukerjee, *Comparative Economics*, 2.
62 Mukerjee, *Comparative Economics*, 6.
63 Mukerjee, *Comparative Economics*, 8–10, 11.
64 Mukerjee, *Comparative Economics*, 61, 25, 38.
65 Mukerjee, *Comparative Economics*, 16.
66 Mukerjee, *Comparative Economics*, 25.
67 Mukerjee, *Comparative Economics*, 13–14.
68 Mukerjee, *Comparative Economics*, 75–76.
69 Mukerjee, *Comparative Economics*, 14, 48–51.
70 Mukerjee, *Foundations of Indian Economics*.
71 Mukerjee, *Comparative Economics*, 40.
72 Mukerjee, *Comparative Economics*, 40–44.
73 Mukerjee, *Comparative Economics*, 46.
74 Mukerjee, *Comparative Economics*, 85.
75 Mukerjee, *Comparative Economics*, 73, 92.
76 Madan, "D. P. Mukherjee, 1894–1961."
77 D. P. Mukerjee, "An Economic Theory for India."
78 Mukerjee, "An Economic Theory for India," 83–85.
79 Mukerjee, "An Economic Theory for India," 99. D. P. Mukerjee refers here to the American sociologist Emory Bogardus's conception of "social distance."
80 Mukerjee, *Amra o Tahara* (1931), in Mukhopadhyay, *Dhurjatiprasad Rachanabali*, 2:89–166.
81 Joshi, "Lucknow School of Economics and Sociology," 1–28.
82 Mukerjee, "Arthashastrer Durgati" (1935), in Mukhopadhyay, *Dhurjatiprasad Rachanabali*, 2:513.
83 Mukerjee, *Personality and the Social Sciences*.
84 Mukhopadhyay, *Antahshila* (1935), in *Dhurjatiprasad Rachanabali*, 1:1–168; Mukhopadhyay, *Abarta* (1937), in *Dhurjatiprasad Rachanabali*, 1:169–312; Mukhopadhyay, *Mohana* (1943), in *Dhurjatiprasad Rachanabali*, 1:313–472.
85 Joshi, "Founders of the Lucknow School and Their Legacy."
86 Mukerjee, "Amra o Tahara," 152; translation by author.
87 D. P. Mukerjee, "Manik Bandopadhyay" (*Parichay*, 1940), in Mukhopadhyay, *Dhurjatiprasad Rachanabali*, 2:524–26.
88 Gorky was translated into Bengali as early as 1925.
89 Manik Bandopadhyay, *Janani*, 1935.
90 "Hat" (*Saptahik Agragati*, 1937), in Bandopadhyay, *Manik Rachana Samagra*, 3:333–38.

91 The "Wives" collection was first published in 1940. "Dokanir Bou," in Bandopadhyay, *Manik Rachana Samagra*, 2:11–21.
92 Bandopadhyay, "Keranir Bou," in *Manik Rachana Samagra*, 2:22–28.
93 Bandopadhyay, "Sahityiker Bou," in *Manik Rachana Samagra*, 2:29–46.
94 Bandopadhyay, "Pratibha," in *Manik Granthabali*, 7:365–66.
95 Bandopadhyay, "Lekhaker Samasya," in *Manik Granthabali*, 8:360–64.
96 Poovey, *Genres of the Credit Economy*.
97 Bandopadhyay, "Shilpi" (*Simanta*, 1946), in *Manik Bandopadhyayer Sera Galpo*, 108–13; translation by author.
98 Bandopadhyay, "Lekhaker Samasya," 8:362.
99 Roy, *Harvest Song*.
100 Roy, *Harvest Song*, 115.
101 Roy, *Harvest Song*, 266.
102 Roy, *Harvest Song*, 348.

Chapter 7. People as Party

1 Sartori, *Party and Party Systems*.
2 Gramsci, *Selections from the Prison Notebook*, 253.
3 Bayly, *Caste, Society and Politics in India*.
4 Dean, *Crowds and Party*, 5.
5 Freitag, *Collective Action and Community*.
6 For an early twentieth-century European debate on the age of the masses, see Canetti, "Discussion with Theodor W. Adorno," 1–15.
7 Zaidi and Zaidi, *The Encyclopaedia of Indian National Congress*, 1:167, 1:178.
8 Ramana Rao, *Development of the Congress Constitution*, 5.
9 Ramana Rao, *Development of the Congress Constitution*, 12, 14.
10 Sitaramayya, *The History of the Indian National Congress*, 325–28.
11 Krishna, "The Development of the Indian National Congress as a Mass Organisation," 413–30.
12 Chatterjee, *Congress Politics in Bengal*, 67–100.
13 Minutes of AICC meeting, Calcutta, November 20–24, 1922, AICC 8/1922, Nehru Memorial Museum and Library.
14 Sitaramayya, *The History of the Indian National Congress*, 399.
15 Sitaramayya, *The History of the Indian National Congress*, 398–99.
16 Minutes of AICC meeting, Calcutta, November 20–24, 1922, AICC 8/1922, Nehru Memorial Museum and Library.
17 Sitaramayya, *The History of the Indian National Congress*, 651.
18 "Constitution of the Swarajya Party," AICC 3/1923, Nehru Memorial Museum and Library.
19 "Election Manifesto of the Swarajya Party of the INC," AICC 3/1923, Nehru Memorial Museum and Library.
20 "Programme of Swarajya Party," Allahabad, February 1923, AICC 13/1923, Nehru Memorial Museum and Library.
21 See the voluminous exchange of letters between Bengal leaders and Jawaharlal

Nehru, then INC president, regarding choice of candidates in 1936–37. AICC E5 (part 1)/1936, Nehru Memorial Museum and Library.
22. Kothari, "The Party System," 847–54.
23. Aurobindo, "New Lamps for the Old" (*Indu Prakash*, October 30, 1893), in *Bande Mataram*, 26–33.
24. Zaidi and Zaidi, *The Encyclopaedia of Indian National Congress*, 1:163.
25. Bate, "'To Persuade Them into Speech and Action,'" 142–66.
26. Zaidi and Zaidi, *The Encyclopaedia of Indian National Congress*, 1:239–40.
27. Kothari, "The Congress System Revisited," 1035–54.
28. Misra, *The Indian Political Parties*, 95.
29. Zaidi and Zaidi, *The Encyclopaedia of Indian National Congress*, 2:58.
30. Ambedkar, *What Congress and Gandhi Have Done to the Untouchables* (1945), in *Babasaheb Ambedkar Writings and Speeches*, 9:16.
31. Ramana Rao, *Development of the Congress Constitution*, 2, 18.
32. Karachi Congress resolution, 1931, in Sitaramayya, *The History of the Indian National Congress*, 835.
33. Correspondence with Sant Ram, secretary of Jat-Pat-Todak-Mandal, in Ambedkar, *Babasaheb Ambedkar Writings and Speeches*, 1:27–35.
34. Articles printed in *Harijan* and reprinted in the appendix to *Annihilation*, in Ambedkar, *Babasaheb Ambedkar Writings and Speeches*, 1:81–85.
35. Visvanathan, *Outside the Fold*.
36. Ambedkar, *What Congress Did*, 68.
37. Ambedkar, *What Congress Did*, 70–71.
38. "Constitution of the All India Kisan Sabha," AICC G 13/1936, Nehru Memorial Museum and Library.
39. First meeting of the All India Kisan Sabha Committee, Niyamatpur, July 14–15, 1936, AICC G 13/1936, Nehru Memorial Museum and Library; also see AICC G 15, 18, 21/1936, Nehru Memorial Museum and Library.
40. AIKS Resolution, August 21, 1936, AICC G 18–21/1936, Nehru Memorial Museum and Library.
41. Ramana Rao, *Development of the Congress Constitution*, 45–46.
42. Sitaramayya, *The History of the Indian National Congress*, 609–11.
43. Achhut Patwardhan, Kamaladevi Chattopadhyay, and A. P. Sinha to general secretary, AICC, March 30, 1936, AICC 16/1937, Nehru Memorial Museum and Library.
44. Members included Jairamdas Doulatram, Jayprakash Narayan, and Rajendra Prasad, with later J. B. Kripalani and Jawaharlal Nehru also joining.
45. Bengal PCC Questionnaire, AICC 21/1936, Nehru Memorial Museum and Library.
46. Bengal PCC Questionnaire, AICC 21/1936.
47. Low, "Congress and 'Mass Contacts,'" 142–43.
48. Report of the Constitution Committee, AICC (1st Part) G-30(a)/1937, Nehru Memorial Museum and Library.
49. Low, "Congress and 'Mass Contacts,'" 149.
50. J. P. Narayan, "Letter to Freedom Fighters" and "On Communist Unity," CSP leaflets, serial no. 46, file 250-B-43, 1943, West Bengal State Archives.

51 Pradhan, "Socialist Stirrings within the Congress," 218–304.
52 Political circulars issued by the secret section of the Bengal Labour Party, Police Intelligence Reports 1939, file 726/39, West Bengal State Archives.
53 Lahiri, "Tene namate debo na"; Bhabani Sen's analysis of the difference between the Communist Party and the Labor Party, in Majumdar and Datta, *Banglar Communist Andoloner Itihas Anusandha*, 1:290–92.
54 Majumdar and Datta, *Banglar Communist Andoloner Itihas Anusandhan*, 1:238–51. Also Muzaffar Ahmed, "The New Party," *Ganabani*, April 14, 1927, in Majumdar and Datta, *Banglar Communist Andoloner Itihas Anusandhan*, 1:269–71.
55 Sitaramayya, *The History of the Indian National Congress*, 382.
56 Secy., Congress Swayamsevak Dal, to Nehru, July 13, 1936, AICC G 21/1936, Nehru Memorial Museum and Library.
57 Chatterjee, *Congress Politics in Bengal*, 53–54.
58 Tamluk Swadhinata Sangram Itihas Committee Papers, file 51, 1943, Nehru Memorial Museum and Library.
59 Renu, *Maila Anchal*.
60 Gandhi, "When I Am Arrested" (February 27, 1930), quoted in Sitaramayya, *The History of the Indian National Congress*, 644.
61 Sitaramayya, *The History of the Indian National Congress*, 765.
62 Amin, "Gandhi as Mahatma," 1–71.
63 Ajay Skaria discusses Gandhi's exemplarity in his *Unconditional Equality*. Also Banerjee, "Example and Following," 429–34.
64 Bhaduri, *Dhorai Charit Manas*, 1941.
65 Bishwa Biswas's novel *Mazdoor*, serialized in *Agrani* in 1939–40, depicted the strike as war, supervised by the "workers' army," in Das and Sarkar, *Bangalir Samyabad Charcha*, 248–51. *Lal Paltan* (Red army) was the name of the newspaper run from 1928 by Bimal Roy's Liluah Eastern India Railways Union.
66 Maclean, *A Revolutionary History of Interwar India*; Jalal, *Partisans of Allah*.
67 Chinmohan Sehanobis argued that Indians pitched workers' issues internationally from the late nineteenth century onward; "Brahmo Samaj and Toiling People," *Mainstream*, 1978, in Majumdar and Datta, *Banglar Communist Andoloner Itihas Anusandhan*, 1:63, 66.
68 The first Communist Party of India was founded not in India but in Tashkent, by M. N. Roy, Abani Mukherjee, and others, for the purpose of sending Indian representatives to the Communist International. Quite separately from the above, in December 1925, Satyabhakt, a Congress worker in United Provinces with revolutionary antecedents, Ganesh Shankar Vidyarthi, and Moulana Hasrat Mohani called a conference of communists in Kanpur, where the Congress session was being held. Satyabhakt, V. H. Joshi, and others wanted to set up the Indian Communist Party—named after the Indian National Congress—so as to indicate its autonomy from the Comintern and its commitment to nationalism. Most others, however, insisted on the name Communist Party of India in order to stage Indian peasants and workers as part of the workers of the world rather than only of the nation. When the Communist Party of India (Marxist) split from the Com-

munist Party of India in 1968, it returned to the 1920 Tashkent moment as the founding year of the party, instead of the 1925 Kanpur moment.
69 Provincial letter, 4/43, to party workers, March 4, 1943, in Majumdar and Datta, *Banglar Communist Andoloner Itihas Anusandhan*, 2:439–43.
70 Manjapra, *M. N. Roy*; Sen, *The Traveller and the Road*.
71 Roy, *Fragments of a Jail Diary*.
72 Ghosh, "The History of Revolutionary Terrorism through Autobiography," 60–91.
73 Ahmed, *Amar Jibon o Bharater Communist Party*.
74 Seth, *Marxist Theory and Nationalist Politics*.
75 Namita Wahi, "State, Private Property and the Supreme Court," *Frontline Magazine* 29, no. 19 (September 22–October 5, 2012), Social Sciences Research Network, https://ssrn.com/abstract=2222315, accessed January 12, 2019.
76 Bhattacharyya, "Of Control and Factions," 59–69.
77 Bhaduri, *Jagori*.
78 Arunima, "Friends and Lovers," 139–58.

Chapter 8. People as Fiction

1 Roy, *Cultural Communism in Bengal*.
2 Hillach, Wikoff, and Zimmerman, "The Aesthetics of Politics," 99–119; Spotts, *Hitler and the Power of Aesthetics*.
3 Baycroft and Hopkin, *Folklore and Nationalism in Europe during the Long Nineteenth Century*; Blackburn, *Print, Folklore, and Nationalism in Colonial India*.
4 Sengupta, *Folklorists of Bengal*; Tagore, "Lok Sahitya," in *Rabindra Rachanvali*, 13:663–734.
5 Swadesh Basu (née Shanti Basu), "Pragati Sahityer Atmasamalochona" (*Dak*, 1949), in Das, *Marxbadi Sahitya Bitarka*, 197; Urmila Guha/Pradyot Guha, "Sahitya Bichare Marxiyo Padhhati," in Das, *Marxbadi Sahitya Bitarka*, 75.
6 Ayub, *Modernism and Tagore*; Amal Hom, "Kerani Rabindranath," in Das, *Marxbadi Sahitya Bitarka*, 412–19; Sushobhan Sarkar, "Rabindranath o Agragati," in Das, *Marxbadi Sahitya Bitarka*, 420–25.
7 Datta, *Rabindranath Tagore's Home and the World*, 8–9.
8 Tagore in *Parichay* (1938), cited in Samajdar, *Bangla Upanyase Lokjibon Charjya*, 125.
9 Sengupta, *Kallol Yug*.
10 Das, *Atmasmriti*.
11 Anjaria, *Realism in the Twentieth-Century Indian Novel*.
12 Banerjee, "The Work of Imagination," 280–322.
13 Atulchandra Gupta, "Kavyajignyasha—Prathama Prastab" (*Sabuj Patra* 9, no. 11), *Ashar* (1926), in Datta, ed., *Sera Sabuj Patra Sangraha*, 2:214–22; "Kavyajgnyasha—Dvitiya Prastab," (*Sabuj Patra* 9, no. 12), *Sravan* (1926), in Datta, ed., *Sera Sabuj Patra Sangraha*, 2:250–60.
14 Shulman, *More Than Real*.
15 Radhakamal Mukhopadhyay, "Sahitye Bastabata" (*Sabuj Patra* 1, no. 10), and *Magh* (1914), in Datta, ed., *Sera Sabuj Patra Sangraha*, 1:85–91.

16 Limbale, *Towards an Aesthetics of Dalit Literature*.
17 Kaviraj, *The Invention of Private Life*, 4–6.
18 Bhattacharya and Sen, *Novel Formations*.
19 Chinmohan Sehanobis, "Sahitya o Ganasangram" (*Parichay*, 1948), in Das, *Marxbadi Sahitya Bitarka*, 326–27.
20 Sitangshu Moitra, "Bangla Pragati Sahityer Atmasamalochona" (*Parichay*, 1949), in Das, *Marxbadi Sahitya Bitarka*, 230.
21 Das, *Marxbadi Sahitya Bitarka*, 624.
22 Bandopadhyay, *Amar Sahitya Jibon*.
23 Hiranyakumar Sanyal, "Hansulibanker Upakatha Prasange" (*Parichay*, 1946), in Das, *Marxbadi Sahitya Bitarka*, 544.
24 Nihar Dasgupta, "Saradiya Sahitye Chhotogolpo" (*Parichay*, 1947), in response to Vishnu Dey's appreciation of Achintya Kumar's "*Muchi Bayen*," in Das, *Marxbadi Sahitya Bitarka*, 484–89, 529.
25 The *Natyashastra* is attributed to sage Bharata and is an ancient treatise on the dramatic arts, encompassing poetry, music, dance, and acting. Indologists place the text sometime between 200 BCE to 200 CE. One of its earliest European language translations (1894) was by J. Crosset in French. An authoritative English translation was done by Manomohan Ghosh and published by the Asiatic Society of Bengal in 1951. My discussion is based on the Ghosh edition of the *Natyashastra*.
26 Pollock, "Introduction," in *The Rasa Reader*, 21–23.
27 Demos, *The Affect Theory of Silvan Tomkins for Psychoanalysis and Psychotherapy*.
28 Tomkins and McCarter, "What and where Are the Primary Affects?."
29 Shapiro, *Reinventing Drama*, 87–88.
30 Böhme, "Atmosphere as the Fundamental Concept of a New Aesthetics," 113–26.
31 Fischer-Lichte, *The Transformative Power of Performance*.
32 Bandopadhyay, *Tarashankar Rachanabali*, 18:390.
33 Rancière, *The Politics of Literature*. Also see Yeazell, *Art of the Everyday*.
34 Bhattacharya, "Reading Rancière," 555–80.
35 Chaudhuri, *Gentlemen Poets in Colonial Bengal*.
36 Chaudhuri, *The Literary Thing*, 27–87.
37 Sen, "Re-visioning the Colonial City," 26–35.
38 Mukhopadhyay, "Hemanga Biswas," 197–215.
39 Pradhan, *Koyekjon Lok-kavi*.
40 Letter to Hemanga Biswas, quoted in Dhar, "Hemanga Biswas o Nibaran Pandit," 274.
41 Biswas quoted in Dhar, "Hemanga Biswas o Nibaran Pandit," 267.
42 Biswas, "Gananatya Andolon o Lokgiti," *Hemanga Biswas Rachana Sangraha*, 321–38.
43 Biswas, "Gananatya o Atmakatha," in *Ujan Gang Baiya*, 110.
44 Biswas, "Loksangiter Ragrup o Ritiniti," *Hemanga Biswas Rachana Sangraha*, 303–20.
45 Oppenshaw, *Seeking Bauls of Bengal*, 32–33.

46 Sengupta, "Muchi Bayen," 613–24.
47 Bandopadhyay, "Gayen," in *Manik Granthabali*, 2:50–54.
48 Anilkumar Singha, "Saradiya Sahitye Chhotogolpo" (*Parichay*, 1948), in Das, *Marxbadi Sahitya Bitarka*, 537–38.
49 Bandopadhyay, *Kavi*, first published in 1944.
50 Rancière, *Proletarian Nights*.
51 Naregal, "Performance, Caste, Aesthetics," 79–101.
52 Bhatia, *Acts of Authority/Acts of Resistance*, 16.
53 Dasi, *My Story and My Life as an Actress*. Dasi, literally meaning servant or devotee, was often a last name attributed to subaltern women, contra Devi, literally meaning goddesslike, which was often attributed to more genteel women. Binodini was either known as *nati* Binodini, *nati* simply meaning actress, or as Binodini Dasi, as befitted her subaltern social status, notwithstanding her great fame as an actor.
54 Quoted in Biswas, *Ujan Gang Baiya*, 171.
55 Dutt, "Hamlet o Janapriyata," in *Utpal Datta Gadya Sangraha*, 1:63.
56 Ghosh, *The Natyashastra*, 9–10.
57 Bhatia, *Acts of Authority/Acts of Resistance*, 19.
58 Pradhan, *Marxist Cultural Movements in India*, 136.
59 Dey, "*Nabanna*: After 25 Years," 2.
60 Haldar, "Bangla Natyakalar Pratham Suchana" (*Parichay*, 1945), in Das, *Marxbadi Sahitya Bitarka*, 426–29.
61 Pradhan, *Marxist Cultural Movements in India*, 124.
62 Sushil Jana, "Jabanbandi" (*Arani*, 1944), in Das, *Marxbadi Sahitya Bitarka*, 430–31.
63 Kalidas Ray, "Nabanna" (*Parichay*, 1944), in Das, *Marxbadi Sahitya Bitarka*, 438.
64 Hiranykumar Sanyal, "Natyakala: Nabanna" (*Parichay*, 1944), in Das, *Marxbadi Sahitya Bitarka*, 435.
65 Swarnakamal Bhattacharya, "Nabanna Prasange" (*Parichay*, 1944), in Das, *Marxbadi Sahitya Bitarka*, 436–37.
66 Mitra, *Shambhu Mitra*, 43–55.
67 Report by Charuprakash Ghosh, cited in Pradhan, *Marxist Cultural Movements in India*, xv–xvii.
68 Adhikari, "Gananatya Sangathan," 15–20.
69 Dutt, "Drishyasajja," in *Utpal Datta Gadya Sangraha*, 1:79.
70 In early India, *alankarashastra* (school of metaphor), believed that figurative speech and unusual or deviant expressions (*vakrokti*) constituted the defining feature of *kavya*. In opposition to this argument, the *rasa* school of aesthetics argued against the adequacy of *alankara* for poetics. It believed that *kavya* was fundamentally about the production and generalization of emotion and affect, what I am calling atmospherics here.
71 Dutt, "Angik," in *Utpal Dutt Gadya Sangraha*, 1:71.
72 Dutt, "Drishyasajja," 80–81.
73 Dutt, *Chaer Dhnoya*, in *Utpal Datta Gadya Sangraha*, 1:29–119. Dutt published a series of essays in a volume called *Chaer Dhnoya*, literally meaning "tea smoke," signifying conversations over tea.

74 Dutt, *Chaer Dhnoya*, 1:63.
75 Dutt, "Sangit o Abhinava," in *Chaer Dhnoya*, in *Utpal Dutt Gadya Sangraha*, 1:95–104.
76 Dutt, "Janapriyata o Alamgir," in *Chaer Dhnoya*, in *Utpal Dutt Gadya Sangraha*, 1:43–60. Sombhu Mitra too was highly appreciative of the same play; Mitra, *Shambu Mitra*, 13. Incidentally, in the preface to *Chaer Dhnoya*, Dutt mentions how Tarashankar Bandopadhyay agreed with Dutt's interpretation of *Alamgir*. Dutt, "In Lieu of a Preface," in *Chaer Dhnoya*, in *Utpal Datta Gadya Sangraha*, 1:27.
77 Dutt, "Bastab o Bastabottar," in *Chaer Dhnoya*, in *Utpal Dutt Gadya Sangraha*, 1:109–11.
78 Dutt, "Janapriyata o Alamgir," in *Chaer Dhnoya*, in *Utpal Dutt Gadya Sangraha*, 1:49.
79 Dutt, "Janapriyata o Alamgir," 1:49.
80 Interview with Samik Bandopadhyay, quoted in Bharucha, *Rehearsals of Revolution*, 46.
81 Dutt, "Dharmatalar Hamlet," in *Utpal Dutt Gadya Sangraha*, 1:136.
82 Dutt, "Adhkhana Manush," in *Utpal Dutt Gadya Sangraha*, 1:165–66.
83 Chakrabarti, "Just Words," 244–83.
84 Dutt, "Epicer Sarkatha," in *Utpal Dutt Gadya Sangraha*, 1:281.
85 Das, "Yatra: Utpal Datter," 244–56.
86 Bandopadhyay, "Editor's Introduction," *Nirbachita Bangla Jatra*, 1:11–12.
87 Bandopadhyay, "Editor's Introduction," *Nirbachita Bangla Jatra*, 3:13.
88 Bandopadhyay, "Editor's Introduction," *Nirbachita Bangla Jatra*, 3:32.
89 Dutt, *Towards a Revolutionary Theatre*, 178.
90 Dutt, "The Longest Interview," interviewed by Partha Bandopadhyay (*Parbantar*, 1995), cited in Bandopadhyay, "Editor's Introduction," *Nirbachita Bangla Jatra*, 3:38.
91 Interview, "Theatre as Weapon," cited in Bharucha, *Rehearsal of Revolution*, 92.
92 Interview, "Theatre as Weapon," cited in Bharucha, *Rehearsal of Revolution*, 93.
93 Dutt, "Taking Shakespeare to the Common Man," 19–20.
94 The play was published in 1970 and was first staged by People's Little Theatre Group in 1971.
95 Sarkar, *Three Plays*.
96 Puchner, *Stage Fright*.
97 Puchner, *The Poetry of Revolution*.
98 Puchner, *The Drama of Ideas*.

Epilogue

1 Sarukkai, *Translating the World*.
2 Marks, *Enfoldment and Infinity*.
3 Diagne, *African Art as Philosophy*.
4 Idris, *War for Peace*.
5 Rosanvallon, *Democratic Legitimacy*.
6 Rosanvallon, *Counter-democracy*.

7 Mignolo and Walsh, *On Decoloniality*; Ndlovu-Gatsheni, "Decoloniality as the Future of Africa."
8 Banerjee, Nigam, and Pandey, "The Work of Theory."
9 Runia, *Moved by the Past*.
10 Many of these points emerged in a conversation held at Columbia University with Anupama Rao, Aditya Nigam, Partha Chatterjee, and Sohini Chattopadhyay. They are available as an interview at https://www.borderlines-cssaame.org/posts/2018/11/6/theories-from-the-south-i-an-interview-with-prathama-banerjee.

BIBLIOGRAPHY

Primary Sources

Archival Sources

All India Congress Committee Papers, Nehru Memorial Museum and Library, Delhi, India.
Police and Intelligence Files, West Bengal State Archives, Kolkata, India.
Tamluk Swadhinata Sangram Itihas Committee Papers, file no. 51, 1943. Nehru Memorial Museum and Library, Delhi, India.

Periodicals and Journals

Indian Historical Quarterly
Janjuddha
Parichay

Books and Tracts

Abedin, Zainul. *Zainul Abedin: Great Masters of Bangladesh*. Edited by Rosa Maria Falva. Milan: Skira and Bengal Foundation, 2013.
Adhikari, Mrityunjoy. "Gananatya Sangathan." *Loknatya* 1, no. 1 (1948): 15–20.
Ahmed, Abul Mansur. *Amar Dekha Rajnitir Panchas Bochhor*. First published 1968. Dhaka: Khosraj Kitab Mahal, 1995.
Ahmed, Muzaffar. *Amar Jibon o Bharater Communist Party*. Delhi: National Book Agency, 1969.
Ahmed, Muzaffar. *Kazi Nazrul Islam Smritikatha*. Calcutta: National Book Agency, 1965.
Ambedkar, B. R. *Ambedkar Speaks*. 3 vols. Edited by Narendra Jadhav. New Delhi: Konark, 2013.
Ambedkar, B. R. *Annihilation of Caste: The Annotated Critical Edition*. Edited by S. Anand. New Delhi: Navayana, 2014.
Ambedkar, B. R. *Babasaheb Ambedkar Writings and Speeches*. 17 vols. Edited by Vasant Moon. Mumbai: Ambedkar Foundation, 2014.
Ambedkar, B. R. *The Buddha and His Dhamma: A Critical Edition*. Edited by Akash Singh Rathore and Ajay Verma. Delhi: Oxford University Press, 2011.

Ambedkar, B. R. *What Congress and Gandhi Have Done to the Untouchables: A Mean Deal*. Bombay: Thacker, 1946.

Ambedkar, B. R. *Who Were the Shudras? How They Came to Be the Fourth Varna in the Indo-Aryan Society*. Bombay: Thacker, 1946.

Aurobindo, Sri. *Bande Mataram: Early Political Writings, 1890–1908*. 5th ed. Pondicherry: Sri Aurobindo Ashram, 1997.

Aurobindo, Sri. *Essays on the Gita*. 8th ed. Pondicherry: Aurobindo Ashram, 1970.

Aurobindo, Sri. *Sri Aurobinder Mul Bangla Rachanabali*. Pondicherry: Sri Aurobindo Society, 1969.

Ayub, Abu Sayyid. *Modernism and Tagore*. Delhi: Sahitya Akademi, 1995.

Bagchi, Pradoshkumar. *Banglabhashae Samyabad Charcha*. Kolkata: National Book Agency, 2010.

Bandopadhyay, Devajit, ed. *Nirbachita Bangla Jatra*. 4 vols. Kolkata: Sahitya Akademi, 2008.

Bandopadhyay, Manik. *The Boatman of the Padma*. Translated by Ratan K. Chattopadhyay. New Delhi: Orient Blackswan, 2012.

Bandopadhyay, Manik. *Janani*. Calcutta: Bengal Publishers, 1935.

Bandopadhyay, Manik. *Manik Bandopadhyayer Sera Galpo*. Calcutta: Bengal Publishers, 1950.

Bandopadhyay, Manik. *Manik Granthabali*. Vol. 12. Calcutta: Granthalaya, 1975.

Bandopadhyay, Manik. *Manik Rachana Samagra*. Vols. 2 and 3. Kolkata: Paschimbanga Bangla Akademi, 2001.

Bandopadhyay, Rangalal. *Kabitabali*. Edited by Sajanikanta Das. Calcutta: Bangiya Sahitya Parishad, 1963.

Bandopadhyay, Tarashankar. *Amar Sahitya Jibon*. Calcutta: Paschimbanga Bangla Akademi, 1997.

Bandopadhyay, Tarashankar. *Kavi*. Calcutta: Mitra and Ghosh, 1948.

Bandopadhyay, Tarashankar. *Tarashankar Rachanabali*. Calcutta: Mitra and Ghosh, 1956.

Bhaduri, Satinath. *Dhorai Charit Manas*. Calcutta: Bengal Publishers, 1949.

Bhaduri, Satinath. *Jagori*. Calcutta: Samabay Publications, 1945.

Bhattacharya, Sukanta. *Sukanta Samagra*. Calcutta: Saraswat Library, 1995.

Biswas, Hemanga. *Hemanga Biswas Rachana Samgraha*. Kolkata: Dey's, 2012.

Biswas, Hemanga. *Ujan Gang Baiya*. Edited by Moinak Biswas. Kolkata: Anustup, 2012.

Chakraborty, Shibram. *Moscow Banam Pondicherry*. First published in 1929. Calcutta: Samabay Publications, 1943.

Chattopadhyay, Bankimchandra. *Anandamath, or The Sacred Brotherhood*. Translated by Julius J. Lipner. London: Oxford University Press, 2005.

Chattopadhyay, Bankimchandra. *Bankim Rachanavali*. 3 vols. Edited by Jogeshchandra Bagal. Calcutta: Sahitya Sansad, 1954.

Chittaprasad. *Chittaprasad: A Retrospective 1915–78*. Edited by Sanjay Kumar Mallick. Delhi: Delhi Art Gallery, 2011.

Das, Anamitra, and Sipra Sarkar, eds. *Bangalir Samyabad Charcha*. Kolkata: Ananda, 1998.

Das, Baneswar, ed. *The Social and Economic Ideas of Benoy Sarkar*. Calcutta: Chuckervertty Chatterjee, 1939.
Das, Dhananjay, ed. *Marxbadi Sahitya Bitarka*. Kolkata: Karuna Prakasani, 2003.
Das, Sajanikanta. *Atmasmriti*. 2nd ed. Kolkata: Nath Publishers, 2010.
Das, Suranjan, and Premansu Kumar Bandopadhyay, eds. *Food Movement of 1959: Documenting a Turning Point in the History of West Bengal*. Kolkata: K. P. Bagchi, 2004.
Dasi, Binodini. *My Story and My Life as an Actress*. Edited and translated by Rimli Bhattacharya. New Delhi: Kali for Women, 1998.
Datta, Bhupendranath. *Baishnaba Sahitye Samajatattva*. Calcutta: Bharatiya Sahitya Bhabana, 1945.
Datta, Bhupendranath. *Studies in Indian Social Polity*. Calcutta: Purabi, 1944.
Datta, Bhupendranath. *Swami Vivekananda, Patriot Prophet: A Study*. Calcutta: Nababharat Publishers, 1954.
Datta, Bijitkumar, ed. *Sera Sabujpatra Sangraha*. 2 vols. Calcutta: Mitra o Ghosh, 2000.
De, Sunil Kanti, ed. *Nazruler Langal Patrikae Krishak o Sramik Prasanga*. Dhaka: Nazrul Institute, 2010.
Deshpande, G. P. *Chanakya Vishnugupta*. Translated by Maya Pandit. Calcutta: Seagull Books, 1996.
Devi, Sarala. *Saraladevi Chaudhuranir Nirbachita Prabandha Sankalan*. Kolkata: Dey's, 2004.
Dikshitar, V. R. Ramachandra. "Kautilya and Machiavelli." *Indian Historical Quarterly* 3, nos. 1–2 (1927): 176–80.
Dutt, Utpal. "Taking Shakespeare to the Common Man: An Interview with Utpal Dutt." *Epic Theatre*, March 1999, 19–20.
Dutt, Utpal. *Tiner Talwar*. Calcutta: Jatiya Sahitya Parishad, 1970.
Dutt, Utpal. *Towards a Revolutionary Theatre*. First published 1982. Kolkata: Seagull Books, 2009.
Dutt, Utpal. *Utpal Datta Gadya Sangraha*. 2 vols. Edited by Samik Bandopadhyay. Kolkata: Dey's, 2004.
Elias, Akhteruzzaman. *Khoabnama*. Dacca: Mowla Brothers, 1996.
Gandhi, M. K. *Ashram Observances in Action*. Ahmedabad: Navajivan Publishing House, 1955.
Gandhi, M. K. *The Bhagavad Gita according to Gandhi*. Berkeley, CA: Atlantic Books, 2009.
Gandhi, M. K. *Collected Works of Mahatma Gandhi*. Delhi: Government of India Publications Division, 1963. Also available on https://gandhiheritageportal.org.
Gandhi, M. K. *Discourses on the Gita*. Ahmedabad: Navajivan Publishing House, 1960.
Gandhi, M. K. *From Yeravada Mandir*. Ahmedabad: Jivanji Desai, 1935.
Gandhi, M. K. *Gandhi: Selected Writings*. Edited by Dennis Dalton. Indianapolis: Hackett, 1996.
Gandhi, M. K. *Key to Health*. Ahmedabad: Navajivan Publishing House, 1948.
Gandhi, M. K. *Satyagraha in South Africa*. Madras: S. Ganesan, 1928.

Gandhi, M. K., and Rabindranath Tagore. *The Mahatma and the Poet: Letters and Debates between Gandhi and Tagore, 1915–1941.* Edited by Sabyasachi Bhattacharya. Delhi: National Book Trust, 2011.

Ghosh, Manomohan, ed. *The Natyashastra: A Treatise on Indian Dramaturgy and Histrionics Ascribed to Bharata Muni.* Translated by Manomohan Ghosh. Calcutta: Royal Asiatic Society of Bengal, 1950.

Ghoshal, U. N. *A History of Indian Political Ideas.* Bombay: Oxford University Press, 1959.

Ghoshal, U. N. "More Light on Methods and Conclusions in Hindu Politics." *Indian Historical Quarterly* 3, nos. 3–4 (1927): 625–58.

Ghoshal, U. N. "Reply to Benoy Kumar Sarkar." *Indian Historical Quarterly* 2, no. 2 (1926): 420–30.

Hakim, Khalifa Abdul. *Islam and Communism.* Lahore: Institute of Islamic Culture, 1951.

Harder, Hans, ed. *Bankimchandra Chattopadhyay's* Srimadbhagabadgita: *Translation and Analysis.* New Delhi: Manohar, 2001.

Hashim, Abul. *The Creed of Islam.* First published 1950. Dhaka: Bangladesh Cooperative Book Society, 1997.

Hore, Somenath. *Tebhaga: Artist's Diary and Sketchbook.* Kolkata: Seagull Books, 1990.

Hossain, Abul. *Banglar Balshi.* Dhaka: Fazlul Karim Mullick, 1925.

Iqbal, Muhammad. "Lenin (Khuda ke Hazoor Mein)." First published 1935 in *Bal e Jibril*, https://rekhta.org/nazms/lenin-allama-iqbal-nazms. Accessed September 16, 2017.

Iqbal, Muhammad. *The Reconstruction of Religious Thought in Islam.* First published 1930. Introduction by Javed Majeed. Stanford, CA: Stanford University Press, 2013.

Islam, Kazi Nazrul. *Kazi Nazrul Islam Rachana Samagra.* 12 vols. Kolkata: Paschimbanga Bangla Akademi, 2003.

Janah, Sunil. *Photographing India.* Delhi: Oxford University Press, 2013.

Jayaswal, K. P. *Hindu Polity.* 2 vols. Calcutta: Butterworth, 1924.

Kangle, R. P. *The Kautilya Arthashastra: A Study.* Bombay: University of Bombay, 1965.

Khan, Mohammad Akram. *Samasya o Samadhan.* Calcutta: Mohammadi Book Agency, 1938.

Kidwai, Mushir Hosain. *Islam and Socialism.* London: Luzac, 1912.

Lal, P. *Great Sanskrit Plays, in Modern Translation.* New York: New Directions, 1957.

Majumdar, Manjukumar, and Bhanudeb Datta, eds. *Banglar Communist Andoloner Itihas Anusandhan.* 2 vols. 2nd ed. Kolkata: Manisha, 2014.

Mukerjee, D. P. *Diversities: Essays in Economics, History, Sociology and Other Social Problems.* Delhi: People's Publishing House, 1958.

Mukerjee, D. P. *Personality and the Social Sciences.* Calcutta: The Book Company, 1924.

Mukerjee, Radhakamal. *Daridrer Krandan.* 2nd ed. Calcutta: Girindranath Mitra, 1915.

Mukerjee, Radhakamal. "Faiths and Influences." In *Frontiers of Social Science: In Honour of Radhakamal Mukherjee*, edited by Baljit Singh, 6–20. London: Macmillan, 1955.

Mukerjee, Radhakamal. *Foundations of Indian Economics.* Bombay: Longmans, Green, 1916.

Mukerjee, Radhakamal. *Principles of Comparative Economics*. Vol. 1. London: P. S. King and Sons, 1921.
Mukhopadhyay, Dhurjatiprasad. *Dhurjatiprasad Rachanabali*. 2 vols. 2nd ed. Kolkata: Dey's, 2010.
Mukhopadhyay, Subhas. *Subhas Mukhopadhyay Gadya Samgraha*. Edited by Subir Raychaudhuri and Amiya Deb. 2 vols. 2nd ed. Kolkata: Dey's, 2010.
Nag, Kalidas. "Prof. Benoy Kumar Sarkar and the 'New Machiavelli.'" *Indian Historical Quarterly* 2, no. 3 (1926): 650–54.
Nivedita, Sister. *The Complete Works of Sister Nivedita*. 5 vols. 5th ed. Kolkata: Advaita Ashrama, 2006.
Nivedita, Sister. *The Master as I Saw Him*. First published 1910. Calcutta. Advaita Ashram, 2007.
Odud, Kazi Abdul. *Hindu-Musalmaner Birodh: Nizam Lecture Delivered in Visvabharati, Shantiniketan*. Birbhum: Santiniketan Press, 1935.
Olivelle, Patrick, ed. and trans. *King, Governance, and Law in Ancient India: Kautilya's Arthashastra*. New York: Oxford University Press, 2013.
Phule, Jyotiba. *Gulamgiri*. First published 1885. Delhi: Gautam Book Store, 2004.
Pradhan, Sudhi, ed. *Koyekjon Lok-kavi*. Calcutta: Anti-Fascist Writers and Artists' Association, 1945.
Pradhan, Sudhi, ed. *Marxist Cultural Movements in India*. Kolkata: National Book Agency, 1960
Prasad, Jayashankar. *Sampurra Natak*. Kanpur: Chintan Prakasan, 1998.
Ray, Annada Shankar. *Pathe Prabase*. First published 1931. Calcutta: M. C. Sarkar and Sons, 1949.
Renu, Phanishwar Nath. *Maila Anchal*. First published 1954. Delhi: Rajkamal, 2016.
Roy, D. L. *Chandragupta*. Edited by Sukumar Bandopadhyay. Calcutta: Modern Book Agency, 1969.
Roy, M. N. *Fragments of a Jail Diary*. First published 1950. Delhi: Ajanta, 1982.
Roy, M. N. *Historical Role of Islam: An Essay on Islamic Culture*. Bombay: Vora, 1937.
Roy, Sabitri. *Harvest Song*. Translated by Chandrima Bhattacharya and Adrita Mukherjee. Kolkata: Stree, 2005.
Sahajanand, Swami. *Sahajanand on Agricultural Labour and Rural Poor: An Edited Translation of "Khet Mazdoor."* Edited and translated by Walter Hauser. Delhi: Manohar, 1994.
Sarkar, Badal. *Three Plays: Procession, Bhoma, Stale News*. Translated by Samik Bandopadhyay. Calcutta: Seagull Books, 1983.
Sarkar, Benoy Kumar. *Economic Development: Snapshots of World Movements in Commerce, Economic Legislation, Industrialism and Technical Education*. 2 vols. Madras: B. G. Paul, 1926.
Sarkar, Benoy Kumar. "Hindu Politics in Italian: Part 1." *Indian Historical Quarterly* 1, no. 3 (1925): 545–60.
Sarkar, Benoy Kumar. "Hindu Politics in Italian: Part 2." *Indian Historical Quarterly* 1, no. 4 (1925): 742–56.
Sarkar, Benoy Kumar. "Hindu Politics in Italian: Part 3." *Indian Historical Quarterly* 2, no. 2 (1926): 351–72.

Sarkar, Benoy Kumar. "The Maratha Political Ideas of the 18th Century: The Marathi Rajaniti of Ramachandrapant (1716)." *Indian Historical Quarterly* 12, no. 1 (1936): 88–103.

Sarkar, Benoy Kumar. *Sukraniti*. Allahabad: Sudhindranatha Vasu, 1914.

Sen, Mohit. *The Traveller and the Road: Journeys of an Indian Communist*. Delhi: Rupa, 2003.

Sengupta, Achintya Kumar. *Kallol Yug*. Calcutta: S. C. Sarkar and Sons, 1950.

Sengupta, Achintya Kumar. "Muchi Bayen." *Masik Basumati* 1, no. 6 (1947): 613–24.

Shamashastry, R., ed. *Kautilya's Arthashastra*. Translated by R. Shamashastry. Bangalore: Government Press, 1915.

Shasmal, Birendranath. *Sroter Trina: Swaraj Ashrame Aat Mas*. Calcutta: Gopinath Bharati, 1922.

Shastri, Haraprasad. *Bauddhadharma*. Dhaka: Nabajug Prakashani, 2011.

Shastri, Haraprasad. *Haraprasad Shastri Rachana Sangraha*. Edited by Satyajit Choudhury and Nikhilieshwar Sengupta. Calcutta: Paschimbbanga Rajya Pustak Parshad, 1989.

Shinde, Tarabai. *A Comparison between Women and Men: Tarabai Shinde and the Critique of Gender Relations in Colonial India*. Edited by Rosalind O'Hanlon. London: Oxford University Press, 2000.

Sitaramayya, Pattabhi. *The History of the Indian National Congress, 1885–1935*. Madras: Congress Working Committee, 1935.

Tagore, Rabindranath. *Rabindra Rachanavali*. 27 vols. Calcutta: Visvabharati, 1940.

Tagore, Rabindranath. *Sanchayita*. Kolkata: Visvabharati, 1969.

Tanvir, Habib. "Interview: It Must Flow, A Life in Theatre." *Seagull Theatre Quarterly* 10 (June 1996): 3–38.

Vivekananda. *The Complete Works of Swami Vivekananda*. 9 vols. Calcutta: Advaita Ashram, 1972.

Vivekananda. *The Indispensable Vivekananda: An Anthology for Our Times*. Edited by Amiya P. Sen. Delhi: Permanent Black, 2006.

Vivekananda. *Selections from the Complete Works of Swami Vivekananda*. 25th ed. Kolkata: Advaita Ashram, 2008.

Wilson, H. H. *Select Specimens of the Theatre of the Hindus*. Vol. 1. Calcutta: Holcroft, 1827.

Zaidi, A. Moin, and Shaheda Zaidi. *The Encyclopaedia of Indian National Congress*. 28 vols. New Delhi: S. Chand, 1976.

Secondary Sources

PhD Dissertations

Briggs, Ellen Jane. "Freedom and Desire in the *Bhagavad Gītā*." PhD diss., University of Texas, Austin, 2008.

Chatterjee, Neha. "Sacred Calling, Worldly Bargain: Caste, Self-Cultivation and Mobilization in Late Colonial Bengal." PhD diss., Jawaharlal Nehru University, 2017.

Dasgupta, Ananya. "Labors of Representation: Cultivating Land, Self and Community among Muslims in Late Colonial Bengal." PhD diss., University of Pennsylvania, 2013. http://repository.upenn.edu/edissertations/849.

Dasgupta, Rajarshi. "Marxism and Middle-Class Intelligentsia: Culture and Politics in Bengal, 1920-30." PhD diss., Queen's College, Oxford University, 2003.

McClish, Mark. "Political Brahmanism and the State: A Compositional History of the Arthashastra." PhD diss., University of Texas, Austin, 2009.

Sen, Dwaipayan. "The Emergence and Decline of Dalit Politics in Bengal: Jogendranath Mandal, the Scheduled Castes Federation and Partition, 1932-1968." PhD diss., University of Chicago, 2012.

Articles and Books

Alam, Muzaffar. *The Languages of Political Islam: India 1200-1800*. Chicago: University of Chicago Press, 2004.

Alphonso-Karakala, John B. "Facets of Panchatantra." *Indian Literature* 18, no. 2 (1975): 73-91.

Alter, Joseph. *Gandhi's Body: Sex, Diet and the Politics of Nationalism*. Philadelphia: University of Pennsylvania Press, 2000.

Amin, Shahid. "Gandhi as Mahatma: Gorakhpur District, Eastern UP, 1920-21." In *Subaltern Studies*. Vol. 3. Edited by Ranajit Guha, 1-71. Delhi: Oxford University Press, 1984.

Anjaria, Ulka. *Realism in the Twentieth-Century Indian Novel: Colonial Difference and Literary Form*. New York: Cambridge University Press, 2012.

Ansari, Khizar Humayun. *The Emergence of Socialist Thought among North Indian Muslims, 1917-1947*. Oxford: Oxford University Press, 2015.

Arendt, Hannah. *The Human Condition*. Chicago: University of Chicago Press, 1958.

Arunima, G. "Friends and Lovers: Towards a Social History of Emotions in 19th- and 20th-Century Kerala." In *Women of India: Colonial and Postcolonial Periods*, edited by Bharati Roy, 139-58. Delhi: Sage, 2005.

Badiou, Alain. *Being and Event*. Translated by Oliver Feltham. London: Continuum, 2006.

Badiou, Alain. *Being Singular Plural*. Minneapolis: University of Minnesota Press, 2000.

Balslev, Anindita. "The Idea of Abhyasa." In *Indian Conceptual World: Philosophical Essays*, 91-97. New Delhi: Aditya Prakashan, 2012.

Bandopadhyay, Sarbani. "Another History: Bhadrolok Responses to Dalit Political Assertion in Colonial Bengal." In *The Politics of Caste in West Bengal*, edited by Uday Chandra, Geir Heierstad, and Kenneth Bo Nielsen, 35-59. Delhi: Routledge, 2016.

Bandopadhyay, Shibaji. "Pita Putra Dvairath." *Antahsar* 5, no. 1 (2008): 352-407.

Bandopadhyay, Sukumar. "Editor's Introduction." In D. L. Roy, *Chandragupta*, 1-26. Calcutta: Modern Book Agency, 1969.

Banerjee, Arnab. "Rehearsals for a Revolution: The Political Theater of Utpal Dutt." *Southeast Review of Asian Studies* 34 (2012): 222-30.

Banerjee, Prathama. "The Abiding Binary: The Social and the Political in Modern India." In *South Asian Governmentalities: Michel Foucault and the Question of Postcolonial Orderings*, edited by Stephen Legg and Diana Heath, 81-105. Cambridge: Cambridge University Press, 2018.

Banerjee, Prathama. "Debt, Time and Extravagance: Money and the Making of 'Primitives' in Colonial Bengal." *Indian Economic and Social History Review* 37, no. 4 (2000): 423–45.

Banerjee, Prathama. "Example and Following." *Contemporary South Asia* 25, no. 4 (2018): 429–34.

Banerjee, Prathama. *Politics of Time: "Primitives" and History-Writing in a Colonial Society*. Delhi: Oxford University Press, 2006.

Banerjee, Prathama. "A Social History of Banking in Bengal" (project report). Kolkata: Centre for Study in Social Sciences, 2001.

Banerjee, Prathama. "The Work of Imagination: Temporality and Nationhood in Colonial Bengal." In *Subaltern Studies XII: Muslims, Dalits and Fabrications of History*, edited by Shail Mayaram, M. S. S. Pandian, and Ajay Skaria, 280–322. Delhi: Permanent Black, 2005.

Banerjee, Prathama, Aditya Nigam, and Rakesh Pandey. "The Work of Theory: Thinking across Traditions." *Economic and Political Weekly* 51, no. 37 (2016): 42–50.

Basu, Shamita. *Religious Revivalism as Nationalist Discourse: Swami Vivekananda and New Hinduism in Nineteenth-Century Bengal*. Delhi: Oxford University Press, 2002.

Basu, Sibaji Pratim. "The Chronicle of a Forgotten Movement: The Food Movement of 1959 Revisited." Kolkata: Mahanirban Calcutta Research Group, 2012, 1–18. http://www.mcrg.ac.in/PP56.pdf. Accessed September 20, 2017.

Bate, Bernard. "'To Persuade Them into Speech and Action': Oratory and the Tamil Political, 1905–19." *Comparative Studies in Society and History* 55, no. 1 (2013): 142–66.

Bausani, Alessandro. "The Concept of Time in the Religious Philosophy of Muhammad Iqbal." *Die Welt des Islams*, n.s., 3, nos. 3–4 (1954): 158–86.

Bayat, Asef. *Life as Politics: How Ordinary People Change the Middle East*. Amsterdam: Amsterdam University Press, 2010.

Baycroft, Timothy, and David Hopkin, eds. *Folklore and Nationalism in Europe during the Long Nineteenth Century*. Leiden: Brill, 2009.

Bayly, C. A. "India, the Bhagavad Gita and the World." *Modern Intellectual History* 7, no. 2 (2010): 275–95.

Bayly, C. A. *Recovering Liberties: Indian Thought in the Age of Liberalism and Empire*. Cambridge: Cambridge University Press, 2012.

Bayly, Susan. *Caste, Society and Politics in India: From the Eighteenth Century to the Modern Age*. Cambridge: Cambridge University Press, 1999.

Bharucha, Rustom. *Rehearsals of Revolution: The Political Theatre of Bengal*. Calcutta: Seagull Books, 1983.

Bhatia, Nandi. *Acts of Authority/Acts of Resistance: Theater and Politics in Colonial and Postcolonial India*. Ann Arbor: University of Michigan Press, 2004.

Bhattacharya, Baidik. "Reading Rancière: Literature at the Limit of World Literature." *New Literary History* 48, no. 3 (2017): 555–80.

Bhattacharya, Baidik, and Sambudha Sen. *Novel Formations: The Indian Beginnings of a European Genre*. Delhi: Permanent Black, 2018.

Bhattacharya, Ramkrishna. *Bhupendranath Datta: Itihasbodh o Rashtrachinta*. Kolkata: Anushtup, 2013.

Bhattacharyya, Dwaipayan. "Of Control and Factions: The Changing 'Party-Society' in Rural West Bengal." *Economic and Political Weekly* 44, no. 9 (2009): 59-69.

Blackburn, Stuart. *Print, Folklore, and Nationalism in Colonial India.* Delhi: Permanent Black, 2003.

Böhme, Gernot. "Atmosphere as the Fundamental Concept of a New Aesthetics." *Thesis Eleven* 36, no. 1 (1993): 113-26.

Bose, Neilesh. *Recasting the Region: Language, Culture, and Islam in Colonial Bengal.* Delhi: Oxford University Press, 2014.

Bose, Sanat. *Essays on Indian Labour.* Calcutta: Bingsha Satabdi, 1996.

Bowles, Adam. "The Failure of Dharma." *Seminar: Enduring Epic, a Symposium on Some Concerns Raised in the Mahabharata*, no. 608, April 2010. http://www.indiaseminar.com/2010/608/608_adam_bowles.htm. Accessed November 12, 2013.

Canetti, Elias. "Discussion with Theodor W. Adorno." *Thesis Eleven* 45, no. 1 (1996): 1-15.

Certeau, Michel de. *The Practice of Everyday Life.* Berkeley: University of California Press, 1984.

Chakrabarti, Arindam. "Just Words." In *Mahabharata Now: Narration, Aesthetics, Ethics*, edited by Arindam Chakrabarti and Shibaji Bandopadhyay, 244-83. New Delhi: Routledge, 2014.

Chakrabarty, Bidyut. "The Communal Award of 1932 and Its Implications in Bengal." *Modern Asian Studies* 23, no. 3 (1989): 493-523.

Chakrabarty, Dipesh. "Bidhi Bam? Kolkatae Marx, 1965-75." *Baromas* 13 (2011): 77-82.

Chakrabarty, Dipesh. "Minority Histories, Subaltern Pasts." *Postcolonial Studies* 1, no. 1 (1998): 15-29.

Chakrabarty, Dipesh. *Provincializing Europe: Postcolonial Thought and Historical Difference.* Princeton, NJ: Princeton University Press, 2000.

Chakrabarty, Dipesh. "A Small History of *Subaltern Studies.*" In *Habitations of Modernity: Essays in the Wake of Subaltern Studies*, 3-19. Delhi: Permanent Black, 2004.

Chakravarty, Dilip K. "Readers' Responses." *Indian Literature* 36, no. 4 (1993): 181-84.

Chandra, Bipin. *The Rise and Growth of Economic Nationalism in India: Economic Policies of Indian National Leadership 1880-1905.* Delhi: Har-Anand Publications, 2010.

Chatterjee, Joya. *Bengal Divided: Hindu Communalism and Partition, 1932-47.* Cambridge: Cambridge University Press, 1994.

Chatterjee, Partha. *Lineages of Political Society: Studies in Democracy.* New York: Columbia University Press, 2011.

Chatterjee, Partha. *The Nation and Its Fragments: Colonial and Postcolonial Histories.* Princeton, NJ: Princeton University Press, 1993.

Chatterjee, Partha. "The Religion of Urban Domesticity: Sri Ramakrishna and the Calcutta Middle Class." In *Subaltern Studies VII*, edited by Partha Chatterjee and Gyanendra Pandey, 40-63. Delhi: Oxford University Press, 1992.

Chatterjee, Srilata. *Congress Politics in Bengal, 1919-1939.* London: Anthem, 2002.

Chattopadhyay, Rajagopal. *Swami Vivekananda in India: A Corrective Biography.* Delhi: Motilal Banarasidass, 1999.

Chaudhuri, Rosinka. *Gentlemen Poets in Colonial Bengal: Emergent Nationalism and the Orientalist Project.* Kolkata: Seagull Books, 2002.

Chaudhuri, Rosinka. *The Literary Thing: History, Poetry and the Making of a Modern Literary Culture.* Delhi: Oxford University Press, 2013.

Chousalkar, Ashok S. "The Concept of Apaddharma and the Moral Dilemma of Politics." *Indian Literature* 49, no. 1 (2005): 115–27.

Chousalkar, Ashok S. "Methodology of Kautilya's Arthashastra." *Indian Journal of Political Science* 65, no. 1 (2004): 55–76.

Chousalkar, Ashok S. "Political Philosophy of Arthashastra Tradition." *Indian Journal of Political Science* 42, no. 1 (1981): 54–66.

Chowdhury, Indira. *The Frail Hero and Virile History: Gender and the Politics of Culture in Colonial Bengal.* Delhi: Oxford University Press, 1988.

Chowdhury, Nurul Hasan. *Peasant Radicalism in Nineteenth Century Bengal: The Faraizis, Indigo and Pabna Movements.* Dhaka: Asiatic Society of Bangladesh, 2001.

Dabashi, Hamid. *The World of Persian Literary Humanism.* Cambridge, MA: Harvard University Press, 2012.

Das, Prabhat Kumar. "Yatra: Utpal Datter." *Lokasamskrti Gabesana* 7, no. 2 (1994): 244–56.

Das, Sisir Kumar. *A History of Indian Literature, 500–1399: From Courtly to the Popular.* Delhi: Sahitya Akademi, 2005.

Das, Sisir Kumar. *A History of Indian Literature, 1800–1910: Western Impact: Indian Response.* Delhi: Sahitya Akademi, 1995.

Das, Veena. *Life and Words: Violence and the Descent into the Ordinary.* Berkeley: University of California Press, 2007.

Das, Veena. "Violence and Nonviolence at the Heart of Hindu Ethics." In *Oxford Handbook on Religion and Violence,* edited by Mark Jurgensmeyer, Margo Kitts, and Michael Jerryson, 15–41. New York: Oxford University Press, 2012.

Dasgupta, Hemendra Nath. *The Indian Theatre.* First published 1988. Delhi: Gyan, 2009.

Dasgupta, Rajarshi. "The Ascetic Modality: A Critique of Communist Self-Fashioning." In *Critical Studies in Politics: Exploring Sites, Selves, Power,* edited by Nivedita Menon, Aditya Nigam, and Sanjay Palshikar, 67–87. Shimla: Indian Institute of Advanced Study and Orient Blackswan, 2014.

Datta, Pradip. *Carving Blocs: Communal Ideology in Early Twentieth-Century Bengal.* Delhi: Oxford University Press, 1999.

Datta, Pradip, ed. *Rabindranath Tagore's Home and the World: A Critical Companion.* Delhi: Orient Blackswan, 2003.

Dean, Jodi. *Crowds and Party.* London: Verso Books, 2016.

Deleuze, Gilles. *Nietzsche and Philosophy.* Translated by Hugh Tomlinson. London: Continuum, 1983.

Deleuze, Gilles, and Félix Guattari. *What Is Philosophy?* New York: Columbia University Press, 1994.

Demos, Virginia E. *The Affect Theory of Silvan Tomkins for Psychoanalysis and Psychotherapy: Recasting the Essentials.* New York: Routledge, 2019.

Dey, Bishnu. "*Nabanna:* After 25 Years." *Bohurupee: Nabanna Smarak Sankhya* (June 1970): 2.

Dhar, Prashant. "Hemanga Biswas o Nibaran Pandit." *Anustup* 8, no. 1 (2012): 259–75.

Diagne, Souleymane Bachir. *African Art as Philosophy: Senghor, Bergson and Negritude.* Kolkata: Seagull Books, 2011.

Dirks, Nicholas. *Castes of Mind: Colonialism and the Making of Modern India.* Princeton, NJ: Princeton University Press, 2001.

Dodescu, Anca. "State versus Market: Some Arguments to Surpass the 'Mirror Approach.'" *Theoretical and Applied Economics* 17, no. 9 (2010): 17–32.

Durkheim, Émile. *The Elementary Forms of Religious Life.* Translated by Carol Cosman. Oxford: Oxford University Press, 2001.

Eaton, Richard. *The Rise of Islam on the Bengal Frontier, 1204–1760.* Berkeley: University of California Press, 1993.

Ernst, Carl. "Muslim Studies of Hinduism? A Reconsideration of Arabic and Persian Translations from Indian Languages." *Iranian Studies* 36, no. 2 (2003): 173–95.

Fischer-Lichte, Erika. *Theatre, Sacrifice, Ritual: Exploring Forms of Political Theatre.* London: Routledge, 2007.

Fischer-Lichte, Erika. *The Transformative Power of Performance: A New Aesthetics.* London: Routledge, 2008.

Freitag, Sandra. *Collective Action and Community: Public Arenas and the Emergence of Communalism in North India.* Berkeley: University of California Press, 1989.

Galanter, Marc. *Competing Equalities: Law and the Backward Classes in India.* Berkeley: University of California Press, 1984.

Gandhi, Leela. *The Common Cause: Postcolonial Ethics and the Practice of Democracy, 1900–50.* Chicago: University of Chicago Press, 2014.

Ganeri, Jonardon. *The Concealed Art of the Soul: Theories of Self and Practices of Truth in Indian Ethics and Epistemology.* Oxford: Oxford University Press, 2007.

Ganeri, Jonardon. *The Lost Age of Reason: Philosophy in Early Modern India, 1450–1700.* Oxford: Oxford University Press, 2011.

George, K. M., ed. *Modern Indian Literature: An Anthology.* Vol. 1, *Surveys and Poems.* Delhi: Sahitya Akademi, 1992.

Ghosh, Durba. "The History of Revolutionary Terrorism through Autobiography." In *Gentlemanly Terrorists: Political Violence and the Colonial State in India, 1919–1947,* 60–91. Cambridge: Cambridge University Press, 2017.

Govindu, Venu Madhav, and Deepak Malghan. *The Web of Freedom: J. C. Kumarappa and Gandhi's Struggle for Economic Justice.* Delhi: Oxford University Press, 2016.

Gramsci, Antonio. *Selections from the Prison Notebook.* Translated and edited by Quentin Hoare and Geoffrey Nowell Smith. New York: International Publishers, 1971.

Guha, Ranajit. "Discipline and Mobilise." In *Dominance without Hegemony,* 100–149. Delhi: Oxford University Press, 1998.

Guha, Ranajit. *Elementary Aspects of Peasant Insurgency in Colonial India.* Delhi: Oxford University Press, 1983.

Guha, Ranajit. *History at the Limit of World History.* New York: Columbia University Press, 2002.

Guha, Ranajit. *An Indian Historiography for India: A Nineteenth-Century Agenda.* Calcutta: K. P. Bagchi, 1988.

Gupta, Bina. *The Disinterested Witness: A Fragment of Advaita Vedanta Phenomenology.* Evanston, IL: Northwestern University Press, 1998.

Gupta, Mahendranath. *The Gospel of Sri Ramakrishna.* Translated by Swami Nikhilananda. Madras: Sri Ramkrishna Math, 1974.

Haberman, David L. *Acting as a Way to Salvation: A Study of Raganuga Bhakti Sadhana.* Delhi: Motilal Banarasidass, 2001.

Hadot, Pierre. *Philosophy as a Way of Life: Spiritual Exercises from Socrates to Foucault.* London: Wiley, 1995.

Halbfass, Wilhelm. "Karma, *Apurva*, and 'Natural' Causes: Observations on the Growth and Limits of the Theory of *Samsara*." In *Karma and Rebirth in Classical Indian Traditions,* edited by Wendy Doniger O'Flaherty, 268–302. Delhi: Motilal Banarasidass, 1983.

Halbfass, Wilhelm. "Practical Vedanta." In *The Oxford India Hinduism Reader,* edited by Vasudha Dalmia and Heinrich von Stietencron, 169–86. Delhi: Oxford University Press, 2009.

Hashmi, Taj-ul Islam. *Pakistan as a Peasant's Utopia: Communalization of Class in Bengal, 1920-1947.* Boulder, CO: Westview Press, 1992.

Hegel, G. W. F. *Lectures on the Philosophy of World History.* Cambridge: Cambridge University Press, 1975.

Heidegger, Martin. "The Question Concerning Technology." In *Basic Writings,* edited by David Farrell Krell, 283–317. San Francisco: HarperCollins, 1978.

Herling, Bradley L. *The German Gita: Hermeneutics and Discipline in the German Reception of Indian Thought, 1778-1831.* London: Routledge, 2006.

Hillach, Ansgar, Jerold Wikoff, and Ulf Zimmerman. "The Aesthetics of Politics: Walter Benjamin's 'Theories of German Fascism.'" *New German Critique,* no. 17 (1979): 99–119.

Husserl, Edmund. *The Crisis of European Sciences and Transcendental Phenomenology.* Edited and translated by David Carr. Evanston, IL: Northwestern University Press, 1970.

Idris, Murad. *War for Peace: Genealogies of a Violent Ideal in Western and Islamic Thought.* New York: Oxford University Press, 2018.

Illiah, Kancha. *God as Political Philosopher: Buddhism's Challenge to Brahmanism.* Kolkata: Samya, 2000.

Inston, Kevin. "Inscribing the Egalitarian Event: Jacques Rancière and the Politics of Iterability." *Constellations* 24, no. 1 (2017): 15–26.

Isherwood, Christopher. *Ramakrishna and His Disciples.* Los Angeles: Vedanta Press, 1983.

Jaffrelot, Christophe. *Dr. Ambedkar and Untouchability: Analysing and Fighting Caste.* Delhi: Permanent Black, 2005.

Jalal, Ayesha. *Partisans of Allah: Jihad in South Asia.* Cambridge, MA: Harvard University Press, 2008.

Jodhka, Surinder S. "Nation and Village: Images of Rural India in Gandhi, Nehru and Ambedkar." *Economic and Political Weekly* 37, no. 32 (2002): 3343–53.

Joshi, P. C. "Founders of the Lucknow School and Their Legacy: Radhakamal Mukerjee and D. P. Mukerji: Some Reflections." *Economic and Political Weekly* 21, no. 33 (1986): 1455–69.

Joshi, P. C. "Lucknow School of Economics and Sociology and Its Relevance Today: Some Reflections." *Sociological Bulletin* 35, no. 1 (1986): 1–28.

Jullien, François. *A Treatise on Efficacy: Between Chinese and Western Thinking*. Honolulu: University of Hawaii Press, 2004.

Kantorowicz, Ernst. *The King's Two Bodies: A Study in Mediaeval Political Theology*. Princeton, NJ: Princeton University Press, 1957.

Kapila, Shruti, and Faisal Devji, eds. "Bhagavad Gita and Modern Thought." Special issue, *Modern Intellectual History* 7, no. 2 (2010).

Kaviraj, Sudipta. *The Invention of Private Life: Literature and Ideas*. Delhi: Permanent Black, 2015.

Kaviraj, Sudipta. "An Outline of a Revisionist Theory of Modernity." *European Journal of Sociology* 46, no. 3 (2005): 497–526.

Khare, R. S. *The Untouchable as Himself: Ideology, Identity, and Pragmatism among the Lucknow Chamars*. Cambridge: Cambridge University Press, 1984.

Kolge, Nishikant. *Gandhi against Caste*. Delhi: Oxford University Press, 2017.

Kolsky, Elizabeth. *Colonial Justice in British India: White Violence and the Rule of Law*. Cambridge: Cambridge University Press, 2010.

Kosambi, D. D. *The Culture and Civilisation of Ancient India: A Historical Outline*. Delhi: Vikas, 1970.

Kothari, Rajni. "The Congress System Revisited: A Decennial Review." *Asian Survey* 14, no. 2 (1974): 1035–54.

Kothari, Rajni. "The Party System." *Economic Weekly*, June 3, 1961, 847–54.

Krishna, Gopal. "The Development of the Indian National Congress as a Mass Organization, 1918–1923." *Journal of Asian Studies* 25, no. 3 (1966): 413–30.

Kumar, Aishwary. *Radical Equality: Ambedkar, Gandhi, and the Risk of Democracy*. Stanford, CA: Stanford University Press, 2015.

Kumar, Udaya. "Self, Body and Inner Sense: Some Reflections on Sri Narayanaguru and Kumara Asan." *Studies in History* 13, no. 2 (1997): 247–70.

Kumar, Udaya. *Writing the First Person: Literature, History and Autobiography in Modern Kerala*. Delhi: Permanent Black, 2016.

Lath, Mukund. "The Concept of Anrsamsyam in Mahabharata." In *Reflections and Variations on the Mahabharata*, edited by T. R. S. Sharma, 82–89. Delhi: Sahitya Akademi, 2009.

Lederle, Matthew. *Philosophical Trends in Modern Maharashtra*. Bombay: Popular Prakashan, 1976.

Lefort, Claude. *The Political Forms of Modern Society: Bureaucracy, Democracy, Totalitarianism*. Edited by John B. Thompson. Cambridge, MA: MIT Press, 1986.

Lefort, Claude. *Democracy and Political Theory*. Translated by David Macey. Cambridge: Polity Press, 1991.

Limbale, Sharankumar. *Towards an Aesthetics of Dalit Literature: History, Controversy and Considerations*. Delhi: Orient Longman, 2012.

Low, D. A. "Congress and 'Mass Contacts,' 1936–37: Ideology, Interests, and Conflict over the Basis of Party Representation." In *Congress and Indian Nationalism: The Pre-independence Phase*, edited by Richard Sisson and Stanley Wolpert, 134–58. Berkeley: University of California Press, 1988.

Lukács, Georg. *The Ontology of Social Being*. Vol. 3, *Labour*. Translated by David Fernbach. London: Merlin Press, 1980.

MacLean, Kama. *A Revolutionary History of Interwar India: Violence, Image, Voice and Text*. London: Penguin, 2016.

Madaio, James. "Rethinking Neo-Vedānta: Swami Vivekananda and the Selective Historiography of Advaita Vedānta." *Religions* 8, no. 6 (2017). http://www.mdpi.com/2077-1444/8/6/101.

Madan, T. N. "D. P. Mukherjee, 1894–1961: A Centenary Tribute." *Sociological Bulletin* 43, no. 2 (1994): 133–42.

Majeed, Javed. *Muhammad Iqbal: Islam, Aesthetics and Postcolonialism*. London: Routledge, 2008.

Malhotra, S. L. "The Contribution of Gandhi to the Development of the Congress Constitution." In *Mahatma Gandhi and the Indian National Congress*, edited by S. L. Malhotra, 1–40. Chandigarh: Punjab University Publication Bureau, 1988.

Manjapra, Kris. *M. N. Roy: Marxism and Colonial Cosmopolitanism*. New York: Routledge, 2010.

Mantena, Karuna. "Another Realism: Gandhi's Politics of Nonviolence." *American Political Science Review* 106, no. 2 (2012): 445–70.

Marchart, Oliver. *Post-foundational Political Thought: Political Difference in Nancy, Lefort, Badiou and Laclau*. Edinburgh: Edinburgh University Press, 2007.

Marks, Laura. *Enfoldment and Infinity: An Islamic Genealogy of New Media Art*. Cambridge, MA: MIT Press, 2010.

Mazzarella, William. *The Mana of Mass Society*. Chicago: University of Chicago Press, 2017.

McDermott, Rachel Fell. *Singing to the Goddess: Poems to Kali and Uma from Bengal*. New York: Oxford University Press, 2001.

Mehta, Uday Singh. "Gandhi on Politics, Democracy and Everyday Life." *Modern Intellectual History* 7, no. 2 (2010): 355–71.

Michelutti, Lucia. "We the Yadavs Are a Caste of Politicians: Caste and Modern Politics in a North Indian Town." *Contributions to Indian Sociology* 38, nos. 1–2 (2004): 43–71.

Mignolo, Walter, and Catherine Walsh. *On Decoloniality: Concepts, Analytics, Praxis*. Durham, NC: Duke University Press, 2018.

Minkowski, Christopher. "Advaita Vedanta in Early Modern History." *South Asian History and Culture* 2, no. 2 (2009–10): 138–59.

Mishra, S. C. *Evolution of Kautilya's Arthashastra: An Inscriptional Approach*. Delhi: Anamika, 1997.

Misra, B. B. *The Indian Political Parties*. Delhi: Oxford University Press, 1976.

Mitra, Iman. "Exchanging Words and Things: Vernacularization of Political Economy in Nineteenth-Century Bengal." *Indian Economic and Social History Review* 53, no. 4 (2016): 501–31.

Mitra, Saonli. *Shambhu Mitra: Bichitra Jibon Parikrama*. Delhi: National Book Trust, 2011.
Mohanty, Jitendra. "Theory and Practice in Indian Philosophy." In *Explorations in Philosophy: Indian Philosophy, Essays*, 19–32. Delhi: Oxford University Press, 2001.
Mukhia, Harbans, ed. *The Feudalism Debate*. Delhi: Manohar, 1999.
Mukherjee, Janam. *Hungry Bengal: War, Famine, Riots and the End of Empire*. Delhi: Harper, 2015.
Mukhopadhyay, Ashok. "Hemanga Biswas: Loksangit or Ganasangit, Prapti or Proshno." *Anushtup* 8, no. 1 (2012): 197–215.
Nancy, Jean-Luc, and Philippe Lacoue-Labarthe. *Retreating the Political*. Abingdon, UK: Routledge, 1997.
Naregal, Veena. "Performance, Caste, Aesthetics." *Contributions to Indian Sociology* 44, nos. 1–2 (2010): 79–101.
Ndlovu-Gatsheni, Sabelo J. "Decoloniality as the Future of Africa." *History Compass* 13, no. 10 (2015): 485–96.
Nietzsche, Friedrich. *The Birth of Tragedy*. Edited by Michael Tanner. Translated by Shaun Whiteside. London: Penguin, 1993.
Nikhilananda, Swami. *Vivekananda: A Biography*. Calcutta: Advaita Ashrama, 1982.
Olivelle, Patrick. *The Dharmasutras: The Law Codes of Ancient India*. New York: Oxford University Press, 1999.
Olivelle, Patrick. *Pancatantra: The Book of India's Folk Wisdom*. New York: Oxford University Press, 1999.
Omana, S. *Sree Narayana Guru*. Trivandum: Critical Quest, 2005.
Oppenshaw, Jean. *Seeking Bauls of Bengal*. Cambridge: Cambridge University Press, 2002.
Pinch, William. *Peasants and Monks in British India*. Berkeley: University of California Press, 1996.
Pinch, William. *Warrior Ascetics and Indian Empires*. Cambridge: Cambridge University Press, 2006.
Pollock, Sheldon, ed. and trans. *The Rasa Reader: Classical Indian Aesthetics*. New York: Columbia University Press, 2016.
Poovey, Mary. *Genres of the Credit Economy: Mediating Value in Eighteenth- and Nineteenth-Century Britain*. Chicago: University of Chicago Press, 2008.
Prabhakar, Vishnu. *Awara Masiha*. Delhi: B. R. Publications, 1989.
Pradhan, Atul Chandra. "Socialist Stirrings within the Congress (1934–40)." In *A Centenary History of the Indian National Congress*, vol. 3, 1935–47, edited by B. N. Pande and M. N. Das, 218–304. Delhi: Vikas Publishing House, 1985.
Puchner, Martin. *The Drama of Ideas: Platonic Provocations in Theater and Philosophy*. New York: Oxford University Press, 2010.
Puchner, Martin. *The Poetry of Revolution: Marx, Manifestos, and the Avant-Gardes*. Princeton, NJ: Princeton University Press, 2006.
Puchner, Martin. *Stage Fright: Modernism, Anti-theatricality and Drama*. Baltimore: John Hopkins University Press, 2002.
Raha, Bipasha. *The Plough and the Pen: Peasantry, Agriculture and Literati in Colonial Bengal*. Delhi: Manohar, 2012.

Rajadhyaksha, Ashish, and Paul Willeman. *Encyclopaedia of Indian Cinema*. First published 1994. Delhi: Oxford University Press, 2002.

Ramana Rao, M. V. *Development of the Congress Constitution*. New Delhi: All India Congress Committee, 1958.

Rancière, Jacques. *Hatred of Democracy*. Translated by Steve Corcoran. London: Verso, 2006.

Rancière, Jacques. *The Politics of Aesthetics: The Distribution of the Sensible*. Translated by Gabriel Rockhill. London: Continuum, 2004.

Rancière, Jacques. *The Politics of Literature*. Translated by Julie Rose. Cambridge: Polity Press, 2011.

Rancière, Jacques. *Proletarian Nights: The Workers' Dream in Nineteenth-Century France*. London: Verso, 2012.

Rancière, Jacques. "Ten Theses on Politics." In *Dissensus: On Politics and Aesthetics*, translated by Steven Corcoran, 35–52. London: Bloomsbury, 2013.

Rao, Anupama. *The Caste Question: Dalits and the Politics of Modern India*. Berkeley: University of California Press, 2009.

Rao, V. N., and Sanjay Subrahmanyam. "An Elegy for *Niti*: Politics as a Secular Discursive Field in the Indian Old Regime." *Common Knowledge* 14, no. 3 (2008): 396–423.

Ray, Debes. *Barisaler Jogen Mandal*. Kolkata: Dey's, 2010.

Rosanvallon, Pierre. *Counter-democracy: Politics in the Age of Distrust*. Cambridge: Cambridge University Press, 2008.

Rosanvallon, Pierre. *Democratic Legitimacy: Impartiality, Reflexivity, Proximity*. Princeton, NJ: Princeton University Press 2011.

Roy, Anuradha. *Cultural Communism in Bengal: 1936–52*. Delhi: Primus, 2014.

Roy, Parama. *Indian Traffic: Identities in Question in Colonial and Postcolonial India*. Berkeley: University of California Press, 1998.

Runia, Eelco. *Moved by the Past: Discontinuity and Historical Mutation*. New York: Columbia University Press, 2014.

Samaddar, Ranabir. *Emergence of the Political Subject*. Delhi: Sage, 2010.

Samajdar, Kamal. *Bangla Upanyase Lokjibon Charjya*. Calcutta: Mukherjee Publications, 1986.

Sanyal, Shukla. *Revolutionary Pamphlets, Propaganda and Political Culture in Colonial Bengal*. Cambridge: Cambridge University Press, 2014.

Sarkar, Sumit. "'Kaliyuga,' 'Chakri' and 'Bhakti': Ramakrishna and His Times." *Economic and Political Weekly* 27, no. 29 (1992): 1543–59, 1561–66.

Sarkar, Sumit. "Renaissance and Kaliyuga: Time, Myth and History in Colonial Bengal." In *Writing Social History*, 186–215. Delhi: Oxford University Press, 1998.

Sarkar, Sumit. *Swadeshi Movement in Bengal, 1903–1908*. Delhi: People's Publishing House, 1973.

Sarkar, Sumit. "Two Muslim Tracts for Peasants: Bengal 1909–10." In *Beyond Nationalist Frames: Relocating Postmodernism, Hindutva, History*, 96–111. Delhi: Permanent Black, 2002.

Sarkar, Sumit, and Tanika Sarkar, eds. *Women and Social Reform in Modern India: A Reader*. Delhi: Permanent Black, 2008.

Sarkar, Tanika. "Birth of a Goddess: 'Vande Mataram,' *Ananadamath*, and Hindu Nationhood." *Economic and Political Weekly* 41, no. 37 (2006): 3959–69.

Sarkar, Tanika. *Hindu Wife, Hindu Nation: Community, Religion and Cultural Nationalism*. Delhi: Permanent Black, 2001.

Sarma, R. N. *Mīmāṁsā Theory of Meaning*. Delhi: Sri Satguru Publications, 1988.

Sartori, Andrew. *Bengal in Global Concept History: Culturalism in the Age of Capital*. Chicago: University of Chicago Press, 2008.

Sartori, Andrew. *Liberalism in Empire: An Alternative History*. Oakland: University of California Press, 2014.

Sartori, Andrew. "The Transfiguration of Duty in Aurobindo's Essays on the Gita." *Modern Intellectual History* 7, no. 2 (2010): 319–34.

Sartori, Giovanni. *Party and Party Systems: A Framework of Analysis*. Cambridge: Cambridge University Press, 1976.

Sarukkai, Sundar. *Translating the World: Science and Language*. Lanham, MD: University Press of America, 2002.

Schmitt, Carl. *The Concept of the Political*. Translated by George Schwab. Chicago: University of Chicago Press, 1996.

Scott, James C. *Weapons of the Weak: Everyday Forms of Peasant Resistance*. New Haven, CT: Yale University Press, 1985.

Sen, Amiya P. "Editor's Introduction." In Vivekananda, *The Indispensable Vivekananda: An Anthology for Our Times*, 3–27. Delhi: Permanent Black, 2006.

Sen, Sambudha. "Re-visioning the Colonial City: Local Autonomy versus the Aesthetics of Intermixtures in the Age of Circulating Print Culture." *Literature Compass* 11, no. 1 (2014): 26–35.

Sen, Sudipta. *Empire of Free Trade: The East India Company and the Making of the Colonial Marketplace*. Philadelphia: University of Pennsylvania Press, 1998.

Sengupta, Shankar. *Folklorists of Bengal*. Calcutta: Indian Publications, 1965.

Seth, Sanjay. *Marxist Theory and Nationalist Politics: The Case of Colonial India*. Delhi: Sage, 1995.

Shapiro, Bruce G. *Reinventing Drama: Acting, Iconicity, and Performance*. Westport, CT: Greenwood, 1999.

Shingavi, Snehal. *The Mahatma Misunderstood: The Politics and Forms of Literary Nationalism in India*. London: Anthem Press, 2014.

Shulman, David. *More Than Real: A History of the Imagination in South India*. Cambridge, MA: Harvard University Press, 2012.

Singh, Navjyoti. "Role of Good Manners as a Bridge between World Religions in the Sanatana Tradition." In *Philosophy Bridging the World Religions: A Discourse of the World Religion*, edited by Peter Koslowski, 66–95. Dordrecht: Kluwer Academic, 2003.

Singh, Upinder. "Politics, Violence and War in Kamandaka's *Nitisara*." *Indian Economic and Social History Review* 47, no. 29 (2010): 29–62.

Sinha, Debabrata, "Theory and Practice in Indian Thought: Husserl's Observations." *Philosophy East and West* 21, no. 3 (1971): 255–64.

Sinha, Mrinalini. *Colonial Masculinity: The "Manly Englishman" and the "Effeminate Bengali" in the Late Nineteenth Century*. Manchester: Manchester University Press, 1995.

Sinha, Mrinalini. *Specters of Mother India: The Global Restructuring of an Empire*. Durham, NC: Duke University Press, 2006.

Skaria, Ajay. "Ambedkar, Marx and the Buddhist Question." *South Asia* 38, no. 3 (2015): 450–65.

Skaria, Ajay. *Unconditional Equality: Gandhi's Religion of Resistance*. Delhi: Permanent Black, 2016.

Sloterdjik, Peter. *The Art of Philosophy: Wisdom as a Practice*. New York: Columbia University Press, 2012.

Smith, Brian K. "Eaters, Food, and Social Hierarchy in Ancient India: A Dietary Guide to the Revolution of Values." *Journal of the American Academy of Religion* 58, no. 2 (1990): 177–205.

Spotts, Frederick. *Hitler and the Power of Aesthetics*. New York: Overlook Books, 2003.

Srinivas, M. N. *Caste in Modern India and Other Essays*. Bombay: Asia Publishing House, 1962.

Srivatsan, R. "Concept of 'Seva' and the 'Sevak' in the Freedom Movement." *Economic and Political Weekly* 41, no. 5 (2006): 427–38.

Subrahmanyam, Sanjay. "Connected Histories: Notes towards a Reconfiguration of Early Modern Eurasia." *Modern Asian Studies* 31, no. 3 (1997): 735–62.

Tambe, Ashwini. "Gandhi's 'Fallen' Sisters: Difference and the National Body Politics." *Social Scientist* 37, nos. 1–2 (2009): 21–38.

Tellmann, Ute Astrid. *Life and Money: The Genealogy of the Liberal Economy and the Displacement of Politics*. New York: Columbia University Press, 2018.

Tomkins, S. S., and R. McCarter. "What and where Are the Primary Affects? Some Evidence for a Theory." *Perceptual and Motor Skills* 18, no. 1 (1964): 119–58.

Visvanathan, Gauri. *Outside the Fold: Conversion, Modernity, and Belief*. Princeton, NJ: Princeton University Press, 1998.

Weber, Max. *The Vocation Lectures*. Edited by David Owen and Tracy B. Strong. Translated by Rodney Livingstone. Indianapolis: Hackett, 2004.

Weil, Simone. *On the Abolition of All Political Parties*. Translated by Simon Leys. New York: New York Review Books, 2013.

Wood, Ellen Meiksins. "The Separation of the Economic and the Political in Capitalism." In *Democracy against Capitalism: Renewing Historical Materialism*, 19–30. Cambridge: Cambridge University Press, 1995.

Yeazell, Ruth. *The Art of the Everyday: Dutch Painting and the Realist Novel*. Princeton, NJ: Princeton University Press, 2008.

Ypi, Lea. "Commerce and Colonialism in Kant's Philosophy of History." In *Kant and Colonialism: Historical and Critical Perspectives*, edited by Katrin Flikschuh and Lea Ypi, 99–126. Oxford: Oxford University Press, 2015.

INDEX

Abhinavagupta's concept of free will, 74
activism, 16, 33–34, 42, 67,69, 75, 78, 84, 102, 183, 216; hyperactivism, 41, 159
Advaita, 33, 61, 125–27, 129–30, 234n15. *See also* nondualism; Vedanta
aesthetic judgment, 196, 212
affect theory: *rasa* and, 52; theater and, 195; of Silvan Tomkins, 243n27
agency, 42, 68, 74; B. R. Ambedkar and, 113; Aurobindo Ghosh and, 80
ahimsa, 69. *See also* nonviolence
Ahmed, Abul Mansur, 131–32, 235n32, 236n15, 236n20
Ahmed, Muzaffar, 113, 179, 231n9, 233n72, 241n54
Akbar, translation of Mahabharata, 71
Ambedkar, B. R., 4, 12, 16, 18, 27, 49, 56–57, 119, 153, 220, 233n67; Bengal and, 146–47; on Bhagavad Gita, 86; as Dalit leader, 24; John Dewey and, 112; on general strike, 144, 236n12; on graded inequalities, 82; on Kautilya, 58; on labor, 105–6, 110, 178; *Manusmriti*, burning of, 46; Round Table Conference and, 174; on rules versus principles, 113–14; on social reform, 24, 173–74, 240n33; on spirituality, 123, 136–41, 235n57; on state, 112, 124, 134; on war, 110–11. *See also karma*: B. R. Ambedkar and; means and ends: B. R. Ambedkar and
Anandamath (Bankimchandra Chattopadhyay), 29–30, 76–78, 223n29, 229n50-52, 229n56
anarchism, 67; hyperactivism and, 74; Radhakamal Mukerjee and, 156; Vivekananda and, 39
anarchy: free action and, 74; Islam and, 133; realpolitik and, 51, 55
anchal, 196, 200, 202. *See also* region
Annihilation of Caste (Ambedkar), 137–38, 174, 222n10, 232n62, 233n87, 235n51
anrsamsata versus *ahimsa*, 69
anushilan, 72–75, 77–78, 228n25; by Anushilan Samiti, 169
apaddharma: as exception, 71, 228n22
Arendt, Hannah, 67–68, 114, 227n2
artha, 15, 76, 142; *arthashastra* and, 45, 60, 70, 76, 218. *See also* Arthashastra
Arthashastra (Kautilya), 46–51, 56, 58, 60, 223n21, 225n2, 226n10, 226n17, 226n34, 228n19
ashram: Hemanga Biswas and, 30; of M. K. Gandhi, 29, 98–99, 181, 229n63, 230n2, 231n30; of Aurobindo Ghosh, 80, 237n39; nationalist, 169, 186; as stages of life, 46; of Rabindranath Tagore, 191
askēsis, 36, 70. *See also* discipline
association: party and, 167–72, 175, 177, 185
atman (self), 33–34, 80–81, 126, 137, 223n42
atmospherics, 195–96, 199, 206–7, 244n70
Ashoka, 27, 48
Aurangzeb: novel and, 76; theater and, 207–8

Badiou, Alain, 7, 221n12, 221n14
Bandopadhyay, Manik, 104, 158–60, 196, 201–2, 238n87, 238nn89-95, 239n97-98, 244n47, 244n49

Bandopadhyay, Tarashankar, 194, 196–97, 201–3, 213, 243n32; Utpal Dutt and, 245n76
"Bangadesher Krishak" (Bankimchandra Chattopadhyay), 145, 234n11
Bengal Labor Party, 178, 241n52
Bhaduri, Satinath, 181–82, 186–88, 241n64, 242n77
Bhagavad Gita, 227n44, 227n47, 228n24, 228nn37–38, 229n42, 229n71; B. R. Ambedkar and, 86, 137; *Arthashastra* and, 58–63; Shibram Chakraborty and, 151; Jnaneshwar and, 126; political action and, 71–75, 77, 79–80, 227n51, 228n25, 228n26, 228nn29–30, 229n43, 229nn54–55, 229nn61–69, 229nn73–78, 230nn82–83, 230n2; translation of, 227n43, 227n49; Vivekananda and, 40, 225n81
bhakti, 37, 54, 58–59, 76, 89, 124, 182, 223n20, 225n2 ; *karma* and, 73–75; *rasa* and, 195; Vedanta and, 126
Bharatanatyashastra, 52, 195–96, 243n25, 244n56
Bhasi, Thoppil, 187–88
Bhattacharya, Sukanta, 101, 232n41
bhava, 52, 192, 194–95, 213; *bhakti* and, 74
Biswas, Hemanga, 30, 90, 97, 199–201, 203, 223n35, 231nn11–12, 231n26, 241n65, 243n38, 243nn40–44, 244n54
body: crowd and, 19, 171, 182, 200, 210; M. K. Gandhi and, 88, 98, 181; labor and, 17, 67, 90, 97–98, 102–3, 107, 150, 159, 161; party and, 19; self and, 33, 35, 73, 75, 80–81, 125
Bolsheviks: as individuals, 151; Muslims as, 182; peasants as, 132; revolution, 149
Bose, Subhas, 171, 176, 178, 180
Brahman: as supreme self, 80, 125, 127
Brahminism, 123; and labor, 106, 161; and Vedanta, 126
Brahmins, 12, 25, 28, 33, 36, 39, 56, 60–62, 86, 138–39, 191, 202, 227n37; and caste war, 111; and economic reason, 142; as exceptions to law, 46; and law, 152; Jyotiba Phule and, 150; as political being, 44, 53–57, 75, 78. *See also dharmashastra*
Brecht, Bertolt, 51, 209–10, 212
Buddha: B. R. Ambedkar and, 86, 111–12, 114, 124; Chanakya and, 56–58; equality and, 122–23, 137–38; renunciation and, 28, 39, 75, 83; Vivekananda and, 27, 41. *See also Buddha and His Dhamma*; "Buddha or Karl Marx"
Buddha and His Dhamma (Ambedkar), 86, 119, 137–39, 141, 153, 230n96, 235nn52–56
"Buddha or Karl Marx" (Ambedkar), 110, 134, 233n74, 233n77, 233n82–84, 233n90, 234n14
Buddhism, 17, 27, 30, 53, 56–57, 60–61, 123–25, 151, 222n15; B. R. Ambedkar and, 113, 124, 135–39, 141, 153; Shastri and, 139–40. *See also* Buddha

capitalism, 4–5, 12, 89, 133, 135, 149, 152, 155–56, 159, 160, 178; B. R. Ambedkar and, 106–7, 114; 219, 236n5; primitive accumulation and, 143–44
caste, 2, 4, 15–18, 26, 28–29, 46, 59, 61–62, 70, 82–83, 85, 96, 101, 104, 126–27, 129, 131–32, 137–39, 145–47, 149–50, 155, 157, 160–61, 166–67, 173–75, 179, 182, 186–87, 194–97, 201–3, 222n4, 222n8, 222n10, 227n53, 232n62, 233n69, 234n12, 237n33, 239n3, 244n51; B. R. Ambedkar and, 24–25, 105–6, 135, 145, 174–75; Bankimchandra Chattopadhyay and, 75–79, 120–21, 123; Chanakya and, 53–54, 56–58, 62; Haraprasad Shastri and, 139; Sree Narayana Guru and, 127; Vivekananda and, 25–26, 35–36, 39–40, 126
Castes in India (Ambedkar), 233n85
causality, 122; and political action, 16, 73–74, 84, 102, 112; and life, 70, 72, 85
celibacy, 29, 30, 40, 42, 46, 88, 98, 107
Chakraborty, Shibram, 142, 149, 151–53, 237nn40–50
Chanakya, 15, 28, 44–63, 216, 226n30, 226n33, 227n41, 227n46
Chanakyasutra, 47, 63

charka, 88–90, 96–97, 169, 231n18, 231nn20–21, 231n25, 231nn27–28
Chattopadhyay, Saratchandra, 30, 194, 213
Choudhury, Pramatha, 191, 233n71
civil disobedience, 13, 41, 169–70, 181
class, 4, 16–18, 39, 41, 56, 79, 87–89, 98, 104, 106–7, 114, 120, 124, 126, 128, 140, 145–47, 149–50, 152, 154, 157, 165–68, 175, 177–80, 212; Depressed Classes, 147, 174; middle, 2, 25, 37, 40, 56, 59, 102–3, 157–58, 172, 190–91, 200, 203, 205; music, 199; war, 110–11, 113, 141, 144, 151, 156, 182, 184, 187, 204. *See also* proletariat
commerce, 105; Kant and, 143, 236n4; war and, 152
Communist Manifesto, The: translations of, 150
Communist International, 123, 184
Communist Party of India, 19, 166, 168, 178–88, 205, 207, 240nn50–51, 241nn53–54, 241n65, 241nn67–74
communists, 17–18, 49, 79, 147–48, 157, 175–78, 187, 237nn24–27, 237n30, 237n32, 237nn34–37; and food activism, 101–3, 232n42; and labor, 87–90, 96–97, 104, 106; and literature, 158–61, 189, 193–94, 196, 199, 203, 205, 208–9, 239nn89–92, 239nn93–102, 242n1, 241nn5–6, 243nn19–21, 243nn23–24, 244n48, 244nn58–65, 244nn67–68; and religion, 123, 126–29, 132–33, 144–46, 151–54; and renunciation, 26–27, 30, 39–40, 42–43, 225n80. *See also* struggle; violence
community, 2, 6–7, 9, 13, 18–20, 25, 33, 60, 62, 99, 127–28, 132, 136, 140, 150, 153, 167, 186, 189–91, 193–94, 195–96, 199, 202, 206–9, 211–13, 239n5
conceptual personae, 119, 220
Congress Socialist Party (CSP), 177–79, 184–86, 240n50
contingency, 62, 73, 80, 83, 111–12, 114, 125, 161
cooperativism, 97, 146–47, 150, 154
crowd, 14, 18, 30, 89–90, 155, 165–67, 170–72, 180, 210–11, 239n4
culturalism, 2, 39, 166, 189, 190

Dalit, 13, 24, 41, 147, 174, 193, 221n4, 236nn18–19, 242n16, 234n12. *See also* Ambedkar, B. R.: as Dalit leader; untouchable
dandaniti: 50. *See also arthashastra*
Das, C. R., 170–71
Datta, Bhupendranath, 39, 179, 225n77–78
Debi Chaudhurani (Bankimchandra Chattopadhyay), 75–76, 229n49
decolonial, 3, 219, 246n7
dependent origination: B. R. Ambedkar and, 138
desire, 27, 36, 39, 40–41, 56, 59, 74–75, 80, 82–83, 107, 151, 155, 162, 166, 193, 195, 202–3, 209, 218; and freedom, 228n24, 228nn37–38, 229n42, 229n71; as meaning of *artha*, 45
desirelessness, 38, 62, 73–74, 77, 87. *See also nishkama karma*
Dewey, John: B. R. Ambedkar and, 18, 112
dhamma, 27, 43, 139. *See also Buddha and His Dhamma*
dharma, 48, 61, 80–81; as caste order, 58, 77; crisis of, 71–72, 110; as end of life, 45; versus *artha*, 46–47. *See also dharmashastra*
dharmashastra, 46, 48–49, 55, 228n18. *See also* law
difference, 9, 105, 132; colonial, 3–4, 17; equality and, 17–18, 120–27, 129–30, 134, 140, 153; and indifference, 34, 38, 83, 128, 208
discipline: as governmental technology, 8–9, 181, 230n94; of knowledge, 10–11, 50, 131, 148, 158, 219; of self-making, 34, 49, 63, 73–74, 76, 88–89, 98–99, 107, 160–61, 172, 225n2
division of labor, 105, 160
domesticity, 9, 76, 89, 131, 150, 158–59, 161–62, 186–87, 223n20
drama, 19, 47–48, 51–52, 56, 60–62, 67, 69, 71, 74, 76, 82, 127, 160, 194, 195–99, 201, 204, 206, 208–10, 212, 218, 243n25, 243n29, 245n95–98
Dramatic Performances Act, 167, 204, 210

Durkheim, Émile, 12–13, 214, 221n23
Dutt, Utpal, 30, 203, 206–11, 244n55, 244n69, 244n71–73, 245nn74–94
duty, 16, 27, 34, 53, 72, 74, 81, 224n71, 227nn49–50

East India Company, 29, 132, 142
economics, classical, 154–57, 160
economic justice, 147, 154
economism, 2, 106, 144, 146, 179
efficacy, 2, 15, 42, 44–46, 62, 69–73, 88, 102, 112–13, 151, 172, 207, 225n2, 228n20
election, 6–7, 29, 106, 132, 170–72, 178, 208, 239n19
electorate, separate, 99, 106, 147, 174–75. *See also* Ambedkar, B. R.: and Round Table Conference
encounter, 12–13, 35, 41, 60, 73, 83, 134, 184, 211; equality and, 140–41; sexual, 152, 191
energy, 69, 125; economics and, 154–55; of masses, 170, 186; and self, 32, 52
epics, 62, 71, 127, 151–52, 158, 181–82, 209, 245n84. *See also* Mahabharata; Ramayana
equanimity, 33, 73, 81, 122, 126, 224n53
ethnography, 19, 69, 190–92, 194, 196–200
event, 5, 7, 11–12, 16, 62, 68–69, 110, 121, 136, 196–97, 211, 213, 219, 221n14, 221n17
everyday, 10, 49, 63, 101, 149, 182–82, 218; action and, 14, 16, 75, 77–78, 82, 84–87, 90, 96–99, 106–7, 110, 115, 126, 137–38, 222n6, 227n3, 243n33; economics and, 149, 153, 157, 159; event and, 221n21; literature and, 192, 194–95, 198, 201, 213. *See also* event
exception, state of, 5–6, 16, 46, 57, 69, 77, 79, 85, 98–99, 110, 129, 154, 169, 228n11. See also *apaddharma*
experience, 1, 3, 18, 23–24, 27, 37, 39, 61, 70, 73–74, 81, 83, 85, 87, 98, 102, 106–7, 110, 112, 119, 120, 122, 126–27, 129, 131, 144, 151–52, 161, 183, 190, 192–93, 195, 207, 209–10, 212–13, 217, 219
extrapolitical, 11–12, 14–15, 17–18, 32, 54–55, 57, 83, 98, 141, 162, 215–16, 218

famine, 29, 76, 98, 101–2, 161, 199, 204–5, 210, 228n14, 232n40
Faraizi, 131–32, 211, 235n33
fast, 13, 41, 87, 135; B. R. Ambedkar and, 153, 174; communists and, 103; M. K. Gandhi and, 42, 88, 101–2, 107, 187; hunger strike and, 98–99
folklore, 45, 190, 194, 242n3
food movement, 102, 232nn40–44. *See also* famine
force, 2, 6, 8, 15, 17, 35, 79, 102–3, 130, 136, 143, 145, 161–62, 173, 178, 184, 197, 207, 211, 217; action and, 67–69, 71–73, 85, 89–90, 96, 98–99, 106–7, 112, 114; spirituality and, 26, 32, 36, 41, 80–83; time and, 83–84
franchise, 2, 7; labor, 89, 172, 175–76; limited, 147, 170; universal, 89, 106. *See also* electorate; vote
freedom, 2, 13, 30, 50–51, 54, 56, 90, 169, 176, 182, 233n69, 238n58, 240n50; of action, 16, 68, 72, 74–75, 85, 96, 111, 113–14, 228n24, 228nn37–38, 229n42, 229n71; and equality, 17, 24, 38, 120, 130–31, 152–53, 173, 175
front: political party and, 166, 182, 184–85

Gandhi, M. K., 4, 12, 24, 48, 59, 107, 113, 123, 178, 182, 194, 212, 218, 231n13, 233n68; and action, 69, 79–80; and body, 42, 90, 230n3, 231n30; and caste, 24, 106, 149, 152, 173–75, 222n11, 233n69, 240n30; and equality, 18, 135, 144–48, 154; and Indian National Congress, 168–72, 176, 178–79, 181, 186–87, 241nn60–61; and labor, 16, 86–90, 96–97, 101, 104–7, 230nn1–2, 230nn4–6, 231nn16–25, 231nn27–29, 231nn31–33, 232nn37–39, 232nn60–61; and nonviolence, 107–13, 176, 225n92; and *satyagraha*, 42, 80, 98, 99, 110, 144, 169, 181; and self, 29–30, 42–43, 114, 222n6, 223n26, 225n91, 229n63. *See also* body: M. K. Gandhi and; fast: M. K. Gandhi and
gender, 15, 62, 70, 76–77, 82, 167, 187; and equality, 17, 120–21, 127, 137, 160; and

labor, 16; and political party, 174–75; and spirituality, 35, 37. *See also* work: of women

Ghosh, Aurobindo, 59, 61, 112, 223n31, 237n39; action and, 79, 80–86, 229nn61–70, 229nn72–78, 230n83, 230n92–93; political party and, 172, 240n23; renunciation and, 27, 40–41, 225n84, 227n49, 227n51

Ghosh, Girish, 53, 59, 204, 207, 222n15

Ghoshal, U. N., 50, 57, 226nn23–25, 227n39

Global South, 3–4, 6, 215–17, 220

god, 57, 59, 61, 71–72, 74–76, 80–84, 96, 123–25, 128, 130, 133–38, 153, 158–59, 180–81, 200, 202, 204, 208, 211, 219, 227n37, 227n40

goddess, 26, 30, 35, 76, 78, 158, 199, 223n30, 229n50, 244n53. *See also* Kali

governmentalization, 2, 24, 156

Gramsci, Antonio, 166, 239n2

Guha, Ranajit, 12–13, 214, 221n19, 222n25, 227n7, 230n89, 230n94

Hashim, Abul, 129–30, 133–34, 140, 234n24, 234n26, 235n40

Hegel, G. W. F., 49, 59, 61, 69, 198, 220, 227n9

Hinduism, 15, 25–26, 35, 38–39, 69, 73, 86, 105, 110–11, 113, 132, 135–37, 174, 228n23. *See also Philosophy of Hinduism*

historicism, 48, 51, 57, 84, 97, 208

household, 1, 15, 30, 46, 76, 78, 82–83, 85, 139, 149, 159, 161–62, 187, 194, 197

hunger strike. *See* fast

Husserl, Edmund, 69, 227n9, 228n10

ideology, 2, 6, 13–14, 86, 152, 196; norm and, 119, 162; philosophy and, 4–5

Independent Labour Party, 105

India and the Prerequisites of Communism (Ambedkar), 233n86

Indian Bolshevik Party, 185

Indian National Congress, 145, 147–48, 166–86, 189, 194, 223n25, 230n6, 237n24, 239nn7–21, 240n22, 240nn24–29, 240nn31–32, 230nn41–49, 240n51, 241nn55–58, 241nn60–61, 241n68. See also *What Congress and Gandhi Have Done*

Indian National Social Conference, 173, 222n14

Indian People's Theatre Association (IPTA), 189, 199–200, 204–6, 210, 244n68

Islam, 3, 17, 46, 136, 216, 225n6, 230n86; economics and, 105, 140, 147, 152–53, 235n30, 235n33, 235n40, 237nn51–57; equality and, 122, 124–25, 127–35, 151, 234nn24–28, 235n43, 235n45; Vivekananda and, 33. *See also tawhid*

Islam, Kazi Nazrul, 89–90, 127–29, 132–35, 140, 179, 231n10, 234nn22–23, 235nn38–39, 235n48

itihasa (history), 71, 195

Jabanbandi (Bhattacharya), 205

jati: as caste, 60, 77, 132, 139, 235n58, 236n60; as nation: 229n73. *See also varna*

jatra: as journey, 84, 209, 230n91; as theater, 59, 103, 209–11, 245nn85–88, 245n90

jihad, 13, 131–32, 182, 241n66

Kali, 26, 35–37, 40–41, 55, 59, 81–83, 128, 159, 230n80

kaliyuga (age of decline), 30, 55, 57–58, 79, 83, 139, 223n20, 223n36, 230n84

Kamandaka, 47, 226n8

Kangle, R. P., 48–49, 226n17

Kant, Immanuel, 10, 72, 143, 153, 196, 236n4

karma, 16, 96, 210; as action, 69–70, 87, 115, 214, 228nn13–15; B. R. Ambedkar and, 85–86, 137. *See also nishkama karma*

karmayoga, 34, 72–73, 78, 85, 224nn51–52, 225n87, 225n90

Kautilya. *See Arthashastra*; Chanakya

kavya (literature), 48, 52, 71, 75, 195, 242n13, 244n70

Khan, Akram, 132, 169, 235n36

Index 269

kinesis, 81, 90, 96–98, 107, 154
king, 15, 27–28, 31, 41, 44, 53–56, 62, 70–71, 75–76, 82, 84, 96, 123, 133, 136, 138–40, 142, 146, 204, 208–11. *See also* kingship
kingship, 46, 49–50, 57, 225n1, 228n14. *See also* sovereignty
Kisan Sabha (peasant league), 175, 177–78, 194, 200, 240nn38–40
Koran, 131, 133–34, 216
Kosambi, D. D., 61, 227n48, 227n52
Krishak Praja Party (KPP), 131–32, 146–47
Krishna, 76, 79–82, 137, 199, 202; Chanakya and, 58–62; Mughals and, 71. *See also* Bhagavad Gita; Mahabharata; Vaishnava
Kshatriya, 79, 111; vis-à-vis Shudras, 28, 39, 53, 70, 145
Kurukshetra, 61, 79, 86, 110, 151

landlord, 5, 12, 56, 101, 120, 142, 144–46, 155, 161, 170, 172, 176, 178, 185, 209. *See also* peasant; *zamindar*
law, 6–7, 101, 106; *Arthashastra* and, 45, 49–50, 70; caste and, 46–47, 111, 113; religion and, 25, 31, 80, 84, 86, 122, 124, 129–31, 137; colonial, 24. *See also* dharmashastra; sovereignty
Lefort, Claude, 6–7, 31, 221n10, 223n41
Lenin, V. I., 67, 79, 129, 140–41, 144, 150, 154, 182–83, 187; Muhammad Iqbal and, 134, 235n47
liberalism, 4–5, 17, 25, 33, 39, 121, 123, 125, 148, 219, 221n7, 235n31
life, 1, 2, 4, 7, 12, 25, 45–46, 48, 50, 165, 183–84, 187, 220; and action, 11, 13–16, 49, 67–89, 115, 216, 218, 222n26, 222n6, 227nn3–4, ; and conflict, 110–11; and economics, 145, 149, 151–59, 162, 236n1; and labor, 96–99, 101, 103, 107; and literature, 189, 191, 193–96, 198, 201, 205, 207–8, 210–13, 242n17; and religion, 125–26, 129–31, 135–39; and renunciation, 27–28, 31, 34–35, 38, 223n16, 223n38, 225n88, 228n16. *See also* everyday

Machiavelli, Niccolò, 48–49, 226n15, 226n19
Mahabharata, 52, 59–60, 62, 69, 71, 73, 79, 86, 111, 152, 199, 209, 227n15, 228n22, 245n83. *See also* Bhagavad Gita
Mandal, Jogendranath, 146–47, 236nn18–19
market, 47, 58, 76, 101, 105, 143, 149, 151, 154–55, 157, 161, 209, 217; colonial, 142, 236nn2–3; literature and, 160, 203; state and, 11, 221n22
martyrdom, 12, 132. *See also* sacrifice
Marx, Karl, 4, 18, 114, 220; B. R. Ambedkar and, 105. *See also* "Buddha or Karl Marx"
Marxism, 2, 4, 9, 11, 61, 124–25, 143–44, 148–50, 154, 156–57, 182, 187; and labor, 89, 110; and literature, 51, 56, 104, 149, 191, 210, 242nn5–6, 243nn19–21, 243n24, 244n48, 244n58–65, 244n67; and nationalism, 242n74; and religion, 129–31, 134, 140–41; and renunciation, 30, 40, 42, 57
mass, 7, 14, 18, 25, 36, 62, 79, 87, 90, 97–99, 101, 107, 113, 148, 150–51, 155, 157–58, 160–61, 221n15, 224n71; audience, 53, 55–56, 58, 198, 204, 205, 207, 209, 210, 212; M. K. Gandhi and, 29, 43, 225n92; party and, 19, 165–77, 180–86, 239n6, 239n11, 240n47, 240n49
Maurya: Chandragupta, 44, 48, 51–56, 226n31, 226n33, 227nn35–36; empire, 60, 123. *See also* Ashoka
means and ends, 48, 169, 171, 176, 226n16; B. R. Ambedkar and, 111–14
means of production, 113, 143
military, 24, 71, 96, 142, 180–85, 209
mirror: as inversion, 159, 209, 221n22; as representation, 173, 189, 205; self and, 41, 125, 127, 140
modernism, 198, 212, 236n9, 242n6, 245n96
monotheism: M. N. Roy's theory of Islam and, 153
moral, 17, 39, 43–45, 48, 61, 74, 97, 112, 131, 134, 136–37, 140, 149, 191, 203, 212, 223n16, 223n38, 228n22

motherland, 36, 38, 76, 82
"Mr Russell and the Reconstruction of Society" (Ambedkar), 111, 233n76, 233n81, 233nn88–89
Mudrarakshasa (Vishakhadatta), 47, 51–52, 54
Mughals, 46, 56, 71, 76, 128, 207–8
Mukerjee, Dhurjatiprasad, 156–58, 238nn77–80, 238nn82–84, 238nn86–87
Mukerjee, Radhakamal, 149, 154–56, 158, 237n26, 238nn59–76, 242n15
Mukhopadhyay, Subash, 102–4, 110, 150, 232nn46–55
Muslim League, 103, 129, 132, 146, 174, 232n42

Nabanna (Bhattacharya), 204–6, 208, 210, 244n59, 244n63–65
Nag, Kalidas, 48, 226nn14–15
Narayan, Jaiprakash: left isolationism, 178, 240n44, 240n50
nationalism, 2, 4, 13, 17, 24–25, 28, 30–31, 33, 35, 38–40, 105, 144–45, 148, 150, 175, 183–85, 199, 222n1, 236n10, 237n29, 241n68, 242n3, 243nn35–36
Nehru, Jawaharlal, 4, 145, 147, 176, 178, 185, 227n41, 239n21, 240n44, 241n56
Nehru, Motilal, 170. *See also* Swarajya Party
Nietzsche, Friedrich, 67, 151, 212, 227n1
nishkama karma: as desireless action, 75, 77–78, 80–81, 90, 114. *See also karma; karmayoga*
niti, 50, 56, 62, 143, 218, 225n5, 226n8. *See also artha; arthashastra*
nitishastra. *See niti*
Nivedita, Sister (Margaret Noble), 27–28, 31, 35–38, 40, 223nn17–19, 223n39, 223n41, 224n53, 224nn55–56, 224nn59–61, 224nn63–64, 224nn66–68, 225n74, 225nn85–86
noncooperation, 29, 42, 129, 148, 168–71, 183, 210, 225n92
noncruelty. *See anrsamsata*
nondualism, 39, 125–28, 156; dualism and, 224n42; Muhammad Iqbal, Henri Bergson, and, 234n25. *See also* Advaita; Vedanta
nonpolitical, 4, 9–11, 14–15, 18–19, 32, 68, 97, 144, 178, 213, 215, 236n1, 236n9
nonviolence, 29, 42, 59, 72, 89, 101, 110–11, 154, 170, 176, 180. *See also ahimsa*
norm, 2, 5–6, 9, 15, 17–18, 44, 48–49, 51, 63, 68–69, 71, 77, 79, 81–83, 86, 119, 162, 173, 217, 228n11
novel: as literature, 29, 30, 52–53, 59, 75–78, 83, 85, 89, 102–4, 110, 132, 149, 158–59, 161–62, 181–82, 186–89, 191, 193–95, 197–98, 202, 205–7, 212–13, 226n31, 241n65, 242n11, 243n18

Panchatantra, 45, 47, 216, 225n3, 228n19
parliament, 26, 165, 172, 175, 226n14; versus military, 182
party society, 185, 224n76
passive resistance, 69, 85, 98, 230n93, 231n32
peasant, 2, 36, 56, 104, 120, 145, 157, 161, 185, 214, 222n25; and communist politics, 90, 101, 241n68; M. K. Gandhi and, 29, 88, 145, 181, 225n92; and literature, 191, 199–201, 204–5, 211; and low-caste politics, 28, 147, 223n23–24; and Muslim politics, 131–33, 140, 146, 149, 235nn31–34, 236n17; organization, 19, 131, 175–78; property, 5, 142–44; rebellion, 12–13, 25, 29, 102, 144, 167, 170, 186. *See also* Kisan Sabha; Mandal, Jogendranath; *praja*; Worker and Peasant Party
Permanent Settlement, 101, 156
philosophy: politics and, 1, 3–7, 13, 15, 23, 33–34, 36, 47–62, 72, 74, 79, 125–26, 129–30, 134, 138, 140–41, 153, 182, 193, 203, 212–13, 216, 219–20, 222n24, 224n49, 224n67, 227n1, 227nn8–9, 228n10, 228n12, 228nn16–17, 228n19, 230nn87–88, 234n1, 236n4, 245n3
Philosophy of Hinduism (Ambedkar), 110, 135, 222n11, 233n65, 233n75, 233nn73–79, 235nn49–50

Index   271

poets and poetry, 12, 13, 17, 24, 30–31, 48–49, 62, 71, 75, 82, 89, 97, 101–2, 112, 115, 189, 191–92, 195, 207, 216, 220, 230n4, 231nn15–25, 231nn27–28, 243n25, 243n35, 244n70, 245n97; and equality, 126–28, 130, 132–35, 141; and modernism, 198; people's, 19, 149, 199–203, 210; and time, 84, 234n25

politic, being, 45, 60, 62, 71, 76–77, 218

political society, 168; B. R. Ambedkar and, 136; Antonio Gramsci and, 166; Partha Chatterjee and, 185, 221n8, 228n11

political theology: B. R. Ambedkar and, 136–37; Ernst Kantorowicz and, 225n7

politicization, 1, 12, 18, 29, 38, 87, 106, 110, 119–20, 206, 218

population, 14, 24, 46, 101, 148, 166–67, 171; colonial demographics and, 147, 167

postcoloniality, 3, 5, 11, 51, 69, 221n1, 221n16, 223n26, 225n83, 229n79

power, 5–6, 25, 27–28, 34, 79, 86, 97, 105, 107, 119, 134, 136, 169, 186; aesthetic, 190, 196, 205, 207, 210, 242n2, 243n31; *artha* and, 45–46, 54–57, 61, 79, 83, 137; economic, 142–43, 146, 148–50, 152, 155, 160; Michel Foucault's concept of, 8; social reform and, 31, 33; political party and, 166, 175, 185; self and, 34, 37–38, 40, 42, 62, 85, 126; will and, 74–77. *See also* force; sovereignty

praja, 146–47, 179, 210. *See also* Krishak Praja Party; peasant

presence, 5, 18, 19, 54, 58, 122, 132, 147, 174, 202, 205, 208, 211–12, 220

primitive, 13, 54, 73, 125, 136, 152, 223n36, 236n3

productivity, 89–90, 114, 143, 147, 154–55, 177

proletariat, 13–14, 19, 104, 112, 124, 140, 145–46, 150, 165–66, 206; as universal class, 19, 96, 101, 104–7, 168, 178–79. *See also* work; workers

Purana, 30, 195; *Bhagavata*, 71; *Markandeya*, 210; *Shunya*, 127

Quit India Movement, 181, 183, 186, 205

race, 13, 17–18, 38, 120, 129, 132, 216

Rajsingha (Bankimchandra Chattopadhyay), 76, 229n53

Ramayana, 71, 152, 182, 199, 209, 228n13

Ramkrishna, 36, 40, 223n20, 224n57

Ranade, M. G.: reform, renunciation, and, 27

Rancière, Jacques, 1, 7–10, 19, 197–98, 203, 206, 221nn14–15, 243nn33–34, 244n50

rasa, 52, 74, 192–96, 202, 206, 209–10, 213, 243n26, 244n70

realism: art and, 19, 192–95, 197–99, 205–8, 211, 242n11, 242n37; politics and, 6, 226n16

reconstruction: B. R. Ambedkar and, 27, 106, 111, 137; M. K. Gandhi and, 170–71, 175–76; Muhammad Iqbal and, 130, 230n86; 234n25; Rabindranath Tagore and, 19. *See also* "Mr Russell and the Reconstruction of Society"

region, 3, 46, 101–2, 132, 155–56, 168, 177, 189–90, 202, 215–16, 222n4, 235n31, 235n35

Renu, Phanishwar Nath, 181, 241n59

representation, 1, 6, 19–20, 33, 134, 146–47, 174, 176, 185, 189, 235n31, 235n33, 235nn41–42, 235n44, 236n16, 236n21; agitation versus, 170–72, 180, 182; imagination versus, 192–97; impersonation versus, 205

revolution, 9, 13, 15, 26, 27, 30, 38–40, 57, 59–60, 68–69, 79–80, 82–83, 90, 107, 126, 130–31, 133, 135–38, 146, 157–60, 162, 169, 180, 182–85, 187, 189, 199, 203, 208, 210, 218, 223n34, 229n60, 230n81, 237n39, 241n66, 241n68, 242n72, 245n80, 245n89, 245nn91–92, 245n97; French, 5, 7, 67, 121, 123, 141, 148, 165, 172, 221n18. *See also* Bolsheviks, revolution

Revolutionary Socialist Party, 103, 185

Rowlatt Satyagraha, 99

Roy, M. N., 148, 152–54, 183, 237nn51–57, 241n68, 242n70

Roy, Sabitri, 161–62, 239nn99–102

sacrifice, 14, 37–38, 40–41, 54, 56, 61, 70, 76, 81, 83, 96–97, 101, 113–15, 131, 137, 151–52, 182, 187, 197, 208, 223n42. *See also* martyrdom
samaj (society), 24, 28, 32, 150, 190, 210, 222n4, 225n78, 233n63, 237n30, 237n32
samya, 73, 120, 122–23, 126, 128, 145, 234nn1–6, 234nn8–11
"Samya" (Bankimchandra Chattopadhyay), 12–23, 234nn2–6, 234nn8–11
samyabad (socialism), 132–33, 150, 230nn7–8, 231nn9–10, 231n14, 232nn56–58, 233nn71–72, 234n39, 237n25, 237n27, 237n30, 237nn34–37, 241n65. *See also* socialism
Sankhya (philosophy), 33–34, 51, 81, 223n42
sannyas, 15, 26, 28–30, 35, 38–39, 46, 76, 78, 224n65
Saraswati, Swami Sahajanand, 29, 177, 223n27
Sarkar, Benoy Kumar, 47–50, 56–57, 61, 143–44, 226n9, 226nn11–12, 226n15, 226n18, 226nn20–23, 227nn38–39, 236nn7–9, 236n11
satyagraha, 42, 46, 69, 80, 98–99, 110, 144, 169, 181, 229n63, 231nn32–33, 232n34, 233n64, 233n73
Schmitt, Carl, 6–7, 67, 72, 110, 221n9, 221n20
secular, 1, 5, 11–12, 25, 29, 35, 46, 81–82, 123–25, 129, 136, 136, 140, 225n15
Sengupta, Achintyakumar, 149, 194, 202, 242n9, 243n24, 243n46
sense: common, 2, 5, 8, 13, 17, 27, 68, 129, 214, 216, 219; popular, 58, 62, 217
senses, 81, 103, 131, 190, 207, 212, 223n28
service: as *seva*, 15, 29, 38, 62, 78, 85, 133, 146, 161, 180, 225n87
seva (public service), 42, 107, 180, 210, 233n69. *See also* service
Shankara, 125, 127
shariat, 122; versus *siyasat*, 46
Shudra, 12, 15, 28, 33, 39, 42, 54–55, 57–58, 62, 84, 104–5, 111, 121, 123, 126, 128, 139, 140, 150, 152–52; Namashudra as, 145–47. *See also* *Who Were the Shudras?*

shunya (void), 138–40
slave, 28, 37–38, 111, 123, 156, 158; and Islam, 133, 156
social: distance, 157, 238n79; reform, 27, 31–33, 37, 39, 99, 127, 131–32, 146, 173–74, 205, 222n9, 223n37, 223n40; versus political, 24–25, 222n2
socialism, 4, 13, 15, 29, 39, 110, 122, 124, 126, 133, 156, 176, 178, 183, 185, 219, 233n63, 235n43, 237n32
sovereign, 1, 6, 9, 18, 24–25, 31, 46, 50, 57, 84, 110, 124, 133, 148, 156, 218, 225n7
species, 69, 88, 125, 127, 130, 137, 155, 162
state, 8–11, 15, 19, 23–26, 28, 31–32, 44–45, 47, 50, 57, 106, 112–13, 124, 133–34, 142–43, 145, 147–48, 156, 165–69, 178, 183, 185–87, 210, 221n22, 222n4, 222n7, 225n4, 242n75
strike, 13–14, 41–42, 69, 97–99, 101–4, 144, 149, 156, 160–61, 179, 232nn37–39, 232n56, 236n12, 241n65
subaltern studies, 2, 145, 221n3, 223n20, 241n62, 242n12
Sufi, 36, 89, 124, 131, 169, 195, 234n29
Sukraniti, 48, 143. *See also* niti
sultan, 46, 84, 133
surrender: and agency, 74–75. *See also* Bhagavad Gita; *bhakti*

Tagore, Rabindranath, 4, 12, 17, 24, 53, 69, 102, 199, 201, 207, 218, 227n8; on folk literature, 190, 201, 242n4; on history, 52, 84, 222n5, 226n29, 230nn89–90; on labor, 96–97, 107, 150, 230n4, 231n14–25, 231n27, 233n70, 237n34; on modern literature, 191–94, 242nn6–8
Tanvir, Habib, 51–51, 226n27
tawhid (unity of being), 128, 131, 140–41, 234n23, 234n29
Tebhaga (sharecroppers' movement), 132, 161, 231n13
theater, 1, 6, 30, 53–63, 103, 167, 189, 203–13. *See also* drama
theatricality, 195, 198, 203, 205, 207–9, 211–13, 245n96
Tilak, Bal Gangadhar, 43, 59, 168, 173

Index 273

time: history and, 223n36, 230n85, 236n3; labor, 89, 96, 148–49; philosophy, religion, and, 5, 9, 48, 57–58, 61, 70, 83–84, 113, 135, 220, 230nn87–88. *See also kali-yuga;* historicism

trade union, 19, 96, 103, 106, 178–79, 183

unity, 29, 33, 61, 79, 99, 106, 122, 128, 130, 140, 148, 153, 169–70, 180, 184, 186, 196, 204–5, 207, 240n50. *See also* community; *tawhid*

universal: economic theory, 141, 144, 146, 148, 154–56, 162; equality, 38, 133, 136, 138; political theory, 2–5, 7, 9–11, 14, 16, 18, 48, 50, 58, 68–70, 172, 187, 199, 215–17, 220, 228n11; self, 34, 39, 61–62, 77, 79–81, 125, 128. *See also* franchise: universal; proletariat: as universal class; philosophy

untouchable, 2, 28, 36, 39, 55, 83, 85, 89, 99, 103, 105–7, 111, 133, 138–40, 145–46, 149, 153, 160, 173–75, 180, 187, 191, 194, 202, 203, 225n76, 233n66. *See also* Dalit

Upanishad, 151, 223n42; and Dara Shukoh, 128, 216, 234n21

utility, 31, 154, 157

Vaishnava, 29, 36–37, 58–59, 74, 76, 150, 202, 209. *See also* Krishna

Vaishya, 39, 149–50

value, 154–57, 160, 162, 239n96

vanguard, 19, 39, 131, 166, 170, 179–85

varna (caste), 46, 60, 72, 77, 79, 132, 237n32. *See also dharmashastra;* caste

Veda, 28, 53, 70, 83, 137, 195, 223n42

Vedanta, 17, 29, 36, 42, 223nn43–45, 224nn47–48, 225n88, 227n6, 227n8, 234n18. *See also* Advaita; nondualism

violence, 25, 68–69, 79, 85–86, 99, 107, 110–12, 114, 128, 134, 143, 169, 186, 208, 222n7, 222n26, 226n8, 227n5. *See also* nonviolence; *ahimsa*

Vivekananda, Swami, 15, 23, 25–42, 55, 78, 82, 125–28, 130, 140, 222nn13–14, 223n16, 223nn37–38, 223n40, 224nn43–45, 224nn47–48, 224nn50–52, 224n54, 224n65, 224nn69–71, 225nn72–73, 225n77, 225n81, 225nn87–90, 234n17

voluntarism, 67, 69, 74

volunteer, 180–82. *See also* vanguard

vote, 89, 147, 171–72, 175. *See also* franchise; election

wage theory. *See* work: wage and

Wahabi, 161, 169

wahdat ul wajood (unity of being). *See tawhid*

war, 13, 28, 41–42, 45, 56, 216, 223n24, 226n8, 245n4; caste, 39, 70, 110; epic, 60–62, 71–72, 75, 79–80, 86, 209; and equality, 128, 132, 135, 141, 152, 241n65; revolutionary, 67, 69, 76, 78; and struggle, 17, 87, 103, 107–12, 114–15; world wars, 101, 161, 169, 183, 186, 189. *See also* Ambedkar, B. R.: on war; class: war

Weber, Max, 10, 48, 172, 216, 226n13

What Congress and Gandhi Have Done to the Untouchables (Ambedkar), 173, 222n11, 240n30, 240nn36–37

Who Were the Shudras? (Ambedkar), 227n42

Women. *See* work: women and

work: Islam and, 131, 135, 152; knowledge and, 121, 207; labor and, 16, 62, 68, 82, 87, 89–90, 96–97, 103–7, 144; wage and, 99, 154, 156, 157, 160; women and, 158–62. *See also* workers

Worker and Peasant Party (WPP), 179–80

workers, 2, 13, 41–41, 65, 87–89, 96, 99, 101–2, 106, 113–14, 128, 142, 145–50, 157–58, 168; and art, 191, 196–99, 200, 202–3, 209, 212; party, 175–80, 184–86. *See also* proletariat; work

yoga, 33–34, 61, 72–75, 83, 85, 126, 223n42, 224nn50–52, 225n87, 225n90

zamindar, 147, 191, 236n9. *See also* landlord

www.ingramcontent.com/pod-product-compliance
Lightning Source LLC
Chambersburg PA
CBHW070756230426
43665CB00017B/2379